The Fraunhofer IESE Series on Software and Systems Engineering

Series Editors

Dieter Rombach
Peter Liggesmeyer

Editorial Board

W. Rance Cleaveland II
Reinhold E. Achatz
Helmut Krcmar

Adam Trendowicz

Software Cost Estimation, Benchmarking, and Risk Assessment

The Software Decision-Makers' Guide to Predictable Software Development

Springer

CoBRA®

Adam Trendowicz
Fraunhofer IESE
Kaiserslautern
Germany

ISSN 2193-8199   ISSN 2193-8202 (electronic)
ISBN 978-3-642-43365-8   ISBN 978-3-642-30764-5 (eBook)
DOI 10.1007/978-3-642-30764-5
Springer Heidelberg New York Dordrecht London

ACM Codes: D.2.9, K.6.1, K.6.3

About this Series

Whereas software engineering has been a growing area in the field of computer science for many years, systems engineering has its roots in traditional engineering. On the one hand, we still see many challenges in both disciplines. On the other hand, we can observe a trend to build systems that combine software, microelectronic components, and mechanical parts. The integration of information systems and embedded systems leads to so-called cyber-physical systems.

Software and systems engineering comprise many aspects and views. From a technical standpoint, they are concerned with individual techniques, methods, and tools, as well as with integrated development processes, architectural issues, quality management and improvement, and certification. In addition, they are also concerned with organizational, business, and human views. Software and systems engineering treat development activities as steps in a continuous evolution over time and space.

Software and systems are developed by humans, so the effects of applying techniques, methods, and tools cannot be determined independent of context. A thorough understanding of their effects in different organizational and technical contexts is essential if these effects are to be predictable and repeatable under varying conditions. Such process-product effects are best determined empirically. Empirical engineering develops the basic methodology for conducting empirical studies, and uses it to advance the understanding for the effects of various engineering approaches.

The series presents engineering-style methods and techniques that foster the development of systems that are reliable in every aspect. All the books in the series emphasize the quick delivery of state-of-the-art results and empirical proof from academic research to industrial practitioners and students. Their presentation style is designed to enable the reader to quickly grasp both the essentials of a methodology and how to apply it successfully.

Scientists build to learn; Engineers learn to build.

Frederick P. Brooks

Foreword by Prof. Dr. Dieter Rombach

Software Engineering is concerned with the development of large and complex software-intensive systems and services in an economical and timely manner by following engineering principles and applying best practice methods, techniques, and tools. Software is entering domains it never belonged to in the past and must face challenges it never had to confront before. High demands on software-intensive systems and increasing competitiveness within the software business have triggered a push towards systematic software engineering approaches, including techniques for managing software projects.

Applied research institutions such as the Fraunhofer Institute for Experimental Software Engineering (IESE) support software organizations in transferring into daily practice innovative, empirically proven software engineering solutions that are driven by their specific needs.

This book is the result of a successful collaboration between the process management division of Fraunhofer IESE and many software companies in the field of software engineering technology transfer. The book introduces an innovative software management technology called CoBRA, which has been deployed in a number of software companies.

Fraunhofer IESE developed the Cost Estimation, Benchmarking, and Risk Assessment method (CoBRA) driven by industrial needs with respect to managing software project resources. In addressing project management objectives, CoBRA goes far beyond simply predicting the development effort. It supports project decision-makers in negotiating the project scope, managing project risks, benchmarking productivity, and directing improvement activities. At the same time, it meets typical constraints encountered in software engineering contexts where other estimation methods typically fail. The method requires neither large amounts of project measurement data nor extensive involvement of human experts. While many leading software engineering researchers and practitioners agree on the need for a systematic approach for combining quantitative data with human judgment, CoBRA is actually doing it.

What makes this book special is that it is driven by industrial practice and aimed at industrial practice. The book introduces the principles of the CoBRA method followed by the basic procedures for applying the method. The methodological concepts are illustrated by a number of practical examples, and the use of the method is exemplified by several case studies from various software organizations.

For any software organization that does not want to leave the success of its software projects to chance, this book should serve as a standard handbook.

Kaiserslautern, Germany   Prof. Dr. Hans Dieter Rombach
                                                                    Executive Director
                         Fraunhofer Institute for Experimental Software Engineering

Foreword by Dr. Koichi Matsuda

Recently, we experienced the so-called 2007 Problem in Japan. Within a short period of time, the Japanese industry, including the software companies, lost a complete generation of highly skilled senior professionals. Born during the time of the baby boom, they now turned 60 and left their jobs to retire. The Software Engineering Center (SEC) was asked to undertake activities to prevent a negative impact of the "2007 Problem" on the software industry. One such undertaking was skill and technology transfer between age groups. Still, in many software engineering areas, professional expertise is rather hard to grasp and to share. Software project effort estimation is one such area. The success of estimation is heavily dependent on human expertise, which is hidden in the experts' minds and is difficult to grasp. This book is unique in that it provides a practical solution to this problem.

Today, software processes benefit greatly from advanced methodological and tool support. Many process areas that used to rely heavily on human knowledge and skills are now largely independent of it. However, the area of project estimation is still largely dependent on experienced engineers. The CoBRA method presented in this book is unique in that it systematically acquires expertise hidden in the minds of human experts and transforms it into explicit knowledge that is easier to share between people and projects.

In Japan, the term KKD is often used in the context of software development. The first "K" stands for *Keiken* (*experience*), the second "K" stands for *Kan* (*intuition*), and "D" stands for *Dokyo* (*courage*). CoBRA improves the *courage* element by combining quantitative project data with the *experience* and *intuition* of human experts. In CoBRA, project estimation *intuition* is enhanced by a systematic, yet comprehensible, methodology for acquiring and documenting the qualitative knowledge of experienced engineers and by integrating it with quantitative data. In this sense, CoBRA introduces a scientific basis to the KKD paradigm.

I am convinced that the software industry, not only in Japan, can greatly benefit from using the CoBRA method for managing the greatest organizational asset, which is knowledge. This book explains the CoBRA method and shows how to use it to achieve and maintain software project excellence.

Tokyo, Japan   Dr. Koichi Matsuda
                                            Director, Software Engineering Center
                                        Information-technology Promotion Agency

Quotes from Industry

The CoBRA method is a way of integrating the "Art" and the "Science" of software estimation, which is usually believed to be a "Black Art." The CoBRA method demystifies the Black Art of software estimation.

-Yasushi Ishigai
Research Director at Research Center for Information Technology
Mitsubishi Research Institute, Inc., Japan

We had not been able to imagine building our own software estimation models until we encountered the CoBRA method. As far as combining project data and expert judgment for the purpose of software effort estimation is concerned, we can definitely say that there are no other methods that are comparable to CoBRA.

-Morihiko Shinoda, Deputy Department Manager
-Yutaka Masaoka, Senior Engineer
Government, Public Sector Systems Division
Hitachi Solutions, Ltd, Japan

We used the CoBRA method for early-stage estimation of system integration projects. We were very satisfied with CoBRA because we could easily model relevant cost drivers that are specific to our own context as well as base development productivity. From limited use in one group, we have now expanded its use to department-wide activities.

-Yasushi Aizaki
Manager at Systems Development Division
NTT Data Sekisui Systems, Japan

I am convinced that the CoBRA method has a high potential of resolving "acquisition issues" related to the accountability of software costs in IT business, which enduringly persist on the side of IT customers. That's because the models are very simple and easy to build and can be understood even by non-IT professionals.

-Hiroshi Iwakiri
General Manager
Information Systems Business Unit
Mitsubishi Electric Corporation

Preface

What This Book Is About?

In this book, we present a method for estimating the effort required to successfully complete a software development project. The method is called Cost Estimation, Benchmarking, and Risk Assessment—CoBRA for short—and combines human judgment and measurement data in order to systematically create a custom-specific effort estimation model.

The book provides a comprehensive specification of processes for developing the CoBRA effort model and for applying the model in a number of different project management scenarios. For each of these processes, we describe detailed activities that need to be performed as well as associated techniques. We illustrate the presented concepts with a number of examples and graphical illustrations. More-over, we provide a series of practical guidelines on how to apply these processes, based on industrial experiences regarding project effort estimation in general, and on using the CoBRA method in particular.

Furthermore the book reports several real-world cases where the CoBRA method was applied in various industrial contexts in order to illustrate the practical usage of the method. The cases represent different estimation contexts in terms of software project environment, estimation objectives, and estimation constraints.

Objectives of This Book

The main objective of this book is to present the Cost Estimation, Benchmarking, and Risk Assessment Method (CoBRA) in a way that allows for applying it successfully in practical situations. Consequently, the key goals we are aiming at with this book include:

- Complete and comprehensible specification of all relevant CoBRA processes such as developing and applying the effort estimation model. This includes the

description of process activities, their inputs and outputs, the personnel involved, and the theories and techniques employed.
• Comprehensive explanation of the presented concepts through practical examples, graphical illustrations, and guidelines from practice.
• Illustration of real-world CoBRA usage through exemplary application cases from various industrial contexts.

After reading this book a reader should understand the principles of the CoBRA method, know the basic CoBRA processes, and be able to adapt and use the method in a specific context.

To Whom This Book Is Addressed

Software Practitioners

We addressed this book to all software practitioners who deal with planning and managing software development projects as part of their daily work. This group includes primarily—but is not limited to—project managers and project estimators. In order to facilitate understanding and practical application of the concepts presented in the book, we illustrate them with a number of practical examples and guidelines. In particular, the book is addressed to those software practitioners who would need an alternative to expensive estimation based on expert judgment, yet who do not have sufficient measurement data to employ analytical effort estimation.

Students

The book is also addressed to students of software engineering and of associated courses. In order to support in-depth study of the concepts presented in the book, we include descriptions of associated theoretical foundations and refer to appropriate further readings.

Key Terminology Used in This Book

In this book, we use several basic terms that in other literature and in practice are often used interchangeably, although they do have different meanings. In order not to confuse the reader, we would like to start by clarifying the most important terms we will use throughout the text. For a more comprehensive dictionary of the employed terms, please refer to the Glossary at the end of the book.

Cost Versus Effort

Although principally and intuitively different, the terms "cost" and "effort" are usually used as synonyms in the software project management area. Webster's dictionary defines cost as "the amount or equivalent paid or charged for something" and effort as "conscious exertion of power" or "the total work done to achieve a particular end." In the software engineering domain, cost is defined in a monetary sense, and with respect to a software development project, it refers to the partial or total monetary cost of providing (creating) a certain product or service. Effort, on the other hand, refers to manpower spent on performing activities aimed at providing a certain product or service. In consequence, project cost includes, but is not limited to, project effort. In practice, cost includes such elements as fixed infrastructure and administrative costs. Moreover, depending on the project context (e.g., currency or cost of manpower unit), project costs may differ even if the project effort is the same.

In software engineering literature and practice, "cost" is often used as a synonym for "effort." One way to notice the difference is to look at units used. Cost in a monetary sense is typically measured in terms of certain currencies (e.g., $, €, ¥, etc.), whereas cost in an effort sense is typically measured as manpower (e.g., person-hours, person-days, person-months, etc.).

In this book, we focus on estimating software development effort, and we consistently differentiate between cost and effort.

Estimation Versus Prediction Versus Planning

In software engineering, effort estimation, prediction, and planning are related to each other; yet, they have different meanings, i.e., they refer to different project management activities. Actually, the dictionary definitions perfectly reflect the differences between these three processes:

- *Estimation*: "the act of judging tentatively or approximately the value, worth, or significance of something"
- *Prediction*: "the act of declaring or indicating in advance; especially foretelling on the basis of observation, experience, or scientific reason"
- *Planning*: "the act or process of making or carrying out plans; *specifically* the establishment of goals, policies, and procedures for a social or economic unit"

Adam Trendowicz

Acknowledgments

This book is not the fruit of one man's work—although it has one author. A number of great people have made their explicit or implicit contribution to this book. Here I would like to thank them for their efforts.

First of all I would like to thank Prof. Dr. Dieter Rombach for creating the Fraunhofer Institute for Experimental Software Engineering—a great environment for innovative work.

I would like to express thanks to Mr. Yasushi Ishigai for his great support in deploying the CoBRA method in Japan and for many inspiring discussions regarding the method. I would also like to thank Mr. Ishigai for his great dedication in reviewing the initial version of this book and making superb comments, which helped me to greatly improve the book.

Furthermore, I would like to thank the representatives of various software companies where the CoBRA method was applied. They provided great support in transferring the CoBRA method into industrial practice and provided valuable feedback about the method from a practical perspective. In particular, I would like to thank Mr. Hisato Hatano, Dr. Nahomi Kikuchi, Mrs. Haruka Nakao, and Mr. Debanjan Ray.

I would like to express many thanks to the reviewers of the book, Mr. Michael Kläs and Mrs. Sylwia Kopczyńska, for their valuable remarks.

Last but not least I would like to thank Mrs. Sonnhild Namingha, the very first reader of the complete book, who revised its spelling and copyedited it.

Contents

Acronyms

Allette	Allette Systems Pty. Ltd (company name)
ARE	Acceptable Risk Exposure
ARL	Acceptable Risk Level
CMMI	Capability Maturity Model Integrated
CoBRA	Cost Estimation, Benchmarking, and Risk Assessment
DF	Direct effort Factor
EF	Experience Factory
EMB	Embedded Software Systems
EO	Effort Overhead
Ext	Extreme
FhG/IESE	Fraunhofer Institute for Experimental Software Engineering
GUI	Graphical User Interface
IF	Indirect effort Factor
IPA/SEC	Information-technology Promotion Agency, Software Engineering Center
ISO	International Standardization Organization
IV&V	Independent Verification and Validation
JAMSS	Japan Manned Software Systems (company name)
LHRO	Performance-Optimized Latin Hypercube (simulation technique)
Max	Maximal
MC	Monte Carlo (simulation technique)
MCDA	Multiple Criteria Decision Analysis
Min	Minimal
MIS	Management and Information Systems
ML	Most Likely
MMRE	Mean Magnitude of Relative Error (or Mean Magnitude of Relative Estimation Error)
MRE	Magnitude of Relative Error (or Magnitude of Relative Estimation Error)
Nom	Nominal
Oki	Oki Electric Industry, Ltd (company name)
PERT	Program Evaluation and Review Technique
PMBOK	Project Management Body of Knowledge

PMI	Project Management Institute
PMO	Project Management Office
RE	Relative Error (or Relative Estimation Error)
sd&m	software design & management AG (company name; currently Capgemini Deutschland Holding GmbH)
SEPG	Software Engineering Process Group
SISL	Siemens Information Systems, Ltd (company name)

Part I
Predictable Software Development

Failing to plan is planning to fail.

Alan Lakein

Software effort estimation is a key element of software project planning and management. Yet, in industrial practice, the important role of effort estimation is often underestimated and/or misunderstood. The first part of this book introduces software effort estimation and motivates the CoBRA method within the landscape of multiplier effort estimation methods offered by the software engineering community. In particular:

- Chapter 1 sketches typical challenges of software development projects and explains the essential role of effort estimation in managing successful software projects.
- Chapter 2 addresses the question of "what is a good estimate?," which is essential for estimation. The chapter uncovers the simplistic view on the goodness of estimation held by the research community and provides practice-oriented criteria for good estimates.
- Chapter 3 introduces the hybrid estimation method called CoBRA, which represents an alternative to estimation methods based strictly either on expert judgment or analysis of quantitative project data. The chapter summarizes the most important benefits of the CoBRA method.

Why Software Effort Estimation?

1

1.1 Software Is Getting Complex

Software is everywhere. Most of today's goods and services are realized, at least in part, either by means of or with the help of software systems. Our dependency on software is increasing continuously. On the one hand, progress in the domains where software has traditionally been playing a key role entails increasing pressure upon software to progress. On the other hand, in domains that were traditionally reserved for hardware, software has become the major driving force of the overall progress in the meanwhile. For example, it is said that 60–90 % of all advances in the automotive domain nowadays are due to software systems. Some products and services that would have traditionally been realized through "hardware" solutions are now realized through software systems. Other products and services are only possible through software systems and could not have been realized by other means. One way or another, the size and complexity of software systems in various domains are increasing rapidly.

The increasing complexity of software systems entails a fundamental shift in their cost, time-to-market, functionality, and quality requirements. Software is required to support a wide variety of domains, must be ever faster, must be more intelligent, must be more dependable, require fewer hardware resources, must be ever easier to maintain, etc. The wish list is typically quite long and ends with "the software must cost less and get on the market before our competition even think about something similar."

1.2 Software Development Is Getting Complex

In addition to rigid requirements on software functionality, quality, cost, and time to market, there are a number of external constraints that make software development a very complex task. Let us just name a few of the most important ones.

A. Trendowicz, *Software Cost Estimation, Benchmarking, and Risk Assessment*,
The Fraunhofer IESE Series on Software and Systems Engineering,
DOI 10.1007/978-3-642-30764-5_1, © Springer-Verlag Berlin Heidelberg 2013

Development Technologies and Paradigms Change Rapidly Software development teams must strive to achieve software development objectives by exploiting the impressive advances in continuously changing—and thus often immature—technologies and development paradigms. In fact, mastering rapidly changing technologies and processes is often considered as the most important challenge differentiating software development from other domains. Without counting the minor changes in methods and tools, over the past 50 years, the software industry has roughly gone through at least four generations of programming languages and three major development paradigms.

Development Distribution Increases Together with the increased variety of software products, technologies, and processes, development distribution is growing constantly. Development is shifting from single contractors to distributed projects, where teams are scattered across multiple companies, time zones, cultures, and continents. The global trend towards software outsourcing has led to software companies needing a reliable basis for making make-or-buy decisions or for verifying the development schedule and cost offered by contractors if they decide to buy parts of a software product.

Software Development Is still Largely a Human-Intensive Process Moreover, software development is a human-based activity with extreme uncertainties from the outset. Rober Glass (2002) recapitulated this fact by saying *"Eighty percent of software work is intellectual. A fair amount of it is creative. Little of it is clerical."* As such, software development depends on the capabilities of the developers on the one hand and on the capabilities of the customers and other involved parties on the other hand.

Software Products Have an Abstract Character Yet, probably none of the aforementioned aspects have as large an impact on the difficulty of software production as the abstract character of software products. This is the "softness" of software products that make software engineering different from other, "classical," engineering domains. To create software, developers start with customer requirements and go through a sequence of transformations during which all involved parties create, share, and revise a number of abstract models of various, usually increasing, complexities. In addition, individual project tasks in a transformation sequence are usually highly interdependent. The intangible and volatile character of software products—especially requirements—makes them difficult to measure and control. This contributes to software development being a mixture of science and art.

1.3   Project Management Is a Key Success Factor

The complex and multidependent character of software development makes managing software projects a challenging task. In today's competitive software development market, an organization's survival and growth require effective means for managing software projects. A software project should, like any other project, be considered in terms of a business case. It should therefore lay out the reason(s) for the investment, the expected benefits of the initiative, the costs expected to make it happen, an analysis of risks, and the future options that will be created. A software project also requires, as one of its key success factors, effective management. Effective project management requires considering numerous issues. It must focus on areas that are critical for financial success, on the effective use of resources, on an analysis of market potential and opportunities for innovation, on the development of a learning environment, etc.

1.4   Effort Estimation Is the Basis for Effective Project Management

Software project management is a key project success factor, and as aptly pointed out by Barry Boehm (1981), *"Poor management can increase software costs more rapidly than any other factor."* A number of bad practices may contribute to poor project management, which in consequence will lead to failed projects. One of the most common aspects of poor project management, which typically results in a project crisis, is poor effort estimation. For example, Glass (2002) points out poor effort estimation as one of the two most common causes of runaway projects, besides unstable requirements. Rosencrance (2007), in her survey of more than 1,000 IT professionals, reports that two out of the three most important causes of IT project failure are perceived to be related to poor effort estimation, in particular insufficient resource planning and unrealistic project deadlines.

Effective project management requires reliable effort and schedule estimation support. On the one hand, project managers need a reliable basis for developing realistic project effort, schedule, and cost plans. On the other hand, as project management is to a large extent a political game, they need a reliable and convincing basis for negotiating project conditions with project owners and/or customers. In the latter scenario, simple estimates that "feel" good are definitely insufficient to justify realistic project plans against the demands and expectations of other project stakeholders.

Yet, independent of these findings, many software organizations are still proposing unrealistic software costs, work within tight schedules, and finish their projects behind schedule and budget, or do not complete them at all.

Further Reading

- E. Yourdon, *Death March, 2nd Edition*, Prentice Hall, November 2003.

  This book is one of the software engineering and project management classics, which, although technologically not quite up to date, discusses timeless traps in software project management. The author discusses the reasons why software projects what he calls "death march" projects, that is, projects that are sentenced to fail from the very beginning because of their unrealistic setup. Typical symptoms of a death march project are: schedule, budget, and staff are about half of what would be necessary, the planned product scope is unrealistic, and people are working 14 h a day, 6 or 7 days a week. The author suggests a number of useful solutions to avoid and, if this is not an option, to rescue death march projects. The example aspects the author discusses as worth considering include project politics and negotiations, team management, process management, project scheduling and time management, and application of tools and technologies.

- S. McConnell, *Software Project Survival Guide, 1st Edition*, Microsoft Press, October 1997.

  This book provides a set of guidelines on how to successfully perform software projects. For each major stage of software development, the author refers to the most common weaknesses that software projects typically face, and he discusses ways of addressing them in order to successfully go through the project. The book focuses on the level-2 key process areas defined within SEI's Capability Maturity Model, such as requirements management, project planning, project tracking and oversight, quality assurance, and change control.

- T. DeMarco and T. Lister, *Peopleware: Productive Projects and Teams, 2nd Edition*, Dorset House Publishing Company, Inc., February 1999.

  This book is another software engineering and project management classic. Although technologically not quite up to date, it discusses timeless human aspects of software engineering. The authors address human factors as key determinants of a software product's quality and, ultimately, of a software project's success. Example aspects the authors discuss include the role of outstanding individuals and teamwork in software development project. Although the authors do not give any ready-made recipe for creating a great team, as a counterexample, they point to a number of ways bad project managers prevent a team from becoming great or that can even destroy a team that is already great.

- F. P. Brooks, *The Mythical Man-Month: Essays on Software Engineering, Anniversary Edition, 2nd Edition*, Addison-Wesley Professional, August 1995.

  This book is another software engineering and project management classic, which although technologically not quite up to date, discusses timeless human aspects of software engineering. Fred Brooks makes a simple conjecture that an intellectual job, such as software development, is completely different from physical labor jobs, such as traditional manufacturing—although both jobs may be human-intensive. Using this assumption, the author discusses in a number of short essays people- and team-related aspects of a software development project. He explains why the simple arithmetic of completing the same job twice as fast with twice as many people does not work in the software engineering. The book discusses many important issues of managing human resources, such as work environment, team building, and organizational learning. Finally, the author outlines important pitfalls of managing software projects and development teams and suggests a number of interesting solutions to these pitfalls.

- J. E. Tomayko and O. Hazzan, *Human Aspects of Software Development*, Charles River Media Inc., 2004.

  The authors devote their book to software engineering as a human-intensive activity. They discuss a number of social and cognitive aspects of software engineering such as teamwork, customer–developer relationships, and learning processes in software development. In particular, they look at individual software development and project management processes, both heavyweight and agile ones, from the human-resource perspective. In doing so, they consider different groups of software stakeholders, such as developers and customers, and interactions within as well as between these groups. The book also addresses human-related aspects of a software product, such as the abstract character of software and different perceptions of various software products. Finally, the book discusses learning issues in software engineering.

- S. Berkun, *Making Things Happen: Mastering Project Management, Revised Edition*, O'Reilly Media, March 2008.

  This book is a collection of essays, each of which addresses selected aspects of project management—its challenges, example solutions, and practical guidelines. The essays are organized around three major project aspects: plans, skills, and management. With respect to plans, the author shows how to lay out best plans and what the reasons of failed plans are. The part devoted to skills discusses the basic abilities of a project manager, such as writing good project and product specifications. In this part, the author also covers soft management skills such as e-mail and meeting etiquette. Finally, regarding the management aspect, Bercun addresses leadership issues such as trust, power, prioritizing, sanity checks, and project politics. For each discussed aspect, the author considers key success criteria, associated challenges, and best-practice solutions. Moreover, he illustrates the presented issues with a number of real-life examples.

What Is a Good Estimate?

The basic question of software effort estimation is "What is a good estimate?" Traditionally, effort estimation has been used for planning and tracking overall resources, such as manpower, required for completing a project. With this objective in mind, over the years, researchers have been pursuing an elusive target of getting a 100 % accurate estimate in terms of exact number of person-hours required for completing a software project. Effort estimation methods that grew upon this goal focus on providing exact point estimates.

Yet, software practitioners nowadays need effort estimation as comprehensive decision support for a number of project management activities. They have noticed that even the most accurate estimates are worthless if they cannot be reasonably justified to the project sponsor and the customers or if they do not provide guidelines on what to do if the project is not going to meet the estimates. From this perspective, one of the critical characteristics of good estimates is the additional information they provide to support project decision making. On the one hand, project decision makers need to identify project areas that are responsible for increased development effort in order to have a transparent and convincing basis for renegotiating the project resources and/or scope with the project sponsor. On the other hand, they need an indication of the effort-related development processes that can potentially be affected in order to gain the greatest improvement in development productivity at the lowest overhead—the concept of "low-hanging fruits."

Summarizing, a good estimate is one that supports a project manager in successful project management and successful project completion. A good estimation method is thus an estimation method that provides such support, without violating other project objectives such as project management overhead.

A. Trendowicz, *Software Cost Estimation, Benchmarking, and Risk Assessment*,
The Fraunhofer IESE Series on Software and Systems Engineering,
DOI 10.1007/978-3-642-30764-5_2, © Springer-Verlag Berlin Heidelberg 2013

Further Reading

- S. McConnell, *Software Estimation: Demystifying the Black Art*, Microsoft Press, Redmond, MA, USA, 2006.

  In the first chapter of his book, McConnell presents his view on what constitutes a "good estimate." He starts with two basic aspects (1) distinguishing between estimates, plans, and bids and (2) accounting for estimation uncertainty and considering estimates in probabilistic terms. Next, he takes a critical look at the common definitions of a good estimate dominated by the estimation accuracy perspective. He brings up the extent to which estimates support project management activities and project success as a key determinant of a good estimate. He concludes his discussion with a concise definition of what constitutes a good estimate.

Why the CoBRA Method?

3

A number of effort estimation methods have been proposed in recent decades. Still, no "silver-bullet" method has been proposed so far. Each and every estimation method has its strengths and limitations, and its goodness largely depends on the context in which it is applied.

In most of the cases, a method represents one of the two extreme estimation strategies: expert-based and data-driven. The first group bases effort predictions on the judgment of human experts, whereas the latter group uses only measurement data to derive effort predictions. In the light of a lack of consensus on which expert-based or data-driven approaches are "better," Jørgensen and Boehm (2009) propose the hybrid methods, which combine the strengths of both strategies while avoiding their weaknesses. The most important consequence of this finding is that a combination of estimation approaches can substantially improve the accuracy of estimates. The two most important strategies for implementing this idea are (1) combining multiple estimation paradigms, such as expert-based and data-driven methods, into a hybrid method and (2) combining multiple estimates provided by independent estimation methods, preferably representing different estimation paradigms. Although it allows for validating alternative estimates against each other, the combination of multiple methods requires much project overhead for applying multiple methods and combining their outputs. From this perspective, we should consider using multiple estimation methods only when the corresponding benefit justifies its high costs. For example, if estimation quality is very critical, there is no single estimation method that meets all our estimation objectives.

However, the typical situations where resources for estimation are limited, hybrid methods offer the best cost–benefit trade-off. They combine multiple information sources and estimation paradigms at reasonable cost, within a single estimation procedure.

Paradoxically, very few hybrid methods have been proposed over the years—among them the Cost Estimation, Benchmarking, and Risk Assessment method (CoBRA). Throughout numerous industrial applications, CoBRA has proven to be an effective and efficient solution for software project effort estimation. The particular strengths of the method include:

A. Trendowicz, *Software Cost Estimation, Benchmarking, and Risk Assessment*,
The Fraunhofer IESE Series on Software and Systems Engineering,
DOI 10.1007/978-3-642-30764-5_3, © Springer-Verlag Berlin Heidelberg 2013

- *High estimation accuracy*: The CoBRA method has proven in a number of industrial applications that it provides highly accurate estimations, with estimation error ranging from 9 to 14 %.
- *Minimal data requirements*: The CoBRA method requires only information on size and effort from about ten already completed ("historical") projects. Even though these data are not available at the time of estimation, they can typically be easily elicited postmortem. Actual project effort is typically documented, and software size can be measured based on the project outcomes such as requirements specification or software code.
- *Reusable cost model*: The CoBRA effort model can be reused, completely or in parts across similar projects.
- *Organizational learning*: The CoBRA method provides a systematic process for eliciting knowledge hidden in the experts' minds and in measurement data and for documenting it within a transparent and intuitive effort model.
- *Comprehensive project management support*: The CoBRA method supports a number of project management activities such as estimation, project scope negotiations, risk analysis, benchmarking, and process improvement.
- *Organizational growth*: The CoBRA method provides a systematic and intuitive approach for analyzing factors that influence the performance of software development processes and project effort. In that sense, it supports the understanding of development processes and helps to identify important improvement potentials.
- *Building up of a measurement system*: The CoBRA method helps to find those factors that have the greatest impact of the performance of software development processes. These factors are potential subjects for measurement and quantitative project control. In that sense, CoBRA supports focusing measurement activities on the most relevant aspects and limiting overhead spent on collecting, analyzing, and maintaining unnecessary measurements.

Further Reading

- L.C. Briand and I. Wieczorek, "Resource Modeling in Software Engineering," in J.J. Marciniak (ed.) *Encyclopedia of Software Engineering, 2nd Edition.* Wiley, 2002.

  The authors present a comprehensive discussion of the most common effort estimation methods. First, they classify existing estimation methods and discuss the basic characteristics of each class. Next, they present the basic principles of the most commonly used effort estimation methods. Finally, the authors define a framework for evaluating estimation methods and use it to subjectively compare selected estimation methods.

Part II
The CoBRA Method

The best forecasting approach is one that takes advantage of the strengths of both [quantitative and judgmental] forecasting approaches.

N. R. Sanders and L. P. Ritzman

The CoBRA method, to which this book is devoted, applies systematic procedures for combining judgmental and analytical strategies to software project effort estimation. This second part of the book describes in detail all the procedures that are necessary to understand the method and apply it in practice. In particular:

- Chapter 4 introduces the basic terminology used within the CoBRA method and provides an overview of the main components of the method.
- Chapter 5 describes the detailed process of developing a CoBRA effort estimation model. For each process step, we describe its objective, inputs, elementary activities, resources, tools, and outcomes.
- Chapter 6 describes the detailed process of applying the CoBRA effort model for the purpose of software project effort estimation. Moreover, the chapter presents typical scenarios of applying the CoBRA model for different estimation purposes.

Principles of the CoBRA Method

4

The Cost Estimation, Benchmarking, and Risk Assessment (CoBRA) method combines multiple prediction approaches in that it aggregates techniques representing expert-based and data-driven estimation paradigms, within one hybrid estimation method. This chapter introduces the basic idea and terminology of the CoBRA method. Moreover, this chapter specifies the basic roles considered in the CoBRA method and the essential conceptual elements of the method.

4.1 Terminology

Briand et al. (1998) proposed CoBRA as a hybrid method that combines data-driven and expert-based paradigms for effort estimation. The core idea of CoBRA is to model software development effort as consisting of two elements: nominal effort and effort overhead.

Nominal effort ($Effort_{Nom}$) is the engineering and management effort spent on developing a software product of a certain size in the context of a nominal project. A *nominal project* is a hypothetical "ideal" project in a certain environment of an organization (or business unit). It is a project that runs under optimal conditions, that is, a project where all environmental characteristics having an impact on project effort are at their "best" levels ("perfect") from the start of the project. Note that "best" refers to realistic levels that are possible in a certain context, not to the best imaginable levels. For instance, the project objectives are well defined and understood by all staff members and the customer, and all key people in the project have appropriate skills to successfully conduct the project.

Effort overhead (EO) is the additional effort spent on overcoming imperfections of a real project environment, such as insufficient skills of the project team. Effort overhead refers to a nonproductive project effort spent in addition to the nominal effort. In CoBRA, effort overhead is quantified as the percentage of additional effort compared to the nominal one. For example, if a project's $EO = 50$ %, this would mean that the project actually requires 150 % of the nominal effort, that is, 50 % more than it would require if it was a nominal project.

A. Trendowicz, *Software Cost Estimation, Benchmarking, and Risk Assessment,*
The Fraunhofer IESE Series on Software and Systems Engineering,
DOI 10.1007/978-3-642-30764-5_4, © Springer-Verlag Berlin Heidelberg 2013

Nominal productivity (P_{Nom}) refers to development productivity under optimal project conditions, that is, the productivity of a nominal project where all effort factors have their best levels. In general, productivity refers (IEEE-1045 1993) to the ratio between a project's output and input. In the concrete case of software projects, development productivity is computed as the ratio between the size of delivered software products and the effort consumed to develop these products (4.1).

$$Productivity = \frac{Size}{Effort} \qquad (4.1)$$

In real software projects, actual development productivity (P_{Act}) is decreased by nonproductive effort spent on overcoming the imperfect character of the project. For example, a certain effort must be expended to train the development team. The factor by which productivity is decreased depends on the specific characteristics of an individual project. The difference between nominal and actual productivity (*productivity loss*) is proportional to the portion of additional nonproductive effort. In CoBRA, the additional nonproductive effort is accounted for through the effort overhead. In general, the higher the effort overhead, the higher the actual project effort and the lower the actual development productivity.

4.2   Components of an Effort Model

CoBRA implements the idea of nominal project effort and effort overhead through two basic components of an effort model (Fig. 4.1): the effort overhead model and the productivity model.

The *effort overhead model* (or *causal effort model*) produces an estimate of the project effort overhead. The effort overhead model consists of factors affecting the project effort within a certain context (so-called *effort factors* or *effort drivers*). The causal model is obtained through expert knowledge acquisition (e.g., involving experienced project managers). An example is presented in Fig. 4.2. The arrows indicate direct relationships. "+" indicates a positive relationship, and "−" indicates a negative relationship. One arrow pointing to another indicates an interaction effect. For example, an interaction exists between "disciplined requirements management" and "requirements volatility." In this case, a decreased level of disciplined requirements management magnifies the negative influence of volatile requirements on project effort; that is, it causes an increase of development effort. In CoBRA, we refer to effort factors directly linked to effort as *direct effort factors* and to effort factors linked to direct factors as *indirect effort factors*. In the aforementioned example, "requirements volatility" is a direct effort factor, whereas "disciplined requirements management" is an indirect effort factor.

The qualitative information concerning a factor's influence on effort is quantified by assigning so-called *effort multipliers* to each factor directly influencing effort. For a given effort factor, its effort multipliers refer to the percentage of effort overhead

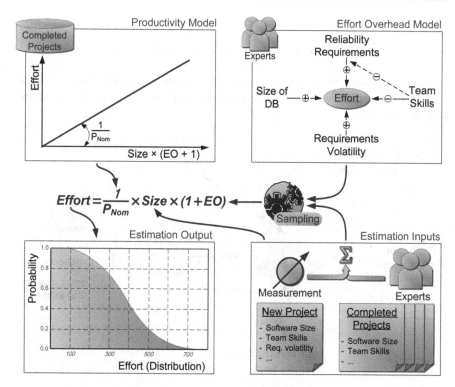

Fig. 4.1 Components of the effort estimation with the CoBRA method

that this factor introduces above that of nominal effort. The value of an effort multiplier depends on the factor's value and is elicited through expert judgment. The multipliers for the effort factors are modeled as distributions to capture the uncertainty inherent in expert opinion. Triangular distributions can be used to reflect the experts' opinion about each effort factor's impact on cost by giving three values: minimum, most likely, and maximum value of a multiplier.

In CoBRA, effort factors directly influencing effort are assumed to be orthogonal to each other. Based on this assumption, the total effort overhead ("EO" in the basic effort equation in Fig. 4.1) can be computed as the sum of the effort overhead (effort multipliers) associated with all effort factors directly influencing effort.

Effort overhead (EO) represents the percentage increase of effort in a real project relative to a nominal project and is expressed as the percentage portion of a nominal project's effort: $EO \times Effort_{Nom}$, where $0 \leq EO \geq 1$. Consequently, the actual effort of a real project, $Effort_{Act}$, is equal to the effort of a nominal project $Effort_{Nom}$ plus the effort overhead EO. We can express this mathematically as

$$Effort_{Act} = Effort_{Nom} + (EO \times Effort_{Nom}) \qquad (4.2)$$

which is equivalent to

$$\text{Effort}_{Act} = \text{Effort}_{Nom} \times (1 + \text{EO}) \tag{4.3}$$

Simply speaking, (4.2) and (4.3) reflect basic mathematics, according to which increasing a certain value by x % corresponds to multiplying this value by (*100 % + x %*).

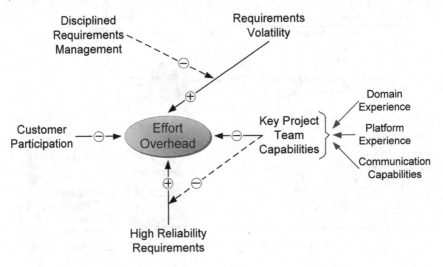

Fig. 4.2 Example of effort overhead model

The ***productivity model*** is the second base element of the CoBRA effort model. The productivity model uses data from past similar projects for identifying a relationship between effort overhead and actual project effort and for determining the productivity of a hypothetical nominal project—*nominal productivity*. We illustrate the idea of CoBRA's productivity model in Fig. 4.3.

The actual development productivities of multiple software projects are represented by gray dots around the *Actual Productivity* regression line. In CoBRA, nominal development productivity is assumed to be constant across projects in the same context and is used as a baseline for estimating new projects. Therefore, we can theoretically determine nominal productivity using the actual development productivity and actual effort overhead of any project. We need to merely increase the project's actual development productivity by the factor represented by its actual effort overhead (4.4).

$$P_{Act} = \frac{P_{Nom}}{(1 + EO)} \tag{4.4}$$

In real software projects, computing nominal productivity using project-specific actual productivity and effort overhead will lead to nominal productivity that varies across projects. This phenomenon is represented in Fig. 4.3 by the diamond-shaped

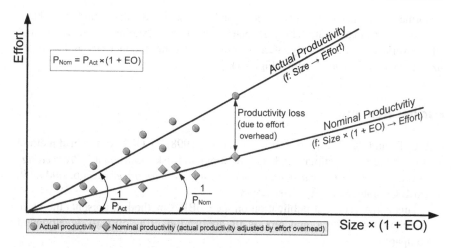

Fig. 4.3 Nominal productivity versus actual productivity

dots spread around the *Nominal Productivity* regression line. This happens because the effort overhead computed using CoBRA's effort overhead model does not account for the true project's effort overhead. The main causes of this deviation are (1) modeling error, in that an imperfect effort overhead model does not correctly and completely cover all true causal effort dependencies, and (2) measurement error in the project data used for computing nominal productivity.

In order to determine *baseline productivity* for estimating future projects, CoBRA synthesizes project-specific nominal productivities computed across multiple historical projects for which actual development productivity and effort overhead are already known. Traditionally, this is accomplished using the linear regression model *f: Size × (1 + EO) → Effort*. The model represents the basic idea of the CoBRA method that nominal effort is linearly dependent on size and that actual nonlinearity is caused by environmental influencing characteristics represented by effort factors. The slope of the regression line in the model approximates the inverse hypothetical nominal development productivity and is used in CoBRA as a baseline for estimating new projects.

Note that the nominal productivity regression line represents a simple bivariate relationship that does not require a large data set. This is important, as it explains why CoBRA does not have demanding data requirements, as opposed to data-driven estimation techniques. In order to build up such a regression model, data from merely about ten historical projects are needed.

The effort estimate for a new project is then determined by its size, its effort overhead, and the baseline nominal productivity determined from historical projects. The project's effort overhead is determined based on its actual characteristics. Since not all of them are known at the time of estimation, which is typically at the very beginning of the development process, value distributions instead of exact values are given to cover their uncertainty. Running a Monte Carlo simulation, sampling is performed from each of the distributions, and each sampled value is added to obtain an effort overhead estimate. This is repeated many times, resulting in a distribution of effort overhead and ultimately, after considering nominal productivity and software size, in the distribution of effort (Fig. 4.1).

Further Reading

• L.C. Briand, K. El Emam, and F. Bomarius (1998), "COBRA: a hybrid method for software cost estimation, benchmarking, and risk assessment," *Proceedings of the 20th International Conference on Software Engineering*, pp. 390–399. IEEE Computer Society Press, 1998.

This is the very first publication on the CoBRA method. It presents the basic principles of CoBRA and reports its application in a software development company.

Model Development and Validation

5

The CoBRA method represents a model-based approach to software effort estimation. In this approach, before we can predict the effort for a new project, we need to first build an effort estimation model. In general, the effort model reflects past experiences regarding effort relationships in similar situations, that is, within projects of a similar kind. Preconditions of reliable estimates are that (1) the estimation model considers all relevant factors influencing the project effort and (2) the estimated project corresponds to the situation represented by the model. In a typical data-driven approach, the effort model arises from the analysis of measurement data from multiple projects. The CoBRA effort model captures believed and actual causal effort dependencies observed in the past in a certain organization's context. Believed dependencies are represented by expert judgments, whereas actual dependencies are represented by measurement data collected in already completed software projects.

In this chapter, we present the detailed step-by-step procedure of developing and initially validating a CoBRA effort estimation model. For each step, we specify the inputs, outputs, and resources needed to complete it. Moreover, we describe the analysis and modeling techniques employed in each step and discuss alternative implementations of the step if multiple options are possible. Finally, we share the experiences we gained using the CoBRA method and give a number of tips on implementing the model development process in industrial practice.

5.1 Process Overview

5.1.1 Model Development Steps

Developing a CoBRA effort estimation model consists of several steps. Figure 5.1 provides an overview of the overall process of building and enhancing a CoBRA effort model.

In the subsequent sections, we describe in detail the elements of each step including its inputs, outputs, activities, involved roles, and relevant constraints to

A. Trendowicz, *Software Cost Estimation, Benchmarking, and Risk Assessment,*
The Fraunhofer IESE Series on Software and Systems Engineering,
DOI 10.1007/978-3-642-30764-5_5, © Springer-Verlag Berlin Heidelberg 2013

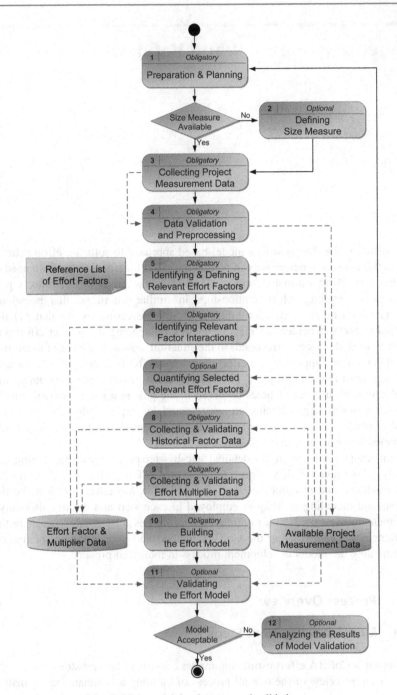

Fig. 5.1 Overview of the CoBRA model development and validation process

consider. The model development process includes the initial validation of the effort model. In the last two steps, the model's performance is validated using historical project data.

After these steps, an analyst may decide to improve the model and revalidate it. In this sense, the development of the CoBRA effort model might be (and from our practical experience should be) an iterative process. Inspired by agile software development, we recommend developing the CoBRA effort model in a series of small increments. In each increment, only a very limited part of the model is changed, with changes including additions, deletions, and modifications of basic model elements. In particular, we recommend developing the CoBRA model in two stages:

- *Incremental construction*: We start with a very small model consisting of just a few of the most relevant effort factors directly influencing project effort. In the subsequent iterations, we can gradually extend the model by adding new factors and indirect influences. We should keep the extent of model changes small in order to control the effects of changes on the model's performance. As we perform subsequent iterations and the CoBRA model grows larger, we should shift the focus from extending to revising the model while keeping its size and complexity at a constant level.
- *Iterative revision*: After a few initial iterations dominated by model additions, we should consider revising the model instead of extending it furthermore. In practice, the "20/80" rule applies to the CoBRA models in that modeling 20 % of the most relevant effort factors in the model usually suffices to account for 80 % of the effects with respect to project effort. In other words, with 20 % of the most relevant effort factors in the CoBRA model, we are able to reliably estimate new projects. Investing further effort into extending the CoBRA model does typically not pay off in increased model performance; conversely, the model's performance decreases as we add new elements. The major reason is that the larger the model, the less comprehensible it is and the more misleading effects it may represent.

Tip

▶ Develop the CoBRA effort model in an iterative manner. Validate the model obtained at the end of each iteration by using historical project data, and improve the model in the next iteration if its performance does not meet predefined acceptance criteria.

5.1.2 Roles in the CoBRA Method

Employing the CoBRA method requires involving personnel with different kinds of expertise depending on whether the method is introduced into an organization for the first time or has already been used. Table 5.1 presents three general roles

Table 5.1 Roles in the CoBRA method

Role	Description and responsibilities
Analyst	Description: A person knowledgeable in the CoBRA method and with experience in building and using CoBRA models. The main job of the analyst is to provide expertise and experience regarding the CoBRA method. The analyst is typically involved in creating all CoBRA models within an organization and is responsible for transferring knowledge to other involved personnel appropriate to the character of their involvement, with personnel comprising the role of estimator and domain expert.
	In large organizations, the analyst is typically a dedicated role that is responsible for all project estimation methods, processes, and models. In small organizations, the role of the analyst may be combined with other responsibilities such as project management or process measurement and improvement. Yet, there should be one person responsible for the CoBRA activities within a certain context, such as a business unit or application domain.
	The analyst will typically be a member of the project management office (PMO) group, the software engineering process group (SEPG), or the measurement group. The analyst may also be a person external to the organization in which CoBRA is applied. In that case, the analyst plays the role of a consultant and transfers CoBRA knowledge to a person who will later on take over the role of analyst within the organization. Major responsibilities of the analyst role include:
	• Training estimators and domain experts in the CoBRA method,
	• Building and maintaining organization-wide CoBRA models,
	• Adapting organization-level CoBRA models to the specific estimation context, objectives, and capabilities of individual projects,
	• Coaching estimators in using the CoBRA models and interpreting the outcomes of estimation,
	• Maintaining the CoBRA method and associated estimation processes.
Estimator	Description: A person who uses CoBRA models for estimating project effort. Typical users of CoBRA are project managers who collect inputs to the model, estimate effort, and interpret the results of the estimation for the purpose of planning and managing a project. In practice, the role of the estimator is typically played by the project manager. Major responsibilities of the estimator include:
	• Applying the CoBRA models for the purpose of project effort estimation,
	• Optionally, the estimator may build and tune a project-specific effort estimation model. The estimator should, however, communicate with the analyst in order to keep the analyst informed about the CoBRA activities within the organization.
Domain expert	Description: A person with significant project experience within the context where a CoBRA model is to be built. Project experience should comprise knowledge of project-specific and cross-project effort dependencies, in particular (1) factors that have a relevant impact on variations in development productivity and project effort, (2) the impact of these factors on project effort, (3) potential interdependencies between these factors, and (4) the values of these factors in at least part of the historical projects used for developing the CoBRA models. As for typical positions in an organization, the role of domain expert comprises project managers and quality engineers. Major responsibilities of the domain expert comprises:
	• Providing expertise for building the CoBRA model (factors influencing software effort and their interactions).
	• Providing historical project data for quantifying the CoBRA model (impact of effort factors on project effort, values of effort factors in historical projects, if not already measured in the organization's project data repository).
	• Supporting the project manager in acquiring data for estimating a new project, in particular software size and values of effort factors.

distinguished within the CoBRA method. Each role is briefly described and major responsibilities that the role is associated within CoBRA are listed.

5.2 Step 1: Preparation and Planning

In order to end up with beneficial results, we need to set up an environment for successfully applying the CoBRA method. Table 5.2 summarizes the most important elements of this step. We provide a detailed description of each activity in the following subsections.

In the following subsections, we present the major activities that comprise the "preparation and planning" step of the CoBRA model development process.

Table 5.2 CoBRA model development process: preparation and planning

Step 1: Preparation and planning	
Objective	The objective of this step is to determine the scope of the CoBRA application, identify potential constraints concerning the method's application, prepare an appropriate infrastructure, and plan the method's application.
Personnel	• *Analyst*: The analyst is responsible for preparing and planning the CoBRA model development process. If CoBRA is applied in an organization for the first time, two analysts will be typically involved in preparation and planning: an external and an internal analyst. The external analyst is responsible for planning, and the internal analyst assists the external analyst in that he/she provides organization-specific information necessary for planning the CoBRA modeling. This information includes the specification of estimation context and goals. Moreover, the internal analyst is responsible for preparing the infrastructure necessary for successfully performing the CoBRA model development process. • *Domain experts*: The involvement of the domain experts in this step is reduced to informing the analyst of their availability for the appropriate activities within the CoBRA model development process. The analyst must consider these constraints when planning resources and scheduling model development activities that require the involvement of domain experts.
Inputs	• Documented relevant context characteristics and assumptions. • Context-specific estimation objectives. • CoBRA learning materials: tutorials (for different target groups), examples of CoBRA inputs and outputs. • Typical scenarios of project effort estimation, that is, scenarios for estimating project effort and using estimation outcomes.
Activities	1. Introducing CoBRA to involved stakeholders. 2. Preparing CoBRA instruments. 3. Planning CoBRA model development.
Tools	• Tools for documenting estimation scope, constraints, and objectives. Example tools include standard office software packages such as MS Word, MS Excel, or MS PowerPoint. • Tools for planning CoBRA model development. Example tools include dedicated time and resource planning tools such as MS Project. Since planning the CoBRA model development is relatively simple, it can also be supported by more general tools supporting basic sequencing and calculation activities, such as MS Excel.
Outputs	• CoBRA model development plan, including work activities, resources assignment, and time schedule.

5.2.1 Introducing CoBRA to Involved Stakeholders

Effective use of the CoBRA method requires that all involved stakeholders possess appropriate knowledge of the method. The objective of this activity is to provide training to different groups of stakeholders depending on their role in the CoBRA model development process. This training for the purpose of developing a CoBRA estimation model should cover the following aspects:

- *Analysts* need in-depth knowledge of the theoretical and practical aspects of the CoBRA method. An appropriate training process consists of two parts: a theoretical and a practical one. In the theoretical part, the candidate for analyst participates in a comprehensible tutorial, which presents the theoretical fundamentals of the CoBRA method including the detailed CoBRA activities, the techniques employed, and the underlying rationales. In the second part, the future analyst is coached by an experienced analyst through the CoBRA activities in an exemplary method application. The application should preferably be a pilot usage of the CoBRA method within the very organization in which the person is going to assume the role of the analyst. Appropriate training can be acquired from external analysts proficient in the theory and practice of the CoBRA method.
- *Domain experts* need only a basic understanding of the CoBRA method and its purposes. Most of all they need to understand their role in developing the effort model, what inputs they should provide, and how they should provide these inputs. The objective of the training for domain experts is therefore to get them accustomed to the method and motivate them to provide proper inputs for the CoBRA modeling. In particular, we should make clear what information the experts should provide and ensure, for example, through practical exercises, that the experts consistently understand what inputs they are required to provide.
- *Estimators* need a basic understanding of the CoBRA method's principles and in-depth knowledge about applying the CoBRA model for the purpose of project effort estimation. The objective of the training for estimators is to present the CoBRA effort model and how to apply it for different project management purposes. The training should also include an introduction to software tools supporting effort estimation with the CoBRA model.

5.2.2 Preparing CoBRA Instruments

As with any other technology, the users' acceptance of the CoBRA method depends to a large extent on the level of tool support the method offers. Appropriate software tools do not only increase the efficiency of the method's usage but also its effectiveness by preventing errors in error-prone human activities and facilitating validation analyses. The objective of this activity is to select appropriate tools for supporting the further steps of the CoBRA model development.

Based on the information we gathered on context-specific constraints and objectives, we may adjust the standard CoBRA processes and associated instruments. For example, we may want to support expert judgment with knowledge learned from additional project measurement data, if such data are available. For this purpose, we may need to set up appropriate data analysis techniques and tools first. Moreover, we may want to reuse the outputs of earlier CoBRA applications, such as effort models, experiences, and guidelines. This requires preparing reusable artifacts so that they can be easily used for creating a new effort model. Finally, we should consider translating the CoBRA instruments into the native language of the organization in which we apply the method.

5.2.3 Planning CoBRA Model Development

Finally, we have to plan the detailed work activities of the CoBRA model development. Planning includes defining and scheduling the individual work activities of the CoBRA process, assigning the necessary resources, and communicating the plan to the involved parties. We should keep in mind the limited availability of experienced personnel, who are typically overloaded with everyday project activities. Therefore, we should plan CoBRA activities that require involving domain experts as soon as possible and synchronize the plan with the affected experts.

Last but not least, planning CoBRA model development also includes ensuring that the necessary infrastructure, such as meeting and working spaces, office hardware facilities, and software tools, is available.

Basic inputs to the planning are the CoBRA modeling process as described in the next sections as well as context-specific objectives and constraints identified during the previous activities of the preparation and planning step. For the purpose of planning, we can use basic planning approaches known from the project management area. Consider the Project Management Body of Knowledge Guide (PMI 2007) as an example reference.

Please note that if CoBRA model development is to be run by an external analyst in a foreign country, then we should consider that potential communication overhead may be needed for overcoming potential language and cultural differences.

Tip

▶ If CoBRA model development is going to be performed by an external analyst in a foreign country, then we should consider potential communication overhead related to language and cultural differences between the analyst and other personnel involved in the CoBRA estimation.

Example 5.1 illustrates the coarse plan for CoBRA model development. It is based on the typical course of actual modeling activities we observed across multiple CoBRA applications in various software development organizations.

Example 5.1. Simple Plan for CoBRA Model Development

In this example, we present a coarse plan for developing a CoBRA model. The plan is based on the experiences we gained developing CoBRA models in several different software organizations.

Let us first define a fictive environment for developing a CoBRA effort estimation model. We take a software organization that develops management and information software systems using Java and C/C++. Software development involves both creating new products and enhancing existing ones. The software organization has defined two major estimation objectives for applying the CoBRA method: estimating project effort and analyzing resource-related project risks. The resources available for developing an appropriate CoBRA model include:

- An external analyst and an internal assistant
- Four domain experts
- Fifteen historical projects for which measurement data are available for software size, for project effort, and for about 10–15 additional aspects of software project environment.

The CoBRA model development process is led by an external analyst with a lot of experience in the CoBRA method. The analyst is assisted by a person from the software organization who is learning CoBRA in order to take over the role of analyst in future applications of CoBRA in this organization.

Table 5.3 summarizes the approximate efforts that are typically required for performing the major activities of CoBRA model development. The information in the table is based on experiences we gained while applying the CoBRA method in various contexts. We distinguish between the first and subsequent (next) iterations of CoBRA model development, as they usually require different amounts of effort. In several cases, in particular for subsequent modeling iterations, we approximate the range of effort required by modeling activities. In these cases, effort $\neq 0$ for the analyst and the domain expert refers to the situation where a certain activity needs to be performed by the analyst and requires the involvement of domain experts. Otherwise effort $= 0$. Specifically, in subsequent iterations of model development, some steps do not need to be performed if model validation has not indicated activity-specific deficits of the model. For instance, if validation has not indicated any issues concerning project measurement data or if the indicated issue can be resolved by the analyst, then domain experts do not have to be involved in the "data validation and preprocessing" step.

Regarding the optional step "defining size measure," we assume for the first iteration that the software organization has already a defined size measure and that the analyst needs to merely prove whether it is appropriate for the effort estimation with CoBRA. An example aspect that the analyst checks here is whether the size measure considers all relevant products of the software processes for which effort is to be estimated using the developed CoBRA model. Additionally, the analyst may check—possibly together with the organization's

Table 5.3 CoBRA model development: example efforts in person-days

Model development step	Effort: first iteration		Effort: next iterations	
	Analyst	Domain expert	Analyst	Domain expert
Preparation and planning (Sect. 5.2)	1.5	0.1	1.0	0.1
1. Defining size measure (Sect. 5.3)	1.0	–	0–1.0	–
2. Collecting project measurement data (Sect. 5.4)	0.5	–	0–0.5	–
3. Data validation and preprocessing (Sect. 5.5)	1.0	0–0.5	0–1.0	0–0.5
4. Identifying and defining relevant effort factors (Sect. 5.6)	1.0	0.5	0.5	0–0.5
5. Identifying relevant factor interactions (Sect. 5.7)	1.0	0.25	0–0.5	0–0.25
6. Quantifying selected relevant effort factors (Sect. 5.8)	1.0	0.5	0–0.5	0–0.5
7. Collecting and validating historical factor data (Sect. 5.9)	1.0	0.1	1.0	0.1
8. Collecting and validating effort multiplier data (Sect. 5.10)	1.0	0.15	1.0	0.15
9. Building the effort model (Sect. 5.11)	0.5	–	0.25	–
10. Validating the effort model (Sect. 5.12)	0.5	–	0.25	–
11. Analyzing results of model validation (Sect. 5.13)	1.0	0.5	1.0	0.5
Total effort [PD]	11	2.1–2.6	5–8.5	0.95–2.6

measurement team—whether the size measure is well defined and appropriately quantifies relevant software products. If the software organization does not have a defined size measure, then "defining size measure" step would require significantly more effort. Yet, our experiences indicate that this is a rather rare situation.

The efforts we present in this example represent a typical case of CoBRA model development. However, it should not be adopted uncritically when planning a specific CoBRA application. We should always consider context-specific objectives and constraints.   ∎

5.3   Step 2: Defining Size Measure

This step is optional and should be performed if valid and consistent measurement data for considered historical projects are not available.

Software size is the major determinant of software project effort. Effectively measuring software size is thus a key element of successful effort estimation. Failed

Table 5.4 CoBRA model development process: defining size measure

Step 2:	<Optional> Defining size measure
Objective	The objective of this step is to define the size measure in order to consistently measure the size of historical projects as input to building the CoBRA effort estimation model. This step is optional and should be considered if no valid size measure is defined in the estimation context and/or no consistent size measurements are available for the historical projects, on which the effort estimation model is to be developed and validated.
Personnel	• *Analyst*: The analyst reviews the measurement data collected for the historical projects considered within the scope of the CoBRA effort estimation. He checks whether valid and consistently measured size and effort data exist.
Inputs	• Measurement data from about ten historical projects. • The organization's project repository: software artifacts delivered in the considered historical projects.
Activities	1. Identify measureable project deliverables. 2. Define software size measure. 3. Apply size measure.
Tools	• Tool supporting the documentation and communication of the definition of the software size measure. Example tools include standard office packages such as MS Word. • Software measurement tool for collecting software size according to the size measure defined in this step.
Outputs	• Software size measure.

software sizing is often the main contributor of failed effort estimates and, in consequence, failed projects. Measuring software size is a challenging task, and not all software organizations do it properly, if they even measure size at all. The CoBRA method requires size data from about 10 (or more) historical projects completed in the context for which we are building an effort estimation model. If such data are missing or we know they are inconsistently measured—for example, using different size measures—we can collect software size using artifacts delivered by the considered historical projects. What we need to do is to:

1. Decide on the artifacts we want to measure
2. Define an appropriate size measure
3. Apply the defined measure to the identified artifacts to collect software size data

Table 5.4 summarizes the most important elements of this step. We provide a detailed description of each activity in the following subsections.

In the following subsections, we present the major activities comprising the "defining size measure" step of the CoBRA model development process.

5.3.1 Identify Measureable Project Deliverables

The purpose of measuring software size in the software effort estimation context is to obtain an indicator of the gross volume of the work required to complete a software project. Since the objective of a project is to deliver a set of software artifacts, the common way of quantifying a project's volume is to measure the size of its deliverables. Yet, measuring the size of all software artifacts a project delivers would be too expensive—if not unfeasible at all. Therefore, a typical approach is to measure the size of those software artifacts that best indicate the volume of work in a project.

When adapting a particular size measure, we need to ensure that its associated software artifacts are (1) proper indicators of the total size of all project deliverables and (2) available in the same form and volume throughout historical projects. For example, if we decide to measure the size of a software use case specification, we need to ensure that use cases available for a historical project consistently cover the same part of the software system—at best the complete software—and that they describe the software system at the same level of detail and using the same modeling notation. Otherwise, even for the same software system, the size measurements will differ dependent on the completeness and precision of its use case specifications.

Tip

▶ For each project artifact that could potentially be the basis for size measurement, check (1) the consistency of the notation used to model this artifact across the available project data, (2) the consistency of the portion of the software system that is modeled by this artifact across the available project data, and (3) the level of detail at which this artifact models a software system across the available project data.

5.3.2 Define Software Size Measure

A number of methods for measuring software size have been proposed over the years. Yet, none of them seem to be the "silver bullet" that solves all problems and serves all purposes. Please refer to Laird and Brennan (2006) or to Jones (2007) for example reviews of software size measures, including their major strengths and weaknesses.

Depending on the particular situation at hand, we should typically use different size measures. Example criteria already mentioned above are (1) the extent to which the size measure indicates the size of all project outcomes and (2) the availability and consistency of given artifacts to which the size measure is applied. A number of different measure validity criteria have been defined in the software engineering context. Considering them is beyond the scope of this book. Please refer to Meneely et al. (2010) for a comprehensive review. For the sake of simplicity, let us conclude that a size measure should be useful for our particular purposes—here effort estimation—and be relatively easy to collect.

Tip

▶ When defining the size measure, make sure that it is useful for the purpose of effort estimation and that it is relatively easy to collect.

5.3.3 Apply Size Measure

Finally, we collect project size data by applying the defined size measure on the deliverables we identified for the historical projects considered. We store the collected size measurement in the organization's project data repository for further reuse. Note that the use of software size data is not limited to effort estimates. Quantitative software project and product management uses software size for a wide spectrum of applications. For example, software size is widely employed to normalize other software products' characteristics, such as software defects in defect density measurement.

5.4 Step 3: Collecting Project Measurement Data

The measurement of project data is an important source of knowledge for the CoBRA model development. The CoBRA method requires size and effort measurement to base the coarse effort estimation model on. Domain experts typically provide the remaining input information to the CoBRA modeling. However, we may use any other quantitative information that is available from historical projects to support the domain experts or to validate the judgments they provide.

The objective of this step is to collect measurement data from the historical projects considered. On the one hand, we must collect the size and effort measurements CoBRA requires. On the other hand, we may look for any other measurement data that might be useful for the purpose of building the CoBRA effort model. Example additional data may include quantitative information on the project's environmental factors. We can analyze these data in order to identify potentially relevant factors influencing project effort.

Table 5.5 summarizes the most important elements of this step. We provide a detailed description of each activity in the following subsections.

In the following subsections, we present the major activities comprising the "collecting project measurement data" step of the CoBRA model development process.

5.4.1 Collect Size and Effort Data

In this activity, we collect mandatory measurement data regarding software size and project effort for the historical projects upon which we will build the CoBRA effort estimation model. Note that even if the size and effort data we can find in the organization's data repository are incomplete, we can usually easily elicit them postmortem—based on the artifacts delivered by the historical projects. We can get project effort from project management documentation, and we can measure the size of the deliverables the project created.

Table 5.5 CoBRA model development process: collecting project measurement data

Step 3: Collect project measurement data

Objective	The objective of this step is to collect available measurement data for the historical projects considered, at least 10. Besides the mandatory size and effort data, we should look for any other measurement data that might be useful for developing the CoBRA effort estimation model. Example additional measurements comprise project environmental characteristics that may potentially influence project effort, that is, potential effort factors.
Personnel	• *Analyst*: The analyst looks through the organization's project repository for measurement data and documentation of the historical projects considered in the CoBRA model development. If the analyst is not responsible for measurement or is external to the organization, then the responsible measurement specialist from the organization should support the analyst.
Inputs	• The organization's project repository, comprising project characteristics, project deliverables, and project measurement data.
Activities	1. Collect software size and project effort data. 2. *<Optional>*Collect additional project measurement data.
Tools	• Tools supporting the storage and reuse of the organization's project assets, such as project deliverables and project measurement data.
Outputs	• Software size and project effort data for the historical projects considered in CoBRA effort modeling. • *<Optional>* Additional measurement data available for the historical projects considered, for example, environmental project characteristics.

5.4.2   *<Optional>* Collect Additional Project Measurement Data

Besides size and effort data, we should look through the organization's measurement repository and documentation of historical projects for potentially useful information regarding project environmental characteristics. Especially interesting are factors that may explain variances in development productivity across the historical projects considered. Therefore, before searching for additional project data, we should compute the actual productivity of each historical project by simply dividing the size of its project deliverables by the project effort—using the measurement size and effort we collected. While analyzing available project information, we should focus on those elements of the project environment that change as the development productivity changes. Later on, we may verify the potential impact of these factors on project effort either through formal analysis or through consultation with domain experts.

5.5   Step 4: Data Validation and Preprocessing

Before we can use measurement data for creating CoBRA effort estimation model, we first need to ensure that (1) the data are valid and (2) they are in the right form. *Data validity* refers to the general correctness of the data, whereas *data form* refers to the structure of the measurement data. The objective of this step is to validate the

Table 5.6 CoBRA model development process: data validation and preprocessing

Step 4: Data validation and preprocessing	
Objective	The objective of this step is to validate and prepare the measurement project data for the purpose of building the CoBRA effort estimation model.
Personnel	• *Analyst*: The analyst performs data validation and preparation. If the analyst is not responsible for measurement or is external to the organization, then the responsible measurement specialist from the organization should support the analyst.
Inputs	• Measurement data from historical projects considered in the CoBRA model development.
Activities	1. Preprocess measurement data. 2. Validate measurement data.
Tools	• Data analysis and visualization tools. • Specialized data preprocessing tools such as data imputation to cope with missing project data.
Outputs	• Valid project measurement data prepared for building the CoBRA effort estimation model.

correctness of the collected measurement data and preprocess them so that they can be accepted by the analysis techniques and tools used during the CoBRA development process.

Tip

▶ Before using measurement data for the purpose of building an effort estimation model, ensure that the data are valid and have a consistent format that is acceptable by the employed analysis techniques and support tools.

Table 5.6 summarizes the most important elements of this step. We provide a detailed description of each activity in the following subsections.

In the following subsections, we present the major activities comprising the "data validation and preprocessing" step of the CoBRA model development process.

5.5.1 Preprocess Measurement Data

Data preprocessing consists of transforming measurement data into a consistent format that is acceptable by the analysis techniques and tools used during the CoBRA development process. Common data preprocessing activities useful in the context of effort modeling and estimation include formatting, integrating, cleaning, and transformation.

Data Formatting
Data formatting refers to simple adjustments of the data format. The purpose of this adjustment is to ensure that data are accepted and properly interpreted by particular

analysis tools. Typical formatting activities cover aspects such as changing representation format, capitalization, concatenation and splitting, and character cleanup.

Changing Representation Format

This preprocessing activity refers to changing the data format. For example, project duration might be measured in terms of project start and end date. Duration can then simply be computed by calculating the time span between start and end date. Yet, dates can be given using different notations, such as European (day-month-year) or US (month-day-year). Inconsistent formats are a common issue in a global development project where projects or parts of a large project are realized in different locations worldwide. Feeding an analysis and effort modeling tool with unpreprocessed data may lead to invalid results.

Capitalization

This preprocessing activity refers to changing the case of data strings. Although it may seem unimportant from the human analyst's perspective, inconsistent capitalization of strings in the project measurement data may lead to serious errors while applying automatic analysis tools. Data analysis tools are case sensitive when working with nominal or ordinal data. This means that strings that differ only with respect to their capitalization and which convey the same information will be interpreted as different by analysis tools. For example, let us consider project measurement data that provide total project effort and specify the exact range of the life cycle phases this effort encompasses, by giving the first and the last phase. A typical analysis tool will distinguish between "requirements-testing" and "Requirements-Testing" as two different ranges of project phases, although they refer to exactly the same part of the development life cycle.

Concatenation and Splitting

This preprocessing activity refers to joining multiple data fields into one or splitting complex data field into several ones. For example, project measurement data may include a field that stores a list of programming languages used in the project. This may lead to fine-granular data that may be useless for the purpose of effort modeling and estimation. For instance, the data for two projects might be "Java, C++" and "Java, C++, C". An analysis tool will consider these two projects as different, although in the latter case only a few lines of software code out of several thousand might have been implemented using "C." From the perspective of impact on development effort, considering these two projects as similar would, however, be more appropriate. In this case, we may want to split the programming language field into "primary" and "secondary" and set up thresholds on the minimal portion of the software that must be implemented using a given programming language in order to consider it as primary or secondary.

Character Cleanup

This preprocessing activity refers to removing extraneous characters that are not accepted by automatic analysis tools. Example characters include currency symbols such as dollar (\$), euro (€), or yen (¥), which may not be interpreted as non-numeric by certain analysis tools. In order to ensure that data fields representing monetary cost are treated as numeric fields, we should remove currency symbols. Note that before doing so, we need to ensure that all values refer to the same currency. If not, we need to first convert all measurements into a common unit—in this case into a common currency.

Data Integration

Data integration refers to adjusting data extracted from multiple data sources. In such cases, the data must be merged, redundancies must be removed, and value conflicts must be resolved. Typical preprocessing activities related to integrating project measurement data include merging data, removing data redundancies, and removing data conflicts.

Merging Data

This preprocessing activity refers to matching up equivalent attributes covered by different data sources and merging them into one data set. To help solve this problem, some databases carry metadata, which are data about the data. By using and comparing these metadata, attributes can be matched up and errors in integration can be avoided. The problem is more complex if adequate attributes have different names or inadequate attributes have similar names and attributes are not clearly described. In order to deal with such issues, the support of data maintainers is usually required. They should provide the definitions and the meaning of the measured attributes.

Removing Data Redundancies

This preprocessing activity refers to removing data fields that refer to the same measurement aspect. In such cases, redundant measurement data do not provide any useful information but increase the complexity of the data analysis. Note that some analysis techniques explicitly require measurement data to be free from collinearities and will provide invalid results if data do not fulfill this prerequisite.

Removing Data Conflicts

This preprocessing activity refers to dealing with conflicts that result from merging data of different representation, scaling, or encoding. For instance, one source of project data provides project effort measured in person-months, whereas the other source provides it in person-days. Merging these two data sets would result in a scale conflict and in inconsistent data. Such an inconsistency will falsify the results of effort modeling; in this particular example, projects where effort was measured in person-months would apparently have very high development productivity relative to projects where effort was measured in person-days. In general, we can cope with conflicting data by transforming them into a consistent representation. We will discuss common data transformation approaches later in this section. Yet, not all data conflicts are so easy to remove. Let us consider another example concerning merging project effort data. A much less obvious and difficult-to-detect problem with merged project data we observed in practice is the inconsistent scope of effort measurement. For example, project effort measured in one business unit comprises requirements, design, and coding phases, whereas effort measured for the same type of project in another business unit comprises design, coding, and testing phases. In addition to being quite difficult to detect, this inconsistency is also very difficult to handle, particularly when the distribution of effort per phase— absolute or percentage—is not known.

Data Cleaning

Data cleaning provides methods for coping with three common problems of real-world data sets. The first problem is that data may be incomplete, meaning that a considerable number of values are missing. To solve this problem, we have to look at means of how to best approximate the missing data. The second problem deals with errors in data values or so-called noisy data. In order to remove these errors, several smoothing methods are available. The third problem deals with data inconsistencies, which occur mostly when data are merged from different sources. Typical data cleaning activities include handling missing data and data smoothing (i.e., handling noisy data).

Handling Missing Data

This preprocessing activity refers to dealing with incomplete data. Missing data are the most common and most difficult problem to cope with. In the real world, collected data almost never are complete. Certain values might be missing for several reasons, most of all because they were never recorded. Other common reasons are the following:

- Data collection equipment malfunction.
- Data were inconsistent with other recorded data and thus were deleted.
- Data were not entered due to a misunderstanding.
- Certain data were not considered to be important at the time of data collection.

Nevertheless, many data analysis algorithms require a complete set of data to run. To solve this problem, all tuples with missing values can obviously be simply ignored. This method is, however, not very efficient though, because large amounts of valuable data (information) might be thrown away.

There are numerous alternative strategies for handling missing data (Schafer 1997). The most popular approaches include:

- *Manually fill in missing values*. In this approach, domain experts fill in missing project data based on their knowledge of particular projects. In CoBRA, data acquisition based on human judgment is actually part of the method. For example, domain experts usually provide project data for most of the effort factors because they were first considered during the building of the CoBRA effort model and thus were never measured before. The procedure of manual imputation of missing project data might be tedious and unfeasible for larger data sets. Yet, this does not apply to CoBRA, which only involves about ten historical projects. We merely need only to ensure that when the CoBRA effort estimation model has been built, the project data for all effort factors the model comprises are systematically and completely collected for future projects.

- *Use a global constant to fill in missing values.* In this approach, we use a global "dummy" constant to encode missing values. Example constants may be "unknown" or "missing" for string parameters or numerical value forms outside the range the parameter is measured on (e.g., "−9" for a positive integer parameter). This method is very simple and allows using analysis methods that would be unable to cope with missing data points. Yet, it does not solve the problem of missing information.
- *Estimate missing values based on the known values of a considered attribute.* In this approach, the distribution of known values about the considered project attribute is used to estimate the missing values for this attribute. A simple instantiation of this idea is to fill in missing values using the statistical mean for known values on this attribute.
- *Estimate missing values based on known values of other attributes.* This is a promising and hence very popular strategy in which unknown values for one attribute are estimated based on known values for other attributes in the data set. Estimates can be based either on inference models, such as the Bayesian formula, decision trees, or correlation models. This is done by constructing a model of the attribute and its relationship to other attributes, that is, estimation models in which the attribute with the missing value is considered as a dependent variable while attributes with known values are considered as independent variables. By constructing a model of the attribute, we can typically approximate any missing values efficiently.

Please refer to Strike et al. (2001), Van Hulse and Khoshgoftaar (2008), and Khoshgoftaar and Van Hulse (2008) for a detailed review and comparison of techniques for handling missing data in the context of software engineering and project estimation. The latter two studies additionally investigate the impact of data quality on the performance of data imputation techniques.

Handling Data Noise

This preprocessing activity refers to handling noisy data, that is, data with random error or variance in a measured variable. Common sources of data noise are faulty data collection instruments or data entry problems. The common approach for removing data noise is called smoothing. Example smoothing techniques include clustering and human inspection. Clustering divides data into groups of similar data (clusters) and removes data points that do not fall into any group. In the human inspection technique, human experts review data and decide about modifying, retaining, or removing noisy data.

Handling Data Outliers

Data outliers are a special case of noisy data. The term outlier refers to data points that fall outside the main body of data. Outliers may have a significant impact on the estimation results provided by prediction methods. In the context of data-driven effort estimation, the effectiveness of effort estimation can be significantly improved by resolving data outliers. Handling data outliers consists of two steps:

detecting outliers and resolving outliers. In the context of CoBRA, we consider data outliers in two places.

The first place where we should consider data outliers is when we analyze size and effort data from historical projects in order to detect projects that are outliers with respect to the development productivity. Yet, we do not resolve these outliers before applying CoBRA for building an effort estimation model. In fact, it is the objective of CoBRA modeling to resolve these outliers. More precisely, the objective of the CoBRA effort model is to explain the variance of productivity across historical projects, that is, model effort factors that cause development productivity to vary.

The second place where we should consider outliers is when we analyze inputs to the CoBRA model development provided by multiple domain experts. At this point, we are interested in judgments that are different from the opinion of the majority of the experts. We resolve potential outlier judgments by investigating the rationale behind them. Our experience shows that the majority is not always right. Moreover, it is also not a rule that more experienced expert are right. We will discuss these issues in more detail in Sects. 5.9 and 5.7.

Tip

▶ Always investigate outliers carefully because they may contain valuable information. Before considering the possible elimination of outliers from the project data,
try to understand why they appeared and whether they may be correct and other
data may be wrong.

There are a number of ways we can detect outliers. The simplest one is visual analysis of graphical data representation, for example, in the form of a histogram. Examples of more formal techniques for detecting outliers include:

- *Box plot analysis*: In this approach, we draw a box plot and look for the data points that fall outside the main body of data determined by a middle point and acceptable deviation from it. Typically, these are represented by (1) data mean and standard deviation or (2) data median and quartiles. For example, data points that are outside the range of ±2 standard deviations (or even ±1.5 SDs) are commonly considered as outliers.
- *Statistical testing*: In this approach, we use formal statistical tests to identify data points outside the main body of data. Similar to the box plot approach, statistical tests are often based on the criterion of "distance from the mean." For example, the Grubbs test statistic calculates the ratio of the largest absolute deviation from the data mean to the data standard deviation.
- *Distance analysis*: This approach is based on the same principle as the box plot analysis, namely, measuring a range of data points from the main body of data. This approach uses formal distance measures such as Mahalanobis distance, which calculates how far a given point is from the center of the complete data set. The advantage of distance-based outlier analysis is that it considers multi-variate outliers, that is, data that are outliers for more than one attribute.

Tip

▶ Use an appropriate method for detecting data outliers. Remember that some methods are designed to detect the presence of a single outlier, while others detect the presence of multiple outliers. Moreover, some methods can consider only one attribute at a time, while others can detect data points that are outliers only when multiple attributes are considered.

Data Transformation

Data transformation refers to data conversions that adapt characteristics to input requirements of a certain analysis method. This includes such transformations as data normalization, data discretization, scale augmentation, unit conversion, aggregation, generalization, and attribute construction.

Data Normalization

This preprocessing activity refers to scaling attribute values to fall within a specified range, for example [0, 1]. During the CoBRA model development, normalization has rather little usage. We may use it for anonymizing project data, such as development productivity, before communicating it across the software organization. We should consider it if we do not want CoBRA to be a tool for assessing personnel.

Data Discretization

This preprocessing activity refers to transforming continuous-scale data into discrete-scale data. We can use discretization for reducing the continuous or multiple-value discrete scale of an effort factor comprised of project data into the simple 4-point approximately interval scale used by the CoBRA method, where 0 refers to the worst-case value (extreme project) and 3 refers to the best-case value (nominal project).

The most common approaches for discretizing data are to consider *expert opinion* or the distribution of the data values in the repository. In the expert opinion method, an expert would be asked to subjectively determine what range of values should be considered worst, what best, and what as discrete values between worst and best. This approach is very useful when an organization already uses a similar kind of mapping in their day-to-day operation.

Distribution-based approaches reduce the continuous scale by dividing its range into a set of intervals, which represent values on a discrete scale. Interval labels can then be used to replace actual data values. There are several strategies for dividing the range of continuous variables into discrete intervals. Simple examples of discretization approaches are based on binning or clustering.

In *binning*, attribute values are sorted and then divided into bins, which make up the neighborhood of the data points inside. Bins may be equi-width (distance), equi-depth (frequency), or just arbitrary, depending on the application. Equi-width partitioning divides the range into N intervals of equal size, meaning that if A and B are the lowest and highest values of the attribute, the width of the intervals will be $W = (B - A)/N$. Equi-depth partitioning divides the range into N intervals, each containing approximately the same number of data points. Arbitrary partitioning divides the data range into intervals of different size and frequency, for instance, depending on the expert's decision.

After partitioning, all points are smoothed by means of binning:

- *Means*: We replace all individual data points inside a bin with the bin's mean value.
- *Medians*: We replace all individual data points inside a bin with the bin's median value.
- *Boundaries*: We first identify the boundaries of a bin (the range of values it contains) and then replace each data point inside the bin with the value of the closest bin's boundary.

In the end, all bins are again merged, resulting in a discrete data set. The intensity of the smoothing depends mostly not on the smoothing operation but on the width of the bins. In general, the larger the width, the greater the effect of the smoothing will be.

Example 5.2. Discretization Through Binning

Let us consider the following set of data: 2, 4, 5, 6, 9, 10, 12, 16, 17, 19, 23, 26, 27, 28, 31, 33, 35. Table 5.7 illustrates the results of discretizing this data set by means of equi-depth bins and smoothing using bin means and boundaries.

Table 5.7 Example discretization through equi-depth bins

Bins	Partition into equi-depth bins	Smoothing by means	Smoothing by boundaries
Bin 1	2, 4, 5, 6, 9, 10	6, 6, 6, 6, 6, 6	2, 2, 2, 2, 10, 10
Bin 2	12, 16, 17, 19	16, 16, 16, 16	12, 19, 19, 19
Bin 3	23, 26, 27, 28	26, 26, 26, 26	23, 28, 28, 28
Bin 4	31, 33, 35	33, 33, 33	31, 31, 35

After merging the bins again, the resulting discretized data sets are as follows:

- Original set: 2, 4, 5, 6, 9, 10, 12, 16, 17, 19, 23, 26, 27, 28, 31, 33, 35
- Set smoothed by means: 6, 6, 6, 6, 6, 6, 16, 16, 16, 16, 26, 26, 26, 26, 33, 33, 33
- Set smoothed by boundaries: 2, 2, 2, 2, 10, 10, 12, 19, 19, 19, 23, 28, 28, 28, 31, 31, 35

As we can see, smoothing by bin neighbors preserves more variance in the data than smoothing by bin means. ∎

Scale Augmentation

This preprocessing activity refers to the transformation between textual data and numerical data. For example, in CoBRA, we code ordinal levels of effort factors;

however, they are textually defined using numerical values {0, 1, 2, 3}. We may also want to code other project data such as context information in order to anonymize their meaning.

Unit Conversion

This preprocessing activity refers to the transformation between measurement units. A typical example from effort estimation might be converting project effort data into consistent units. For example, after merging several sources of project data, we may obtain a mixture of effort units such as person-hours, person-days, and person-months. We need to convert these data into a consistent unit in order to avoid an invalid effort model. A critical issue when converting between different units may be the determination of the proper conversion coefficient. In case of trivial conversions such as between LOC and kLOC, the conversion ratio is obvious—in this case, $LOC = 1,000 \times kLOC$. Yet, in case of project effort, conversion rates might not be so obvious anymore because it differs from organization to organization.

Aggregation and Generalization

These preprocessing activities refer to moving up in the concept hierarchy on numeric, respectively nominal attributes. In the context of effort estimation, this issue refers to changing the granularity level of the prediction model. We may, for example, estimate complete project effort instead of effort per project phase. In this case, we need to sum up phase-wise project efforts. An example of a quite common problem when synthesizing effort data into a higher granularity level is that some of the detailed effort data are missing. For example, we cannot easily compute total project effort because effort for some development phases is not available. In this case, we need to approximate the missing effort data. A simple way of accomplishing this is to use projects where complete phase-wise effort is available and compute the percentage effort distribution per project phase. We may then use this information to extrapolate phases where effort data are missing based upon the phases for which effort has been measured.

Attribute Construction

This preprocessing activity refers to replacing or adding new attributes inferred by existing attributes. A basic example of this operation in the context of CoBRA is the construction of the development productivity attribute based upon software size and development effort attributes. We compute productivity because it is much easier and more practical to identify potentially relevant effort factors by analyzing development productivity than by analyzing project effort. In CoBRA, we assume software size to be the major determinant of development effort, and we are interested in other project characteristics that make effort differ for projects of the same size, meaning the characteristics that make development productivity vary.

Example 5.3. Data Preprocessing

In this example, we illustrate some common deficits of project data and exemplary preprocessing steps to handle these deficits. Let us consider project data as presented in Table 5.8.

Table 5.8 Example deficits of project data

Project	Size (kLOC)	Size (FPA)	Effort [PM]	Primary OS
P1	–	1,275	PM = 21	Windows 系
P2	15,000	192	3	Win-2000
P3	15.000	180	3	Windows2000
P4	87	–	PD = 2,280	Windows 2000
P5	73	930	MM = 13	Win2000
P6	38	460	16	2000, NT, 98
P7	–	360	5	Win/Solaris
P8	8	–	2	Win2000
P9	–	1,670	30	Windows-2000
P10	141	1,745	34	MsWindows 2000

Basic deficits of these data include:

- *Primary OS*: The field uses inconsistent coding for the same value. "Windows 2000" is coded using different strings. Moreover, for project P1, a special Asian character is used which might cause interpretation problems for analysis tools that cannot handle Asian coding. Finally, several operating systems are given as primary OS for projects P6 and P7. In case of P7, we propose looking at the project objectives to see whether both operating systems were, in fact, considered as equally important targets. If not, we propose extending the project data table by adding a project attribute "Secondary OS" and including the less important target OS in this field. In the case of P6, we propose investigating how much different, from the perspective of project effort, the development of software for the three versions of Windows OS named in the measurement data is. If there is no significant difference, we propose generalizing this measurement to the MS Windows operating system, excluding versions and coding it with a "Windows" string.
  Preprocessing: We use the consistent string "Win2000" for generalizing and consistent coding of all inputs referring to the Windows 2000 operating systems. Moreover, we create an additional project attribute in the data set for storing information on the operating system.
- *Size [kLOC]*: The use of periods and commas in the software size measurements for projects P2 and P3 may potentially be wrong. Since the effort consumed by these two projects is almost identical, we can suspect that the size of a product of these projects will not differ by any order of magnitude. If we compute development productivity for the remaining projects using kLOC size, we would get an approximate range of productivity of between 4 and 6 kLOC per person-month. This would suggest that 15,000

is the correct measurement and 15.000 results from the erroneous use of the period instead of the comma. In the first case, productivity would be 5, which would correspond to the range of productivity for the remaining projects, rather than 15.000, for which productivity would be 0.005.

Preprocessing: We exchange commas for periods in the kLOC size measurement for project P3.

- *Size [kLOC]*: Size measurements are missing for projects P1, P7, and P9. If we want to build an estimation model based on LOC size, we need to handle the incomplete measurements on this attribute. One option would be to look for project deliverables and measure their size. In our example, size is additionally measured using Function Point Analysis (FPA). If FPA size is available for the project where LOC size is missing, we may want to convert FPA size into LOC size using backfiring. For this purpose, we can use the backfiring coefficients published in the related literature, such as Jones (2007), or use our internal project data to compute an appropriate coefficient.

Preprocessing: Since for several historical projects in our example project data set both size in LOC and size in FPA are available, we can compute our context-specific backfiring conversion rate. The LOC per FPA rate computed on projects for which both LOC and FPA measures are available ranges between 78 and 83 LOC/FPA. In order to compute missing LOC data from available FPA measurements, we use the rate 81, which is close to the value of 80. Jones (2007) gives for third-generation languages and IFPUG FPA.[1]

- *Size[FPA]*: Size measurements are missing for projects P04 and P08. If we want to build an estimation model based on function point size, we need to handle the incomplete measurements on this attribute. One option would be to look for project deliverables, such as requirements specification or design, and count software functional size. Another possibility is to use backfiring for converting LOC size data available for these two projects into PFA counts.

Preprocessing: We use the same backfiring rate as in the previous preprocessing activity for approximating missing LOC data.

- *Effort*: The effort fields for projects P1, P4, and P5 contain non-numerical data (strings). Moreover, effort for project P4 is given in person-days, which is inconsistent with the other projects, for which effort is measured in person-months (man-months).

Preprocessing: We remove string data and retain only numerical information on project effort. Moreover, we convert the effort unit for project P4 from person-days (PD) into person-months (PM). For this purpose, we use the conversion rate of 152 PD/PM defined within the context of the historical projects considered.

---

[1] Refer to the website of Software Productivity Research, Inc. (http://www.spr.com/programming-languages-table.html) for the current backfiring rates.

Table 5.9 Example deficits of project data

Project	kLOC	FPA	LOC/FPA	Effort	Prod	Primary OS	Secondary OS
P1	*103*	1,275	–	21	4.9	Win2000	–
P2	15	192	78	3	5.0	Win2000	–
P3	15	180	83	3	5.0	Win2000	–
P4	87	*1,074*	–	*15*	5.8	Win2000	–
P5	73	930	78	13	5.6	Win2000	WinNT, Win98
P6	38	460	83	16	2.4	Win2000	Solaris
P7	*29*	360	–	5	5.8	Win2000	–
P8	8	*99*	–	2	2.7	Win2000	–
P9	*135*	1,670	–	30	4.5	Win2000	–
P10	141	1,745	81	34	4.1	Win2000	–

- *Productivity*: We derive a development productivity attribute such as $Prod = LOC/Effort$. We will use this attribute to identify potential project outliers and investigate the causes of their extreme productivity values.

After applying basic preprocessing operations, we obtain data as presented in Table 5.9.

A visual analysis of the software development production rate, represented by the scatter plot in Fig. 5.2, shows two phenomena. First, illustrated by the dashed line, is the slight diseconomies-of-scale effect shown by the projects, in that their effort grows disproportionally (nonlinearly) relative to the size of the delivered software. The diseconomies-of-scale effect is often observed in software development projects. It is caused by increased project communication and coordination overhead as project and team size increase and is displayed as a decrease in development productivity as the project size increases.

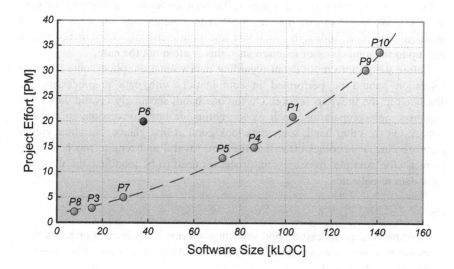

Fig. 5.2 Production rate represented by a scatter plot of software size and project effort

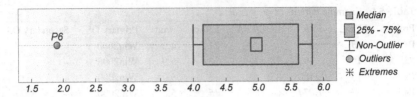

Fig. 5.3 Distribution of development productivity

The second phenomenon we are actually interested in is project P6, which seems to cost more effort than would be suggested by the distribution of effort in other historical projects. In order to verify our observation regarding outlier project P6, we analyze the development productivity of the historical projects considered using a box plot analysis. An appropriate box plot presented in Fig. 5.3 shows project P6 having, in fact, extremely low productivity relative to other historical projects from the same context.

In the next preprocessing steps, we should investigate the potential causes of the outlier productivity in project P6. First, we need to ensure that the project data that generated these outliers are correct. Next, we should search for project characteristics that make P6 different from other historical projects. These characteristics will then be first candidates for the effort factors we should include in the CoBRA effort estimation model.   ∎

5.5.2 Validate Measurement Data

Even the most comprehensive project data will not be worth much if they are incorrect, leading to an incorrect effort estimation model and wrong project decisions. An example of incorrect data we often observed in software industry refers to counting software requirements. Software organizations count the number of functional requirements, nonfunctional requirements, and the total count of requirements. Now, although functional and nonfunctional requirements should sum up to the total count of requirements, this is often not the case.

Before we go into more detail regarding data validation, please note that data validation should be performed in combination with data preprocessing, as discussed in the previous section. On the one hand, seemingly invalid data often require simple preparation, such as formatting or unit conversion, to make it correct. On the other hand, some data look good at first glance, but already after preprocessing, it becomes clear that they are invalid and require much work to correct—for example, measurement processes need to be modified and measurement data re-collected.

Tip

▶ Combine data preprocessing and validation activities. Simple data preparation may remove what seems to be invalid data or reveal that what seems to be correct data is actually invalid.

At this point, let us also make a clear distinction between valid data and the data that represent true (valid) causal effort dependencies for the considered historical projects. Although we would gladly ensure that project data reflect true causal effort relationships, this is, in practice, quite difficult, if not impossible. The theory of statistics and causal modeling shows that covering true causal relationships would require collecting infinite amounts of data on a potentially infinite number of factors, which may influence project effort. Clearly, we cannot ensure such data. What we can ensure is the basic correctness and consistency of the data we already have or may obtain at reasonable cost. We can accomplish this objective in two ways:

- *Directly*, by analyzing the measurement data. In this case, we analyze the data independent of other project measurements on the one hand. On the other hand, we analyze the project data with respect to potential relationships to other project measurements. For example, let us consider the number of hazardous requirements (#HR). On the one hand, we can look at the distribution of #HR across historical projects for potential outliers and check if invalid data are responsible for this. On the other hand, we can perform a simple cross-check of #HR against the total number of requirements. If #HR exceeds the total count of requirements, which we have observed in practice, there is obviously something wrong with the data, and they need to be corrected.
- *Indirectly*, by evaluating the measurement processes applied for collecting the data. In this case, we analyze the definitions and measurement procedures employed to collect the project data that we suspect, for example, following a visual analysis of their distribution, to be invalid. For example, in case of the number of hazardous requirements (#HR) measure, we can look at the definition of hazardous requirements and the definition of requirements, in general. It may occur, for instance, that the former is defined on a different level of abstraction (detail) than the latter. If hazardous requirements comprise what would generally be considered as sub-requirements, then #HR can be greater than the total number of all requirements—using such measures for the purpose of effort estimation may lead to misleading conclusions and wrong project decisions.

One important aspect to consider is the consistency of the measurement procedure and the resulting data with appropriate measure definitions. For example, we might be interested in the size of software in terms of effective lines of source code. From the perspective of development effort, we are not interested in any elements of software code, such as generated code, that require minimal or no development effort. Yet, the associated measurement procedure might not implement this definition or be inconsistently performed across various development projects. In the first case, we will think that we are considering apples, when in fact we will be considering oranges when estimating project effort. In the latter case, we would compare apples with oranges while we are thinking we were considering apples— or even worse, while thinking we were considering something altogether different, like plums.

Another important aspect to prove while validating project data is that consistency with the defined scope of the CoBRA application should be considered. A common issue we have observed in industrial contexts is that the total project effort collected for multiple projects encompasses the distinct activities of the development process. For example, the project effort for one project comprises requirements specification and systems testing, while for another project, these phases are not considered within the total effort data. It is good when the data repository includes effort per phase or at least information on which phases are covered by the total project effort. Yet, in many cases, a single number for total project effort is given, which encompasses very different project activities, without any information on what these phases are and what part of the effort they contribute to. In such a case, effort data are practically useless.

Tip

▶ Verify that the effort data comprises the same project activities. Make sure that they cover the same range of activities (e.g., the same development phases) and the same type of activities (engineering, management, administrative).

5.6   Step 5: Identifying and Defining Relevant Effort Factors

Software development effort depends on a number of factors. The size of software deliverables is the major effort factor, but it is not the only one. The rate with which we are able to deliver project outputs (known as development productivity) depends on a number of factors. Example factors include product characteristics (other than size), capabilities of the project team, project environment and organization, and external constraints. In essence, we are interested in knowing what factors make project effort differ even though we deliver outputs of the same size. In other words, we are interested in factors that cause development productivity to vary across different projects even though their general context is similar.

Selecting relevant effort factors is one of the keys to successful effort estimation. A typical threat during this step is the selection of a large number of irrelevant or even misleading effort factors while omitting relevant ones. And estimation accuracy is not the only success criterion here. The high costs of collecting, analyzing, and maintaining unnecessary project information may demotivate any effort estimation initiative. In fact, effort estimation overhead has already killed a number of effort estimation initiatives in the software industry.

The objective of this step is to identify and define a minimal set of the most relevant effort factors, that is, factors having the greatest impact on software development effort in a particular context, "minimal" meaning sufficient to achieve our estimation objectives and small enough not to exceed our cost constraints. Since size is the major factor contributing to project effort, we exclude it from consideration and focus on other effort factors, that is, factors which cause variations in development productivity.

In the CoBRA method, the selection of the most relevant effort factors is traditionally based on the judgment of multiple domain experts. Yet, it can and should be supported by an analysis of available project measurement data. We recommend using group consensus techniques for identifying the most relevant effort factors. Although we can perform the selection procedure off-line, for example, in the form of an e-mail survey, we should prefer face-to-face sessions with the domain experts. An exception might be the case when domain experts have already been involved in the building of the CoBRA model and very familiar with it. An advantage of a group session is that the analyst and the domain experts can immediately identify and clarify any issues and misunderstandings as they occur. We suggest using a Delphi-like[2] procedure for selecting the most relevant effort factors. Table 5.10 summarizes the most important activities of this step. We provide a detailed description of each activity in the following subsections.

Table 5.10 CoBRA model development process: identifying relevant effort factors

Step 5: Identifying relevant effort factors	
Objective	The objective of this step is to identify a set of the most relevant effort factors to be considered in the CoBRA effort estimation model.
Personnel	• *Analyst*: The analyst leads a group discussion session during which the domain experts identify the most relevant effort factors. The analyst may prepare an example list of effort factors and present it to the involved domain experts in order to clarify to them the concept of effort factor and the session objectives. Moreover, the analyst computes and analyzes development productivity for the historical projects considered. The analyst presents these results to the domain experts in order to stimulate them in searching for the most relevant factors causing productivity variations. If additional project data are available, the analyst investigates the data using analytical techniques for the purpose of identifying potentially relevant effort factors. Finally, the analyst synthesizes the outcomes of the effort factor identification activities, presents these results to the domain experts, and iterates the whole step (or its parts) if necessary.
	• *Domain experts*: The domain experts identify potentially relevant effort factors, rate their relevancy, and decide on the subset of effort factors to be added to the CoBRA effort estimation model. If the selected effort factors represent complex concepts, the domain experts decompose them into effort variables, representing the most relevant aspect of the effort factor.
Inputs	• Questionnaire for specifying, defining, and rating relevant effort factors.
	• *<Optional>* List of example effort factors, preferably effort factors that are typically used in contexts considered while building the CoBRA effort model (refer to Appendix 13 for an example reference list of effort factors).

(continued)

---

[2] Delphi is a group consensus technique proposed by Boehm (1981). Wideband Delphi is the most recent refinement of Delphi. Wideband Delphi and its variants are widely used in many domains for achieving group consensus.

Table 5.10 (continued)

Step 5: Identifying relevant effort factors	
Activities	1. Identify potentially relevant effort factors. 2. Rate the relevancy of the identified effort factors. 3. Analyze rating consistency. 4. Synthesize multiple ratings. 5. Decide on a set of most relevant effort factors. 6. Decompose complex effort factors.
Tools	• Statistical tools for analyzing the consistency of the judgments provided by the domain experts and (optionally) of the results of the analytical identification of relevant effort factors. Example tools may comprise statistical software packages that support computing Kendall's coefficient of concordance. Alternatively, simple calculation tools, such as MS Excel, can be used to implement the computation of Kendall's coefficient of concordance. • *<Optional>* Software tools that implement analytical techniques for identifying from measurement data those factors that had the greatest impact on development productivity in historical projects. These techniques and tools may include simple multivariate regression analysis, factor weighting and selection tools, and advanced causal analysis tools. • Software tools for visualizing, documenting, and communicating the results of effort factor selection. Basic tools include elements of standard office packages such as MS Excel, MS Word, and MS PowerPoint.
Outputs	• A list of the relevant effort factors with associated definitions and relevancy ratings. • Selection of the most relevant effort factors to be added to the CoBRA effort model. • *<Optional>* A list of variables defined for complex effort factors. • *<Optional>* Results of the analytical identification of relevant effort factors (procedure and outcomes of the analysis of available project measurement data).

In the following subsections, we present the major activities comprising the "identifying and defining relevant effort factors" step of the CoBRA model development process.

5.6.1   Identify Potential Effort Factors

The objective of this activity is to identify project characteristics that are believed to have a significant impact on development productivity in projects within the selected context. The CoBRA method uses two principal approaches for accomplishing this activity: judgmental and analytical. We can combine these two approaches in order to moderate their weaknesses and utilize their strengths and thus optimize the effectiveness of the factor identification step.

Judgmental Approach: Group Consensus Session
The judgmental approach for selecting the most relevant effort factors is the default approach used within CoBRA. In this approach, multiple domain experts identify potentially relevant effort factors during a brainstorming session. The analyst organizes and moderates a group discussion session during which the domain experts specify those effort factors they perceive as relevant based on their individual project experiences.

Threats of Group Discussion

Group discussion sessions are a common technique for eliciting an organization's knowledge and obtaining expert consensus on certain aspects. Group sessions are also commonly regarded as leading to less biased outcomes compared to the judgment of individual human experts. Yet, group consensus techniques are not free from biases. Typical biases of group discussion include:

- *Wishful thinking*: This effect refers to the tendency of humans to make estimates according to what might please the receiver of the estimates (e.g., the customer) or even themselves (overoptimism regarding one's own performance) instead of basing such estimates on evidence or rationality.
- *Group think*: This effect is close to wishful thinking and refers to the situation where people with stronger personalities dominate the deliberations and some group members might be influenced by others. For example, senior and management project members typically have much influence on the young technical staff.
- *Polarization*: This effect is close to the group-think effect and refers to the situation where a majority of a group creates the behavior of the whole group. For example, groups in which members are prone to making risky judgments become more prone to making such judgments, while groups with a majority of members who are averse to making risky judgments become more risk averse.
- *Anchoring*: This effect (also known as *focalism*) refers to the common human tendency to rely too heavily on one aspect or piece of information when making estimates. As a result, estimates are biased towards a specific aspect without accounting for other important elements influencing the estimated value.
- *Risk shift:* This effect refers to the tendency of people in a group, where individual responsibility is diminished, to adopt riskier courses of action than they would take on a personal basis. This effect typically leads to unrealistic underestimations.

In the context of a group consensus session, the role of the analyst as the session moderator is essential for avoiding group discussion bias and for obtaining reliable effort factor identification results.

In support of this activity, the analyst can prepare a reference list of example effort factors and present it to the domain experts in order to explain the idea of an effort factor and its proper definition. However, we should be very careful in presenting particular effort factors because they may bias later judgments of the domain experts.

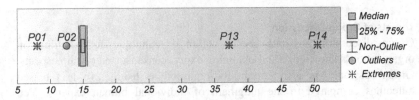

Fig. 5.4 Example distribution of development productivity

As an additional stimulus, the analyst may present to the domain experts the distribution of development productivity—defined as software size divided by project effort—for historical projects and ask them to identify factors that caused the observed productivity variances. For example, if we consider the productivity data illustrated in Fig. 5.4, the analyst may ask the domain experts first what made project P14 and P13 extremely productive and then what made projects P01 and P02 extremely unproductive.

The effort factors identified by the domain experts may, especially at the beginning of the brainstorming session, be quite abstract and actually refer to a composition of multiple less abstract factors. For example, the domain experts may point out team skills as an important effort factor. In this case, the analyst should clarify whether the domain experts have any specific skills of any specific team member in mind? If so, relevant sub-factors of the *"Team skills"* factor should be defined. Example relevant sub-factors may include the work coordination skills of project manager and the technical skills of the software analyst.

Tip

▶ Effort factors may be quite abstract and represent a composition of less abstract concepts. Stimulate the domain experts to exactly define each effort factor they name and ensure that they are aware of the composite nature of specific factors. In case of composite factors, encourage them to decide on the most relevant aspects of the factor and to define these.

Summarizing, the major activities of judgmental effort factor identification are:

1. Schedule an effort factor identification session and invite domain experts.
2. Prepare a template for documenting the effort factors identified during the brainstorming session.
3. Prepare a reference list of example effort factors.
4. Analyze the historical project data and prepare the distribution of development productivity, defined as software size divided by project effort.
5. Run the brainstorming session, during which the involved domain experts shall identify, define, and discuss the potentially relevant effort factors.

The brainstorming session should end with a list of relevant effort factors and associated concise definitions. In this respect, the analyst should ensure that:

- Composite effort factors include a clear definition of all relevant sub-aspects.
- All domain experts agree on the effort factor definitions.
- All domain experts understand the same concept for each defined effort factor.

Violating these requirements may result in inconsistent perception of the effort factors among the domain experts and lead to invalid results of the factor rating activity; by rating the same factors, the experts will actually consider different aspects of the software project.

Tip

▶ Ensure that all domain experts agree with respect to the concept defined by each effort factor identified during the brainstorming session.

Analytical Approach: Analysis of Project Measurement Data

The analytical approach for selecting the most relevant effort factors is optional within CoBRA because it requires the availability of sufficient project measurement data and expertise in certain data analysis techniques—each of which is not always available in software industry contexts.

Simply speaking, in this approach we employ an analytical technique to search for significant relationships between a project's development productivity (dependent variable) and multiple project characteristics (independent variables).

The analytical approach for selecting the most relevant effort factors has several significant advantages over the judgmental approach. First of all, it is objective in that it extracts knowledge represented by quantitative measurement data—unlike the judgmental approach, in which the assessments of human experts are biased by their individual experiences and preferences. The analytical approach will, for example, not omit any relevant knowledge if it is actually present in the data and can be extracted by specific analysis techniques, unlike the human experts who often omit (consciously or unconsciously) relevant information. Furthermore, the analytical approach typically costs much less than that laborious process of a systematic group consensus procedure with human experts. Using the analytical approach merely requires applying an appropriate analysis tool to the measurement data and interpreting the outcome of the analysis provided by the tool. Finally, even though human experts are to be provided with measurement data to base their judgment on, analytical approaches are much more effective (and efficient) in extracting knowledge from measurement data—especially from large, multidimensional data sets whose analysis is beyond the cognitive capabilities of human experts.

Depending on the capabilities of a particular analysis technique, the project measurement data on its input need to accomplish different prerequisites, and it provides different kinds of information on its output.

- *Simple visual analysis* of the measurement data does not impose any particular constraints on the data. It is, however, typically limited to the identification of project characteristics directly influencing development productivity. It is rather infeasible to determine other useful information from simply looking at the data. Even identifying characteristics directly influencing productivity might be quite difficult for a larger amount of data, that is, a larger number of historical projects and their measured characteristics.

- *Statistical methods*, such as multivariate regression analysis, impose a number of constraints on the input data. For example, they require mutual independency of the independent variables (project characteristics). In return, they provide an indication of the most relevant project characteristics that have a direct impact on productivity and the strengths of the impact. For example, stepwise regression selects only those independent variables that provide a significant explanation for the variance of the dependent variable and assigns each selected independent variable a regression coefficient that quantifies the variable's contribution to the variance of the dependent variable.

- *Machine learning methods*, such as feature weighting (Wettschereck et al. 1997), impose fewer constraints on input data than statistical analysis and provide similar outputs (relevant project characteristics having a direct impact on development productivity and the strengths of the impact).

- *Causal modeling methods* represent the most advanced approach (Spirtes et al. 2001). The constraints they impose on the input data depend on the particular modeling technique. On the output, they provide a mode of causal dependencies between dependent and independent variables, including mutual interactions between independent variables and estimates for the strengths of the identified causal relationships. There are several free and commercial software packages[3] that support causal discovery. Most of them, however, focus on discovering the structure of a causal model from the data, that is, on discovering relevant causal interactions between the considered variables, in our case between development productivity and project characteristics. Only a subset of software packages supports the quantification of the discovered causal effect by estimating conditional probabilities[4] for the variables in the causal model. Yet, for identifying the most relevant effort factors, the causal model structure will perfectly suffice for this purpose.

A detailed discussion of particular analysis techniques is beyond the scope of this book. Readers interested in applying analytical methods for the purpose of

---

[3] We do not provide a list of existing software packages supporting causal discovery because they change over the time. As causal modeling has been gaining more and more interest, new software tools are created and existing ones are enhanced by new functionalities. You may easily find appropriate software packages on the Internet using "causal discovery," "learning/discovering causal models," or similar keywords.

[4] For each variable in a causal model, the probability distribution of its values is computed given the values of variables that have a direct causal influence on this variable.

identifying relevant effort factors may refer to the related literature provided at the end of this chapter in the "Further Reading" section.

Example 5.4. Analytical Identification of Relevant Effort Factors

Data Set

Let us assume the project data used in Fig. 5.4. However, we were able to obtain measurement data on seven project characteristics:

- *Team Size*: Peak size of the software development team. This attribute is measured on an absolute scale and ranges between one and infinity.
- *Dom-Skills*: The level of the project team's knowledge and skills with regard to the software application domain. This attribute is measured on a Likert-like[5] approximately interval scale and ranges between 1 and 5, where one refers to a team in which all or most of the members are new to the application domain and five refers to a team in which all or a majority of the members are experts in the application domain.
- *PM-Skills*: The level of the project manager's knowledge and experience with regard to project management. This attribute is measured on a Likert-like approximately interval scale and ranges between 1 and 5, where one refers to a project manager who is inexperienced and has never managed a project and five refers to a project manager who is very experienced and has managed a number of high-priority projects.
- *Q-Reqs*: The extent of quality requirements specified with regard to a software product. This attribute is measured on a Likert-like approximately interval scale and ranges between 1 and 5, where one refers to strict requirements regarding software quality and five refers to low-quality requirements.
- *Reuse-Lev*: The extent of software reuse. This attribute is measured on a Likert-like approximately interval scale and ranges between 1 and 5, where one refers to less than 10 % reuse and five refers to more than 70 % reuse.
- *Prog-Cplx*: The level of software code complexity. This attribute is measured on a Likert-like approximately interval scale and ranges between 1 and 5, where one refers to incomprehensive code with literally no discernible structure and five refers to simple non-procedural code.

---

[5] A Likert scale is considered as an approximately interval scale on which the distance between subsequent values is assumed to be equal. This assumption allows for applying upon Likert-scale measurement mathematical operations that are admitted for interval scales, yet meaningless for ordinal scales. The classical Likert scale contains an odd number of levels where the middle level refers to the neutral value of the measured aspect—neutral in the sense that it is neither positive nor negative. In the example presented here—similar to the typical usage of the CoBRA method—we use an approximately interval scale that does not include any clear "neutral" value. The values typically range between best (nominal) case and worst (extreme) case.

Table 5.11 Example project data

Project	Prod	Team Size	Dom-Skills	PM-Skills	Q-Reqs	Reuse-Lev	Prog-Cplx
P01	7.9	3	2	5	5	1	3
P02	12.3	10	3	3	5	1	2
P03	14.2	4	4	3	5	2	3
P04	14.4	6	4	4	5	2	4
P05	14.4	1	5	4	4	1	2
P06	14.5	4	4	4	5	1	2
P07	14.6	4	4	4	3	1	3
P08	14.7	5	4	4	5	1	3
P09	14.8	12	4	4	5	3	2
P10	15.0	4	3	5	5	2	3
P11	15.1	9	3	4	5	2	2
P12	15.3	1	5	5	5	2	3
P13	37.3	1	5	5	4	3	2
P14	50.7	1	5	5	5	5	4

Table 5.11 provides historical project data sorted with respect to development productivity. The approximately interval character of the Likert-like scale we use allows us to use analysis techniques applicable for interval-scale data—which would not be applicable if we used ordinal scales.

Figure 5.5 presents a scatter plot of the projects' size and effort. As we can see, some projects are outliers with respect to their productivity. The question the project analysis should answer is which of the project characteristics comprised by measurement data are potential causes of the observed productivity deviations?

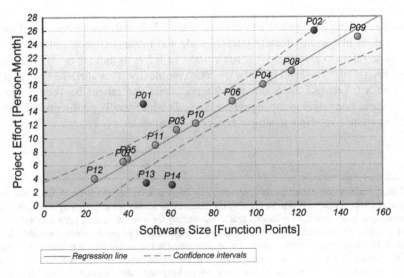

Fig. 5.5 Distribution of development productivity

Visual Analysis

Let us first analyze the data visually and then apply several formal techniques for identifying which of the project characteristics has the greatest impact on productivity according to the available measurement data.

Visual analysis requires neither any particular data preprocessing nor setting method parameters. During the data investigation, we are interested in project outliers with respect to development productivity and characteristics on which these project differ from other, non-outlier, projects. We can easily notice that for the main body of projects (P03–P12), productivity ranges between 14 and 15. Outlying projects include P01 with extremely low productivity, P02 with somehow lower productivity, and P13–P14 with extremely high productivity. Now we look for project characteristics on which these productivity outliers differ from the main body of projects.

The only clear candidate is *Reuse-Lev*. This attribute seems to determine the high productivity of project P14, which is the only project that gained the highest score (5). The second most productive project P13 obtained a score of 3 which is the same as project P09. Both P13 and P09 are similar on other attributes; the slightly higher scores of P13 on *Dom-Skills* and *PM-Skills* may explain its higher productivity relative to P09.

On the lower end of productivity, the outlier projects P01 and P02 obtained the worst scores on *Reuse-Lev*. Yet, since the more productive projects P05–P08 obtained the same score, *Reuse-Lev* is not the only determinant of development productivity. A closer look at the project for which *Reuse-Lev* $= 1$ reveals the *Dom-Skills* attribute as the one that seems to be correlated with the productivity of these projects.

Summarizing, product reuse level (*Ruse-Lev*) and team domain skills (*Dom-Skills*) seem to be relevant effort factors in our example. We must, however, note that even for such a small data set with quite clear trends, identifying relevant effort factors is quite difficult. For larger data sets, visual analysis will not be feasible. Therefore, we need analytical methods that do this job for us.

Multivariate Regression

The first analytical method we use is multivariate regression. For the purpose of analysis, we use the MS Excel application from the Microsoft Office package. Since regression analysis does not handle categorical data, we need to ensure that the project data meet this constraint and preprocess it, if necessary. In our case, none of the project attributes are categorical, so we apply regression analysis on it without extra preprocessing. In the regression analysis, we set development productivity (*Prod*) as an independent variable and measure six project characteristics as independent variables. In addition, we force regression to set intercept to zero (we assume that for the lowest values of the independent variables, productivity is equal to zero). Table 5.12 presents the basic outcomes of the regression analysis.

As we can see, three project characteristics have been assigned positive regression coefficients: *Reuse-Lev*, *Dom-Skills*, and *PM-Skills*. Yet, regression

Table 5.12 Results of multivariate regression analysis

Project characteristic	Regression coefficient	Statistical significance p
Size of software development team (Team Size)	−0.63	0.328
Knowledge and skills on application domain (Dom-Skills)	*2.03*	*0.272*
Project management knowledge and experience (PM-Skills)	*0.91*	*0.713*
Extent of software quality requirements (Q-Reqs)	−0.78	0.773
Extent of software reuse (Reuse-Lev)	***7.73***	***0.002***
Program code complexity (Prog-Cplx)	−0.72	0.782

analysis found only the reuse level (*Reuse-Lev*) as a statistically significant contribution to the variance on development productivity ($p = 0.002$). We may then say that as the reuse level definitely shows an impact on development productivity, domain and project management skills might be the next candidates, although the regression analysis did not indicate them as clear determinants of development productivity.

Feature Weighting with Relief

The next analytical method we try is feature weighting analysis. Feature weighting is commonly used in the context of case-based reasoning, which uses a weighted distance function to generate predictions from known instances. The objective of feature weighting is to find optimal attribute weights that lead to the best predictions. In our example, we use a technique called Relief[6] (Robnik-Sikonja and Kononenko 2003) because it copes with common deficits of software engineering data such as missing measurements, data collinearities, and mixed scales. Moreover, Relief provides an intuitive output, namely, factor weights that represent a percentage contribution of the factors to the variance of the dependent variable.

For the purpose of analysis, we use Weka[7] (Hall et al. 2009), an open source machine learning package. Before using the tool, we need to convert the data into one of the file formats acceptable to Weka. We set all project attributes to a cardinal scale. On the one hand, we would like to be consistent with regression analysis. On the other hand, interpreting Likert-like approximately interval scales as categorical would not be right because in that case, all five values would be considered as equally dissimilar, which is not true. For example, we can definitely say that value 1 is closer to value 2 than to value 3. If we interpreted these values as categories, 1 would be equally dissimilar to 2 and 3. We set the number of the nearest neighbors parameter to $K = 1$ (typical for very small data sets) and left other parameters with their default values proposed

---

[6] More precisely, we use the version of the Relief technique called RReliefF, which copes with both categorical and cardinal data.

[7] http://www.cs.waikato.ac.nz/ml/weka/

Table 5.13 Results of relief feature weighting

Project characteristic	Weight
Size of software development team (Team Size)	−0.087
Knowledge and skills on application domain (Dom-Skills)	−0.079
Project management knowledge and experience (PM-Skills)	*0.083*
Extent of software quality requirements (Q-Reqs)	−0.080
Extent of software reuse (Reuse-Lev)	***0.316***
Program code complexity (Prog-Cplx)	*0.037*

by Weka. Table 5.13 presents the results of the weighting. Attributes with weights equal to or lower than zero are interpreted as irrelevant.

The outcomes of feature weighting are largely consistent with previous analyses. Similar to visual analysis and regression analysis, Relief identified the reuse level (*Reuse-Lev*) as the most relevant and project manager skills as the second most relevant determinant of development productivity. Unlike regression analysis, which identified domain skills (*Dom-Skills*) as the next most relevant effort factor, Relief pointed out program complexity (*Prog-Cplx*).

Causal Modeling with Tetrad

The last analytical method we try in this example is causal discovery. We use the PC algorithm implemented in the free causal discovery software package called Tetrad IV[8] (Scheines et al. 1998). Again, we set all project characteristics to a cardinal scale and formatted the data to a file format acceptable to Tetrad tool. For the PC algorithm, we used the default setting of Tetrad.

The analysis found reuse level (*Reuse-Lev*) and domain skills (*Dom-Skills*) to have a relevant causal influence on development productivity. No other relationships were found.

Summary

Table 5.14 presents an overview of the example effort factor identification using different analytical approaches. We use ranks to indicate the relative importance of the effort factors pointed out by the respective analysis technique. Ranks in

Table 5.14 Summary of analytical identification of relevant effort factors

Project characteristics	Visual analysis	Multivariate regression	Feature weighting	Causal discovery	Summary
Team Size	–	–		–	–
Dom-Skills	(2)	(2)		1	2
PM-Skills	(3)	(3)	2	–	3
Q-Reqs	–			–	–
Reuse-Lev	1	1	1	1	1
Prog-Cplx	–	–	3	–	4

---

[8] http://www.phil.cmu.edu/projects/tetrad/

brackets refer to uncertain results; for example, when using regression analysis, the effort factors were not statistically significant, although regression assigned them the second and third largest coefficients. The summary column illustrates the example decisions regarding the sequence of considering candidate effort factors.

Concluding, we can say that a number of different analytical techniques exist that can support domain experts in identifying relevant effort factors. As we saw in this example, different methods provide largely consistent results when applied to relatively simple measurement data. Yet, when selecting a particular technique, we need to consider the characteristics of the project data and the capabilities of the potential analysis technique.   ∎

The analytical approach for identifying relevant effort factors has several significant weaknesses. First, it cannot identify effort factors that, although being relevant, are not included in the measurement data from historical projects. Second, even though a certain project characteristic contributes to increased project effort (decreased development productivity), it will not be considered as relevant as long as it does not introduce any variance in the measured productivity. For example, requirements volatility is commonly considered as an important factor reducing development productivity. Yet, if for all measured historical projects requirements volatility has been measured as "high," it will be ignored in any kind of analysis because it is not possible to observe no variance on requirements volatility related to variance on development productivity—simply because there is no variance on requirements volatility.

In order to overcome the weaknesses of the analytical approach and exploit its strengths, we suggest using it in combination with the judgmental approach, for example, by supplementing expert judgment with analytical factor identification based on available project measurement data.

Combined Approach: Synthesizing Judgmental and Analytical Approaches

This approach represents an alternative way of performing the group consensus session—alternative to an exclusively judgmental approach. In this approach, the judgment of domain experts is compared to the results of analytical factor selection, and then, this comparison is presented to the domain experts, who discuss the potential reasons of the observed discrepancies. At the end, the domain experts agree on the synthesis of judgmental and analytical factor selection and decide which effort factors are relevant and should be included in the CoBRA model.

As an alternative to a group consensus session, we may consider an analytical way of combining the outcomes of effort factor selection by means of expert judgment and by means of data analysis. Before deciding on an analytical synthesis of expert- and data-based factor selection, we should consider the benefits and drawbacks of this approach. One significant drawback is that we need to master the appropriate theory used for the synthesis. An advantage is that we can avoid judgmental biases by applying a systematic synthesis process based on clear decision criteria for selecting or rejecting particular effort factors. Moreover, we can avoid additional involvement of the domain experts, whose availability is typically very limited. A more detailed discussion of particular theories and techniques that can be employed for synthesizing the outcomes of alternative factor selection approaches is beyond the scope of this book. Let us only mention that one possible approach involves applying the methods of Multicriterial Decision Analysis (MCDA). For example, we have applied this approach for identifying relevant effort factors in the context of an analogy-based and data-driven effort estimation method (Trendowicz et al. 2008a/b).

5.6.2   Rate Relevancy of Identified Effort Factors

The objective of this activity is to rate the relevancy of the initially identified effort factors from the perspective of their usefulness for the CoBRA effort model. The outcomes of the rating will support the selection of a subset of the most relevant factors, which will then be included in the CoBRA model. In a typical case, a judgmental approach is employed in which domain experts assess the relevancy of the relevant effort they initially identified during the group consensus session. Alternatively, an analytical approach can be used in which an analyst checks the measurement data for the relevant factors (if such data are available) with respect to the impact of the factors on project effort. Finally, similar to the factor identification step, judgmental and analytical approaches can be combined to determine the relevancy of effort factors.

Judgmental Approach: Group Consensus Session

In the judgmental approach, the domain experts rate the relevancy of the effort factors in the group session during which these factors were identified. At the end of the session, the analyst presents the consolidated results of the effort factor identification and introduces the rating procedure and the questionnaire to the domain experts. The experts rate each factor individually and return their ratings to the analyst before leaving the session. Optionally, the domain experts may perform the factor rating off-line and submit their individual ratings to an analyst, for example, via e-mail.

In the simplest case, each expert rank-orders the identified factors with respect to their relative impact on development productivity. In this case, a candidate effort factor can be simply put on paper cards—one effort factor per card—and given to the experts to sort the cards in order of the relevancy of the factors on the cards.

Another approach is to rate the relevancy of the candidate effort factors with respect to several aspects. Example aspects may include the factor's impact, measurability, and controllability, where:

- *Impact* represents the strength of a given factor's influence on development productivity and project effort.

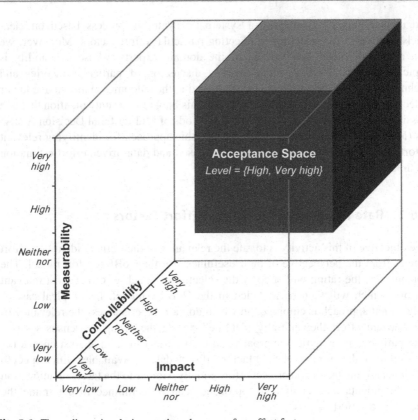

Fig. 5.6 Three-dimensional view on the relevancy of an effort factor

- *Measurability* represents the difficulty (overhead) of collecting factor-related project data. This includes the ease of defining a quantitative measure and collecting corresponding quantitative data. From the perspective of project management overhead, effort factors included in the effort model should be measurable at reasonable cost.
- *Controllability* represents the extent to which a software organization can influence/control the factor's value. For example, a customer's characteristics are usually hard to control. From the perspective of improving development productivity and managing software project risks, project managers must be able to control factors included in the effort model, that is, they must be able to affect their values in order to improve the project's productivity and mitigate associated project risks. On the other hand, from the perspective of negotiating software project costs, a project manager might want to include customer-related effort factors in order to investigate their impact on project effort and thus get the basis for negotiations with a customer.

Figure 5.6 illustrates the three-dimensional space of factor relevancy represented by the aforementioned three aspects. The analyst asks the domain expert to assess each effort factor with respect to each aspect, for example, using a simple 5-point Likert scale as illustrated in Fig. 5.6. In the end, the analyst and the domain experts may agree on including in the CoBRA model only those effort factors that were assessed as at least "high" on each impact, measurability, and controllability aspect (represented by the "acceptance space" in Fig. 5.6).

In both cases, rank ordering or rating effort factors, the analyst should keep the number of candidate factors relatively small in order to allow the domain experts to comprehend them all while assessing the factors' relevancy. Rating or ranking a large number of factors is rather difficult for human experts. Therefore, we recommend considering up to 15 effort factors. However, if the factor identification session resulted in a larger number of factors and the analyst would like to let the domain experts rate them all, he should divide the factors into groups and let the domain experts assess the relevancy of the factors within each group individually. Factors can be grouped according to the project aspects they concern, such as process-, product-, and personnel-related factors.

Note that even though the domain experts have determined the decomposition of complex effort factors into sub-factors (so-called effort variables) before, rating is performed for effort factors. The domain experts may decide on a specific decomposition of effort factors after selecting the most relevant effort factors ("decompose complex effort factors" activity).

Tip

▶ Although factors could represent the composition of less abstract concepts (so-called variables or sub-factors), ranking is done on abstract factors representing n-dimensional concepts. However, decomposition has already been performed (at least gross), and the domain experts are aware of the composite nature of specific factors.

Analytical Approach: Analysis of Project Measurement Data

The assessment of an effort factor's relevancy can be supported through the analysis of project measurement data, if appropriate data are available. Yet, analytical techniques focus on the "impact" aspect of a factor's relevancy, that is, on the strength of the influence a given effort factor has on effort. Other aspects, such as a factor's measurability or controllability, need to be judged by human experts. In the analytical approach, we employ explorative data analysis techniques in order to determine the strength of the relationship between one or more effort factors (independent variables) and effort (dependent variable). In case of one effort factor, we refer to *univariate data analysis*, while for multiple effort factors, we refer to *multivariate data analysis*. Since, in practice, software size is actually the effort factor with the greatest impact on effort, we typically exclude it from the analysis by shifting it to the side of the dependent variable and investigate the relationship between the effort factor and development productivity (computed as effort divided by size).

Example analysis techniques include many of the techniques we already proposed in Sect. 5.6.1 for the purpose of analytical selection of candidate effort factors. Example theories we can consider include statistics, machine learning, or causal modeling. Similar to identifying candidate effort factors, we look at the numerical coefficients that an analysis technique assigns to each effort factor in order to quantify its impact on productivity. These coefficients may include regression coefficients, feature weights, or strength of causal relationships. Yet, in each of these cases, the principal concept is much the same: Each factor is assigned a numerical value that represents the strength of the factor's contribution to the variance in development productivity. Please refer to Example 5.4 for an illustration of popular analytical techniques that may be used for the purpose of rating the relevancy of potential effort factors using available project measurement data.

The credibility of the analysis result depends to a large extent on the amount and quality of the data. Since software engineering data are typically sparse and often inconsistent, we recommend interpreting the results of such a data analysis with great care. At best, the data should be confronted with the judgment of human experts, who ultimately decide on the impact of effort factors.

5.6.3 Analyze Rating Consistency

The objective of this activity is to check for consistency between the factor relevancy assessments provided by multiple domain experts and—optionally— the analysis of the project measurement data. Potential inconsistencies should then be discussed with the domain experts during a group meeting. Usually, such a discussion can take place at the beginning of the factor quantification group session (Step 7 of the model development process discussed in Sect. 5.8). In case of many significant inconsistencies, the analyst may consider holding a separate group session for this purpose.

Consistency Between Experts' Ratings

Domain experts often vary with respect to their individual ratings for the same effort factors. CoBRA offers several possibilities to deal with inter-rater disagreement. The overall consistency check consists of testing Kendall's coefficient of concordance for the experts' agreement (Sheskin 2011). In case of significant disagreement, the analyst may analyze the distribution of the ratings and clarify potentially outlying ratings in a group discussion with the domain experts. One possible source of inconsistent ratings might be the different experiences of the involved domain experts. Example 5.5 illustrates how to check consistency between relevancy ratings, which three independent experts provided for 12 effort factors they had initially identified in a brainstorming session. Kendall's coefficient of concordance among all three experts was equal to $w = 0.33$, meaning little agreement. Yet, after excluding the ratings of the least experienced expert, it increased to $w = 1.00$, meaning perfect agreement.

Consistency Between Judgmental and Analytical Ratings

The ratings of the effort factors' importance judged by the domain experts and those returned by data analysis differ with respect to their scale. Moreover, the concept of a factor's relevancy is typically interpreted differently by human experts and by data analysis techniques. Experts perceive a factor's relevancy from the perspective of its usefulness for effective effort estimation. In consequence, they may consider a number of different aspects of a factor's relevancy, such as its impact on effort, its measurability, or its controllability. Data analysis, on the other hand, typically represents a very narrow view on a factor's relevancy in that it considers solely the extent to which changes on the factor's values contribute to changes in development productivity. Therefore, judgmental and analytical assessments of factor relevancy cannot be compared directly. In CoBRA, we recommend comparing the results of analytical and judgmental factor relevancy assessment on the level of factor rankings. In this approach, we rank-order effort factors using (1) the results of a data analysis and (2) expert judgments with respect to the factor's impact on effort and investigate to which extent these two rank orders are consistent. For this purpose, we can compute Spearman's rank correlation coefficient (Sheskin 2011) and look how close it is to 1, which means perfect agreement between the two rank orders. In case of significant inconsistencies, the analyst should first prove the reliability of the data analysis. If the data analysis proves to be correct, then the analyst should discuss the discovered inconsistencies with the domain experts. It might have simply happened that the measurement data covered different experiences than the experts. In this case, we can treat the expert judgment and the data analysis as complementary sources for the relevancy assessments of the effort factors and should combine them during a group discussion with the domain experts.

In practice, <u>effort factors identified by human experts may differ, at least partially, from factors covered by measurement data</u> (and thus considered by the analytical approach). Usually, only some of the effort factors are shared by both approaches. In this situation, comparing rank orders between the two partially exclusive sets of factors might not be so straightforward. In such a case, we suggest checking consistency between the judgmental and the analytical factor relevancy in two steps:

1. *Compare factor sets*. Analyze how many effort factors were considered by both the judgmental and the analytical approach, meaning how many of the factors initially identified by the domain experts were also covered by the available measurement data, and thus considered in the analytical approach. Additionally, one may check how many factors were considered by both approaches as being of any relevancy, that is, as being different from completely irrelevant. In Example 5.5, the domain experts brainstormed 12 effort factors as potentially relevant, whereas the analytical approach selected 3 out of 6 factors covered by the measurement data as having a nonzero impact on development productivity. Yet, only 3 factors are shared by the factor sets considered by both the experts (3 out of 12 brainstormed factors) and the data analysis (3 out of 6 factors covered by the available project measurement data).

2. *Compare factor ratings/rankings.* Analyze the absolute and relative position of the effort factors shared by the alternative rating approaches in the rank order provided by each individual approach. *Absolute position* refers to the position of factors in individual rank orders, provided independently by the experts and the analytical approach. If we were to rank the effort factors considered in Example 5.5 according to the experts' ratings and the analytical weights, the three effort factors shared by both approaches would be highly ranked in both the expert-based and the analysis-based rank orders. In particular, the three factors would obtain ranks {1, 2, 2} among the 12 factors considered in the judgmental approach and ranks {2, 3, 4} among the six factors considered in the analytical approach. *Relative position* refers to the position of the shared factors in the rank-order sequence relative to one another. Continuing our simple example, if the three shared factors were ranked relative to each other's relevancy within each judgment-based and analysis-based ranking, then the relative ranks (positions in the sequence) would be {1, 2, 2} and {1, 2, 3} for the judgmental and the analytical approach, respectively. From both the absolute and the relative rank perspectives, the human experts are highly consistent concerning the relevancy of three effort factors considered by both approaches. Yet, this might not be the case for all factors considered by the domain experts if they were covered by appropriate measurement data and their relevancy was assessed using the analytical approach.

Example 5.5. Analyzing Consistency of Factor Relevancy Ratings

Let us illustrate the process of checking consistency between effort factor relevancy judged by human experts and the acquired from available project measurement data using a data analysis technique.

Judgmental Approach

In this example, the expert-based selection of relevant productivity factors involved three domain experts with different roles and experience (Table 5.15) and proceeded in two steps.

Table 5.15 Characteristics of involved domain experts

Characteristic	Expert 1	Expert 2	Expert 3
Position/role	Project manager	Developer	Quality manager
Experience [#working years]	8	5	9
Experience [#performed projects]	30	15	40

The first step consisted of a group meeting, during which the domain experts identified an initial set of factors through a brainstorming session. The initial set of 12 factors was then grouped into project-, process-, personnel-, and product-related factors. The first four groups refer to the characteristics of the respective entities (software project, development process, products, and stakeholders).

In the second step, the experts were asked to rate the effort factors using the 5-point Likert scale as illustrated in Fig. 5.6, yet only with respect to a factor's

Table 5.16 Results of judgmental factor selection and rating

Id	Effort Factor	Expert 1	Expert 2	Expert 3
Project				
PROJ.1	Clarity of project team roles and responsibilities	3	1	3
PROJ.2	Development schedule constraints	4	2	3
PROJ.3	Geographic separation of development locations	2	3	2
Personnel				
PERS.1	Communication and team work skills	4	2	4
PERS.2	Knowledge and skills on application domain	3	3	3
PERS.3	Project management knowledge and experience	5	4	4
Process				
PROC.1	Disciplined requirements management	4	4	5
PROC.2	Customer participation	3	1	3
PROC.3	Quality of testing	1	1	2
Product				
PROD.1	Requirements volatility	5	4	5
PROD.2	Product criticality	1	3	1
PROD.3	Program code complexity	4	5	4

impact on development productivity. The five levels of a factor's impact were defined as follows: 1—very low, 2—low, 3—neither nor, 4—high, 5—very high. Table 5.16 summarizes the outcomes of the experts' ratings of the factors they had previously identified during the brainstorming session. The underlined factors are those for which project measurement data had been collected for already completed projects (we assume the data from Example 5.4, Table 5.11).

Checking Consistency Between Expert Judgments

In order to check the overall consistency of the ratings provided by the experts, we compute Kendall's coefficient of concordance. There is little agreement among all three experts (Kendall's $w = 0.33$). Yet, we can observe a certain inconsistency between *Expert 2* and the remaining two experts. We can look for potential reasons of this inconsistency in the experts' characteristics provided in Table 5.15. In fact, *Expert 2* differs from the remaining two experts on two aspects. First, he represents a technical role (developer), whereas the other two experts rather represent managerial and controlling roles. Second, *Expert 2* has relatively little experience compared to the other two experts. We can check our hypothesis by temporarily excluding *Expert 2* and analyzing the agreement between the relevancy ratings of *Expert 1* and *Expert 3*. Indeed, these experts almost perfectly agree with respect to their ratings of relevancy for the 12 effort factors (Kendall's $w = 1.00$). Concluding, we should consider the results of the consistency analysis before synthesizing the relevancy ratings provided by multiple domain experts. We may first consider discussing in a group the exact rationale behind the inconsistent ratings. In our example, it may, for instance, appear that the developer has very important experiences that led him to other ratings than the project manager and the quality manager. In light of these experiences, the latter two experts may revise their relevancy ratings. If, however, the developer had no reasonable support for his ratings, we can exclude them from further consideration and use the ratings of the project manager and those of the quality manager for synthesizing the final ratings of the effort factors' relevancy (see Example 5.6).

Analytical Approach

Regarding the analytical approach for rating the relevancy of the most important effort factors, let us reuse the results from Example 5.4. Let us assume that the available project measurement data consist of 14 already completed projects. For each, data on six characteristics have been collected: *Team size, Domain skills of development team, Project manager's skills, Level of software quality requirements, Extent of software reuse,* and *Software code complexity.* As already noted, three of these factors (marked by underlining) were also considered by the domain experts as being relevant effort factors.

Table 5.17 Results of Relief feature weighting

Project characteristic	Weight	Rank
Size of software development team (Team Size)	−0.087	4
Knowledge and skills in application domain (Dom-Skills)	−0.079	4
Project management knowledge and experience (PM-Skills)	0.083	2
Extent of software quality requirements (Q-Reqs)	−0.080	4
Extent of software reuse (Reuse-Lev)	0.316	1
Program code complexity (Prog-Cplx)	0.037	3

Let us also assume that to rate the relevancy of these potential effort factors, we employed the feature weighting technique called Relief as described in Example 5.4. We decided on this technique because it can be efficiently applied to large data sets (due to its polynomial computation complexity) and because it copes with common deficits of software engineering data, such as missing measurements, data collinearities, and mixed scales. Moreover, Relief is easy to use because it is supported by an open source data mining tool called Weka and provides intuitive outputs (factor weights that represent a percentage contribution of the factors to the variance in development productivity). Table 5.17 summarizes the results of the Relief weighting and the corresponding ranks for the six effort factors covered by the available project measurement data.

Checking Consistency Between Judgmental and Analytical Approach

In order to check consistency between the effort factors selected as relevant by the judgmental and the analytical approach, we consider two aspects: considered factors sets and assigned factor ratings.

With respect to the similarity between the effort factors considered by the domain experts and those selected by the data analysis, the experts identified a lot more factors than the analytical approach. The domain experts identified 12 potentially relevant effort factors, whereas the data analysis considered six project characteristics included in the available project data repository. Yet, this is not an unusual situation in the context of sparse project measurement data.

In our example, the measurement data repository comprises merely six project characteristics, which could be considered as potential factors influencing a project's productivity and effort. In such a case, the advantage of the judgmental factor selection approach is that specific experiences of individual human experts comprise a lot more potential effort factors.

With respect to the factor ratings, we look at the relevancy ratings assigned to the factor shared by both the judgmental and the analytical approaches. These are three effort factors: *"PERS.2. Knowledge and skills in application domain"*, *"PERS.3. Project management knowledge and experience"*, and *"PROD.3. Program code complexity"*. Since comparing the expert ratings on the Likert scale against the ratio-scale weights assigned by the analytical approach is difficult, we would compare the rank order of the three shared factors within both the judgmental and the analytical approach. Table 5.18 illustrates the absolute and relative ranks of the three factors.

Table 5.18 Absolute and relative ranking of shared effort factors

Effort factor	Absolute ranks				Relative ranks			
	Expert 1	Expert 2	Expert 3	Relief	Expert 1	Expert 2	Expert 3	Relief
PERS.2	3	3	3	4	3	2	2	3
PERS.3	1	2	2	2	1	2	1	1
PROD.3	2	1	2	3	2	1	1	2

Concerning the absolute ranks, it is hard to say anything conclusive. We can merely say that the shared effort factors are placed at the top of the rank order determined by the experts' ratings. We cannot draw such a conclusion for the rank order based on analytical weights because there are simply too few factors in total considered in the analytical approach. Concerning the relative ranks, we can say that the domain experts and the data analysis have consistent preferences among the three shared factors. The most relevant factor is *"Project management knowledge and experience"* (*PERS.3*), followed by the *"Program code complexity"* (*PROD.3*) and *"Knowledge and skills in application domain"* (*PERS.2*).

In the next step, the factor relevancy ratings should be combined and presented to the domain experts in order to let them decide about the final set of factors for inclusion in the CoBRA effort model. ■

5.6.4 Synthesize Multiple Ratings

The objective of this activity is to combine the relevancy ratings acquired from different sources and through different methods in order to select the most relevant effort factors. After the domain experts have assessed the relevancy of the candidate effort factors and inconsistent assessments have been clarified, the analyst synthesizes the results in order to come up with an aggregated ranking of the factors' relevancy. Finally, the analyst prepares the results of the aggregation for presentation and discussion with the domain experts during the next group meeting.

Table 5.19 Variants of Borda's approach for scoring ranking results

Ranking (n ranks)	Score (n—rank + 1)	Score (rank/n)
1st	n	1/1
2nd	$n-1$	1/2
3rd	$n-2$	1/3
...	...	...
nth	1	1/n

Synthesizing Judgment-Based Ratings

The CoBRA method uses two simple approaches for aggregating factor relevancy assessments, depending on the form of the assessment. We propose approaches to factors' relevancy assessment using rankings and ratings.

Aggregating Ranking-Based Factor Relevancy Assessments

If the domain experts ranked the candidate effort factors, then the simple method[9] proposed by Borda (1781) can be used for aggregating k rankings provided by k experts. In this method, each factor is assigned a vector of k scores, where the ith score corresponds to a position of the factor in the ranking of the ith domain expert. Each score represents a point count such that the first factor in the ranking gets the largest number of points and each subsequent factor in the rank order obtains smaller number of points, proportionally to its position in the rank order. Table 5.19 illustrates two different variants of Borda's approach for scoring the outcomes of ranking n elements with n ranks (in our case n effort factors).

For the purpose of aggregating the results of the expert-based ranking of effort factors, we propose using the modified version of Borda's method to handle missing ranks[10] and rank ties in the following way:

- *Missing ranks*: For a set of n effort factors, m factors are assigned ranks, where $m < n$. In this situation, the effort factor with the highest rank obtains a score of n or *1* dependent on the scoring variant (see Table 5.19). Each subsequent effort factor in the rank obtains a smaller score, according to the selected scoring variant. The last effort factor in the rank order obtains a score of m–n–1 or $1/m$, respectively. Unranked factors are then assigned a score of 0 in both scoring variants. Such an approach makes two assumptions: (1) that the top-ranked factors are equally important to both groups of experts, who ranked all n and

---

[9] Borda's approach is commonly used for aggregating the results of voting.

[10] We recommend a ranking subset of the initially selected effort factors in case the set is very large. Rating or ranking large sets of effort factors might be difficult for human experts due to their limited cognition capabilities for considering multiple factors at once. In case of rating large sets of effort factorism, the experts may be first asked to select a small subset of the factors they perceive as most relevant and then to rate or rank only this subset of factors. After completing the rating procedure, factors that did not obtain any rating are removed from the set, and the aggregation is performed on the remaining factors.

who ranked m factors, and (2) that factors with missing ranks are equally completely unimportant to the experts who left them unranked.

- *Rank ties*: There exist effort factors F_i and F_j such that $i \neq j$ and *rank* $(F_i) =$ *rank* (F_j). A simple way of determining scores for tie ranks is to compute the scores as if there were no ties in the ranking and then distribute the weights equally for each tied rank, that is, sum the weights across the tied ranks, divide by the number of tied ranks, and assign the resulting average weight equally to each rank. Let us illustrate this idea on a simple example. Let us assume that we have $n = 4$ factors *F1* to *F4* ranked as $\{1, 2, 2, 3\}$. First, we compute the scores as if the four factors were not tied in the ranking, that is, as if the rank order were $\{1, 2, 3, 4\}$. For this purpose, we use a scoring variant in which the highest ranked factor obtains a score equal to n. The resulting "untied" scores would be $\{4, 3, 2, 1\}$. Yet, in order to compute the scores for the tied factors *F2* and *F3*, we would sum their untied scores and divide by 2. The resulting score for the tied factors would then be $(3 + 2)/2 = 2.5$. The final scoring of the four effort factors would then be $\{4, 2.5, 2.5, 1\}$.

After scoring the effort factors, the aggregated score is computed for each factor by summing up the scores it has been assigned based on the rankings of multiple experts. The summary score represents the consensus among the experts. The factors with highest score should be considered as the most relevant ones.

Optionally, one may want to differentiate the impact of an individual expert's assessments on the final result, for example, in order to give preference to the assessment of the more experienced experts. This can be simply achieved by computing the weighted sum over the scores, where higher weights are assigned to the scores of the preferred experts. Please note that in order to preserve the scoring scale, the weights assigned to the experts should be between 0 and 1 and sum up to 1 across all experts.

Aggregating Rating-Based Factor Relevancy Assessments

If the domain experts rated the effort factors using a Likert scale (possible on multiple aspects) or using another approximately interval or interval scale, then a simple statistical median can be used to aggregate the ratings across multiple experts. In this approach, for each candidate effort factor, a median is computed for the ratings provided by multiple domain experts. If the experts rated the factors with respect to different aspects, such as impact, measurability, and controllability, the median of the ratings is computed individually for each aspect. Depending on the estimation purpose, different aspects of relevancy may have different degrees of importance. For example, for the purpose of simply estimating effort, aspects such as controllability of factor values will not be important because we would not be interested in changing its values to affect the estimated effort. Yet, for the purpose of risk mitigation and productivity improvement, the controllability aspect would be important because we would like to change the factors with the greatest negative impact on effort in order to improve development productivity and reduce project risk.

Synthesizing Judgmental and Analytical Ratings: Combined Ratings Approach

Factor relevancy assessments provided by analytical and judgmental approaches cannot be aggregated directly because they represent different concepts of relevancy. In the judgmental approach, relevancy refers to the usefulness of an effort factor for a particular effort estimation purpose and can refer to the factor's impact on effort, its measurability, or the controllability of the factor's values. In the analytical approach, relevancy typically refers to the extent to which a factor's variance "explains" a variance in development productivity. A simple indirect approach for aggregating judgmental and analytical relevancy assessments involves rankings and contains the following steps:

1. Aggregate the relevancy assessments provided by the experts and rank-order the effort factor with respect to the aggregated expert ratings.
2. Rank-order the effort factors using the outcomes of the analytical factor relevancy assessment.
3. Combine the rankings from steps 1 and 2 using Borda's method presented above in the "Synthesizing Judgment-Based Ratings" paragraph for aggregating expert-based factor rankings. Yet, in order not to penalize the rating method that considered fewer effort factors (typically this is the analytical approach), we set the highest score to the cardinality of the overall set of ranked factors, meaning factors that were assigned a relevancy rating within at least one judgmental or analytical approach. In order to favor one rating approach over the other during aggregation, they can be assigned numerical weights. In order to preserve the scoring scale, the weights should be between 0 and 1 and sum up to 1. These weights are then used to multiply the Borda's scores assigned to the factors based on the ranks. For example, the analyst may want to prefer the results of the analytical factor relevancy assessment because the analysis was based on high-quality data, whereas the judgmental assessments involved few domain experts with little experience. After scoring the rated effort factors using their ranks, the total score for each factor is computed through simple sum or weighed sum. The effort factors with the highest total scores are the candidates for inclusion in the CoBRA model. The results of the synthesized assessment of the factors' relevancy are to be discussed in a group meeting with the domain experts, who will decide which effort factors will ultimately be included in the CoBRA model (see Sect. 5.6.5).

Borda's Scoring: Avoiding Penalty on Analytical Ratings

In the traditional Borda's voting method adjusted for missing ranks, the highest score is set to the cardinality of the ranked candidates (m) instead of to the cardinality of all candidates in the voting pool (n). This way, the method penalizes ratings of voters who have not ranked all candidates in the pool (in order to motivate voters to rank all candidates in the pool).

In the context of the CoBRA method, such an approach would in most cases unjustly penalize the results of the analytical approach, which typically considers fewer effort factors than the domain experts due to the limited availability of project measurement data. The number of effort factors rated by the analytical approach concerning their relevancy is always limited by the scarcity of available project measurement data. In contrast, the domain experts may consider any number of potential effort factors, so that the resulting relevancy rating is, in practice, limited only by the effort the domain experts can afford to spend on rating the factors they initially proposed. As a result, a factor ranking provided by analyzing the measurement data would almost always be disfavored to a factor ranking provided by domain experts. In order to avoid this effect in CoBRA, the highest score is always set to the cardinality of the complete set of ranked factors (where each factor has been ranked by at least one voter, that is, a domain expert or a data analysis technique).

An advanced approach for combining multiple assessments of factor relevancy where each assessment makes a different contribution to the final assessment includes using Multicriteria Decision Analysis (MCDA) methods. However, a detailed specification of such approach is beyond the scope of this book. Please refer to Trendowicz et al. (2008a/b) for an example application of an MCDA method for the aggregating results of different approaches to assessing factor relevancy.

Example 5.6. Synthesizing Multiple Factor Ratings

In order to illustrate the synthesizing of multiple ratings of factor relevancy, we will continue our previous example (Example 5.5). In the first step, we will aggregate the outcomes of the judgmental approach, meaning the relevancy ratings provided by the multiple human experts. In the next step, we will synthesize the aggregated outcome of the judgmental factor relevancy assessment with the outcome of the analytical approach.

Synthesizing Judgment-Based Ratings

We aggregated the expert-based assessments of factor relevancy using Borda's approach. Table 5.20 summarizes the results of the aggregation. The aggregation procedure consists of the following steps:

- Determine factors' rank order: For each expert, we use Likert-scale ratings of a factor's relevancy to determine the factors' rank order.
- Determine individual scores: For each factor, we employ Borda's method for deriving numerical scores from the ranks determined for each expert.
- Determine aggregated score: For each factor, we compute the total score using the weighted sum. We assigned weights to experts to reflect discrepancies in their expertise, thus potential discrepancies in the relevancy ratings they provided. We assigned the developer (*Expert 2*) the lowest weight (0.1) and the two managers (*Expert 1* and *Expert 3*) high, yet slightly different, weights (0.4 and 0.5) reflecting the different levels of their experience.

Table 5.20 Synthesizing judgmental factor's relevancy ratings

Effort factor	Expert 1 (0.4)		Expert 2 (0.1)		Expert 3 (0.5)		Borda's weighted score	Final rank
	Rank	Score	Rank	Score	Rank	Score		
PROJ.1	3	5.0	5	2.0	3	5.5	5.0	8
PROJ.2	2	8.5	4	4.5	3	5.5	6.6	6
PROJ.3	4	3.0	3	7.0	4	2.5	3.2	9
PERS.1	2	8.5	4	4.5	2	9.0	8.4	5
PERS.2	3	5.0	3	7.0	3	5.5	5.5	7
PERS.3	**1**	**11.5**	**2**	**10.0**	**2**	**9.0**	**10.1**	**3**
PROC.1	**2**	**8.5**	**2**	**10.0**	**1**	**11.5**	**10.2**	**2**
PROC.2	3	5.0	5	2.0	3	5.5	5.0	8
PROC.3	5	1.5	5	2.0	4	2.5	2.1	10
PROD.1	**1**	**11.5**	**2**	**10**	**1**	**11.5**	**11.4**	**1**
PROD.2	5	1.5	3	7.0	5	1.0	1.8	11
PROD.3	2	8.5	1	12.0	2	9.0	9.1	4

Table 5.20 summarizes the total scores across the considered effort factors and determines the final factor ranking, which we use next for synthesizing the judgmental and the analytical assessments of factor relevancy. We marked the top three effort factors using bold font. According to the domain experts, the three most relevant effort factors are *"PROD.1. Requirements volatility," "PROC.1. Disciplined requirements management,"* and *"PERS.3. Project management knowledge and experience."* Using a weighted average directly upon the Likert-scale relevancy ratings leads to exactly the same rank order of the considered effort factors.

Synthesizing Judgmental and Analytical Ratings

In order to synthesize the judgmental and the analytical assessments of factor relevancy, we employed Borda's method on (1) the rank order of the effort factors assessed by the analytical approach and (2) the rank order of the effort factors assessed by the domain experts. Table 5.21 presents the results of the aggregation. In order to determine the highest score, we consider the complete set of 15 effort factors considered by both domain experts (12 factors) and data analysis (6 factors), where three factors are shared by both sets. Next, we exclude from the consideration the two factors that were not assigned any rank; these are the three factors that were covered by the project measurement but were neither considered by the domain experts nor assigned a weight > 0 by the Relief feature weighting approach (meaning no impact on development productivity and effort). As a result, the aggregation of the relevancy assessments considers 13 effort factors.

We assumed that the judgmental and the analytical assessments are equally reliable and assigned them equal weights (0.5). In consequence, the analytical approach introduced one effort factor (*Reuse level*) into the synthesized top-

Table 5.21 Synthesizing judgmental and analytical factor relevancy ratings

Effort factor	Judgmental (0.5)		Analytical (0.5)		Borda's weighted score	Final rank
	Rank	Score	Rank	Score		
PROJ.1	8	5.5	–	0.0	2.8	8
PROJ.2	6	8.0	–	0.0	4.0	6
PROJ.3	9	4.0	–	0.0	2.0	9
PERS.1	5	9.0	–	0.0	4.5	5
PERS.2	7	7.0	–	0.0	3.5	7
PERS.3	**3**	**11.0**	**2**	**12.0**	**11.5**	**1**
PROC.1	2	12.0	–	0.0	6.0	4
PROC.2	8	5.5	–	0.0	2.8	8
PROC.3	10	3.0	–	0.0	1.5	10
PROD.1	**1**	**13.0**	**–**	**0.0**	**6.5**	**3**
PROD.2	11	2.0	–	0.0	1.0	11
PROD.3	**4**	**10.0**	**3**	**11.0**	**10.5**	**2**
Reus-Lev	**–**	**0.0**	**1**	**13.0**	**6.5**	**3**

ranked effort factor in addition to the three factors that were already top-ranked by the domain experts: "*PROD.1. Requirements volatility,*" "*PROC.1. Disciplined requirements management,*" and "*PERS.3. Project management knowledge and experience.*"

Trendowicz et al. (2008a/b) compared judgmental, analytical, and combined approaches in order to select the most relevant effort factors in the context of Toshiba Information Systems (Japan) Corporation. The authors apply the multicriteria decision analysis (MCDA) approach for synthesizing the outcomes of judgmental and analytical factor rating and for deciding on the final set of effort factors to use for effort estimation purposes. Finally, alternative sets of effort factors obtained with different approaches were compared with respect to the estimation accuracy they provide when applied within the same effort estimation method.   ■

5.6.5   Decide on a Set of Most Relevant Effort Factors

The objective of this activity is to select the most relevant effort factors to be considered in the CoBRA effort model. Usually, this activity is accomplished in a group discussion session. During the meeting, the analyst presents to the involved domain experts the aggregated results of the factor relevancy assessment (obtained using either a judgmental, analytical, or combined approach as discussed in previous sections). The analyst may additionally propose a preselection of the most relevant effort factors. In case of single factor ranking, the analyst may propose qualifying a certain number of the top-ranked factors. In the case of factor ratings on a Likert scale, the analyst may propose a certain rating threshold above which effort factors are qualified. If factor ratings encompass multiple aspects of a factor's relevancy, an individual threshold can be set for each aspect depending on the importance of that particular aspect from the viewpoint of the estimation purpose. Figure 5.6 in Sect. 5.6.2 presents an example threshold for three aspects of a factor's relevancy: factor's impact on effort, factor's measurability, and controllability of factor's values. In this example, the analyst sets equal thresholds for all three aspects. These thresholds determine the "acceptance space" in the three-dimensional area of a factor's relevancy. In order to be accepted for inclusion in the CoBRA model, an effort factor must be rated as "high" or "very high" on all three aspects. Yet, if, for example, some dimensions are not so important for a specific estimation purpose, less rigid threshold should be established.

Next, the analyst and the domain experts discuss the presented results and agree on the final subset of candidate effort factors to be included in the CoBRA effort model. In the iterative CoBRA model, it is recommended adding a limited number of factors in a single model development iteration. Our industrial experiences show that the best practice is to start an initial CoBRA model with up to seven effort factors and then revise it iteratively, with each iteration focusing on modifying—adding, deleting, or modifying—up to three factors. We chose the number seven for the initial set of effort factors as it is traditionally acknowledged as the limitation on a human's cognitive capability for comprehending distinct elements, in this case effort factors. In practice, we observed that depending on the complexity of the concepts represented by the effort factors, selecting 5 to 10 effort factors for the initial CoBRA model works fine. As far as model revisions are concerned, each model's refinement iteration should concentrate on small modifications so that the effects of the change can be easily traced and understood.

5.6.6 Decompose Complex Effort Factors

In practice, while deciding on a candidate and on the most relevant effort factors, the domain experts tend to operate with fairly abstract concepts. At this stage, the analyst should typically allow considering abstract effort factors, as it is easier for domain experts to comprehend and rate the relevancy of a few abstract effort factors. Yet, after selection of the most relevant factors, the analyst needs to tackle the issue that the selected effort factors actually represent complex concepts, which are difficult to operationalize. Therefore, the analyst should ensure that the experts decompose such factors into variables that specify the most relevant aspects for each complex factor. For example (Fig. 5.7), the domain experts may select the *"Key Project Team Capabilities"* factor, which refers to the skills of the project team. Yet, from among many possible team skills, only few may actually be relevant for the purpose of effort estimation. In this case, the experts should decide which skills exactly should be considered.

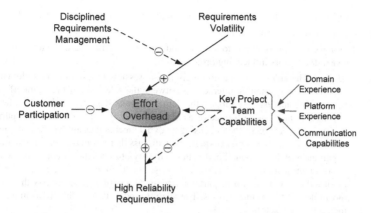

Fig. 5.7 Example of effort overhead model with complex effort factor

5.7   Step 6: Identifying Relevant Factor Interactions

In a CoBRA model, we distinguish between direct and indirect effort factors. Moreover, direct effort factors are assumed to be independent of each other. The practical consequence of this assumption is that the total effort overhead is the sum of the effort overheads (effort multipliers) associated with the effort factors directly influencing effort.

The objectives of this step are (1) to identify potential interactions among effort factors selected in the previous step, (2) to model the most relevant factor interactions through indirect effort factors, and (3) to ensure that the remaining direct effort factors are orthogonal to each other.

Table 5.22 summarizes the most important elements of this step. We provide a detailed description of each activity in the following subsections.

In the following subsections, we present the major activities comprising the "identifying relevant factor interactions" step of the CoBRA model development process.

5.7.1   <Optional> Analyze Existing Project Data

Traditionally, identification of relevant factor interactions takes place during a group meeting in which the domain experts and the analyst discuss potential interactions among already identified effort factors and decide on the most relevant interactions to be modeled in the CoBRA effort overhead model. Optionally, the analyst may—prior to the meeting—analyze available historical project data with respect to potential dependencies. The analyst may then use the results of the analysis during the meeting as alternative source of information—an alternative to the judgment of the involved domain experts.

Table 5.22 CoBRA model development process: identifying relevant factor interactions

Step 6: Identifying relevant factor interactions	
Objective	The objective of this step is to identify and model the most relevant interactions between the factors influencing project effort.
Personnel	• *Analyst*: The analyst leads a group discussion session, during which the domain experts identify potential interactions between the selected most relevant effort factors. The analyst may support the domain experts with the results of the factor dependency analysis performed on available historical project data. For this purpose, the analyst investigates the data using analytical techniques and presents the results of the analysis to the domain experts, who discuss them from the perspective of their experiences and judgment. Finally, the analyst synthesizes the outcomes of the effort factor identification activities, presents these results to the domain experts, and iterates the whole step (or its parts), if necessary, in order to come up with set of the most relevant factor interactions. The analyst models these interactions in terms of indirect effort factors. • *Domain experts*: The domain experts identify and discuss the potential interactions between the most relevant effort factors they identified in the previous step. Finally, they decide on which factor interactions are most important and thus should be considered in the CoBRA model. In this step, the experts may add new effort factors—not considered so far—if they have a relevant indirect or direct impact on project effort.
Inputs	• Selection of the most relevant effort factors to be added in the CoBRA effort model. • <*Optional*> A list of variables defined for the complex effort factors. • <Optional> Project measurement data. • <Optional> Historical factor data collected in the previous model development iterations.
Activities	1. <Optional> Analyze existing historical project data. 2. Identify potential factor interactions. 3. Decide on the most relevant factor interactions. 4. Ensure independency of direct effort factors.
Tools	• Software tools for visualizing, documenting, and communicating the results of the identified factor interactions. Basic tools include elements of standard office packages such as MS Excel, MS Word, and MS PowerPoint. • <*Optional*> Software tools that support the analysis of measurement data for the purpose of identifying dependencies between effort factors. These techniques and tools may include simple correlation and covariance analysis tools as well as advanced causal analysis tools.
Outputs	Qualitative effort overhead model, meaning the structure of the causal effort model: • Modified set of the most relevant direct effort factors. • Set of the most relevant indirect effort factors and their relationships to the direct factors.

The investigated historical project data may include project measurement data collected and validated in Step 3 and Step 4 of the CoBRA modeling process and historical factor data collected in previous modeling iterations (Step 8). In order to identify dependencies among the factors encompassed by the available measurement data, the analyst can use one or more analysis techniques. In the simplest case, the analyst can investigate the dependencies between pairs of measured factors using basic correlation analysis. A more sophisticated investigation of the dependencies between more than two factors at a time will, for example, involve causal analysis.

A detailed discussion of particular analysis techniques and their usage is beyond the scope of this book. Please refer to the literature on multivariate data analysis and on inferring causal dependencies from data.

5.7.2   Identify Potential Factor Interactions

The main part of the factor interaction identification step takes place during a group meeting with the domain experts. At the start of the meeting, the analyst presents to the domain experts the effort overhead model developed so far; this includes the effort overhead model developed in previous modeling iterations and the direct effort factors selected in Step 5 of the current modeling iteration. Next, the analyst motivates the domain experts to identify and discuss potential interactions among the effort factors considered in the model. At that point, the domain experts may add new effort factors to the effort overhead model if they agree that some relevant factors (direct or indirect ones) are missing in the model. The domain experts should define each newly added effort factor and decompose it into variables if necessary. The analyst should ensure that only very few changes are made to the effort factors already considered in the model. If the domain experts decide that a major revision of the effort factors is necessary, the analyst should suggest repeating Step 5 (Sect. 5.6) of the model development process.

The analyst may support the identification of potential factor interactions by providing the results of the data analysis. On the one hand, the analyst may present factor dependencies indicated by the analysis of the historical project data to initiate discussion among the domain experts. On the other hand, the analyst may compare the factor interactions identified by the domain experts against the factor dependencies indicated by the data analysis. The commonalities and discrepancies between these two sources of information can then be discussed with the experts.

Possible Versus Allowed Factor Interactions
In CoBRA, two basic types of indirect causal effort effects are considered. They represent explicit and implicit dependency between effort factors, respectively. Figure 5.8 illustrates these two types of interactions.

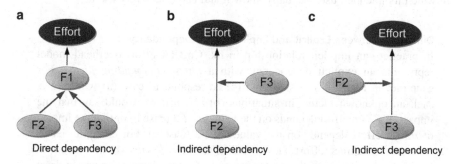

Fig. 5.8 Indirect causal effort effect considered in CoBRA

Explicit dependency (**Fig. 5.8a**): The value of a factor directly contributing to project effort overhead (*F1*) depends on one or more other factors (*F2* and *F3*), which thereby indirectly contribute to project effort overhead. In CoBRA, this dependency embodies the situation in which an effort factor (*F1*) represents a complex concept, encompassing multiple aspects. In this situation, such a complex factor is decomposed into multiple sub-factors (so-called effort variables), each of which represents one aspect of the factor. In Fig. 5.8a, factor *F1* would be associated with two effort variables *F2* and *F3*, and the effort overhead of *F1* would be the sum of the effort overhead on *F2* and F3 (*F2* and *F3* are assumed to be independent of each other). For example, in Figs. 5.10 and 5.11, the effort factor (*F1*) *"Project team capabilities,"* which directly influences effort, is associated with two sub-factors, which represent particular team capabilities having relevant impact on project effort (*F2* and *F3*): *"Domain experience"* and *"Platform experience."*

Implicit dependency (**Fig. 5.8b, c**): The impact of a factor directly influencing effort is influenced by another, indirect, factor. In other words, the magnitude of the direct factor's contribution to the total effort overhead depends on the value of another (indirect) effort factor. In principle, one or more indirect factors may be considered in the CoBRA effort overhead model. However, expanding the number of the indirect factors considered entails exponential growth in the complexity and costs of eliciting effort multipliers for individual direct effort factors and in computing total effort overhead data. According to our experience, the practical benefit from considering more than one implicit dependency is very limited. Therefore, in practice, we strongly recommend restriction to a single indirect factor for each direct effort factor. Figure 5.10 illustrates two examples of implicit dependency. In the first example, the impact of *"Customer participation"* on the project effort is influenced by the *"Customer skills."* This reflects the practical situation in which a skilled customer may boost project performance by providing appropriate project input at the appropriate time; in contrast, the involvement of an unskilled customer may significantly hinder project progress. In the second example, the impact of *"Tool usage"* on the project effort is influenced by *"Tool experience."* This represents a common observation from the practice "a fool with a tool is still a fool." In other words, the extent to which a tool can be effectively used within the project and boost its performance depends on the extent to which its intended users actually know it and can effectively use it.

Difference Between Explicit and Implicit Factor Dependency

In practice, an implicit relationship in the CoBRA effort overhead model represents an explicit dependency with a *latent confounding factor*. For example, in Fig. 5.8, cases (b) and (c) correspond to case (a) when *F1* is such an unknown factor. In situations (b) and (c), we would say that the impact of *F2* on effort depends on the values of *F3* (case b) or that the impact of *F3* on effort depends on the values of F2 (case c). For example, let us consider the direct effort factor "*F2. Customer Participation*" factor in Fig. 5.9. The impact of this factor on project effort depends on the indirect

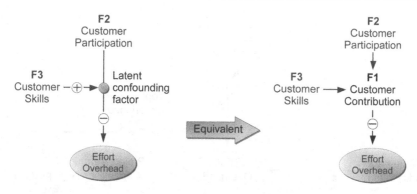

Fig. 5.9 Explicitly modeling a latent effort factors in an implicit dependency

factor "*F3. Customer Skills.*" Behind this indirect dependency exists a latent effort factor, which we can model explicitly by adding a composed factor "*F1. Customer Contribution.*" This composed factor represents a project situation in which contribution of the customer to the project (in terms of added value) depends on two aspects: the extent to which the customer participates in the project whenever such participation is needed and the level of the required customer's skills. The explicit model deliberately does not specify the type of impact of *F2* and *F3* on *F1*, because the impact of the customer's participation (*F2*) on his overall contribution to the project (*F1*) depends on whether the customer has appropriate skills (*F3*) or not. This relationship should be represented by an appropriate effort overhead computation formula defined for *F1*.

In principle, explicit and implicit dependencies can be combined in that a direct effort factor is decomposed into variables and, at the same time, interacts with indirect effort factors. In practice, however, not all possible combinations of factor interactions are beneficial. Modeling complex dependencies increase the costs of developing, applying, and maintaining CoBRA models without proportionally increasing estimation performance. On the contrary, modeling complex factor interactions usually contributes to decreased estimation performance of CoBRA models. Therefore, complex factor interactions are not considered in CoBRA models. Figure 5.10 illustrates the different types of factor interactions in CoBRA.

Case 1 is allowed in CoBRA because the effort variables associated with a direct effort factor without any associated indirect factors can be modeled as direct effort factors. Since, in CoBRA, the impact of a composite direct effort factor is the sum of its impacts across its variables, the variables can actually be modeled as effort factors directly influencing effort. Figure 5.11 illustrates this equivalence.

Case 2 is allowed in CoBRA because decomposing a direct effort factor with an associated indirect factor into effort variables corresponds to associating the

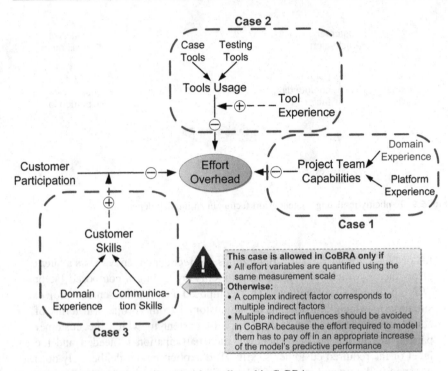

Fig. 5.10 Factor interactions allowed and not allowed in CoBRA

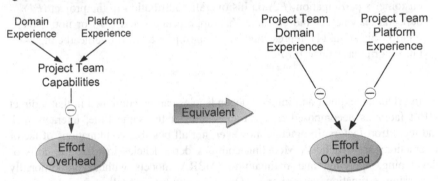

Fig. 5.11 Equivalence of direct effort factor with indirect factor and variables

indirect factor with each variable the direct factor is decomposed into. Figure 5.12 illustrates this equivalence.

The impact of a direct factor on effort is the sum of its impacts across the variables into which the factor is decomposed. The effort overhead introduced by each variable is a conditional effort overhead depending on the indirect factor. Consequently, the total effort overhead introduced by the composed direct effort factor corresponds to the sum of conditional effort overheads of the associated variables (given the indirect factor, which interacts with each component variable).

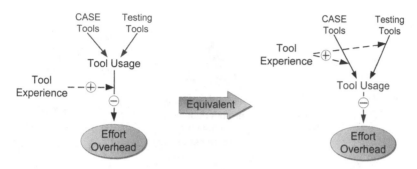

Fig. 5.12 Equivalence of direct effort factor with variables

Case 3 is <u>conditionally</u> allowed in CoBRA because in certain conditions it may lead to a substantial increase in the model's complexity, which in practice increases modeling costs and does not result in increased model performance; on the contrary, it often leads to a decrease of the goodness of the estimates. The condition for decomposing an indirect effort factor is consistent scaling of the variables resulting from such decomposition. The reason is the complexity of computing the effort overhead with which the composite factor contributes to the overall effort overhead. Specifically:

- <u>Decomposing an indirect factor is allowed</u> if all effort variables associated with such a factor are quantified using the same measurement scale. In this case, the values of the associated effort variables can be easily summed up. Furthermore, if a factor's variables are measured on the same scale, the conditional effort multiplier of the direct effort factor (*"Customer Participation"*) can be considered given the summary value of the associated indirect effort factor (*"Customer Skills"*).
- <u>Decomposing an indirect factor is not allowed</u> if all effort variables associated with such a factor are quantified using different measurement scales. In such a case, the associated effort variables must not be simply summed up. Furthermore, if a factor's variables are measured on different scales, computing the effort multiplier of the direct effort (*"Customer Participation"*) factor would require considering its conditional effort multiplier given each variable one by one (given *"Customer's Domain Experience"* and given *"Customer's Communication Skills"*). This would correspond to a situation in which the direct effort factor interacts with two indirect effort factors, which is not allowed in CoBRA. Figure 5.13 illustrates this situation.

5.7.3   Decide on the Most Relevant Factor Interactions

After identifying and discussing potential factor interactions, the domain experts decide on the final set of indirect effort factors to be considered in the model. Since modeling each factor interaction increases the complexity of the model and

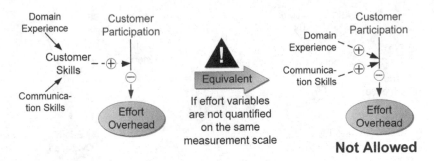

Fig. 5.13 Equivalence of indirect effort factor with variables

the costs of collecting effort multiplier data, the analyst should ensure that only very few most relevant indirect effort factors are considered in the effort overhead model.

Tip

▶ Ensure that only a very limited number of the most relevant indirect factors are considered in the CoBRA effort overhead model. In practice, considering indirect factors of little or no relevancy significantly increases the cost of developing and maintaining CoBRA models without any relevant increase in the model's predictive performance.

For example, if all experts immediately agree on the high relevancy of a certain indirect effort factor, the analyst can include it in the model. If, however, a certain indirect factor invokes many discussions and is the subject of significant disagreement among the domain experts, the analyst should avoid including this factor in the model. In practice, modeling irrelevant indirect factors significantly increases the cost of developing and maintaining the CoBRA model but does not provide proportional benefits in terms of increased predictive performance of the model.

A good practice is to start with an initial CoBRA model that does not contain any factor interactions (a so-called *naive causal model*). If, after validating the model, the experts are still convinced that modeling a particular factor interaction will improve estimation performance, the model should be modified appropriately during the next modeling iterations. There are two potential benefits of such a strategy:

- It may happen that a model without factor interactions will suffice to meet the estimation goals. In such a case, the estimation goals are achieved while the costs of modeling unnecessary model elements are saved.
- An initial naive effort overhead model can serve as a baseline for subsequent model refinements, including the modeling of factor interactions. In this case, after introducing factor interaction, in a subsequent modeling iteration, the analyst and the experts have the chance to see the difference in the model's estimation performance before and after the interaction was introduced.

5.7.4   Ensure Independency of Direct Effort Factors

Finally, the analyst should ensure that all direct effort factors are de facto independent of each other. For this purpose, the analyst and the domain experts together go through the definitions of the direct effort factors and prove that a factor does not address the same aspects of the project environment. If appropriate project measurement data for the considered effort facts are available, the analyst may analyze it with respect to potential correlations prior to the meeting with the domain experts.

The analyst ends the group discussion session by presenting and confirming the structure of the effort overhead model, that is, direct effort factors, indirect effort factor, factor variables, and interactions between direct and indirect effort factors.

5.8   Step 7: Quantifying Selected Relevant Effort Factors

In the CoBRA method, effort estimation is developed using the data from already completed projects. For each already completed project, project effort, software size, and the values of all effort factors considered in the effort overhead model need to be provided. In addition, the impact of each factor on effort—the so-called effort multiplier—is quantified as a function of the effort factor's values—in the simplest case, the effort overhead associated with the worst-case factor's value is specified.

The objective of this step is to define appropriate measures for each effort factor that is considered in the effort overhead model. In practice, quantifying an effort factor consists mainly of defining an appropriate measurement scale, which will be used for collecting the factor's project data (Step 8) and effort multipliers (Step 9).

This step is optional and there is no need to define metrics for factors that are already covered by existing measurement processes. For the remaining factors, the experts provide the metric definitions. Ratio- and interval-scale metrics are preferred. Since measurement data for those factors must be collected from the experts, the granularity of the defined scale depends on how much confidence the experts have regarding the project data.

The definition of measures is a critical element of the CoBRA process. Dependent on the consistent understanding of the defined scales, the experts will later give consistent effort multiplier and project data. Therefore, it is recommended defining each value on the scale in such a way that all experts will relate the value to the same project situation. The more quantitative the value description, the less room for subjectivity and the fewer deviations in the experts' answers during later data collection steps.

Table 5.23 summarizes the most important elements of this step. We provide a detailed description of each activity in the following subsections.

In the following subsections, we present the major activities comprising the "quantifying selected relevant effort factors" step of the CoBRA model development process.

Table 5.23 CoBRA model development process: quantifying selected relevant effort factors

Step 7: Quantifying selected relevant effort factors	
Objective	The objective of this step is to quantify the effort factors selected for inclusion in the CoBRA effort model. Factor quantification refers to defining measures for each selected factor. These measures will be used later to collect project data (for already completed and new projects) and effort multiplier data for each effort factor in the CoBRA model.
Personnel	• *Analyst*: The analyst leads a group discussion session during which the domain experts define measures for the effort factors considered in the effort overhead model. The analyst may prepare and propose to the domain experts example measures. The analyst documents the outcomes of the session.
	• *Domain experts*: The domain experts decide on the measures used for quantifying the effort factors and support the analyst with their expertise when defining the measures.
Inputs	• Selection of the most relevant effort factors to be added in the CoBRA effort model
	• *<Optional>* A list of variables defined for the complex effort factors
Activities	1. Decide on measurement scale.
	2. Define factor measures.
Tools	• Software tools for visualizing, documenting, and communicating the results of the quantification of the selected relevant effort factors. Basic tools include elements of standard office packages such as MS Excel, MS Word, and MS PowerPoint.
Outputs	• Measures for effort factors considered in the effort overhead model.
	• <Optionally> Measures for effort variables defined for complex effort factors in the effort overhead model.

5.8.1 Decide on Measurement Scale

Based on the definition of the effort factors considered in the CoBRA effort overhead model and the available measurement data, the analyst selects the most appropriate measurement scales for quantifying the factors. This initial selection regarding the measurement scales will then be next used as a starting point during a group session with the domain experts to define measurement scale for each considered effort factor.

In general, effort factors in CoBRA can be quantified using any measurement scale (Table 5.24). Yet, in practice, not all measurement scales are reasonable or useful. Example issues include:

- *Collecting factor project data*. In practice, measurement data for effort factors are rarely available. Therefore, they need to be quantified by the domain experts, and the domain experts need to provide historical project data for effort factor. In order to increase reliability and limit the effort required for defining effort factor scales, an approximately interval scale with approximately equidistant values is typically considered. The benefit is that the domain experts must consider only a very limited number of possible values when providing historical project data in Step 8 of the CoBRA model development process (Sect. 5.9. Step 8: Collecting and Validating Historical Factor Data). Low granularity of the measurement scale supports consistent measurements when data are acquired

Table 5.24 CoBRA model development process: effort factor measurement scales

Scale	Definition	Usage in CoBRA
Nominal	Numbers or symbols are assigned to represent class memberships. Thus, the scale consists of different classes, and no ordering among these classes exists. Allowed operations: $=$, $<>$.	Nominal-scale measures are typically used to quantify context factors. If we identify a factor influencing project effort and the factor is of a nominal nature, we should consider it as a context factor. Typical nominal-scale context factors include application domain, development type, software life cycle model, and programming language.
Ordinal	Used for rank orderings. The size of the interval between different ranks cannot be determined. Allowed operations: $=$, $<>$, $<$, $>$.	Ordinal-scale measures are not used in the CoBRA method for quantifying effort factors. One reason is the inherent subjectivity of ordinal scales and the undefined distance between subsequent values on the scale. Moreover, using ordinal-scale measures would require collecting effort multipliers for each value on the scale. Instead, an approximately interval scale should be defined in that each value on the "ordinal" scale is defined in such a way that the distance between subsequent values remains approximately equal.
Interval	Intervals between any two consecutive integers represent equal amounts of measured attribute. Thus, the order is preserved as well as differences so that we can understand the size of the jump from one class to another. Allowed operations: $=$, $<>$, $<$,$>$,$+$, $-$.	Interval-scale measures are usually used for quantifying effort factors in CoBRA. Actually, n-point approximately interval-scale measures are defined in that the domain experts define each of the n possible values so that the distance between subsequent values remains equal. The experts typically define each level by describing a corresponding project situation.
Ratio	Interval scale with an absolute zero point that represents a total lack of the measured attribute. The scale must start at zero and increase at equal intervals known as units. All arithmetic operations can be meaningfully applied: $=$, $<>$, $<$, $>$, $+$, $-$, $*$,$/$.	Ratio-scale measures are rather rarely used for quantifying effort factors. A typical case of using such measures includes a situation in which historical project data for the effort factor has already been collected using a ratio-scale measure. Still, in this situation, the domain experts must decide on the worst-case factor value that is realistic in the effort estimation context. This worst-case threshold is needed for specifying the factor's effort multiplier data.

from multiple human experts. In principle, the more measurement values can be selected, the higher the probability of disagreement among multiple experts with respect to the value of the same factor in the same project. Therefore, the use of ratio-scale measures should be limited to cases where corresponding historical project data are already available or can be easily collected in an automatic and objective way.

- *Collecting factor effort multiplier data.* The usefulness of nominal- and ordinal-scale effort factors is limited due to the relatively high effort needed to collect effort multiplier data in Step 10 of the CoBRA model development process

(Sect. 5.10. Step 9: Collecting and Validating Effort Multiplier Data). In such a case, effort multipliers for each value on the measurement scale need to be specified by one or more human experts. In case of at least interval-scale measures, it is typically sufficient for a given effort factor to specify its worst-case value and the functional dependency between the factor's value and the effort multiplier. In CoBRA, we typically use interval-scale measures and assume linear dependency between a factor's value and the value of its effort multiplier. Moreover, the basic assumption in the CoBRA method is that an effort factor does not introduce any additional effort (effort multiplier = 0) in its best-case value. Given these assumptions and worst-case effort multipliers, we can easily compute the effort multipliers for the other factor values (between best and worst case).

Granularity of Approximately Interval Scale
The granularity of the interval—or approximately interval—scale used for quantifying effort factors in CoBRA has certain consequences with respect to the cost of defining the measure and the feasibility of collecting credible data to build the CoBRA model on. The three major aspects to consider when deciding on the number of levels on the measurement scale include:

- *Defining the measure.* The first aspect is definition of the measure itself. The more the levels on the measurement scale, the more expensive the definition of such a scale, because the domain experts must define each level on the scale.
- *Collecting project data.* With respect to collecting historical project data, the granularity of the measurement scale has an influence on the credibility of the historical project data collected retrospectively by means of expert judgment. Typically, human experts are capable of recalling the gross values of an effort factor in an already completed project. The more time has passed since project completion, the more uncertain the expert judgments will be. In consequence, the experts are better able to provide historical project data on a gross scale rather than on a detailed scale. If we do, for example, quantify an effort factor using a 15-point scale, the experts might have problems in recalling if the factor's value in a project that was completed a few years ago was 13 or 14. Yet, if we reduce the scale to 3 levels—each level corresponding to 5 levels of the detailed 15-point scale—then the experts can judge with high confidence that the factor has the value 3.
- *Collecting effort multiplier data.* If the experts decide about the nonlinear dependency between an effort factor quantified on an interval scale and this factor's effort multiplier, they must define an effort multiplier for each possible value of the factor (except for the best-case value, for which the effort multiplier is assumed to be equal to zero percent). The more levels on the factor's measurement scale, the more effort the experts have to spend on specifying effort multiplier data.

In the end, practical experiences with the CoBRA method show that the risks related to using high-granularity measures for quantifying effort factors compensate for the potential benefits in the form of increased precision of effort estimates. Therefore, we recommend using 4- or 5-point interval scales.

Tip

▶ Use a 4-point approximately interval scale for quantifying effort factors for which ratio-scale measurement data neither exist nor can be automatically collected.

In fact, there are two types of approximately interval scales we may consider in CoBRA: non-Likert and Likert scale.

Default 4-Point Approximately Interval Scale

Industrial experiences have shown that a 4-point approximately interval scale is the best trade-off between precision of input data for effort estimation and acceptable effort required to collect these data. The default measurement scale in CoBRA goes from level "0," which represents the best case and goes through levels "1" and "2" to level "3," which represents the worst case. The domain experts define each level by characterizing the specific project situation a given level represents.

Often, experts refer to a ratio-scale measure when defining the interval scale levels. Let us consider the example effort factor "requirements volatility," which represents the extent of changes to requirements after their freeze. The experts may quantify this factor using a 4-grade approximately interval scale in that they define each value on the interval scale in terms of the range of percentage changes to requirements after the requirements freeze. For example, in Table 5.25, a factor's value of "0" may be defined as 0–10 % changed requirements, a value of "1" as 11–20 % changes, a value of "2" as 21–30 % changes, and a value of "3" as 31–40 % changes.

Table 5.25 Example 4-point approximately interval scale

Extent of changes to software requirements during the development life cycle, after requirements freeze			
0	1	2	3
0–10 % requirements changed (*best case*; *nominal situation*)	1–20 % requirements changed	21–30 % requirements changed	31–40 % requirements changed (worst case; *extreme situation*)

Alternative 5-Point Likert Scale

As alternative to a 4-point interval scale, a so-called Likert scale can be employed for quantifying effort factors. A Likert scale is a type of psychometric scale frequently used in psychology questionnaires. It was developed by and named after organizational psychologist Rensis Likert (1932), who proposed quantification through conceptual levels. The general advantage of this scale is that levels on the scale can be assumed to be equidistant, which means that a Likert scale can be treated in practice as being approximately interval. In a Likert scale, an expert is presented a questionnaire with one or more phrases. Each phrase represents a certain thesis or question and comes with a number of answers, each of which is associated with a numeric score. Answers and scores are values (levels) on the measurement scale. The answers in the scale are approximately equally spaced conceptually; thus, associated scores represent an approximately interval scale. It is a characteristic of a Likert scale that it consists of an odd number of levels, where the middle level represents a "neutral" answer. The neutral answer represents that the measured concept has neither a good nor a bad value. Since a Likert scale requires an odd number of levels, we recommend using a 5-point Likert scale. Table 5.26 presents an example quantification of the "requirements volatility" effort factor using a Likert scale. The standard scoring schema used within the Likert scale used integer numbers beginning from "1," where this value may refer to the best- or to the worst-case value. In order to use a Likert scale for computing the parameters of the CoBRA estimation model, the scoring should begin from the worst-case value, to which the score "0" is assigned.

Table 5.26 Example Likert scale

After freezing software requirements, they change during the development life cycle				
1	2	3	4	5
Never (*best case; nominal situation*)	Sometimes	Average (*neutral case*)	Often	Very often (*worst case; extreme situation*)

Specialist literature defines several standard Likert scales that can be used as templates and adapted for quantifying different concepts.

The advantage of a Likert scale over the CoBRA default 4-point approximately interval scale is that it does not require defining a specific project situation for each measurement level. It is sufficient to define the main phrase and select appropriate answers defined on one of the standard Likert scales. The disadvantage of the Likert scale is its high subjectivity. Answers to standard Likert-scale questions may depend a lot on their interpretation by a specific domain expert. This is not the case in a 4-point approximately interval scale, where each level is precisely defined in a group meeting involving all experts. We recommend using Likert scales for quantifying factors only when it is not possible to define 4-point approximately interval scales, for example, because no domain experts are available for defining factor measurement scales since their availability is very limited (insufficient for a detailed definition of scales of all factor measures).

5.8.2 Define Factor Measures

After deciding on the appropriate measurement scale to quantify the effort factors considered in the CoBRA model, the analyst and the domain experts define exact measurement scales for each effort factor.

Typically, the domain experts define measures for the effort factors during a group meeting moderated by the analyst. The analyst starts the meeting by presenting the proposed measurement scales to the domain experts. The experts discuss the proposed measurement scales with respect to their appropriateness for quantifying the associated effort factors and from the perspective of the feasibility of defining these scales during the session. Next, the domain experts define the measures for the effort factors considered in the CoBRA effort overhead model:

- *4-Point approximately interval scale*: An effort factor is assigned four measurement levels between 0 and 3, where 0 refers to the best-case and 3 to the worst-case level. The best case refers to a nominal project situation in which the factor has a nominal value and does not introduce any additional project effort. The worst case refers to an extreme project situation in which the factor introduces the maximal effort overhead possible in the CoBRA estimation context. For each value on the factor's measurement scale, the domain experts describe a project situation that corresponds to this value. The analyst moderates the discussion among the experts and ensures that (1) each level is unambiguously defined so that all involved domain experts associate the same project situation with a given level and (2) the distance between any two subsequent factor values is (conceptually) approximately equal.
- *5-Point Likert scale*: An effort factor is assigned a 5-point Likert scale. The domain experts define a phrase that characterizes or asks for a certain project situation and select an appropriate set of standard Likert-scale answers. The analyst ensures that (1) the phrase is unambiguous and that all involved domain experts associate with it the same project situation and (2) a correct set of answers is selected. Finally, the analyst associates the scores 0–4 with Likert-scale answers, where 0 and 4 refer to the values of the best- and worst-case factor, respectively.
- *Other scales*: If the experts decide to quantify some effort factors using measurement scales other than an interval one, they specify these scales appropriately. For nominal scales, the experts need to characterize each nominal value. For ratio scales, experts define the measurement unit and the best- and worst-case thresholds.

5.9 Step 8: Collecting and Validating Historical Factor Data

In the CoBRA method, an effort model for the estimation of future software project is developed based upon actual information from already completed similar projects—so-called historical projects. The historical project data used for developing the CoBRA model include software size, project effort, and effort factors considered in the CoBRA effort overhead model. Size and effort are collected and validated in Step 3 and Step 4 of the model development process (Sect. 5.4. Step 3: Collecting Project Measurement Data and Sect. 5.5. Step 4: Data Validation and Preprocessing).

The objective of this step is to collect historical project data regarding effort factors considered in the effort overhead model. If measurement data for some effort factors have already been collected or can be automatically collected based on existing project artifacts, then we use these measurement data. Yet, typically effort factors considered in the CoBRA model have neither been the subject of measurement nor can they be easily collected in an automatic manner. In this case, historical factor data must be acquired from domain experts who are familiar with the historical projects used for developing the CoBRA model. In this section, we focus on acquiring factor data from domain experts.

Table 5.27 summarizes the most important elements of this step. We provide a detailed description of each activity in the following subsections.

In the following subsections, we present the major activities comprising the "collecting and validating historical factor data" step of the CoBRA model development process.

Table 5.27 CoBRA model development process: collecting and validating historical factor data

Step 8: Collecting and validating historical factor data	
Objective	The objective of this step is to collect historical project data regarding the effort factors considered in the effort overhead model.
Personnel	• *Analyst*: The analyst prepares data collection and validation tools based upon the quantified effort overhead model, in particular, the considered effort factors and the associated measures. After preparing the tools, the analyst acquires historical factor data from domain experts familiar with the historical projects considered for developing the CoBRA effort model. If the CoBRA method and the modeling process are new to the domain experts, the analyst acquires the factor data in a face-to-face interview with each domain expert individually. If the domain experts are already experienced with the factor data acquisition procedure, the analyst can provide the experts with an appropriate questionnaire and ask them to deliver the factor data by means of an off-line survey, for example, via e-mail. Finally, the analyst checks the collected historical factor data for potential threats and, if any are found, clarifies them with the appropriate experts Optionally, prior to the judgment-based factor data acquisition, the analyst may look through already available historical project measurement data to see whether they can be used for determining the values of the modeled effort factors. In addition, the analyst may investigate whether useful measurement data can be easily measured retrospectively across the considered historical projects. If appropriate historical project data are available or can be collected in retrospect, the analyst can use these instead of the expert judgments or in addition to the expert judgments (in order to validate the expert judgments against the project data as discussed it in Sect. 5.9.3: Validate Historical Project Data).
	• *Domain experts*: The domain experts provide the effort factor data for the historical projects they are familiar with, at best because they were involved in managing these projects.
Inputs	• Quantified effort overhead model, in particular effort factors (direct and indirect), effort variables (if any are defined), and measures specified for factors and variables.
	• <Optional> Available measurement data from the historical projects used for developing the CoBRA effort model.
	• <Optional> Artifacts from the considered historical projects that can be easily measured to acquire needed factor data.

(continued)

Table 5.27 (continued)

Step 8: Collecting and validating historical factor data
Activities	1. Prepare data collection and validation tools. 2. Collect historical factor data. 3. Validate historical factor data.
Tools	• Software tools for preparing data collection instruments. In the simplest case, MS Word or MS Excel to create data collection questionnaires. In advanced cases, a dedicated CoBRA tool, which automatically generates data collection forms based upon the quantified effort overhead model modeled in the tool. • Basic data analysis and visualization tools such as MS Excel or specialized statistical analysis tools such as R, SPSS/PASW, or Statistica.
Outputs	• Historical project data for effort factors considered in the CoBRA effort overhead model.

5.9.1   Prepare Data Collection and Validation Tools

The analyst prepares instruments for collecting and validating historical factor data. For the purpose of data collection, CoBRA uses a questionnaire that consists of two sections:

- *General information.* This section asks for a unique identifier of the historical project for which factor data are being collected and the domain expert who provides the data. Moreover, this section collects basic characteristics of the domain expert, such as position in the historical project or domain experience, which can be used as context information while analyzing the acquired factor data.
- *Factor data.* This section provides a definition and measurement scale for the effort factors considered in the effort overhead model and asks for the value of each factor. For the interval-scale factors, the questionnaire specifies the value on the scale; factor data are provided by simply checking the appropriate value. In order to account for judgment uncertainty, each factor's value can be associated with a confidence field. In this case, the experts can check more than one factor's value and specify the percentage confidence for each selected value; for a single factor, the confidence percentages across all selected values must sum up to 100 %.

The factor data collection can be prepared manually by the analyst in electronic or paper form. It could also be generated automatically by an appropriate CoBRA tool based upon the quantified effort overhead model.

5.9.2   Collect Historical Factor Data

The analyst acquires historical factor data from the domain experts using the data collection questionnaire prepared in the previous activity. It is important that the expert providing the project data knows the project. In order to increase the validity of the expert assessment, more than one domain expert should (if feasible) provide data for the same project. In this case, each expert should provide data independently of the other experts.

Depending on the familiarity of the involved domain experts with the factor data acquisition procedure, the analyst decides between two alternative ways of collecting the data:

- *Interviews*: If the factor data acquisition procedure is new to the domain experts, it is highly recommended that the domain experts provide the data individually in a face-to-face interview with the analyst. During a personal interview, the experts still have an opportunity to clarify potential doubts with respect to the definition and/or quantification of effort factors.
- *Survey*: If the domain experts are already familiar with the factor data acquisition procedure, for example, because it is already a subsequent model development iteration they are involved in, the analyst may collect factor data off-line in an e-mail or Web-based survey. In this case, the domain experts fill in data acquisition forms off-line and send them back to the analyst. The advantage of this approach to factor data collection is its relatively low cost, compared to time-consuming interviews.

The quality of the factor data is influenced by two facts: The expert judgments may be biased by the subjective perception and preferences of a particular expert, or a domain expert might not be able to exactly recall the project in order to provide precise information with respect to a certain effort factor. In order to address these issues, CoBRA proposes:

- *Collecting redundant factor data*: For a given factor and historical project acquire data from more than one domain expert. This will later allow analyzing consistency of multiple judgments, clarify underlying reasons, and coming up with consensus value.
- *Collect uncertainty assessments*: In order to account for the uncertainty of expert judgment, the analyst may allow the domain experts to deliver multiple values for a certain factor, where each value is associated with a percentage confidence by the expert. Note that the confidence percentages across the provided factor's values should sum up to 100 %. For example (Table 5.28), for an effort factor measured on the 4-point interval scale, an expert may select more than one value and assign it with a percentage confidence level quantifying how certain the expert is of this factor's value.

Table 5.28 Example element of factor data collection questionnaire

Effort Factor: requirements volatility

Question: Please assess the percentage of software requirements that changed after requirements freeze, during the development life cycle. If you are not certain of one value, please select multiple values; please specify how confident you are of each selected value (note that the confidences must sum up to 100 %)

Factor's measurement scale	Expert's assessment	Confidence
0–10 % of requirements changed	❏ <0> best case	___%
11–20 % of requirements changed	❏ <1>	___%
21–30 % of requirements changed	❏ <2>	___%
31–40 % of requirements changes	❏ <3> worst case	___%

In addition to the factor data, the analyst should acquire the basic characteristics of the domain experts, such as domain experience and position in the historical project for which the expert provided the factor data. This additional information may later on help to explain potential inconsistencies in the factor data; for example, the level of involvement in the particular project and the understanding of its application domain may influence the assessment of a particular expert.

5.9.3 Validate Historical Project Data

After collecting the historical factor data, typically from multiple domain experts, the analyst first integrates the data and investigates it completeness. The analyst ensures that for each effort factor considered in the CoBRA effort overhead model, data from all historical projects used for developing the effort model have been provided by at least one domain expert. Moreover, the analyst checks the typographical correctness of the data, that is, if the data are free from typing errors.

Next, the analyst investigates the factor data concerning potential inconsistencies. There are two ways of checking the consistency of the project data provided by the experts:

- *Against project data*: The project data provided by the domain experts are compared to existing measurement data (if available). Even though measurement data exist for a certain effort factor, it is recommended eliciting corresponding data from the domain experts. A common experience is that there is a significant discrepancy between existing measurement data and the data provided by the domain experts. On the one hand, domain experts tend to provide inaccurate data for historical projects—especially if they were completed a long time ago. On the other hand, the measurement and data collection processes may be invalid, resulting in invalid data—in this case, the experts may prevent the uncritical acceptance of existing measurement data. Potential inconsistencies can then be discussed with the experts in order to identify the sources of inconsistency and come up with reliable project data.
- *Between domain experts*: In cases where more than one domain expert provided data for the same project, the data can be compared against each other. Potential inconsistencies can then be discussed with the respective experts in order to identify the source of inconsistency and come up with reliable project data. According to our experience, the most common source of data inconsistency is incoherent interpretation of a factor's definition.

5.10 Step 9: Collecting and Validating Effort Multiplier Data

In CoBRA, the domain experts quantify the impact of an effort factor on effort by specifying so-called effort multipliers. The objective of this step is to acquire effort multipliers from one or more domain experts.

An effort multiplier is assigned to each effort factor directly influencing effort. It refers to the percentage increase of effort that this particular effort factor introduces independently of other direct effort factors, potentially given the associated indirect factors.

Table 5.29 CoBRA model development process: collecting and validating effort multiplier data

Step 9: Collecting and validating effort multiplier data	
Objective	The objective of this step is to collect valid effort multiplier data.
Personnel	• *Analyst*: The analyst prepares effort multiplier collection and validation tools based upon the quantified effort overhead model, in particular the considered effort factors and their associated measures. After preparing the tools, the analyst acquires the effort multiplier data for the direct effort factors from the domain experts. If the CoBRA method and the modeling process are new for the domain experts, the analyst acquires factor data in a face-to-face interview with each domain expert individually. If the domain experts are already experienced with the factor data acquisition procedure, the analyst can provide the experts with an appropriate questionnaire and ask them to deliver the effort multiplier data by means of an off-line survey, for example, via e-mail. Finally, the analyst checks the collected effort multiplier data for potential threats and, if any are found, clarifies them with the appropriate experts. • *Domain experts*: Domain experts provide effort multiplier data based on their personal experiences in the domain addressed by the developed CoBRA model.
Inputs	• Quantified effort overhead model, in particular effort factors (direct and indirect), effort variables (if any are defined), and measures specified for factors and variables.
Activities	1. Prepare multiplier data collection and validation tools. 2. Collect effort multiplier data. 3. Validate effort multiplier data.
Tools	• Software tools for preparing data collection instruments. In the simplest case, MS Word or MS Excel to create data collection questionnaires. In advanced case a dedicated CoBRA tool, which automatically generates multiplier data collection forms based upon the quantified effort overhead model modeled in the tool. • Basic data analysis and visualization tools such as MS Excel or specialized statistical analysis tools such as R, SPSS/PASW, or Statistica.
Outputs	• Effort multipliers for direct effort factors considered in the CoBRA effort overhead model.

Table 5.29 summarizes the most important elements of this step. We provide a detailed description of each activity in the following subsections.

In the following subsections, we present the major activities comprising the "collecting and validating effort multiplier data" step of the CoBRA model development process.

5.10.1 Prepare Multiplier Data Collection and Validation Tools

The analyst prepares the data collection, storage, and validation instruments. Since effort multiplier data in CoBRA are acquired from one or more domain experts, the analyst must prepare an appropriate data collection questionnaire. This questionnaire will later be used to document the assessed effort multipliers, either during interviews or in an off-line survey. The effort multiplier questionnaire contains two blocks:

• *General information*. This section asks for basic information on the domain expert who provides the multiplier data. In addition to the unique identifier of the expert, one may ask for basic characteristics that may have an impact on the expert's assessments. Example characteristics include the expert's position in the organization, the domain in which the expert is most experienced, and the expert's seniority. This information can be used while validating the data to explain potential inconsistencies between the assessments of multiple experts.

- *Multiplier data.* This section asks for the effort multipliers associated with the direct effort factors considered in the effort overhead model. In principle, the domain experts are asked to specify the percentage of additional effort introduced by each direct factor under the condition that all other direct effort factors have their best-case values, meaning they do not introduce any additional effort. For a given direct effort factor, the exact effort multiplier query depends on several aspects: (1) uncertainty of expert assessment, (2) factor's measurement scale, (3) existence of associated indirect factors, and (4) factor's decomposition into variables. We will discuss these issues in the next paragraphs.

Uncertainty Considerations

In order to account for the uncertainty of human judgment, the domain experts are asked to provide three values of the effort multipliers for each direct effort factor:

- *Min*: Minimal believed percentage of additional effort introduced by the effort factor
- *Max*: Maximal believed percentage of additional effort introduced by the effort factor
- *ML*: Most likely believed percentage of additional effort introduced by the effort factor

While building a CoBRA model, the three effort multiplier values are interpreted as a triangular or beta-Pert probability distribution of the effort multipliers.

Figure 5.14 illustrates an example result of acquiring three values of an effort multiplier, which are then interpreted as a triangular distribution. The example

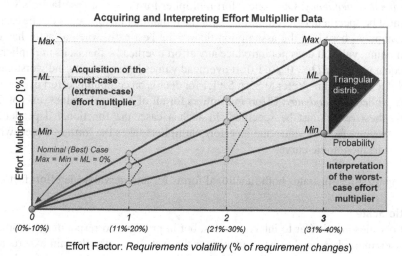

Fig. 5.14 Example triangular distribution of effort multipliers

assumes that the effort factor is measured on a 4-point interval scale and that the effort multiplier is linearly dependent on the factor's value. In this case, the domain experts solely need to provide the effort multipliers (Min, Max, and ML) for the worst-case factor's value. Under the assumption that the effort multiplier for the best-case (nominal) factor's value is equal to zero, one may easily compute the triangular distributions of the effort multiplier for the intermediate factor's values.

Scale Considerations
Depending on the factor's measurement scale, the domain experts must provide different numbers of multipliers.

Nominal Scale
The use of nominal-scale factors in CoBRA is limited to context factors. Because of their inability to build an order, nominal-scale effort factors are not used in CoBRA.

Ordinal Scale
Although theoretically feasible, ordinal-scale factors are not used in CoBRA because of the undefined distance between subsequent values on the ordinal measurement scale. Instead, approximately interval or interval scales are used for which an equal distance between subsequent values on the scale is assumed.

Interval Scale
For interval-scale effort factors, an equal distance between the subsequent factor's values is assumed. Depending on the assumed functional form of the dependency between the factor's values and its effort multipliers, one or more effort multipliers need to be specified:

- *Linear dependency*: Only one effort multiplier for the worst-case factor's value must be specified. Effort multipliers for the remaining factor values can be easily computed based on the assumption that in the best case, when a factor has its nominal value, it does not introduce any effort overhead—that is, its multiplier is equal to zero ($EO = 0\ \%$). Effort overhead values between best- and worst-case values form a line. Refer to Sect. 5.11.1 for details on computing effort overhead.
- *Nonlinear dependency*: Effort multipliers for all of a factor's values, except for the best case, must be specified. In such a case, the functional dependency between a factor's value and its effort multipliers takes the form of a piecewise linear, monotonic curve.

Figure 5.15 illustrates both functional forms for an interval-scale effort factor.

Ratio Scale
Ratio scales are similar to interval scales, but in practice, corresponding historical measurement data need to be available for the fact. If not, the domain experts are typically not capable of recalling the historical project data for factors defined on a continuous scale. If a ratio scale is justified, it is sufficient to collect the worst-case multiplier and compute the intermediate multipliers based upon:

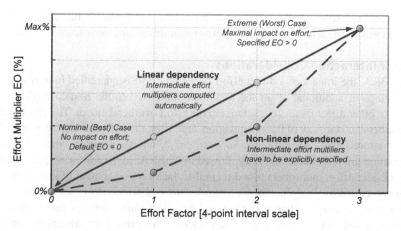

Fig. 5.15 Effort multiplier curves for an interval-scale effort factor

- *The assumption* that in the best case, when the effort factor has its nominal value, it does not introduce any effort overhead, meaning its effort multiplier is equal to zero ($EO = 0\%$).
- *The functional dependency* between the factor's value and the effort overhead it introduces. In principle, any monotonic function can be employed. Yet, one must take into account that the functional form is defined by the domain experts, who might find it difficult to consider functions other than linear. The analyst may support the selection of the appropriate function dependency by analyzing whether there is a sufficient amount of historical data on the factor's value and the associated effort overhead. Yet, in practice, such amounts of data would require multiple CoBRA applications and thus will be available rather rarely.

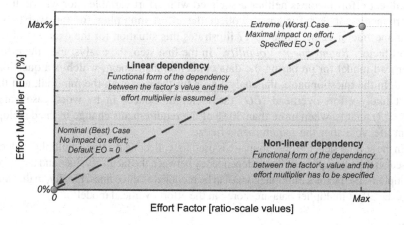

Fig. 5.16 Effort multiplier curves for interval-scale effort factor

Figure 5.16 illustrates an example of a nonlinear and a linear functional dependency between a factor's value and its effort multiplier for a ratio-scale effort factor.

Factor Interaction Considerations

In CoBRA, the impact of a direct effort factor on effort is quantified in terms of the percentage of additional effort the factor introduces given the best-case (nominal) value of other direct factors considered in the effort overhead model. The exact effort multipliers and the way of their acquisition depend on the potential interactions of the direct effort factor. As discussed in Sect. 5.7.2, not all possible types of factor interaction are reasonable and thus allowed in CoBRA. In the following paragraphs, we consider effort multipliers of a direct effort factor in the context of three types of factor interactions. In doing so, we consider interval-scale effort factors and linear dependency between a factor's value and its effort multipliers, as these are most commonly used in practice. The basic principles we present are also applicable to ratio-scale factors and nonlinear effort multipliers. Yet, as these are complex and rarely used in practice, we will not consider them in this book.

We will illustrate each discussed situation with a figure that presents an example of an appropriate effort overhead model, a corresponding effort multiplier data collection questionnaire, and the outcome effort multiplier data. In the first step, the analyst uses the effort overhead model to prepare the data collection instrument, which is a questionnaire. In the questionnaire, the analyst asks for the minimal, the maximal, and the most likely effort overhead introduced by direct effort factor given the value of the associated indirect effort factor. In the second step, the analyst uses the questionnaire for acquiring the multiplier data from the domain experts. Based on the assumption of linear dependency between a factor's values and its effort multipliers, the factor's multiplier data can be modeled as three lines. Finally, effort multiplier data are stored in the effort overhead model.

Direct Impact

If a direct effort factor is neither associated with effort variables nor with indirect effort factors, it is sufficient to collect the effort multiplier for the worst-case (extreme) factor value. Figure 5.17 illustrates this situation for the example of the effort factor "*Requirements Volatility*." In the first step, the analyst uses the effort overhead model for preparing the data collection instrument, which is a questionnaire. In the questionnaire, the analyst asks for the maximal, the minimal, and the most likely effort overhead (*EO*) the factor introduces in its worst-case value ($F1 = 3$), that is, when more than 30 % of the requirements change in the development lifecycle after the requirements freeze.

In the second step, the questionnaire is used for collecting the three multiplier values. Based on the assumption of linear dependency between the factor's values and the effort multipliers, the factor's multiplier data can be modeled as three lines. Finally, in the third step, the effort multiplier data are stored in the effort overhead model.

Indirect Impact

In CoBRA, only one-way interactions are allowed, that is, one direct effort factor can be associated with at most one indirect effort factor. This is a practical

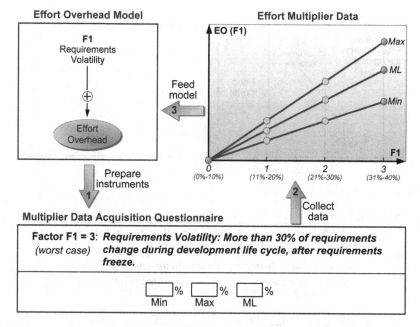

Fig. 5.17 Effort multipliers for a direct effort factor with no interactions

limitation which originates from the observation we made across multiple applications of the CoBRA method. Our experience shows that modeling multiple indirect factors increases the cost of developing, applying, and maintaining CoBRA models. Yet, it does not result in an appropriate increase in the estimation performance—on the contrary, confused by complex factor interactions, the domain experts provide inconsistent information on other factors, and on factor and multiplier data, which results in decreased estimation performance.

If a direct effort factor is associated with an indirect effort factor, the effort overhead of the direct factor depends on the values of the indirect factor. Assuming linear influence of the indirect factor and the direct factor's overhead, only two boundary values of indirect effort factors need to be considered: nominal (best case) and extreme (worst case).

Depending on what particular direct effort we are considering, conditional effort multipliers for either the extreme or the nominal value of the direct effort must be collected. In CoBRA, we refer to these cases as *indirect impact with influence on extreme case* and *indirect impact with influence on nominal case*, respectively.

Indirect impact with influence on extreme case refers to a situation where conditional effort multipliers are collected for the worst-case (extreme) value of the direct effort factor given:

- The best-case (nominal) value of the associated indirect factor
- The worst-case (extreme) value of the associated indirect factor

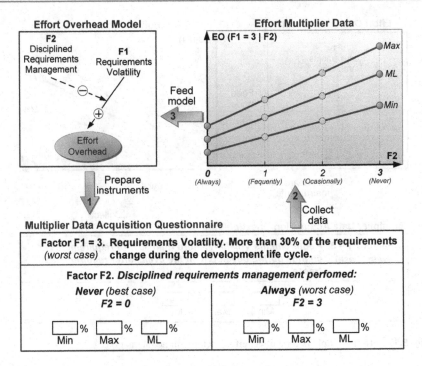

Fig. 5.18 Effort multipliers: indirect impact with influence in extreme case

Figure 5.18 illustrates such a situation on an example effort overhead model where the direct effort factor "*F1. Requirements Volatility*" interacts with the indirect effort factor "*F2. Disciplined Requirements Management.*" This simple effort overhead model can be interpreted such that the negative impact of volatile requirements on project effort depends on the level of disciplined requirements management. The more intensive and systematic disciplined requirements management is, the less negative impact do volatile requirements have on project effort. As we can see, considering the impact of disciplined requirements management when requirements do not change does not make much sense because the resulting effort multiplier would be zero anyway.

Indirect impact with influence on nominal case refers to a situation where conditional effort multipliers are collected for the best-case (nominal) value of the direct effort factor given the worst-case (extreme) value of | the associated indirect factor. In this case, no effort multiplier for the nominal value of the direct effort factor given the best-case (nominal) value of the indirect factor needs to be collected because it is per default equal to 0 %. Additionally, however, the unconditional effort multipliers for the worst-case (extreme) value of the direct factor must be collected.

Figure 5.19 illustrates such a situation on an example effort overhead model where the direct effort factor "*F1. Customer Participation*" interacts with the indirect effort factor "*F2. Adequacy of Customer's Inputs.*" This simple effort

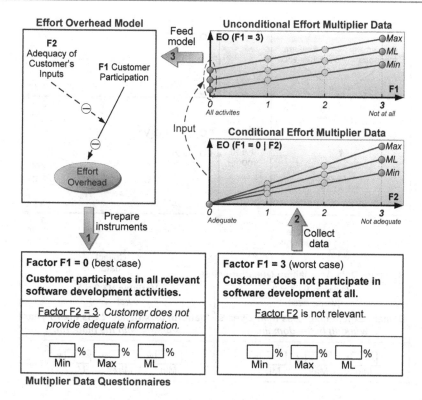

Fig. 5.19 Effort multipliers: indirect impact with influence in nominal case

overhead model can be interpreted such that the positive impact of a customer participating in software development depends on the adequacy of the information the customer provides. The more adequate the information the customer provides to the development, the more benefit is gained from the customer's involvement in the development. As we can see, considering the impact of information adequacy in case when customer does not participate in the development—thus does not provide any information—does not make sense. In such a case, the worst-case effort overhead introduced by *F1* will not depend on *F2*.

Conditional multipliers collected for the nominal case of a direct factor are then used as input for computing the factor's unconditional multipliers for the nominal case; unconditional effort multipliers for the factor's extreme case are collected using a questionnaire. The two unconditional effort multipliers—computed for the nominal case and collected for the extreme case—then serve as input for building the CoBRA model.

Composite Direct Impact

If a direct effort factor is decomposed into multiple effort variables, the effort multiplier data for each effort variable must be collected. The factor's multipliers

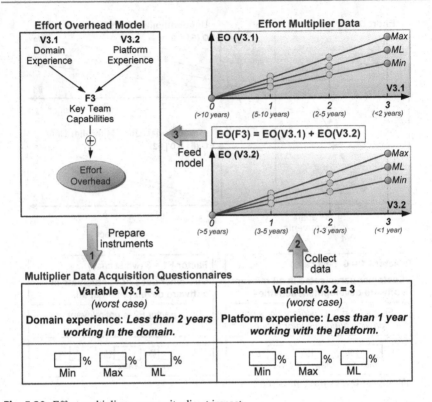

Fig. 5.20 Effort multipliers: composite direct impact

do not have to be collected because they can be simply computed as the sum of the effort multipliers on its variables. Refer to Sect. 5.11.1 where we present details on computing the actual effort overhead for historical projects.

Figure 5.20 illustrates this situation on a simple effort overhead model in which the direct effort factor "*F3. Key Team Capabilities*" is decomposed into two effort variables "*V3.1. Domain Experience*" and "*V3.2. Platform Experience.*" This simple effort overhead model can be interpreted such that the two most relevant capabilities of software development team that have an impact on project effort are domain and platform experience.

In this example, the analyst collects the effort multipliers for each variable, given its worst-case (extreme) value. The worst-case effort multiplier of the direct effort factor *F3* is then assumed to be the sum of the multipliers on *V3.1* and *V3.2*.

Composite Indirect Impact

The CoBRA method allows for composite indirect factors under the condition that all effort variables that consist of composite factors are quantified using the same measurement scale; thus these values can be added. If there exist composite indirect factors, the analyst collects conditional effort multipliers for the direct effort factor analog to the case of indirect impact (non-composite indirect factor). However, now the nominal or extreme case of the indirect factor refers to the nominal or, respectively, the extreme case of all associated effort variables.

Depending on whether the composite indirect factor influences the nominal or the extreme case, the analyst collects conditional effort multipliers:

- <u>Indirect impact with influence on nominal case:</u> Conditional effort multipliers are collected for the best-case (nominal) value of the direct effort factor given the worst-case (extreme) value of all effort variables the indirect factor is composed of.
- <u>Indirect impact with influence on extreme case:</u> Conditional effort multipliers are collected for the worst-case (extreme) value of the direct effort factor given:
  - The best-case (nominal) value of all effort variables the indirect factor is composed of
  - The worst-case (extreme) value of all effort variables the indirect factor is composed of

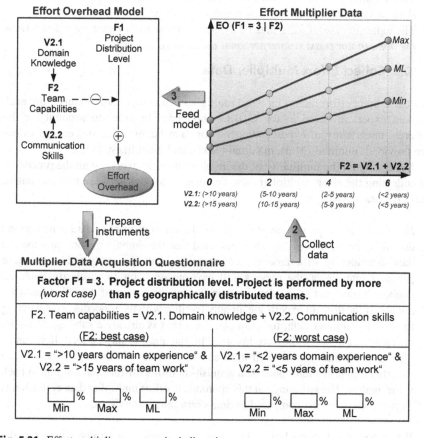

Fig. 5.21 Effort multipliers: composite indirect impact

Figure 5.21 shows an example that illustrates indirect impact with influence on extreme case. In the example, the impact of the direct effort factor "*F1. Project Distribution Level*" on project effort is influenced by the indirect factor "*F2. Team Capabilities*," which is composed of two variables "*V2.1. Domain Experience*" and "*V2.2. Communication Skills*." This simple effort overhead model can be interpreted such that the negative impact of the large number of geographically distributed project teams on the project's effort depends on the capabilities of the members of the distributed development team. In particular, the negative effect of team distribution on project effort can be alleviated if team members can efficiently and effectively communicate with each other and coordinate their work. Two particular team capabilities contribute to efficient and effective communication: very high domain experience and excellent communication skills.

In this example, the analyst collects conditional effort multipliers for the extreme case of *F1* (*project work is performed by more than five geographically distributed teams*) given:

* The nominal case of *V2.1* and *V2.2* (*development team members possess high domain knowledge and excellent communication skills*)
* The extreme case of *V2.1* and *V2.2* (*development team members neither know the domain nor possess interpersonal communication skills*)

5.10.2 Collect Effort Multiplier Data

For each direct effort factor, its effort multiplier is acquired individually from each domain expert involved in the CoBRA modeling. In order to account for the inherent uncertainty of expert judgment, for each factor, three percentage values are provided: minimal (Min), maximal (Max), and most likely (ML).

Depending on the familiarity of the involved domain experts with the procedure of collecting the effort multiplier data, the analyst decides between two alternative ways of data acquisition:

* *Interviews*: If the procedure of collecting the effort multiplier data is new to the domain experts, it is highly recommended that the domain experts provide the data individually in a face-to-face interview with the analyst. During these personal interviews, the experts still have an opportunity to clarify potential doubts with respect to the definition and/or quantification of the effort factors.
* *Survey*: If the domain experts are already familiar with the procedure of collecting the effort multiplier data, for example, because it is already a subsequent model development iteration they are involved in, the analyst may collect effort multiplier data off-line in an e-mail or Web-based survey. In this case, the domain experts fill in effort multiplier data acquisition forms off-line and send them back to the analyst. The advantage of this approach to effort multiplier data collection is its relatively low cost compared to time-consuming interviews.

We recommend considering face-to-face interview sessions whenever the CoBRA modeling process is new to the involved experts; off-line questionnaires can be used otherwise.

Tip

▶ While acquiring effort multiplier data, prefer face-to-face interviews with domain experts wherever it is feasible. Collect effort multipliers in an off-line survey only when the domain experts are very familiar with the data acquisition procedure.

5.10.3 <Optional> Validate Effort Multiplier Data

The purpose of the consistency check is to identify any potentially invalid factor impact quantification provided by the experts. Two methods are proposed for identifying potential data inconsistencies: internal consistency check and external consistency check.

Internal Consistency Check

The internal consistency check focuses on investigating the extent to which the domain experts agreed with respect to the impact of the same effort factors on effort. For each direct effort factor, the analyst compares the values of the effort multipliers (Min, Max, and ML) that different experts provided. The purpose of the analysis is to identify potential outlier values. Minimal, maximal, and most likely values are analyzed individually. Quantifications lying far from the main body of data should be discussed during a group meeting with the domain experts. Note that outlier effort multipliers are, in principle, allowed because they may cover different experiences. They do, however, require justification.

In general, any known outlier analysis technique can be applied; please refer to the appendix for a brief overview of several approaches to detecting data outliers. In CoBRA, we propose using the Mahalanobis distance (Mahalanobis 1936) and box plot analysis. In this approach, the Mahalanobis distance of each judgment (in this case the single effort multiplier value) to other judgments is computed.

Figure 5.22 illustrates an example outlier analysis of effort multiplier data provided by five domain experts. In addition to the percentage multipliers, the domain *experience* of the experts has been measured in terms of number of years working in the domain. A simple visual analysis of the triangular distributions constructed upon the multiplier data already shows that *Expert 3* differs noticeably in his judgment from the other experts. In particular, *Expert 3* seems to be an outlier with respect to the most likely effort multiplier (ML) and the judgment uncertainty reflected by the *range* of estimated multipliers, where *Range = Max−Min*.

A formal analysis of the Mahalanobis distance confirms the informal observations. *Expert 3* differs from the other experts with respect to the maximal and the most likely effort multipliers. Moreover, the expert is distinguished by the large uncertainty of this multiplier assessment, which is reflected by the large distance between the minimal and maximal effort multiplies.

In order to identify the potential causes of outlier judgments, the analyst may investigate the values of the Mahalanobis distance of the judgments to the quantitative characteristics of experts who provided particular judgments. Continuing the example in Fig. 5.22, we can check the association between the domain experience

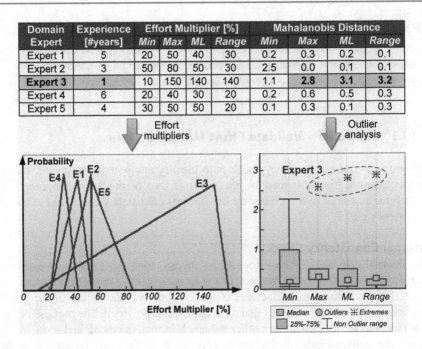

Domain	Experience	Effort Multiplier [%]				Mahalanobis Distance			
Expert	[#years]	Min	Max	ML	Range	Min	Max	ML	Range
Expert 1	5	20	50	40	30	0.2	0.3	0.2	0.1
Expert 2	3	50	80	50	30	2.5	0.0	0.1	0.1
Expert 3	**1**	10	150	140	140	1.1	**2.8**	**3.1**	**3.2**
Expert 4	6	20	40	30	20	0.2	0.6	0.5	0.3
Expert 5	4	30	50	50	20	0.1	0.3	0.1	0.3

Fig. 5.22 Using Mahalanobis distance for identifying outlier expert judgments

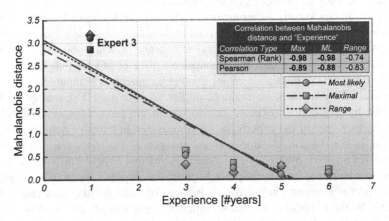

Fig. 5.23 Correlating experts' judgments to experts' experience

of experts and the Mahalanobis distance of their judgments. Figure 5.23 illustrates the results of such an analysis.

We used a simple statistical correlation to check if there is any relationship between the experience of an expert and the extent to which the expert's judgments differ from those of other experts. The results of the analysis suggest that the level of agreement among the experts may have something to do with their individual experience. In such a case, the analyst should look closer at the characteristics of the outlier expert and consider two possible responses:

- *Accept outlier inputs*: If the experiences of an outlier domain expert correspond to the estimation context of the developed CoBRA model, the outlier inputs should be considered within the modeling process. In this case, the outlier expert may simply have gained experiences in other situations than the remaining experts. In this sense, the outlier data are a valuable source of information complementing the experiences of the majority. It may be that the outlier data represent a rare and exceptional project situation, which may however recur in the future. In this case, excluding such data from consideration would expose the developed CoBRA model to the risk of poor performance when applied in such an exceptional project situation.
- *Exclude outlier data*: If the experiences of an outlier domain expert represent a project situation that is rather unlikely to recur in the future project in which developed CoBRA model will be used, the data should be excluded from further consideration. In an extreme case, if the expertise of the outlier expert does not fit the considered estimation context or is not credible because of low work experience of the expert, the analyst may decide to exclude the expert from the model development process.

External Consistency Check

The external consistency check involves comparing the effort multipliers provided by the domain experts to other indicators of the factors' impact on effort. Two possible indicators of the factors' impact on effort include (Fig. 5.24) experts' ratings of the factors' importance and statistical association of the factors with development productivity.

A factors' importance ratings refer to the ratings that domain experts assigned to the candidate effort factors in Step 5 of the model development process when selecting the most relevant effort factors to consider in the effort overhead model (Sect. 5.6.2: Rate Relevancy of Identified Effort Factors).

A factors' association with development productivity refers to the strength of the statistical association between the effort factors and development productivity obtained by analyzing the historical factor data collected in Step 8 of the model development process (Sect. 5.9. Step 8: Collecting and Validating Historical Factor Data). In order to quantify a factor's impact on effort, the analyst can employ one or more multivariate analysis techniques proposed within statistics and data mining theories upon the historical project data. Effort factors represent then independent variables, and development productivity (computed as software size divided by project effort) represents the dependent variable.

Because effort multipliers, impact ratings, and association strength differ with respect to the measurement scale and to the concept they represent, they cannot be compared directly. In order to check the consistency between these various indicators of a factor's impact on effort, the analyst can use one of the statistical measures of association (Sheskin 2011) to test the overall agreement between the impact of various factors using their raw impact quantifications. The analyst must

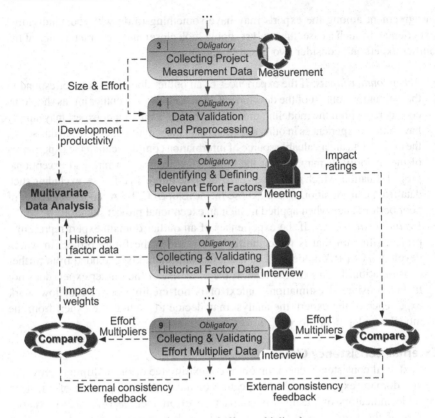

Fig. 5.24 Checking the external consistency of effort multiplier data

ensure that the used measure of association is appropriate for the measurement scales represented by the analyzed data. For example, the association between the interval-scale ratings and the ratio-scale effort multipliers can be tested using the Pearson coefficient of correlation (Sheskin 2011).

Alternatively, the analyst may rank-order the effort factors using alternative impact quantifications and then check the consistency of the resulting rankings. Additionally, the analyst may use a simple rank correlation coefficient known from statistics to test overall agreement between factor rankings.

5.11   Step 10: Building the Effort Model

In CoBRA, the effort of a new project is estimated using two inputs: (1) the baseline nominal development productivity observed across already completed projects from the same context and (2) the new project's effort overhead computed on the basis of the specific characteristics of the project. The baseline nominal productivity is a part of the CoBRA model and is determined during the model development

Table 5.30 CoBRA model development process: building the effort model

Step 10: Building effort model	
Objective	The objective of this step is to determine the baseline nominal productivity of the already completed projects considered in the model development process.
Personnel	• *Analyst*: The analyst synthesizes the data collected throughout previous steps of the model development process. In particular, the analyst uses the quantified effort overhead model and the factor data for each historical project considered and computes the project's effort overhead. Using the total project overhead and the project's actual size and effort data, the analyst determines the nominal productivity for each historical project. Finally, the analyst synthesizes the nominal productivities across all considered historical projects and computes the baseline nominal productivity, which will then be used for estimating new projects. • *Domain experts*: The domain experts are not involved in this step of the CoBRA model development process.
Inputs	• Quantified effort overhead model, in particular effort factors (direct and indirect), effort variables (if any are defined), and measures specified for factors and variables. • Historical factor data. • Effort multiplier data. • <Optional> Factor importance ratings provided by the domain expert while selecting the most relevant effort factors in Step 5 of the model development process (Sect. 5.6.2: Rate Relevancy of Identified Effort Factors).
Activities	1. Compute actual effort multipliers for historical projects. 2. Simulate effort overhead distributions for historical projects. 3. Determine nominal productivity baseline.
Tools	• Software tools for preparing data collection instruments. In the simplest case, MS Word or MS Excel to create data collection questionnaires. In advanced cases, a dedicated CoBRA tool, which automatically generates multiplier data collection forms based upon the quantified effort overhead model modeled in the tool. • <Optional> Multivariate data analysis tools for quantifying the relationship between project development productivity (dependent variable) and effort factors (independent variables). Two groups of tools to consider include statistical analysis tools such as R, SPSS/PASW, or Statistica and data mining tools such as Weka, KNIME or the data mining modules of the SPSS/PASW and Statistica packages.
Outputs	• CoBRA effort estimation model: effort overhead model and baseline nominal development productivity.

process, whereas the new project's effort overhead is determined when the CoBRA model is applied.

The objective of this step is to determine the baseline nominal productivity of the already completed projects considered in the model development process.

Table 5.30 summarizes the most important elements of this step. We provide a detailed description of each activity in the following subsections.

In the following subsections, we present the major activities comprising the "building the effort model" step of the CoBRA model development process.

5.11.1 Compute Actual Effort Multipliers for Historical Projects

In this activity, the analyst calculates—using an appropriate software tool—the actual effort multipliers for the historical projects considered in the CoBRA model

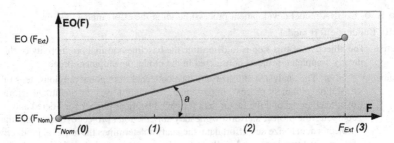

Fig. 5.25 Effort multiplier curve

development process. Using the generic effort multiplier data provided by the domain experts (Step 9) and the project-specific historical factor data (Step 8), the project-specific actual effort multiplier for each effort factor directly influencing effort is calculated. In other words, a factor-specific contribution to the total effort overhead in a specific project is computed.

For the sake of simplicity, we assume a typical case of a CoBRA application, in which (1) the effort factors and variables are measured on a 4-point interval scale and (2) a factor's effort overhead (EO) is linearly dependent on this factor's value (Fig. 5.25).

Basic Idea
The idea of computing the actual effort multipliers is to apply the actual factor's value in a specific project to the effort overhead function defined for this very factor. In order to explain the basic effort overhead computations in CoBRA, we assume a typical case of linear dependency between a factor's value and its effort overhead. For each effort factor, the exact dependency (linear function) has been specified by the domain experts in Step 9 of the CoBRA model development process through two boundary values of effort overhead: for the nominal (best-case) and for the extreme (worst-case) factor's value. Figure 5.25 illustrates such simple dependency.

The effort overhead associated with an effort factor is computed using simple linear dependency (5.1)

$$EO(F) = aF + EO_{Nom},   \tag{5.1}$$

where a is the slope of the linear relationship between the factor's effort overhead EO and the factor's value F. The slope of the effort overhead curve can be easily computed (5.2) using the factor's nominal and extreme effort multipliers (EO_{Nom} and EO_{Ext}).

$$a = \frac{EO_{Ext} - EO_{Nom}}{F_{Ext}}   \tag{5.2}$$

The intercept EO_{Nom} represents the minimal value of the factor's effort overhead $EO(F)$ in the best case, where the factor F has its nominal value (F_{Nom}); if the impact of the direct effort factor F is not influenced by an indirect effort factor, then $EO_{Nom} = 0\,\%$. EO_{Ext} represents the maximum value of the factor's effort overhead in the worst case, where the factor has its extreme value (F_{Ext}). The value of EO_{Ext} has been provided by the domain experts in Step 9 of the model development process (Sect. 5.10. Step 9: Collecting and Validating Effort Multiplier Data).

Exact calculations depend on whether the effort factor is a stand-alone factor or a factor to which an indirect factor or effort variables are associated. The following paragraphs present three basic cases of computing project-specific effort multipliers for an effort factor directly influencing effort. For each direct effort factor, three values of the effort multiplier are computed: minimal, maximal, and most likely effort overhead introduced by the factor in a specific project, given the factor's value in this very project.

Single Direct Impact

In this case, we consider a single stand-alone direct effort factor $F1$, meaning the factor with which neither effort variables not indirect effort factors are associated. In other words, neither the impact of $F1$ on effort is a composition of impacts of multiple effort variables nor is the impact of $F1$ influenced by the value of an indirect effort factor. Figure 5.26 illustrates the corresponding effort overhead model, the multiplier data collection questionnaire, and the factor's effort multiplier (effort overhead) curves.

For the sake of simplicity, in the following paragraphs, we do not individually consider minimal, maximal, and most likely effort overhead. Instead, we simply refer to effort overhead (EO). Yet, all the considerations we present apply to

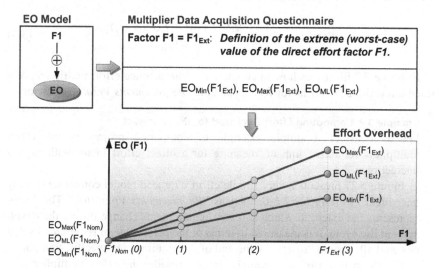

Fig. 5.26 Calculating effort multipliers: simple direct impact

minimal, maximal, and most likely effort overhead (EO_{Min}, EO_{Max}, and EO_{ML}, respectively). For example, we refer to EO in the mathematical formulas we define for calculating a project-specific factor's effort overhead. In order to use these formulas for computing the appropriate minimal, maximal, and most likely effort overheads, one must simply instantiate the generic identifier "EO" with "EO_{Min}", "EO_{Max}", or "EO_{ML}", respectively.

The actual effort overhead introduced by the effort factor $F1$ in a particular project depends on the value of $F1$ in the project and is computed in two steps.

Step 1: *Construct the effort overhead curve for the direct effort factor.* In this step, we construct effort overhead curve based upon the boundary effort multipliers acquired for $F1$ in Step 9 of the CoBRA model development process (Sect. 5.10. Step 9: Collecting and Validating Effort Multiplier Data). The two boundary values include:

- *Extreme-case multiplier*: The effort overhead introduced by $F1$ given its worst-case factor's value ($F1_{Ext}$). This effort overhead (EO_{Ext}) has been acquired in Step 9 of the CoBRA model development, typically from the domain experts.
- *Nominal-case multipliers*: The effort overhead introduced by $F1$ given its best-case factor's value ($F1_{Nom}$). According to the principles of the CoBRA method, the best-case effort overhead (EO_{Nom}) of any single direct effort factor is, per default, equal to zero, meaning that in the nominal case, an effort factor does not introduce any effort overhead.

Step 2: *Compute the effort multiplier of the direct factor given its actual value.* Based on the effort overhead curve constructed in the previous step and on the actual value of $F1$ in a particular project, we compute the actual effort overhead the factor introduces. Equation (5.3) provides the generic formula for computing the effort multiplier for a particular value x of direct effort factor $F1$ (for $F1 = x$).

$$EO(F1 = x) = x \cdot \frac{EO(F1_{Ext}) - EO(F1_{Nom})}{F1_{Ext}} \qquad (5.3)$$

Example 5.7 illustrates how to compute the intermediate effort multipliers of a stand-alone direct effort factor for an example "*Requirements Volatility*" factor.

Example 5.7. Computing Effort Overhead for Direct Impact

Let us consider a simple example of computing project-specific effort multipliers for direct impact, meaning for a direct effort factor without any interactions.

Figure 5.27 presents a very simple effort overhead model consisting of only one direct effort factor $F1$ defined as "*Requirements Volatility*." The factor represents the extent to which software requirements change during the development life cycle. It is measured in terms of the percentage of requirements that changed after being "frozen" at the end of the requirements specification phase.

For the purpose of our example, let us consider the effort multiplier data provided for $F1$ by only one domain expert. The effort multiplier data consist of the minimal, maximal, and most likely effort overhead introduced by $F1$ in the

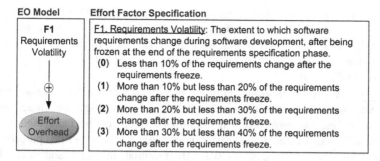

Fig. 5.27 Example: effort overhead model with direct impact

extreme (worst) case. An expert has assessed the respective extreme effort overhead values as 30 %, 100 %, and 50 %. Figure 5.28 illustrates the procedure of computing the project-specific effort multiplier associated with *F1* given the value of *F1 = 2* in the project.

Computing project-specific effort multipliers consists of two steps:

- *Step 1*: *Construct the effort overhead curve for the direct effort factor.* We use the effort multiplier data acquired from the domain experts to construct the

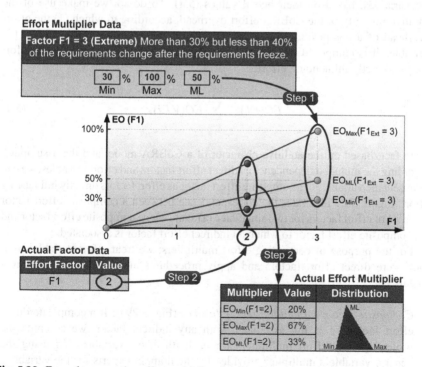

Fig. 5.28 Example: computing effort multipliers for direct impact

effort overhead function. In doing so, we assume linear dependency between the values of $F1$ and its effort overhead. Moreover, we follow the basic assumption of CoBRA in that for the nominal case of the effort factor $F1$, we presume the factor's effort overhead to be equal to 0 %—formally written as $EO(F1 = 0) = 0\ \%$.

- *Step 2: Compute the effort multiplier of a direct factor given its actual value.* We compute the actual effort overhead of $F1$ in a specific project based on the linear function constructed in the previous step for the factor and on the factor's actual value in the project (in our case $F1 = 2$). For this purpose, we employ a simple formula (5.3) for the minimal, maximal, and most likely effort overhead, respectively.

After performing simple calculations, we obtain the actual effort multipliers for $F1$ equal to 20, 33, and 67 %. This means that in the project in which $F1 = 2$, the factor will increase project effort minimally by 20 %, maximally by 67 %, and most likely by 33 %.   ∎

Composite Direct Impact

If a direct effort factor $F1$ is composed of n effort variables $V1.1, \ldots V1.n$, we compute the factor's actual effort overhead as the sum of the actual overheads on the variables, based on their actual values (5.4). To do so, we make use of the additive property of the CoBRA effort overhead, according to which (1) the effort overhead of a composite effort factor is the sum of the effort overheads on the variables it is composed of and (2) total effort overhead is the sum of the effort factors directly influencing effort.

$$EO(F1) = \sum_{i=1}^{n} EO(V1.i). \tag{5.4}$$

In fact, based on the additive character of a CoBRA model and the assumption regarding the mutual independence of direct effort factors and effort variables, we can represent the variables of a composite effort factor as effort factors directly influencing effort. Figure 5.29 illustrates the correspondence between a composite effort factor and a set of effort factors for two situations: (a) stand-alone composite effort factor and (b) composite effort factor to which an indirect effort factor is associated.

For the purpose of computing effort multipliers, we treat effort variables as if they were direct effort factors and apply procedures analog to those for direct factors:

- *Composite factor without indirect influences* (Fig. 5.29a): If a composite direct effort factor $F1$ is not associated with any indirect factor, we compute the project-specific effort multipliers for each ith effort variable $V1.i$ using the generic variable's multiplier provided by the domain experts for the variable's worst-case value and the variable's value in the project.

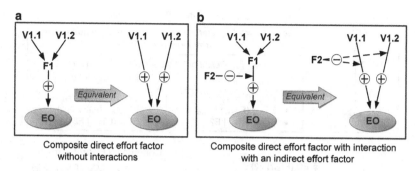

Fig. 5.29 Equivalence of composite direct effort factors

- *Composite factor associated with an indirect factor* (Fig. 5.29b): If a composite direct effort factor *F1* interacts with an indirect factor *F2*, we treat each *i*th variable of the direct factor *F1* variable as a direct effort factor. Each such factor interacts with the indirect factor *F2*. We compute the project-specific conditional effort multipliers for each *i*th effort variable *V1.i* given the value of *F2*. In the following two paragraphs, we discuss how to compute the effort multipliers for the case of indirect impact.

Indirect Impact with Influence on Extreme Case

In this paragraph and the next two, we consider the interaction between a direct effort factor *F1* and an indirect effort factor *F2*. This interaction refers to a situation where the impact of *F1* on project effort (meaning the effort multiplier of *F1*) depends on the value of *F2*. We denote this conditional effort overhead as *EO(F1/ F2)* and read it as *the effort overhead of factor F1 given the value of factor F2*. In this paragraph, we consider factor interaction in which the extreme (worst-case) effort multiplier of *F1* depends on the value of *F2*; the nominal (best-case) effort multiplier of the direct factor *F1* does not depend on the indirect factor and is, per default, assumed to be equal to 0 %.

Figure 5.30 illustrates the corresponding effort overhead model, the effort multiplier data collection questionnaire, and the factor's effort multiplier (effort overhead) curves. For the sake of simplicity, in the following paragraphs, we do not individually consider minimal, maximal, and most likely effort overhead. Instead, we simply refer to effort overhead (*EO*). Yet, all the consideration we present applies to minimal, maximal, and most likely effort overhead (*EO_{Min}*, *EO_{Max}*, and *EO_{ML}*, respectively). For example, we refer to *EO* in the mathematical formulas we define for calculating a project-specific factor's effort overhead. In order to use these formulas for computing the appropriate minimal, maximal, and most likely effort overheads, one must simple instantiate the generic identifier "*EO*" with "*EO_{Min}*", "*EO_{Max}*", or "*EO_{ML}*", respectively.

Computing the actual effort overhead introduced by the direct effort factor *F1* in a particular project, given its actual value, the actual value of the associated indirect factor *F2* proceeds in three steps.

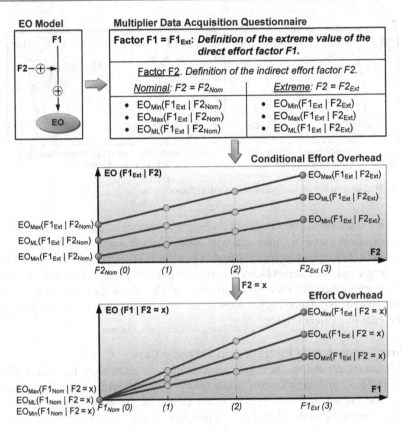

Fig. 5.30 Calculating effort multipliers: direct effort factor with indirect impact on extreme case

Step 1: Construct a conditional effort overhead curve for the extreme case of the direct effort factor. In this step, we use the conditional effort multipliers acquired in Step 9 of the CoBRA model development process to construct a conditional effort overhead curve for the extreme case of the direct effort factor $F1$.

Step 2: Compute the extreme multiplier of direct effort factor given the actual value of the indirect factor. In the next step, we consider the actual project value of the indirect effort factor $F2$ in order to compute the unconditional extreme (worst-case) effort multiplier for the direct factor $F1$. For this purpose, we use the effort overhead curves for the extreme case of the direct factor given the value of the indirect factor. We denote this conditional effort overhead of $F1$ given the value of $F2$ as $EO\ (F1_{Ext}/F2)$.

We compute the extreme multiplier of $F1$ given a particular value x of $F2$ using the two parameters of the $EO\ (F1_{Ext}/F2)$ curve: its slope and its intercept. The slope of the curve can be determined using the generic equation (5.5).

$$\frac{EO(F1_{Ext}|F2_{Ext}) - EO(F1_{Ext}|F2_{Nom})}{F2_{Ext}} \tag{5.5}$$

The intercept of the linear function $EO\ (F1_{Ext}/F2)$ is equal to EO $(F1_{Ext}/F2_{Nom})$, which is already available because it has been directly collected in Step 9 of the CoBRA development process.

Having the slope and intercept of the $EO\ (F1_{Ext}/F2)$ curve, the extreme multiplier of $F1$ given $F2 = x$ can be simply computed by multiplying the slope by x and adding the intercept.

$$EO(F1_{Ext}|F2 = x) = \left(\frac{EO(F1_{Ext}|F2_{Ext}) - EO(F1_{Ext}|F2_{Nom})}{F2_{Ext}} \cdot x \right)$$
$$+ EO(F1_{Ext}|F2_{Nom}) \qquad (5.6)$$

Step 3: Compute the effort multiplier of a direct factor given its actual value. After considering the actual value of the indirect factor $(F2 = x)$, we can construct the curve for the unconditional effort overhead of the direct factor $F1$. The curve is defined by two boundary values of the direct factor $F1$: the extreme effort multipliers we have just computed and the nominal effort multipliers, which are assumed to be equal to 0 %.

The effort multiplier value for a particular value y of the direct factor $F1$, given the value x of $F2$ can then be computed analog to computing simple direct impact (5.7).

$$EO(F1 = y|F2 = x) = \frac{EO(F1_{Ext}|F2 = x) - EO(F1_{Nom}|F2 = x)}{F1_{Ext}} \cdot y \qquad (5.7)$$

Example 5.8 illustrates how to compute the intermediate conditional effort multipliers of a direct effort factor "_Requirements Volatility_" interacting with an indirect factor "_Disciplined Requirements Management._"

Example 5.8. Computing Effort Multiplier for Indirect Impact on Extreme Case
Let us consider a simple example of computing project-specific effort multipliers for indirect impact on an extreme case, meaning for a direct effort factor whose impact on effort in an extreme case is influenced by an indirect effort factor.

Figure 5.31 presents a very simple effort overhead model consisting of only two effort factors. The direct effort factor "_F1. Requirements Volatility_" interacts with the indirect effort factor "_F2. Disciplined Requirements Management._" This interaction can be interpreted in the following way: "The impact of volatile requirements on project effort depends on (is influenced by) the extent of disciplined requirements management."

The "_Requirements Volatility_" factor is specified and measured in terms of the percentage of requirements that changed after being "frozen" at the end of the requirements specification phase of software development. The "_Disciplined Requirements Management_" factor is specified and measured in terms of the

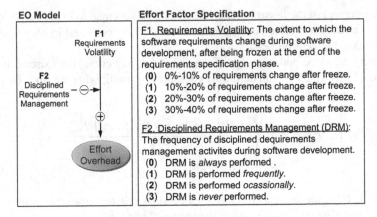

EO Model

Effort Factor Specification

F1
Requirements
Volatility

F2
Disciplined
Requirements
Management

Effort
Overhead

F1. Requirements Volatility: The extent to which the software requirements change during software development, after being frozen at the end of the requirements specification phase.
(0) 0%-10% of requirements change after freeze.
(1) 10%-20% of requirements change after freeze.
(2) 20%-30% of requirements change after freeze.
(3) 30%-40% of requirements change after freeze.

F2. Disciplined Requirements Management (DRM): The frequency of disciplined dequirements management activites during software development.
(0) DRM is *always* performed .
(1) DRM is performed *frequently*.
(2) DRM is performed *ocassionally*.
(3) DRM is *never* performed.

Fig. 5.31 Example: effort overhead model with indirect impact on an extreme case

frequency of disciplined requirements management activities during software development.

For the purpose of our example, let us consider the effort multiplier data provided for *F1* by only one domain expert. The effort multiplier data for *F1* consist of the minimal, maximal, and most likely effort overhead introduced by *F1* in the extreme case given the nominal and the extreme case of *F2*. An expert assessed the respective conditional effort overhead values as <10 %, 50 %, and 30 % > and <30 %, 100 %, and 50 %>. Figure 5.32 illustrates the procedure of computing the actual effort multiplier of *F1* given *F2* using factor data from an example software project. Let us assume the following project-specific factor values: *F1* = 2 and *F2* = 1. Computing the actual effort multiplier consists of three steps.

Step 1: Construct the conditional effort overhead curve for the extreme case of the direct effort factor. We use the conditional effort multiplier data acquired from a domain expert to construct the effort overhead curve for the extreme case of *F1* given two boundary values of *F2*: nominal ($F2_{Nom}$) and extreme ($F2_{Ext}$). In this case, we assume linear dependency between the extreme effort overhead of *F1* and the values of *F2*.

Step 2: Compute the extreme multiplier of the direct effort factor given the actual value of the indirect factor. We determine the actual extreme-case effort overhead of *F1* based on the conditional effort overhead function constructed in the previous step and on the actual value of the indirect effort factor *F2* = 1. For this purpose, we employ formula (5.6) for calculating the minimal, maximal, and most likely effort overhead of *F1* in its extreme case given *F2* = 2. Based on the calculated extreme effort multipliers, we construct the unconditional effort overhead function for *F1*, using the CoBRA's assumption that in the nominal case (*F1* = 0), the factor's effort overhead is equal to 0 %.

Step 3: Compute the effort multiplier of the direct factor given its actual value. We compute the actual effort overhead of *F1* based on the linear function

Effort Multiplier Data

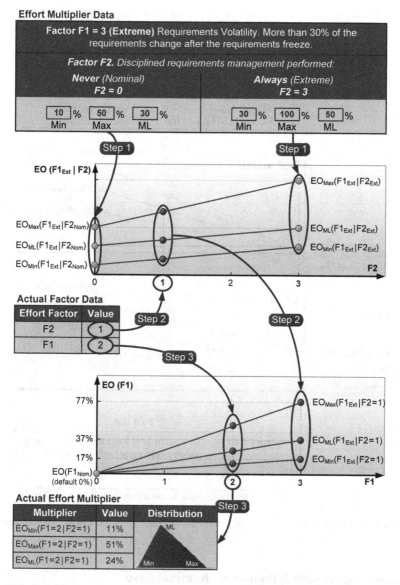

Fig. 5.32 Example: computing the effort multiplier for indirect impact on the extreme case

constructed in the previous step and on the actual project data for $F1 = 2$. For this purpose, we employ a simple formula (5.7) for the minimal, maximal, and most likely effort overhead, respectively.

After performing simple calculations, we obtain the actual effort multipliers for $F1$ equal to 51 %, 11x %, and 24 %. This means that in a project in which $F1 = 2$ and $F2 = 1$, $F1$ will contribute to an increase in project effort of minimally 11 %, maximally 51 %, and most likely 24 %. ∎

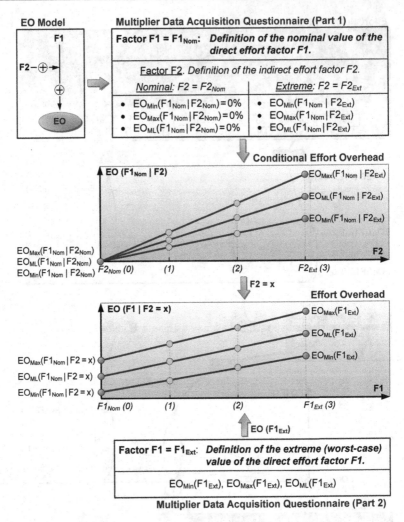

Fig. 5.33 Calculating effort multipliers: direct effort factor with indirect impact on the nominal case

Indirect Impact with Influence on Nominal Case

In this paragraph, we consider the interaction between a direct effort factor $F1$ and an indirect effort factor $F2$, in which the nominal (best-case) effort multiplier of $F1$ depends on the value of $F2$; the extreme (worst-case) effort multiplier of the direct factor $F1$ does not depend on the indirect factor and has been directly collected in Step 9 of the CoBRA model development process. Figure 5.33 illustrates the corresponding effort overhead model, the effort multiplier data collection questionnaire, and the factor's effort multiplier (effort overhead) curves.

For the sake of simplicity, in the following paragraphs, we do not individually consider the minimal, maximal, and most likely effort overhead, respectively. Instead, we simply refer to effort overhead (EO). Yet, all the consideration we present applies to minimal, maximal, and most likely effort overhead (EO_{Min}, EO_{Max}, and EO_{ML}, respectively). For example, we refer to EO in the mathematical formulas we define for calculating the project-specific factor's effort overhead. In order to use these formulas for computing the appropriate minimal, maximal, and most likely effort overheads, one must simply instantiate the generic identifier "EO" with "EO_{Min}", "EO_{Max}", or "EO_{ML}", respectively.

Computing the actual effort multiplier for the direct effort factor $F1$ given the value of $F2$ proceeds in four steps.

Step 1: *Construct the conditional effort overhead curve for the nominal case of the direct effort factor given the extreme value of the indirect effort factor.* In this step, we use the conditional effort multiplier data acquired from the domain experts for constructing the nominal effort overhead curve of $F1$ given the values of the associated indirect effort $F2$. The curve is based on two points: (1) the acquired conditional nominal effort multiplier of $F1$ given the extreme value of $F2$ and (2) the default value (0 %) of the nominal effort multiplier of $F2$ given the nominal value of $F2$.

Step 2: *Compute the nominal multiplier of the direct effort factor given the actual value of the indirect effort factor.* First, we consider the actual project value of the indirect effort factor in order to compute the unconditional nominal (best-case) effort overhead for the direct factor. For this purpose, we use the effort overhead curves for the nominal direct factor given the value of the indirect factor, which we denote as $EO(F1_{Nom}/F2)$.

The nominal multiplier of $F1$ given a particular value x of $F2$ is computed using simple linear dependency (5.8).

$$EO(F1_{Nom}|F2 = x) = x \cdot \frac{EO(F1_{Nom}|F2_{Ext}) - EO(F1_{Nom}|F2_{Nom})}{F2_{Ext}} \qquad (5.8)$$

Step 3: *Construct the unconditional effort overhead curve for the direct effort factor.* After considering the actual value of the indirect factor ($F2 = x$), we can construct the curve for the unconditional effort overhead of the direct factor $F1$. The curve is defined by two boundary values of the direct factor $F1$: on the nominal effort multipliers computed in the previous step and on the unconditional extreme effort multipliers, which were collected directly in Step 9 of the CoBRA model development process.

Step 4: *Compute the actual effort overhead for the direct effort factor given its actual value.* Finally, we compute the actual effort multiplier value for a particular value y of the direct factor $F1$. For this purpose, we use the slope and the intercept of the unconditional effort overhead curve for $F1$ determined in the previous step. The first component of the appropriate sum (5.9) represents the slope and the second component the intercept.

$$EO(F1 = y|F2 = x) = \left(\frac{EO(F1_{Ext}) - EO(F1_{Nom}|F2 = x)}{F1_{Ext}} \cdot y \right)$$
$$+ EO(F1_{Nom}|F2 = x) \tag{5.9}$$

Example 5.8 illustrates how to compute the intermediate conditional effort multipliers of a direct effort factor "*Customer Participation*" interacting with an indirect factor "*Adequacy of Customer's Inputs.*"

Example 5.9. Computing Effort Multipliers for Indirect Impact on the Nominal Case
Let us consider a simple example of computing the actual effort multipliers for indirect impact on the extreme case, meaning for a direct effort factor whose impact on effort in the nominal case is influenced by an indirect effort factor.

Figure 5.34 presents a very simple effort overhead model consisting of only two effort factors. The direct effort factor "*F1. Customer Participation*" interacts with the indirect effort factor "*F2. Adequacy of Customer's Inputs.*" This interaction can be interpreted in the following way: "The impact of customer participation in the software development project on its effort depends on (is influenced by) the adequacy of the inputs the customer provides to the project."

The "*Customer Participation*" factor is specified and measured in terms of the portion of relevant software project activities the customer participates in. The "*Adequacy of Customer's Inputs*" factor is specified and measured in terms of the perceived adequacy of the inputs to the project the customer provides while participating in relevant project activities.

For the purpose of our example, let us consider the effort multiplier data provided for *F1* by only one domain expert. The effort multiplier data for *F1* consist of the minimal, maximal, and most likely effort overhead introduced by *F1* in two cases: (1) the nominal case given the extreme case of the interacting factor *F2* and (2) the extreme case. Note that in the extreme case of *F1*,

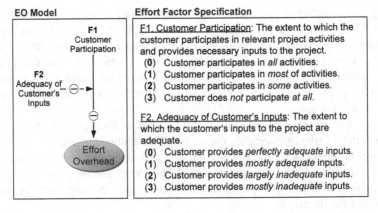

Fig. 5.34 Example: effort overhead model with indirect impact on the nominal case

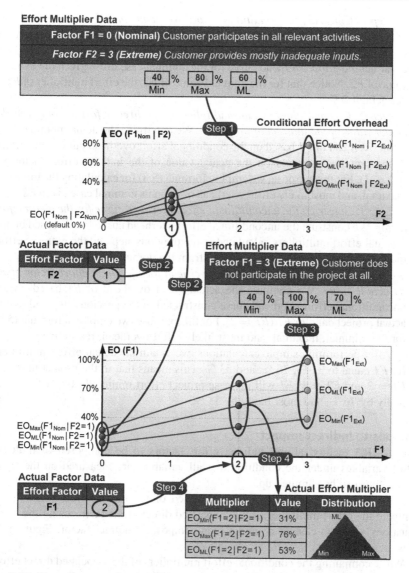

Fig. 5.35 Example: computing the effort multiplier for indirect impact on the nominal case

considering *F2* does not make sense; if the customer does not participate in the project, this does not provide any inputs, so considering the adequacy of the inputs makes no sense. An expert assessed the respective conditional effort overhead values as <40 %, 80 %, and 60 % > and <40 %, 100 %, and 70 %>. Figure 5.35 illustrates the procedure of computing the actual effort multiplier of *F1* given *F2*, using example factor data from one software project. We take $F1 = 2$ and $F2 = 1$.

Computing the actual effort multiplier consists of four steps.

Step 1: *Construct the conditional effort overhead curve for the nominal case of the direct effort factor given the extreme value of the indirect effort factor.* We use the conditional effort multiplier data acquired from the domain experts to construct the effort overhead curve for the nominal case of *F1* given the extreme value of *F2*. Notice that for the nominal value of *F2*, the effort multiplier of *F1* is per default 0 %.

Step 2: *Compute the nominal multiplier of the direct effort factor given the actual value of the indirect effort factor.* We determine the actual nominal-case effort overhead of *F1* based on the conditional effort overhead curve constructed in the previous step and on the actual value of the indirect effort factor *F2* (*F2* = *1*). For this purpose, we employ formula (5.8) for calculating the minimal, maximal, and most likely effort overhead of *F1* in its nominal case given *F2* = 2.

Step 3: *Construct the unconditional effort overhead curve for the direct effort factor.* We construct the unconditional effort overhead curve for *F1* based on the nominal effort multipliers calculated in the previous step and the extreme effort multipliers that were acquired directly from the domain experts.

Step 4: *Compute the actual effort overhead for the direct effort factor given its actual value.* We compute the actual effort overhead of *F1* based on the unconditional effort overhead curve constructed in the previous step and on the actual project data for *F1* (*F1* = *2*). For this purpose, we employ a formula (5.9) for the minimal, maximal, and most likely effort overhead, respectively.

After performing simple calculations, we obtain the actual effort multipliers for *F1* equal to 31 %, 76 %, and 53 %. This means that in the project in which *F1* = 2 and *F2* = *1*, *F1* will increase project effort minimally by 31 %, maximally by 76 %, and most likely by 53 %.   ∎

Composite Indirect Impact

The CoBRA method allows indirect effort factors to be composed of multiple effort variables under the condition that all variables are measured on the same scale—thus can be summed up.

If an indirect effort factor *F2* is composed of *n* variables *V2.1* to *V2.n*, we compute the effort multiplier of the associated direct effort factor using the same equations as in the case of a simple (non-composite) indirect factor. Figure 5.36 illustrates the idea.

While computing the conditional effort multipliers of the associated direct effort factor *F1*, we simply consider *F2* in terms of its variables:

- The nominal and the extreme cases of *F2* refer to the nominal and extreme cases of all its *n* variables, respectively.
- The value of *F2* is simply the sum of the corresponding values of its variables (5.10).

$$F2 = \sum_{i=1}^{n} V2.n \tag{5.10}$$

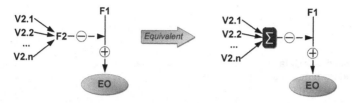

Fig. 5.36 Calculating effort multipliers: composite indirect impact

An example consequence is that the nominal and the extreme values of a composite indirect effort factor are assumed to be the sum of the nominal and extreme values of its variables. Using the traditional 4-point interval scale, the nominal factor's value would then be equal to 0 (*n* times the value "0" on *n* variables) and the extreme value would be *3n* (*n* times the extreme value "3" on *n* variables).

5.11.2 Simulating Effort Overhead Distributions for Historical Projects

In this step, the analyst applies a simulation technique upon the actual effort overheads computed in the previous activity. The purpose of this step is to come up with a distribution of total effort overhead for each historical project considered in the CoBRA model development process.

In a single simulation run, two types of sampling take place for each direct effort factor (or variable in case of composite factors) considered in the effort overhead model (Fig. 5.37):

1. *Select domain expert.* This sampling is performed in cases where multiple domain experts have provided their assessments of minimal, maximal, and most likely effort overhead (conditional or unconditional effort multipliers). In a single simulation run, one domain expert is randomly sampled from among the experts who provided the effort overhead data for the effort factor. Typically, all experts associated to a given factor are equally likely of being chosen. Yet, another likelihood distribution can be considered; for example, the sampling procedure may prefer more experienced domain experts.
2. *Sample effort overhead.* In this sampling, a simulation procedure picks a crisp value from the triangular (or beta-PERT) distribution of the effort overhead constructed upon the minimal, maximal, and most likely multiplier values provided by the domain experts. The sampling procedure follows the Monte Carlo (MC) simulation technique. Klaes et al. (2008) suggest using the Performance-Optimized Latin Hypercube (LHRO) realization of the Monte Carlo simulation as the most appropriate technique because for the same sampling accuracy the LHRO proved to be more efficient, in terms of runtime, than classical MC.

In each simulation run, the effort overhead values sampled for all effort factors directly influencing effort (unconditionally and conditionally) are summed up into the

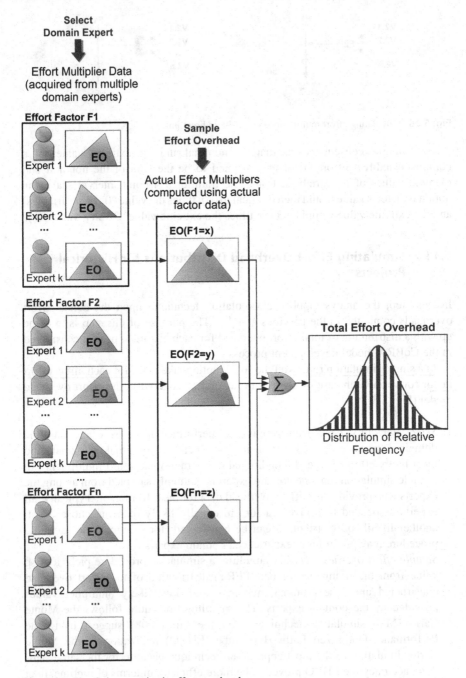

Fig. 5.37 Simulating a project's effort overhead

total effort overhead value. The result of multiple simulation runs (e.g., 10,000 runs) is a relative frequency distribution of total overhead. The relative frequency distribution approximates the probability distribution of total overhead.

5.11.3 Determining Nominal Productivity Baseline

In this activity, the analyst determines nominal productivity, which will be used as baseline productivity for estimating future software projects. Using the simulation approach described in the previous section, the analyst first computes the distribution of the actual effort overhead for each historical project considered in the CoBRA model development process. Next, using the actual values of effort overhead (*EO*), software size (*Size*), and project effort (*Effort*) for all historical projects, the analyst determines the baseline nominal productivity (P_{Nom}) for estimating future projects. Figure 5.38 illustrates the basic idea of determining the baseline nominal productivity.

In a perfect case, nominal productivity across the historical projects should be constant. This means that the CoBRA model should account for the complete effort overhead for each historical project. In reality, however, this is not the case and

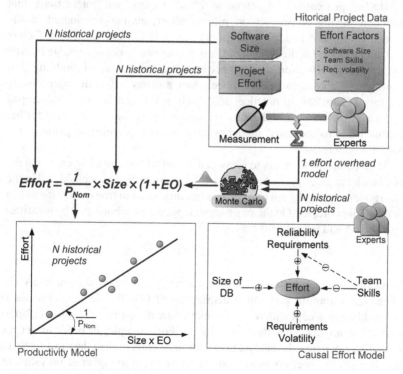

Fig. 5.38 Determining baseline nominal productivity

there is still some variance in nominal productivity left across historical projects. In principle, the cause is the imperfection of the effort overhead model and the data used for developing the CoBRA model.

Imperfect Character of the CoBRA Effort Model

Like any model, the CoBRA effort models have an imperfect character. And this is good, because the purpose of the CoBRA model is to reflect, in a simplified form, those project effort dependencies that are necessary for reliable effort estimation. The CoBRA model does not aim at representing true and complete project effort dependencies. On the one hand, this would probably not be feasible because such true dependencies are not known. On the other hand, this would not be economically reasonable because modeling many, complex effort dependencies would cost too much. The objective of the CoBRA modeling is to obtain a useful model, that is, a model that provides reliable effort estimates at minimal expense for modeling, application, and maintenance. One of the consequences of the imperfect character of the CoBRA models is that the nominal productivity computed across projects using a CoBRA model varies to some extent. In the context of CoBRA, there are two major sources of model imperfection: model incompleteness and model inaccuracy.

Model incompleteness refers to effort factors and interactions that although having an impact on project effort are not considered in the model. On the one hand, it is simply not feasible to identify all such factors and interactions. On the other hand, it is economically not reasonable to even try to model all effort factors because the large cost of building and maintaining a complex effort model does not pay off with appropriately improved estimates. In practice, acceptably good models can be developed using a limited number of the most relevant effort factors; considering further factors leads to increased modeling cost without appropriate gains in the model's performance.

Model inaccuracy refers to measurement effort and modeling error. On the one hand, not all effort factors and their interactions that are considered in the effort overhead model are correct, that is, correspond to true effort effects in a development project. On the other hand, input data are burdened by measurement effort and judgmental biases.

Typically, for each historical project, the analyst selects the most likely effort overhead (*EO*) from the probability distribution of *EO*. Yet, depending on the risk one would like to accept with respect to exceeding the estimated project effort, one may also use an *EO* other than most likely. For example, in order to get more conservative estimates, the analyst may take an *EO* higher than the most likely one. This will result in lower nominal productivity and lead to higher effort estimates.

Point Nominal Productivity

The basic approach in the CoBRA method is to determine a crisp-value baseline nominal productivity. For this purpose, the analyst may use either the regression or the median approach.

The regression approach looks at the regression line *f: Size x EO → Effort* that best fits the actual data observed across historical projects (Fig. 5.39). In CoBRA, the line's intercept is assumed to be equal to zero. The inverse of the regression line's slope is then adapted as baseline nominal productivity. Since simple ordinary least square regression is susceptible to data outliers, we recommend using a robust regression analysis for this purpose.

The median approach first computes the nominal productivities for each historical project using the selected point value of the effort overhead (EO) and the actual project effort and size using the transformed basic CoBRA equation (5.11).

$$P_{Nom} = \frac{Size \cdot EO}{Effort} \tag{5.11}$$

Next, the statistical median of the nominal productivities is taken as the baseline for estimating future projects. By taking the median (instead of, for instance, the mean), one avoids bias towards outlier nominal productivities, if such occur among

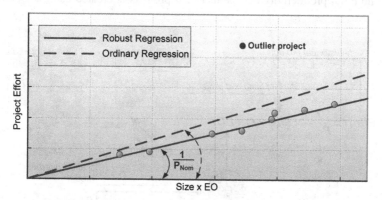

Fig. 5.39 Regression approach for determining baseline nominal productivity

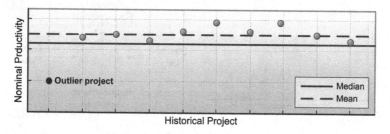

Fig. 5.40 Median approach for determining baseline nominal productivity

historical projects. Figure 5.40 illustrates the median approach for the historical projects from Fig. 5.39.

In case of outlier nominal productivities, we should ideally first investigate the reasons for these outlier nominal productivities and correct or remove them before computing the baseline nominal productivity. Yet, taking the simple median typically works in practice. If the final CoBRA model did not meet the estimation objectives, an analysis of the distribution of the nominal productivities across historical projects would be one of the first means to find potential sources of the model's unsatisfactory performance. Refer to Sect. 5.13 for more details on analyzing the results of the performance of a CoBRA model.

Distribution of Nominal Productivity: Bootstrapping Approach

Computing the crisp value of the baseline nominal productivity—using a regression or median approach—has the drawback that information about the estimation uncertainty caused by the imperfection of the estimation model is lost. This may result in a probability distribution for the predicted project characteristics that is too narrow and, consequently, overconfident regarding the provided estimate.

In order to account for the model's uncertainty, CoBRA proposes an advanced approach to determining the baseline nominal productivity, in which a distribution of the nominal productivity across historical projects is created using a Bootstrap

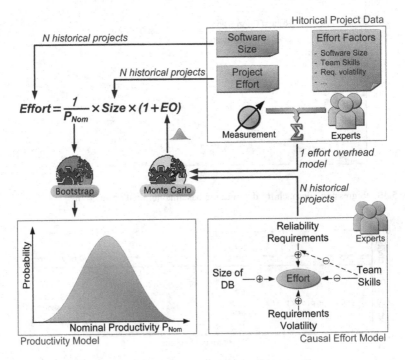

Fig. 5.41 Determining baseline nominal productivity using Bootstrapping

technique. This approach helps to account for the uncertainty of the CoBRA model manifested by the variance in nominal productivity across historical projects.

Bootstrap sampling (Efron and Tibshirani 1994) is performed upon the nominal productivities of historical projects in order to come up with a distribution of the relative frequency (Fig. 5.41). This distribution is taken as an approximation of the probability distribution of nominal productivity across historical projects, where the distribution's width reflects the uncertainty of the effort overhead model. This distribution is then the basis for estimating future projects. When used in various industrial contexts, the bootstrapped baseline nominal productivity has proved to lead to more realistic estimates (Klaes et al. 2011).

5.12 Step 11: Validating the Effort Model

After developing a new CoBRA model, we need to decide whether it is likely to provide reliable estimates and can thus be released for estimating future software projects or whether we should refine the model in the next development iteration. In other words, we should check whether the model meets our estimation objectives and find out potential improvements if it does not. In practice, new CoBRA models typically require at least two to three iterations before they are sufficiently mature for estimating future projects. For example, in terms of estimation accuracy, our industrial experiences show that initial CoBRA models usually achieve a mean magnitude of relative error MRE of 30–50 %. In very few cases, the estimation error of an initial CoBRA model is larger. Yet, in all cases, performing two to three additional modeling iterations quickly improves the model and reduces its estimation error to MRE of 5–15 %.

The objective of this step is to evaluate the performance of the CoBRA model created in the previous steps of the model development process, using actual project data from already completed historical projects. In particular, the objective of such an initial validation is to show that the developed CoBRA model (1) meets the basic assumptions of the CoBRA method and (2) is capable of providing accurate and precise estimates of project effort.

If the CoBRA model meets the estimation objectives, we can finish the development process and release the model for estimating future projects. Otherwise, we must continue with Step 12 of the development process, in which we analyze the validation results in detail and identify potential causes of the poor performance of the model. Based on the results of the analysis, we refine the model in additional iterations throughout the model development process.

Table 5.31 summarizes the most important elements of this step. We provide a detailed description of each activity in the following subsections.

In the following subsections, we present the major activities comprising the "validating the effort model" step of the CoBRA model development process.

Table 5.31 CoBRA model development process: validating effort model

Step 11: Validating the effort model	
Objective	The objective of this step is to evaluate the CoBRA model created in the previous steps of model development process, using actual project data from already completed historical projects. In particular, validation aims at showing that the developed CoBRA model meets the basic assumptions of the CoBRA method and is capable of providing accurate and precise estimates of project effort.
Personnel	• *Analyst*: The analyst prepares the historical project data and the tools necessary for validating the CoBRA model. Next, the analyst runs a cross-validation experiment, in which he builds and applies multiple CoBRA models using different subsets of historical project data. Finally, the analyst collects the outcomes of the validation and prepares them for analysis in the next (final) step of the CoBRA model development process.
	• *Domain experts*: The domain experts are not involved in this step of the CoBRA model development process.
Inputs	• Quantified effort overhead model, in particular effort factors (direct and indirect), effort variables (if any are defined), and measures specified for factors and variables.
	• Effort multiplier data.
	• Historical project data including effort factor data, software size, and project effort.
Activities	1. Perform cross-validation.
	2. Validate explanatory power.
	3. Validate predictive power.
Tools	• Software tools for implementing the CoBRA model: MS Excel or dedicated tools such as CoBRIX.
	• Software tools for collecting and preparing the outcomes of the model validation data. Typically, MS Excel suffices for this purpose.
	• Basic data analysis and visualization tools such as MS Excel or specialized statistical analysis tools such as R, SPSS/PASW, or Statistica.
Outputs	Results of effort model validation when applied upon historical projects, in particular:
	• Projects' actual effort overhead,
	• Projects' nominal productivity,
	• Project effort estimation error (accuracy, precision, and bias).

5.12.1 Perform Cross-Validation

In this activity, the analyst builds and applies the CoBRA model using historical project data and collects information on the model's performance. In order to avoid validating the model on the same project data upon which it was developed, we validate it in a so-called *cross-validation* experiment. In general, a round of cross-validation starts with partitioning the sample project data into two complementary subsets: *training set* and *testing set*. Next, the projects in the training set are used to build the CoBRA model using Step 10 of the CoBRA model development process (Sect. 5.11). Finally, the model is applied upon projects from the testing set and its performance is evaluated. Cross-validation consists of multiple runs in which different training and testing sets are used. For example, in tenfold cross-validation, the sample set of project data is divided into ten parts, and in each validation, round model is built using the combined nine parts and validated on the tenth remaining part.

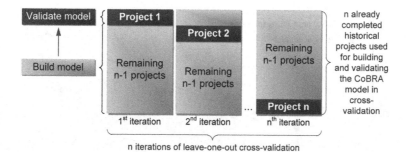

Fig. 5.42 Leave-one-out cross-validation of a CoBRA model

In the context of software engineering, in particular in effort estimation, very scarce project data are available. Therefore, CoBRA proposes using the leave-one-out (or Jacknife) version of cross-validation. Figure 5.42 illustrates this cross-validation schema for n historical projects. In one validation cycle, exactly one project is left for testing the model, and the remaining $n-1$ projects are used for building the model; consequently validation consists of n rounds.

On the output of each cross-validation cycle, the analyst collects information on the particular performance aspects of the CoBRA effort models. In the following subsections, we discuss specific model validation aspects grouped into two categories: *explanatory power* and *predictive power*.

5.12.2 Validate Explanatory Power

The explanatory power of the CoBRA model refers to its capability to capture the relationship between development productivity and effort overhead. This criterion is evaluated by investigating the extent to which the CoBRA model meets two basic assumptions of the CoBRA method:

- *Linear relationship* between project size and nominal development effort,
- *Inverse (nonlinear) relationship* between effort overhead and actual development productivity.

Relationship Between Software Size and Project Effort

The basic assumption of the CoBRA method is that the effort of a nominal project is linearly dependent on its size. In real projects, actual development productivity (a) varies across projects and (b) changes depending on software size. The CoBRA model is supposed to account for both these phenomena so that nominal productivity across projects is constant. We can check the ability of a CoBRA model to explain sources of unstable development productivity by investigating two aspects: (a) the functional dependency between software size and project effort and (b) the functional dependency between development productivity and software size.

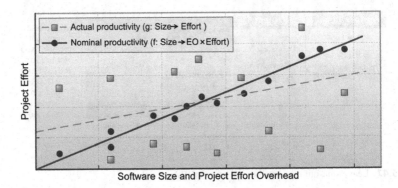

Software Size and Project Effort Overhead

Fig. 5.43 Validating the relationship between software size and project effort

Functional Dependency Between Software Size and Project Effort

We investigate the relationship between software size and project effort. In particular, we look at the spread and linear fit of the project data around the function $f: Size \times EO \rightarrow Effort$. For that purpose, we investigate the coefficient of determination (R^2) of the regression line built on $Size \times EO$ and $Effort$ data for the historical projects available. Moreover, we can compare this tot R^2 of the actual productivity line $g: Size \rightarrow Effort$ in order to test how much of the original productivity variance is explained by the CoBRA effort overhead model. Figure 5.43 illustrates the explanatory power of the CoBRA model in terms of software development productivity curve. The large variance in actual development productivity manifested by the widely spread points of actual development productivity $(g: Size \rightarrow Effort)$ is explained by the CoBRA model through the project-specific effort overhead $(f: Size \times EO \rightarrow Effort)$.

In addition to checking the linear fit, we can use a less stringent correlation coefficient for checking the relationship between software size and project effort. In this approach, we may consider determining either *Pearson's correlation* coefficient or *Spearman's rank correlation* coefficient.

Functional Dependency Between Development Productivity and Software Size

We now investigate the relationship between development productivity and software size. In particular, we look at the spread and direction of the project data around the function $f: Size \rightarrow Nominal\ Productivity$. In order to evaluate these aspects, we can basically look at the correlation between software size and a project's nominal productivity. We test if there is a significant correlation between size and productivity as well as what the sign of the relationship is. If there is a negative relationship, we conclude that there is a *diseconomies of scale* effect; otherwise there is an *economies of scale* effect. In both cases, the model still does not account for project environment aspects responsible for a disproportionate (nonlinear) increase in effort along with an increase in software size.

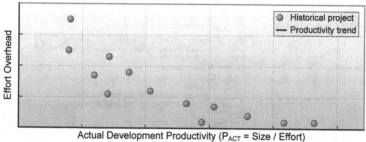

Fig. 5.44 Validating the relationship between project effort overhead and productivity

Inverse Relationship Between Effort Overhead and Actual Productivity

The basic CoBRA assumption regarding the linear functional form of the size–effort dependency implies an inverse, nonlinear ($1/x$) relationship between actual productivity and effort overhead (Fig. 5.44). During the validation of the model, however, we use a less stringent criterion, namely, we assume that the model is valid if there is a significant inverse association between effort overhead and actual productivity. In order to check this assumption, we basically analyze the rank correlation between effort overhead and development productivity across historical projects. If there is a significant negative association between a project's actual effort overhead and its productivity, we can say that the CoBRA model captures, at least partially, the variation in productivity across projects.

Tip

▶ While validating the CoBRA effort model on historical project data, look for unintuitive effects with respect to the development productivity and effort overhead of projects that were assigned by the CoBRA model.

Actual Impact of Effort Factors on Project Effort

An additional approach for validating the explanatory power of a CoBRA model is to check to what extent the effort factors considered in the model actually contribute to the total project effort in each historical project considered in the model development process. In particular, we perform such an analysis if we suspect that the CoBRA effort overhead model considers irrelevant effort factors while missing relevant ones.

For this purpose, for each historical project, we run a sensitivity analysis, in which the actual effort overhead introduced by each effort factor is computed using the effort multipliers provided by the experts and the actual factor data in the project. Next, we can synthesize the sensitivity analysis results for all historical projects in order to rank the effort factors. The greater the impact of an effort factor on project effort across historical projects, the higher the rank this factor obtains. Finally, we can compare the ranking of the factors to their importance ranking

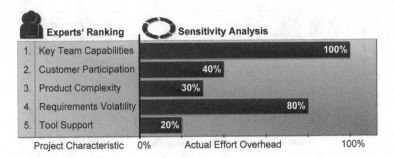

Fig. 5.45 Validating the actual impact of effort factors on project effort

assigned by the domain experts when they selected the most relevant effort factors in Step 5 of the CoBRA model development process (Sect. 5.6.2).

Figure 5.45 illustrates an example situation when factor ranking based upon a sensitivity analysis does not comply with the ranking determined by the domain experts. The major discrepancy is that the domain experts seem to underestimate the impact of volatile requirements on project effort.

Large discrepancies between the impact of actual and assessed factors on project effort should then be investigated in the subsequent step of model development where the results of model validation are analyzed in more detail and appropriate model improvements are identified.

5.12.3 Validate Predictive Power

The predictive power of the CoBRA model basically refers to its capability of providing effort estimates that are close to the actual project effort. We evaluate its predictive power by computing common measures of prediction error for each cross-validation run. For n historical projects, leave-one-out cross-validation delivers n measures of prediction error. We can then analyze these data with respect to three basic aspects of prediction error: accuracy, precision, and bias.

Estimation Accuracy
Estimation accuracy refers to the nearness of an estimate to the true value, that is, a highly accurate prediction method will provide estimates very close to the actual, known values. In order to quantify the summary accuracy of the estimation method, we use the measure of *relative error* (*RE*) or *magnitude of relative error* (*MRE*). For each historical project, *RE* measures the difference between predicted effort (*Effort$_{Est}$*) and actual effort (*Effort$_{Act}$*) relative to the actual one (5.12).

$$RE = \frac{Effort_{Est} - Effort_{Act}}{Effort_{Act}} \tag{5.12}$$

The MRE measures the magnitude of difference ignoring its sign of *RE*, that is, ignoring whether the relative error is positive (CoBRA overestimated) or negative (CoBRA underestimated). In other words, $MRE = |RE|$.

In addition to the project-specific accuracy, we can compute the aggregated measure of accuracy by calculating the mean or median value across the *MRE* measures obtained throughout *n* historical projects.

Estimation Bias

Estimation bias refers to a systematic (constant) error in estimates and is determined as the difference between the average of estimates and the actual, true value. In order to quantify estimation bias, we use the *Prediction at Level m (Pred.m)* measure. The *Pred.m* measures the percentage of estimates that are within *m* % of the actual value (5.13). Commonly, the value of $m = 25$ % is taken. We use *Pred.25* in order to evaluate the ability of an estimation method to consistently estimate within 25 % of error.

$$Pred.m = \frac{k}{m} \tag{5.13}$$

where *k* is the number of projects for which MRE$\leq$25 %.

Estimation Precision

Estimation precision refers to the degree to which several estimates are very close to each other. It is an indicator of the scatter in the estimates. The lesser the scatter, the higher the precision. In order to quantify estimation precision, we can use the *standard deviation (SD)* measure. Standard deviation is a common statistical measure of data spread. In the context of software engineering, where the variance of a data sample is not stable,[11] Foss et al. (2003) proposed using the measure of *relative standard deviation (RSD)* (5.14) instead of basic SD. RSD computes the standard deviation of estimates relative to project size ($Size_{Act}$).

$$RSD = \frac{1}{n-1} \cdot \sqrt{\sum_{i=1}^{n} \left(\frac{Effort_{Act} - Effort_{Est}}{Size_{Act}} \right)^2} \tag{5.14}$$

5.13   Step 12: Analyzing the Results of Model Validation

The deficits of the CoBRA model, either with respect to the basic assumptions of the CoBRA method or the estimation objectives, which are identified during the model's validation upon historical projects should be analyzed in detail. The purpose of this analysis is to identify the sources of the model's deficits and determine potential model improvements.

---

[11] So-called heteroscedastic data sample.

Table 5.32 CoBRA model development process: analyzing the results of model validation

Step 12: Analyzing the results of model validation

Objective	The objective of this step is to analyze the results of the model validation and to identify the sources of the identified deficits of the CoBRA model as well as appropriate improvement potentials.
Personnel	• *Analyst*: The analyst investigates in detail the results of the model validation step and all data collected during the model development process in order to identify potential sources of the model's deficits. The analyst packages the outcomes of the analysis and discusses them with the domain experts during a group meeting. In this meeting, the domain experts discuss the potential causes of the observed poor performance of the CoBRA model and identify potential model improvements.
	• *Domain experts*: The domain experts review the results of the model validation and analysis performed by the analyst in order to identify potential causes of poor performance of the model and to propose appropriate improvements to the model.
Inputs	• Historical project measurement data, in particular software size, project effort, and any other historical measurement data regarding the projects' characteristics.
	• Quantified CoBRA effort overhead model.
	• Results of the effort model validation when applied upon historical projects, in particular actual effort overhead, nominal productivity, and effort estimation error (accuracy, precision, and bias) of the projects.
Activities	1. Analyze explanatory power.
	2. Analyze predictive power.
	3. Package results of analysis.
	4. Discuss results and identify improvement potentials.
Tools	• Software tools for storing and preparing the outcomes of the model validation data. Typically, MS Excel suffices for this purpose.
	• Basic data analysis and visualization tools such as MS Excel or specialized statistical analysis tools such as R, SPSS/PASW, or Statistica.
	• Basic tools for documenting and presenting analysis results. Typically, MS PowerPoint suffices for this purpose.
Outputs	• Documented results of the analysis and group discussion.
	• List of potential improvements to the CoBRA model.

The objective of this step is to analyze the results of the model validation and to identify the sources of the identified deficits of the CoBRA model as well as appropriate improvement potentials.

Table 5.32 summarizes the most important elements of this step. We provide a detailed description of each activity in the following subsections.

In the following subsections, we present the major activities comprising the "analyzing the results of model validation" step of the CoBRA application.

5.13.1 Analyze Explanatory Power

In this activity, the analyst takes a closer look at the results of the model validation with respect to its explanatory power. The objective of this activity is to identify deficits of the CoBRA model and identify appropriate model improvement potentials. For this purpose, the analyst investigates two aspects of the historical projects upon which the model has been applied: development productivity (actual and nominal) and effort overhead.

Analyze the Relationship Between Software Size and Project Effort

Regarding the development productivity of the historical software projects, we compare their actual productivity to their nominal productivity, that is, their productivity after considering the actual project effort overhead provided by the CoBRA model. By comparing actual and nominal productivity, we investigate the ability of the CoBRA model to explain the variance of actual productivity. In particular, we look at the spread of the productivity values and the functional form of their trend. With respect to the spread of the productivity values, we investigate two issues:

- *Overall variance of productivity values*, in particular how large the spread of actual productivity is and whether it decreases on nominal productivity, that is, after considering the projects' effort overhead
- *Data patterns recurring in both actual and nominal productivity data*, in particular outlier projects or groups of projects that are present in the actual productivity data and do not disappear after considering the projects' effort overhead in the nominal productivity data

With respect to the functional form of the projects' productivity trend lines, we expect a linear functional form.

Issues that one should pay attention to and clarify include situations where for two or more projects, the productivity and effort overhead data contradict the basic assumptions of the CoBRA model and are simply counterintuitive. Typical situations include:

- Projects that fall outside of the major (expected linear) trend. In particular, we should focus on projects whose effort is negatively related to the size of the delivered software. For example, for two projects A and B, project A may have consumed significantly more effort than project B, although it delivered a significantly smaller software product than B.
- Projects that consumed a significantly different amount of effort for developing software of approximately equal size.
- Projects that consumed approximately the same amount of effort for developing software of significantly different size.

Figure 5.46 illustrates these issues on example historical project data. In this case, the CoBRA model is able to explain the variance in actual development productivity for the majority of the software projects. The spread of project points around the trend line decreases when the projects' effort overhead is considered. Yet, the model is still not able to explain the extremely low productivity of a group of three projects. After considering effort overhead, these projects remain outliers with respect to productivity. In this situation, the basic question to ask would be, "what characteristics make these projects differ from other projects with respect to development productivity?"

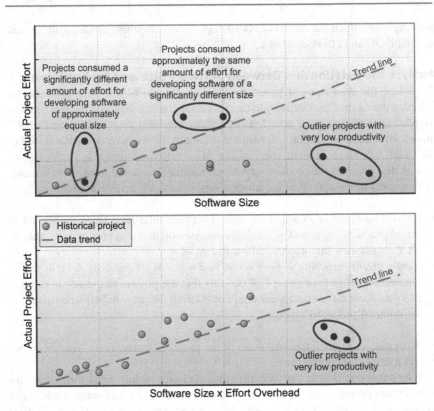

Fig. 5.46 Analyzing productivity outliers

Inverse Relationship Between Effort Overhead and Actual Productivity

Regarding the effort overhead that the CoBRA model provides for each historical project, we investigate the negative inverse relationship between effort overhead and actual development productivity. In particular, we look at the spread of the project data and the functional form of their trend.

With respect to the spread of the project data, we first check if a project's effort overhead and its actual productivity create any clear trend. Then we can check what kind of trend this is. We expect a significant negative dependency between a project's effort overhead and its actual development productivity. The rationale behind this expectation is that the higher effort overhead in the project, the more effort it costs to develop software products of the same size and, thus, the lower the project's development productivity.

In order to analytically check the strength of the relationship, we can look at the coefficient of rank correlation computed in the model validation step. In the best case, the actual development productivity should be nonlinearly (inverse) dependent on the effort overhead. With this relationship in mind, we look for patterns in

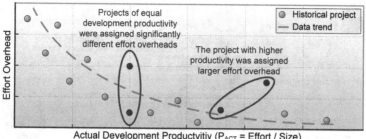

Fig. 5.47 Analyzing effort overhead

the historical project data that may indicate potential deficits of the CoBRA model. Issues that one should pay attention to and clarify include situations where for two or more projects, the productivity and effort overhead data contradict the basic assumptions of the CoBRA model and are simply counterintuitive. Typical situations include:

- Projects for which productivity and effort overhead are positively correlated. For example, for two projects A and B, although the productivity of A is significantly greater than the productivity of B, the CoBRA model assigned A significantly greater effort overhead than B—which would suggest that the productivity of A should actually be significantly lower than that of B.
- Projects that, although assigned approximately equal effort overhead, are characterized by significant differences in development productivity.
- Projects that, although characterized by approximately equal development productivity, were assigned significantly different effort overheads.

Figure 5.47 illustrates some example project data in which two issues require clarification. The first issue is that the CoBRA model assigned significantly different effort overheads to two projects of equal productivity; we would expect that the project with the lower productivity would be assigned higher effort overhead. The second issue relates to the pair of projects of different productivity for which the CoBRA model assigned higher effort overhead to the project with higher development productivity than to the project of lower productivity; we would expect converse assignment. These two issues would, in conjunction with another analysis, require clarification and appropriate improvement of the CoBRA model or input data.

Analyze the Actual Impact of Effort Factors on Project Effort

Finally, we can take a closer look at the results of the sensitivity analysis of the actual impact each effort factor considered in the CoBRA model has on the project effort across historical projects. As already mentioned in the validation step, the results of the sensitivity analysis can be compared to the relative factor importance perceived by the domain experts involved in the historical projects considered.

Potential discrepancies in an actual factor's importance assessed by the experts and obtained through a sensitivity analysis might indicate deficits of the effort

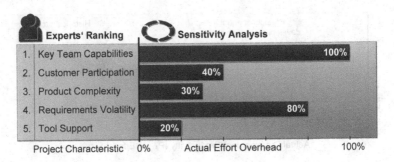

Fig. 5.48 Validating the actual impact of effort factors on project effort

overhead model. In particular, this could mean that some effort factors should have been assigned different effort multipliers in order to account for their actual impact on project effort. For example, Fig. 5.48 illustrates a situation in which the domain experts seemed to underestimate the importance of the *"Requirements Volatility"* effort factor. They ranked it as the fourth most important effort factor, while according to the sensitivity analysis, it is the second most important effort factor in the context of the considered historical projects. If *"Requirements Volatility"* was, in fact, the second most important effort factor whose relative impact on effort is significantly larger than that of subsequently ranked effort factors, the domain experts would need to appropriately revise the effort multipliers they assigned to the effort factors.

In addition, we may ask the experts who were involved in the considered historical projects to prioritize the effort factors in retrospect with respect to their impact on effort in each specific project and then compare this prioritization to the result of the project-specific sensitivity analysis. For example, if the model predicts that *"Requirements Volatility"* is the most important factor influencing project cost, then we would expect that the project manager(s) would, in retrospect, also agree that this factor was the most important one. The same argument applies to the least important factor. To generalize this idea, the ranking of factors produced by the model should exhibit high agreement with the ranking that would be produced by the project manager in retrospect.

In practice, sensitivity analysis often helps to explain the causes of unintuitive effects observed in other analyses of the effort model's explanatory power. For instance, it may help to explain why the CoBRA model assigned higher effort overhead to one project than to another, although the latter actually had higher development productivity.

In case of inconsistencies in a factor's impact on project effort, model improvement activities should focus on revising the effort multipliers assigned to the effort factors and the historical project data. Moreover, we may review the effort overhead model to see whether it contains irrelevant elements while missing relevant ones. By elements we mean not only effort factors but also effort variables and factor interactions.

Tip

▶ If the model's sensitivity analysis showed unexpected impacts of an effort factor on project effort, revise the effort multipliers and the historical project data. Sensitivity analysis uses both effort multipliers and project data for determining a project's actual effort overhead.

5.13.2 Analyze Predictive Power

In this activity, the analyst takes a closer look at the error in the estimates the CoBRA model delivered when applied for the historical projects. In particular, the distribution of absolute and relative estimation error is investigated in conjunction with the projects' actual development productivity and effort overhead.

Similar to the analysis of the explanatory power, we look for unexpected effects manifested by recurring outliers and trends in both estimation error and project data. For example, Fig. 5.49 illustrates a situation where outlier projects with very low actual development productivity remained outliers with respect to estimation error—these were the highly underestimated projects.

In this example, the CoBRA model was clearly not able to account for the project characteristics that were responsible for the extremely low productivity of the three outlier projects. In the cross-validation runs, the baseline nominal productivity for each outlier project was based upon the median nominal productivity of

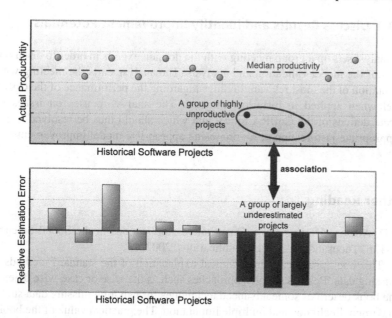

Fig. 5.49 Validating the actual impact of effort factors on project effort

the remaining highly productive projects. This led to a situation in which the outlier projects were estimated using high baseline productivity, yet their effort overhead was not as large as it should be concerning their low actual productivity. In consequence, the estimated effort was much lower than the effort actually consumed. There might be a number of causes for this situation. One potential reason might be a missing effort factor that distinguishes the outlier projects from others. Another might be invalid project effort or size data. For example, the effort measurements for the outlier projects may have omitted important project activities that were considered when measuring the effort of the remaining projects. In fact, our industrial experiences show that the inconsistent scope of size and/or effort measurement is often the major cause of failed estimates.

5.13.3 Package Results of Analysis

In this activity, the analyst synthesizes the results of the analysis and prepares a presentation for the domain experts involved in the CoBRA model development process. The presentation should show, in a clear and concise way, the relevant outcomes of the model validation, their analysis, and their interpretation. In the presentation, the analyst should focus on the effects that indicate potential deficits of the CoBRA model and associated data and that require discussion with the domain experts.

5.13.4 Discuss Results and Identify Improvement Potentials

The analyst sets up a group meeting with the domain experts in order to discuss the results of the model validation and analysis. The analyst starts the meeting with a presentation of the most relevant findings regarding the performance of the CoBRA model when applied to historical projects. The analyst focuses on issues that indicate deficits of the CoBRA model and which should thus be resolved—either by appropriate justification or by proposing appropriate model improvements.

Further Reading

- P.D. Allison, *Missing Data*, Quantitative Applications in the Social Sciences. p. 136. Thousand Oaks: Sage Publications, 2002.

  This book provides a nontechnical explanation of the standard methods for missing data. Besides simple approaches such as list-wise or case-wise deletion, the book describes some advanced techniques for handling missing data such as maximum likelihood and multiple imputation. The practical value of the book is increased by numerous examples and practical tips.

- A. Trendowicz and J. Münch, "Factors Influencing Software Development Productivity—State-of-the-Art and Industrial Experiences," *Advances in Computers*, pp. 185–241. Elsevier, 2009.

  This article provides a comprehensive overview of the factors influencing development productivity and effort. The authors based their survey on a review of related literature and on numerous experiences gained in the software industry. On the one hand, the authors discuss effort drivers that seem to be universally applicable across various project environments; on the other hand, they provide factors that seem to apply only within particular project situations.

- D. Wettschereck, D.W. Aha, and T. Mohri, "A Review and Empirical Evaluation of Feature Weighting Methods for a Class of Lazy Learning Algorithms," *Artificial Intelligence Review*, vol. 11, no. 1-5, pp. 273–314. February 1997.

  This paper provides a comprehensive review of feature weighting techniques developed in the machine learning domain. Feature weighting techniques can be employed in CoBRA for identifying the most relevant effort factors using available project measurement data. In particular, feature weighting techniques can be used to quantify the impact of the measured project characteristics on development productivity.

- N. E. Fenton and S. L. Pfleeger, *Software Metrics: A Rigorous and Practical Approach*. Revised, 2nd ed. Boston, MA, USA: PWS Publishing Co., 1998.

  This book provides the fundamentals of software measurement. In particular, in Chapter 2, the authors explain measurement scales with their associated limitations. The principles of measurement this book presents might be useful when developing CoBRA effort models, in particular (1) when collecting and validating project measurement data and (2) when quantifying the effort overhead model and acquiring corresponding expert knowledge.

Model Application

6

After developing a new or modifying an existing CoBRA effort model, we can directly use it for estimating the effort of individual software projects. Applying the CoBRA model for estimation involves several simple activities.

In this chapter we describe the activities an estimator performs to predict the effort of a software project using the CoBRA model. These activities are common estimation activities that do not depend on any particular purpose of estimation.

6.1 Process Overview

Once developed and accepted, the CoBRA model is used at the project level for estimating individual software projects. Figure 6.1 illustrates the steps involved in applying CoBRA models.

In the first two steps (Steps 1 and 2), the estimation context and the goals within the specific project are determined. Depending on whether the project situation belongs to the range of situations the model was intended for, we can adjust the model or the project situation appropriately in Step 3 of the process (before using the model for estimating the project in Step 4). After project completion, in the last two steps of the estimation cycle (Steps 5 and 6), the performance of the CoBRA model is evaluated based upon the goodness of the estimates it provided for the project. Potential deficits and their possible reasons are packaged and reported, together with information about the project-specific estimation context. Feedback collected on multiple software projects creates a basis for revising the CoBRA model.

Re-estimating Project Effort In practice, estimators will repeat the first four steps of the model application process in order to re-estimate project effort as the project proceeds. Project estimates obtained in very early stages of software development, when relatively little is known about the project scope and environment, are typically burdened by high uncertainty. Therefore, it is a

A. Trendowicz, *Software Cost Estimation, Benchmarking, and Risk Assessment*,
The Fraunhofer IESE Series on Software and Systems Engineering,
DOI 10.1007/978-3-642-30764-5_6, © Springer-Verlag Berlin Heidelberg 2013

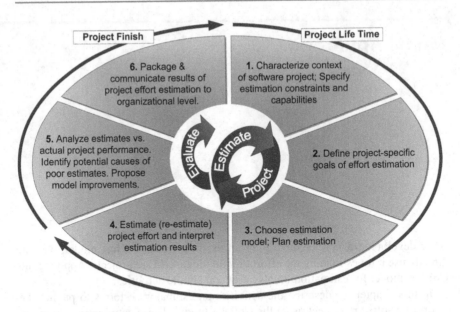

Fig. 6.1 Applying CoBRA models

good practice to repeat the estimation project on a regular basis in order to take advantage of current project information and for project tracking and controlling purposes. As the software project proceeds, more actual information is available. Figure 6.1 illustrates the idea of re-estimating a project during its lifetime and packaging the experiences gained during re-estimation cycles at project finish.

Re-estimating the project using updated information allows for reducing the uncertainty of the estimates and revising the initial estimates, which were based upon incomplete information or upon conditions that have changed along the course of the project. Figure 6.2 illustrates this effect using the so-called "cone of uncertainty" (Boehm 1981; McConnell 2006), which is nothing else but a representation of the decreasing uncertainty of estimates across a software development project.

In addition, we may consider using different size measures at different stages of software development depending on their availability. For example, using common lines of code (LOC) as a measure is in practice limited by the availability of the software code, which is available relatively late during software development. Using LOC in early stages of a software project forces us to estimate the size of the software in terms of LOC and then base our effort estimates on these size estimates. The danger of such an approach is that effort estimates based on size estimates are burdened with a large error, which is the product of two errors: size estimation error and effort estimation effort. In CoBRA, using different size

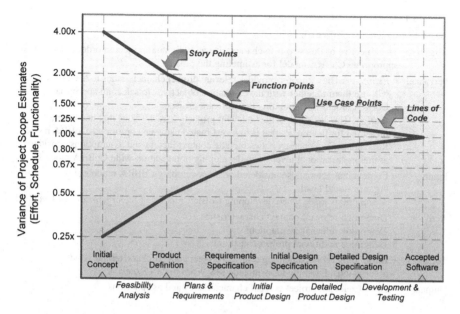

Fig. 6.2 Cone of estimation uncertainty

measures for estimating project effort at different stages of the development life cycle would require constructing multiple CoBRA effort models, where the productivity models would be based upon different size measures and the effort overhead model would remain the same (see basic components of the CoBRA effort model in Sect. 4.2, Fig. 4.1).

6.2 Characterize Project Context

The objective of this step is to characterize an individual project in order to choose an appropriate CoBRA model for estimating the project. For this purpose, we determine the project environment characteristics that determine the applicability of the CoBRA models defined at the organizational level in a specific project. To do so, we should focus on those characteristics of the project environment that were considered when developing the CoBRA models at the organizational level.

If more than one CoBRA model has already been developed within an organization, we may use one that has been created for the context similar to a context of the estimated project. In case of small dissimilarities, minor adjustments of the chosen model and its application process might be necessary. If a CoBRA model that fits the context of the estimated project is not available, then developing a new model should be considered. If developing a new model is not feasible—due to time constraints or lack of necessary inputs to model development—then using an alternative estimation method should be considered.

Table 6.1 CoBRA model application process: characterize project context

Step 4.1: Characterize project context	
Objective	The objective of this step is to characterize an individual project in order to choose an appropriate CoBRA model for estimating the project.
Personnel	• *Estimator*: The estimator provides relevant project characteristics to the analyst who will use them together with the estimation objectives to select an appropriate CoBRA model for estimating the software project.
	• *Analyst*: The analyst specifies relevant project characteristics that need to be measured for the project that is to be estimated using an appropriate CoBRA model. Relevant project characteristics include context factors and assumptions considered at the organizational level when developing organization-wide CoBRA models.
Inputs	• Context characteristics considered when developing CoBRA models at the organizational level.
	• Assumptions made when developing CoBRA models at the organizational level.
Activities	1. Determine relevant context characteristics.
	2. Determine relevant assumptions.
	3. Determine additional project constraints.
Tools	• Basic tools for documenting relevant project context characteristics and assumptions. Example tools include MS Word or MS Excel.
Outputs	• List of relevant project context characteristics and assumptions.

Tip

▶ When using a CoBRA model for estimating an individual project, analyze the characteristics of the project and make sure that they do not differ from the context and assumptions for which the employed CoBRA model has been developed.

In fact, in this and in the next step of the model application process, we characterize a project's estimation context in order to select and apply an appropriate CoBRA estimation model—or identify potential discrepancies between a project-specific situation and the range of project situations for which a given CoBRA model was designed. Typical context characteristics considered here include application domain (embedded vs. information systems), development type (new development vs. enhancement), or development life cycle (waterfall vs. iterative).

Table 6.1 summarizes the most important elements of this step. We provide a detailed description of each activity in the subsequent paragraphs.

6.2.1 Determine Relevant Context Characteristics

In this activity, the estimator assesses the characteristics of the project environment that are relevant for choosing the CoBRA model that will (1) be feasible to apply in the project and (2) provide reliable project estimates. The estimator obtains a list of the relevant characteristics from the analyst who is responsible for managing the CoBRA model within the organization. The list includes known and assumed context factors that were considered at the organizational level for specifying the scope of the applicability of the developed CoBRA models.

Examples of typical context factors considered at the organizational level include "application domain" and "development type." For instance, if at the organizational level, a CoBRA model has been developed for new development projects in the embedded software domain, the estimator should assess the "development type" and "application domain" of the project for which the CoBRA model is to be selected and applied.

With respect to assumptions made at the organizational level, the estimator should verify if these assumptions hold within the specific project. For example, a typical assumption on the organizational level is that the estimation for a project is based on the data that are reliable and close to the actual project characteristics. It may, however, happen that due to low experience of the project staff or poor measurement processes, the inputs for the estimation are of poor quality, leading to poor estimates. In this case, noticing project-specific circumstances will be crucial for explaining the reasons of potentially failed estimates. Instead of looking for deficits in the CoBRA model, we should simply ensure proper data collection and validation processes in the subsequent projects.

6.2.2   Determine Relevant Assumptions

For those project characteristics that are relevant for choosing an appropriate CoBRA model but that are not known at the time of the project characterization, the estimator must make the necessary assumptions. In such a case, the estimator must assess certain project characteristics using the best of his knowledge and experiences.

6.2.3   Determine Additional Project Constraints

Finally, the estimator should consider and document any project-specific characteristics that were not taken into account explicitly during the development of the CoBRA models on the organizational level but which may influence the feasibility or performance of a CoBRA model used in the project. For example, the estimator may notice that there might be some difficulties in reliably measuring software size, which may have an impact on the goodness of the estimates. This issue should be documented as a potential issue to be considered when analyzing the goodness of the estimate at project completion.

6.3   Define Goals of Project Effort Estimation

The objective of this step is to specify the effort estimation goals defined in a particular software development project.

Table 6.2 CoBRA model application process: define goals of project effort estimation

Step 4.2: Define goals of project effort estimation	
Objective	The objective of this step is to specify the effort estimation goals defined in a particular software development project.
Personnel	• *Estimator*: The estimator specifies the project needs with respect to effort estimation and discusses them with the analyst in order to choose the most appropriate CoBRA model and, later on, tailor the model and the estimation process, if necessary.
	• *Analyst*: The analyst supports the estimator in specifying the project-specific goals of the effort estimation. In particular, the analyst provides a list of the estimation goals considered when the CoBRA models were developed at the organizational level.
Inputs	• Estimation goals considered at the organizational level.
Activities	1. Define project-specific goals of effort estimation.
Tools	• Basic tools for documenting project estimation goals. Example tools include MS Word or MS Excel.
Outputs	• List of the project-specific goals of effort estimation.

Defining estimation goals allows not only for selecting the most appropriate CoBRA model but also for identifying potential deviations between project-specific estimation objectives and organizational-level objectives for which the chosen CoBRA model was developed. Based on the identified differences, appropriate tailoring of the CoBRA model and/or estimation process can be performed within the project.

Table 6.2 summarizes the most important elements of this step. We provide a detailed description of each activity in the subsequent paragraphs.

6.3.1 Define Project-Specific Goals of Effort Estimation

In this activity, the estimator specifies the effort estimation goals he aims to achieve in the project and provides them to the analyst, who chooses the most appropriate CoBRA model to use in this particular project. If no CoBRA model is available that perfectly matches the project-specific estimation goals, the analyst looks for the most appropriate model and evaluates the discrepancy. The analyst then considers a potential adaptation of the CoBRA model in order to meet the project-specific effort estimation goals. For example, the best available CoBRA model showed an average estimation error of 20 % in the past, but the project requires 10 % error at most. In this case, the estimator must adjust the existing model in order to ensure that the stringent project-specific goal is met. Another example might be that the existing model focused on estimating project effort and the new project requires the model to support justifying and negotiating the project scope with the customer. In this case, the existing model would most likely focus on the internal, organization-related effort factors such as the capabilities of the development team or the quality of the selected development processes. Meeting the project objective would, however, require that the model considers the impact of customer-related effort factors on project cost. Showing this impact explicitly would form the basis for justifying and negotiating the project budget and scope with the customer. For instance, considering customer involvement in the project as a relevant effort factor may be used as an argument for either more customer involvement in the project or (if this is not possible) an increase in the project budget to compensate for the insufficient involvement of the customer in the project.

If there is no CoBRA model that would meet all project-specific effort estimation objectives, and if the available models would require major modifications, the analyst must suggest using another method for estimating project effort. Alternatively, another estimation method can be used in addition to CoBRA; the project estimates will then result from combining the outcomes of both estimation methods.

The estimator may moderate the goal-related constraints on the CoBRA model and prioritize the project-specific effort estimation goals. In this case, the analyst may choose the CoBRA model that meets the most critical goals or the majority of the project goals. For example, the estimator may use the method of Triage in that he tells what effort estimation goals "*must*," which "*should*," and which "*can*" be fulfilled by the selected CoBRA model based on its past performance.

6.4 Choose Estimation Model and Plan Estimation

The objective of this step is to select an appropriate CoBRA estimation model and to plan the project estimation procedure. The form of both the estimation model and the estimation procedure depends on the project-specific situation, that is, on its estimation context and objectives. The CoBRA model chosen for estimating the project should, if possible, closely correspond to the project's estimation context in terms of its environmental characteristics and its effort estimation goals. Otherwise, the model will be very likely to provide unreliable effort estimates. *Estimation procedure* here refers to the part of the overall project that deals with estimating project effort and using the outcomes of estimation. Planning estimation procedure refers to planning and scheduling the estimation activities and to assigning corresponding responsibilities and required infrastructure.

Table 6.3 summarizes the most important elements of this step. We provide a detailed description of each activity in the subsequent paragraphs.

6.4.1 Select Appropriate CoBRA Model

In this activity, the estimator characterizes the context of a particular project for the analyst who then selects the CoBRA model that is most appropriate for estimating the project. In order to ensure reliable estimations, the project should be within the range of project situations for which the CoBRA model was developed at the organizational level. On the one hand, the analyst should ensure that the estimation context for which the CoBRA model was developed and the project context fit with

Table 6.3 CoBRA model application process: choose estimation model and plan estimation

Step 4.3: Choose estimation model and plan estimation	
Objective	The objective of this step is to select an appropriate CoBRA estimation model and to plan the project estimation.
Personnel	• *Estimator*: The estimator identifies the relevant characteristics of the project and its estimation goals to the analyst, who looks for a CoBRA effort estimation model that is the most appropriate one for estimating this particular project. The estimator plans the estimation in conjunction with the project manager who is responsible for overall project planning and management. Note that typically the project manager also plays the role of the estimator.
	• *Analyst*: The analyst chooses the most appropriate CoBRA model for estimating the project, taking into account the estimation context specified by the estimator. The analyst may optionally locally adjust (within the project) the CoBRA model if it does not comply with the project's estimation context. Finally, the analyst should also be involved in planning the effort estimation by specifying the estimation activities required for achieving the project's estimation goals, capabilities, and constraints.
Inputs	• Project contexts.
	• Project effort estimation goals.
	• Existing CoBRA effort estimation models.
Activities	1. Select appropriate CoBRA model.
	2. <Optional> Adjust project's estimation context.
	3. <Optional> Adjust estimation model.
	4. Plan effort estimation.
Tools	• <Optional> Tool for implementing the adjusted CoBRA model.
	• Tool for planning effort estimation. Typically, this will be the tool used for planning and managing the entire software project.
Outputs	• CoBRA effort estimation model.
	• <Optional> List of adjustments to CoBRA model and their rationales.
	• <Optional> List of adjustments to project's estimation context.
	• Estimation plan.

respect to environmental characteristics, constraints, and estimation goals. On the other hand, the analyst and the estimator should check whether the estimated project is similar to one or more of the historical projects used for developing the CoBRA model under consideration. The more similar the estimated project is to the historical projects, the more likely the CoBRA model is to provide reliable estimates for the project.

In case there is no CoBRA model that perfectly suits the project's specific situation, the analyst should check the following possibilities:

• *Adjust project's context*. If the project manager and the project owner agree, the project environment and the estimation objectives may be modified to fit the available CoBRA model.

• *Adjust CoBRA estimation model*. If the scope of the potentially required changes to the CoBRA model is not too large, the analyst may locally—meaning within the project—adjust the available CoBRA to fit it to the project's estimation context and objectives.

- *Select alternative estimation method.* If neither adjusting the project's context nor adjusting the available CoBRA model is feasible or likely to ensure reliable project effort predictions, then an alternative estimation method should be considered. In this case, the analyst and the estimator choose (after approval by the project owners and managers) and propose the most suitable method and appropriately plan project estimation.

6.4.2 Adjust Project Estimation Context

If none of the available CoBRA model fits the project-specific context, we can try to adjust the project environment so that it is closer to the range of project situations (estimation context) covered by one of the available CoBRA models. Such an adjustment requires the approval of the project owner and the project manager. For example, poor measurement processes—thus poor inputs to estimation—are a common source of poor estimates. If we expect that the measurement procedures used within a particular project will probably not provide us with reliable data for estimation, we may plan alternative ways of obtaining appropriate data or improving the measurement processes beforehand.

6.4.3 Adjust Estimation Model

If adjusting the project environment is not possible or insufficient for ensuring reliable project estimates using a particular CoBRA model, we may consider adjusting the model.

Using the information regarding project context and estimation objectives provided by the estimator, the analyst looks for a CoBRA model that best fits the project situation. After selecting a candidate CoBRA model, we investigate to which extent the project-specific situation differs from the range of situations covered by the "best suitable" CoBRA model. If the discrepancies are not large and can be resolved by small changes to the CoBRA model, the analyst can modify the model appropriately. If the discrepancy between the estimation context of the best suitable CoBRA model and that of the specific project is large and would require major adjustments to the model, the analyst and the estimator should consider employing alternative effort estimation method for that specific project.

Adjusting CoBRA Model Within Specific Project.
The prerequisite for adjusting the CoBRA model within an individual project is that the required adjustments are limited—thus acceptable within the scope of the individual project.

A CoBRA model that has been adjusted within a project <u>should not</u> be automatically used for estimating other models but should be reported to the organizational level. If similar projects are likely to recur in the future, it

(continued)

would make sense to create a suitable CoBRA model. If, however, the project is exceptional and it is rather unlikely to be repeated in the future, it will probably not be worth developing a dedicated CoBRA model. On the one hand, it would be difficult to develop a model based on a single historical project. On the other hand, the effort invested in building such a CoBRA model will probably never be returned because the specific project will not recur in the future. Already when approved on the organizational level, an adjusted model can be released for estimating other projects. Ignoring these rules will in practice lead to an uncontrolled increase of locally modified models, which would increase the cost of their use and maintenance.

6.4.4 Plan Effort Estimation

Planning effort estimation consists of planning the activities, resources, and infrastructure necessary for estimating project effort with the chosen CoBRA model. In terms of planning, planning the effort estimation does not differ from planning any other project activity. In fact, the estimation plan should be aligned with the project activities and be integrated into the project plan. Presenting detailed aspects of project planning goes beyond the scope of this book. Please refer to the related literature, such as PMI (2007), for details regarding the planning of projects.

6.5 Estimate Project Effort

The objective of this step is to obtain project estimates using the chosen CoBRA model and actual project data.

Table 6.4 summarizes the most important elements of this step. We provide a detailed description of each activity in the subsequent paragraphs.

6.5.1 Collect Required Project Data

In this activity, the estimator collects the project data required on the input of the CoBRA effort model. This includes the size of the software and the effort factors considered in the effort model. The data format should comply that defined in the effort model. For instance, the project data should be collected according to the measurement scales defined in the effort model.

If the estimator knows the project, he may provide the project data by himself; otherwise, he should acquire the data from the experts who were involved in the project and know it well. Typically, the project manager, who usually plays the role of the estimator, will provide all inputs to effort estimation. If some inputs are not known at the time of the estimation, the data should be estimated using available

Table 6.4 CoBRA model application process: estimate project effort

Step 4.4: Estimate project effort	
Objective	The objective of this step is to obtain project estimates using the chosen CoBRA model and actual project data.
Personnel	• *Estimator*: The estimator collects actual project data and feeds them to the chosen CoBRA model. The estimator interprets the outcomes of the estimation and runs additional analyses, if necessary.
	• *Analyst* (optional): Involvement of the analyst in the estimation step is optional. The analyst may support the estimator in using the CoBRA model and interpreting its output, in particular when the estimator is not experienced yet in using the CoBRA method for estimating project effort.
Inputs	• CoBRA effort model.
Activities	1. Collect required project data.
	2. Run estimation.
	3. Interpret estimation outcomes.
Tools	• Basic tools for collecting, storing, validating, and preprocessing actual project data.
	• Tool supporting estimation with the CoBRA method. Example tools include implementations in MS Excel or dedicated CoBRA tools such as CoBRIX.
Outputs	• Intermediate project data (collected during project's lifetime).
	• Actual project data (collected at project finish).
	• Outcomes of project effort estimation.
	• Interpretation of project estimation outcomes.

project information. A typical situation where some effort factors might not be already known is estimation in very early phases of software development, when generally little is known about the project. In such cases, the expected or assumed values of certain project characteristics can be used to generate initial project estimates. In the later project stages, when more is known about the project, the actual project characteristics can be used to revise the initial estimates, meaning effort can be re-estimated.

After collecting the project data, the analyst analyzes it with regard to completeness and consistency. In case of any deficits, the estimator should refer to the data provided for clarification. Finally, the estimator prepares the data in order to enter it into the CoBRA model. Depending on the particular tool implementing the model, the input data may require reformatting.

6.5.2   Run Estimation

In this activity, the estimator enters the actual project into the CoBRA model and runs the estimation. Based upon the quantified effort overhead model and the actual project data, (1) actual distributions of effort multipliers for all direct effort factors are computed and (2) a Monte Carlo simulation is executed to determine the distribution of the project's overall effort overhead. Using the simulated project effort overhead and the baseline nominal productivity from the CoBRA model, the distribution of the project's estimated effort is computed. Please refer to Sects. 5.11.1 and 5.11.2 for more details regarding these computations.

Since a CoBRA estimation is computationally intensive—especially due to the Monte Carlo simulation—it should be supported by an automatic tool. If necessary for achieving particular estimation goals, the estimator may run additional analyses. For example, the project risk assessment goal requires running a sensitivity analysis (see Sect. 7.2). At the time of the writing of this book, two software tools supporting the CoBRA method were available:

- A standalone software package called CoBRIX,[1] offered in multiple languages by the Fraunhofer Institute for Experimental Software Engineering (FhG/IESE)
- A tool,[2] based on MS Excel offered in Japanese by the Information-technology Promotion Agency Software Engineering Center (IPA/SEC). In addition, IPA/ SEC offers a web-based CoBRA tool with a predefined set of effort factors

6.5.3 Interpret Estimation Outcomes

Finally, the estimator interprets the outcomes of the estimation and provides them to the project manager. Since, in practice, the project manager typically plays the role of the estimator, the latter activity will usually not be necessary.

6.6   Analyze Estimation Performance

This activity is performed at the end of the project, and its objective is to evaluate the performance of the CoBRA model by comparing the estimates it provided during the project to the actual project outcomes at its finish. In particular, errors in the effort estimates are considered. Furthermore, we identify the potential sources of the identified performance deficits and propose appropriate improvements. These improvements may refer to the CoBRA estimation model and/or to the project environment in which the model has been used. For instance, poor measurement processes—thus poor input data for estimation—may turn out to be the reason for failed estimates. In this case, we should focus our improvement actions on the measurement processes rather than on the CoBRA model.

Note that in this step, the estimation performance of the CoBRA model within a specific project is evaluated. After reporting the model's performance and the project data to the organizational level, the model's performance in the project will be evaluated in the context of other projects the model has been applied in.

In general, this activity is performed by the estimator. Yet, the analyst may support the estimator if he is not yet sufficiently experienced in CoBRA. The analyst may completely take over this step if the estimator's constraints do not

---

[1] *http://www.cobrix.org/cobrix/index.html*

[2] *http://sec.ipa.go.jp/tool/cobra/* (in Japanese; in order to enter the page, a free-of-charge sign in on the IPA/SEC website is required)

Table 6.5 CoBRA model application process: analyze estimation performance

Step 4.5: Analyze estimation performance	
Objective	The objective of this step is to evaluate the performance of the CoBRA model by comparing the estimates it provided during the project to the actual project outcomes at its finish.
Personnel	• *Estimator*: The estimator collects the actual project data at project finish and compares it to the estimates the CoBRA model provided during the project.
	• *Analyst* (optional): Involvement of the analyst in this step is optional. On the one hand, the analyst may support the estimator in analyzing the estimation performance analyses, especially when the estimator is not yet sufficiently experienced in using the CoBRA method. On the other hand, the estimator may delegate the analysis of the estimation performance directly to the analyst, in particular if the role of the estimator is played by a project manager whose time constraints do not allow for analyzing estimation performance.
Inputs	• Actual project data (collected at project completion).
	• Outcomes of project effort estimation.
Activities	1. Analyze predictive performance.
	2. Analyze explanatory power.
Tools	• Basic data analysis and visualization tools such as MS Excel or specialized statistical analysis tools such as R, SPSS/PASW, or Statistica.
Outputs	• Results of estimation performance evaluation.

allow him to perform this activity, for example, because he is the project manager and is committed to project management activities.

Table 6.5 summarizes the most important elements of this step. We provide a detailed description of each activity in the subsequent paragraphs.

6.6.1 Analyze Predictive Performance

Predictive performance refers to the *accuracy* of the effort estimates, meaning the nearness of the estimated project effort to the actual effort reported at project finish. In order to quantify the summary accuracy of the estimation method, we use the *relative error (RE)* measure. For each historical project, *RE* measures the difference between predicted effort ($Effort_{Est}$) and actual effort ($Effort_{Act}$) relative to actual effort (6.1).

$$RE = \frac{Effort_{Est} - Effort_{Act}}{Effort_{Act}} \qquad (6.1)$$

If the estimation error is greater than an acceptable level specified in the project estimation objectives, we should investigate the potential reasons for this. One potential source of low predictive performance might be inappropriateness of the CoBRA model. The model may, for instance, miss effort factors that were actually important determinants of effort in the estimated project. Another potential source of poor estimates might be poor inputs to estimation. For instance, poor measurement processes might have provided unreliable size or factor measurements to the effort model, leading to inaccurate effort estimates.

Failed Estimation Versus Failed Project.
Poor performance of the estimation method is a typical but not the only cause of failed project estimates. The discrepancy between the estimates and the actual performance may be due to a failed project. In such a situation, the CoBRA method would actually have correctly estimated the project if it had run under usual conditions, i.e., conditions that are represented by the CoBRA model.

Recall that a CoBRA model is developed and validated on successful historical projects. It would not make much sense to take failed projects as a reference for the future. The common definition of a successful project in the software community refers to completing a project within budget and time and delivering a software product with the expected functionality and quality. The minimal definition of a successful project may refer to a project that delivered the expected software product without creating substantial financial loss.

Yet, if some exceptional project conditions cause a project to fail and (among the other "losses") does not meet its estimate effort, the estimation method cannot be blamed for this. By exceptional conditions, we mean project-internal and -external events that are difficult to foresee upfront. An internal event might be a wrong decision or a chain of wrong decisions made by the project manager. An external event might be unexpected significant fluctuation within the project team due to structural changes in the whole organization. In the case of a failed project being the cause of "failed" estimates, the causes of the failed project should be documented as potential risks to project success. These risks should then be considered for planning contingency reserves in future projects, not, however, for modifying the estimation method in order to account for project failure.

6.6.2 Analyze Explanatory Power

The analysis of the explanatory power focuses on the ability of the CoBRA model to indicate and explain effort-related project risks. In particular, the actual impact of the effort factors considered in the CoBRA model on project effort is considered here. CoBRA proposes analyzing the explanatory power of the effort model through a feedback session with the project team. During such a session, the project team members assess which aspects of the project environment have the greatest influence on the productivity of their work activities—thus on the effort required to successfully complete these tasks. The estimator compares this feedback against the effort multipliers the CoBRA model actually assigned to the effort factors considered in the effort overhead model. On the one hand, it may occur that the CoBRA model underestimated the impact of some effort factors on project effort while overestimating the impact of other factors. On the other hand, the experts' feedback may reveal that the CoBRA model has missed some relevant effort factors while considering irrelevant ones.

6.7   Package and Communicate Estimation Results

The objective of this step is to synthesize the outputs of the project estimation and the analysis of the estimates that are relevant for improving the CoBRA estimation model and the effort estimation processes within the organization. After packaging the results of the project estimation, the estimator communicates them to the organizational level, where the analyst analyzes them together with the estimation feedback from other software projects.

Table 6.6 summarizes the most important elements of this step. We provide a detailed description of each activity in the subsequent paragraphs.

Table 6.6 CoBRA model application process: package and communicate estimation results

Step 4.6: Package and communicate estimation results	
Objective	The objective of this step is to synthesize the outputs of the project estimation and the analysis of the estimates that are relevant for improving the CoBRA estimation model and the effort estimation processes within the organization.
Personnel	• *Estimator*: Estimator synthesizes outcomes of estimation and reports them to analyst at the organization level. • *Analyst* (optional): The analyst may optionally support the estimator in synthesizing the relevant outcomes of the estimation and in preparing them for reporting.
Inputs	• List of relevant project context characteristics and assumptions. • List of the project-specific goals of the effort estimation. • <Optional> List of adjustments to project's context. • CoBRA effort estimation model used in the project. • <Optional> List of project-specific adjustments to the CoBRA model and their rationale. • Estimation plan. • Actual project data (collected at project completion). • Outcomes of project effort estimation. • Interpretation of project estimation outcomes. • Results of estimation performance evaluation. • <Optional> Guidelines for packaging and reporting the estimation outcomes.
Activities	1. Synthesize estimation results and prepare them for reporting. 2. Communicate packaged results to organizational level.
Tools	• Basic tools for documenting project data and the outcomes of the project estimation. Example tools include MS Word or MS Excel.
Outputs	Packaged outcomes of project estimation that are relevant for improving the CoBRA model and the estimation process: • Project context factors relevant for effort estimation, for example, those that were used for choosing an appropriate CoBRA model, • Project-specific goals of effort estimation, • Any additional project capabilities and constraints considered during effort estimation, • The CoBRA effort model chosen for estimating the project, • Project-specific changes made to the estimation context, the estimation goals, the CoBRA model, or the estimation process—together with their rationale, • Actual project data collected at project finish, including software size and the effort factors considered in the CoBRA model used for estimation, • Project estimates, including the project effort and effort overhead introduced by each direct effort factor considered in the employed CoBRA model, • Indicators of the predictive and explanatory power of the CoBRA model, identified deficits and their potential causes.

6.7.1   Synthesize Estimation Results and Prepare Them for Reporting

In this activity, the estimator reviews the outcomes of the estimation and synthesizes those that are most relevant for improving the CoBRA model and the estimation processes within the organization.

The analyst may optionally provide the estimator with an exact specification of the content and format of the project estimation outcomes that should be reported to the organizational level. Typically, project estimation outcomes reported to the organizational level should include:

- Project context factors relevant for effort estimation, for example, those that were used for choosing an appropriate CoBRA model,
- Project-specific goals of the effort estimation,
- Any additional project capabilities and constraints considered during the effort estimation,
- The CoBRA effort model chosen for estimating the project,
- Project-specific changes made to the estimation context, the estimation goals, the CoBRA model, or the estimation process—together with their rationale,
- Actual project data collected at project finish, including software size and the effort factors considered in the CoBRA model used for estimation,
- Project estimates, including the project effort and effort overhead introduced by each direct effort factor considered in the employed CoBRA model,
- Indicators of the predictive and explanatory power of the CoBRA model, identified deficits and their potential causes.

6.7.2   Communicate Packaged Results to Organizational Level

In this activity, the estimator conveys the packaged results of the project estimation to the organizational level, where the data is used for maintaining the organization's effort estimation processes and the CoBRA effort models.

Further Reading

- V. R. Basili, G. Caldiera, and H. D. Rombach, "The Experience Factory," J.J. Marciniak (ed.), *Encyclopedia of Software Engineering*, vol. 1, pp. 469–476. John Wiley & Sons, 1994.

  This chapter of the Encyclopedia of Software Engineering presents the concept of the *Experience Factory (EF)*. The authors specify a universal framework for capitalizing and reusing the outcomes of the software development life cycle, including experiences and products. The publication discusses the *Quality Improvement Paradigm (QIP)* as one fundamental methodology used within the EF. The QIP represents a universal cycle of continuous improvement, which is also adapted for organizing the overall process of adjusting, applying, and maintaining CoBRA models within a software organization.

- V. R. Basili, M. Lindvall, M. Regardie, C. Seaman, J. Heidrich, J. Munch, H.D. Rombach, A. Trendowicz (2010), "Linking Software Development and Business Strategy Through Measurement," *IEEE Computer*, vol. 43, no. 4, pp. 57–65. April 2010.

  This article presents a systematic approach for specifying quantitative goals in the context of software engineering. The authors present the GQM⁺Strategies® method, which extends the well-known Goal-Question-Metric (GQM) paradigm. The GQM approach provides means for defining measurement objectives, refining those objectives down to specifications of measures to be collected, and then analyzing and interpreting the resulting measurement data with respect to the original goals. GQM goals are defined in terms of purpose, focus, object of study, viewpoint, and context. GQM⁺Strategies® supports aligning and quantifying goals at various levels of a software organization. For example, in the context of effort estimation, the particular effort estimation objectives must be aligned to an organization's business objectives so that the achievement of the estimation objectives clearly contributes to the achievement of the business objectives.

Usage Scenarios of a CoBRA Model

7

The CoBRA method has been designed to provide a project decision maker with comprehensive support regarding estimating, controlling, and managing project effort. The CoBRA model can be used for a number of software estimation purposes.

In this chapter, we present several typical scenarios of using the CoBRA model for different purposes. For each scenario we explain, using an intuitive example, how to interpret appropriately the outcomes of applying the CoBRA model.

7.1 Effort Estimation

7.1.1 Most Likely Effort

Traditionally, the objective of effort estimation has been to evaluate the most likely effort required to successfully complete a project with certain characteristics. The simplest way to obtain an estimate of the most likely project effort is to take the mean value from the distribution of effort provided as output by the CoBRA model (Fig. 7.1).

The CoBRA model consists of a quantified effort overhead model and a *baseline nominal productivity* determined using a set of historical projects. After feeding the effort overhead with actual factor data from the project, it returns a distribution of the project's *effort overhead* (distribution of relative frequency obtained through Monte Carlo simulation). Since usually not all project characteristics are known at the time of effort estimation, some of them may be estimated first and updated later, when project re-estimation is performed.

Effort overhead distribution and baseline nominal productivity are inputs to the basic CoBRA equation (7.1), which we use to estimate the effort required to deliver software products of a particular *size*.

A. Trendowicz, *Software Cost Estimation, Benchmarking, and Risk Assessment,*
The Fraunhofer IESE Series on Software and Systems Engineering,
DOI 10.1007/978-3-642-30764-5_7, © Springer-Verlag Berlin Heidelberg 2013

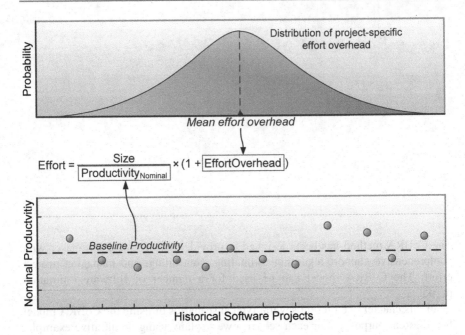

Fig. 7.1 Estimating the most likely effort in CoBRA

$$EffortAct{}_{Act} = \frac{Size}{Productivity_{Nom}} \cdot (EO_{Act} + 1) \qquad (7.1)$$

Let us consider the example distribution of estimated effort in Fig. 7.2. We adapt the mean value over the distribution as the estimate of the most likely project effort. The field under the distribution curve to the left of the mean point represents the probability of project effort being lower than the mean, whereas the field under the curve to the right of the mean represents the probability of project effort being larger than the mean. The latter probability is especially interesting from the point of view of project risk management because, in practice, it represents the probability of exceeding the estimated effort.

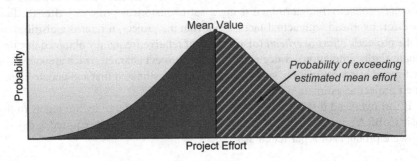

Fig. 7.2 Example distribution of estimated project effort

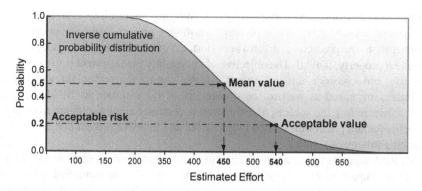

Fig. 7.3 Example cumulative distribution of effort overhead

7.1.2   Effort at a Given Risk Level

In practice, we should avoid estimating project effort by simply taking the mean value over the estimated effort distribution. Instead, we should consider the risk[1] we are willing to take and estimate the effort for a specific probability of exceeding the estimated effort.

Let us consider a simple example. Figure 7.3 illustrates an inverse cumulative distribution of estimated project effort. We use this form of distribution because it is easier to interpret visually.

The most likely mean effort of 450 units means in practice that there is a 50 % chance of exceeding it. If we want to decrease the probability (risk) of running over the planned project budget, we must plan more. If we want to decrease the chance of exceeding the planned budget down to 20 %, we must plan 540 units of effort. In other words, in order to decrease the risk of exceeding the most likely estimate down to 0.2, one has to plan 20 % more effort.

7.2   Risk Management

The CoBRA method supports project risk management with respect to two aspects: (1) it handles the inherent uncertainty of software prediction and (2) it supports the identification of the potential sources of the most critical project risks related to development productivity and effort.

---

[1] In risk-driven estimation with CoBRA, we use the term risk as a synonym for probability. In the risk management domain, risk is defined as the composition of two elements: the probability of an event and the size of (negative) effects of the event.

Managing Estimation Uncertainty Considering uncertainty is an important element of managing risk while planning a software project. Although uncertainty is inherent to the prediction of software effort, estimation methods typically do not handle it properly, if at all. The objective of uncertainty management is to explicitly identify and consider the uncertainty of the input information on which the estimates are based as well as the uncertainty of the estimate itself. Identifying and understanding the sources of estimation uncertainty allows software managers to better handle prediction-related project risks and improve project budgeting and planning processes.

CoBRA supports the handling of estimation uncertainty with several mechanisms. First, the impact of each identified effort factor on effort is quantified using the three values representing a triangular probability distribution. Second, the actual value of each effort factor can be quantified by several values with an associated probability of occurrence. Finally, both the impact and the value of each effort factor can (and should) be quantified by multiple domain experts. Such uncertain input data are subject to a simulation algorithm that provides a probability distribution of estimated effort as its output.

Managing Project Risks The objective of risk management is to determine whether special actions are necessary to reduce effort-related risks in the project. CoBRA supports this objective in two ways:

1. It supports finding out how risky, with respect to effort, the project is going to be. This step consists of setting up a risk baseline of acceptable risk and assessing the risk with respect to this predefined baseline.
2. If the identified level of risk is already unacceptable, then CoBRA supports deciding on actions that should be undertaken to mitigate the risk.

7.2.1   Defining a Baseline for Risk Assessment

In order to perform a risk assessment, we have to build a baseline against which to evaluate individual software projects. We build such a baseline using data from a set of projects, each considered successful according to the organization's understanding of business success. The notion of a successful project may, for instance, at least encompass that the project was completed and did not create substantial financial loss. In cases where no additional project data is available, the same projects that were used for developing the CoBRA effort model can be utilized for setting up a risk baseline.

In CoBRA, we typically define a risk baseline as the median or the mean effort overhead upon the sample of successful historical projects. We explain this approach on an example presented in Fig. 7.4. The threshold T_I represents the

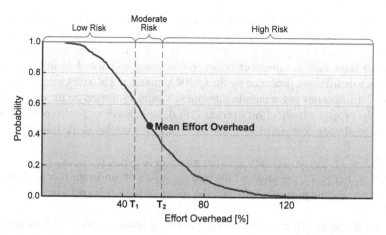

Fig. 7.4 Simple risk assessment using mean effort overhead

median over the effort overheads of a set of historical projects, where for each historical project, the mean effort overhead over the distribution is considered. We may say that T_1 represents a "typical" project. This implies that 50 % of the projects will have a mean effort overhead value greater than T_1 and 50 % will have a mean value up to T_1.

An alternative formulation is to consider the probability of having an effort overhead exceeding the "majority" of projects. For a given sample of historical projects, we can additionally set up a threshold T_2 as the upper quartile upon the mean effort overheads of the historical projects. We may say that T_2 represents the "majority" of the projects. The upper quartile has 75 % of the projects below it and 25 % of the projects above it.

A comparison of a project's actual mean effort overhead against a baseline tells us how risky the project is. There are a number of different ways in which this can be done. In the following paragraphs, we present several approaches, starting from the simplest and progressing to the more complex ones.

7.2.2 Assessing Project Risk Level

The objective of project risk assessment is to evaluate how risky a project is. There are several strategies proposed in CoBRA for assessing the risk level of the software development of a project: based on effort overhead thresholds, based on an acceptable risk probability level, and based on an acceptable risk exposure level.

Risk Assessment Based on Effort Overhead Thresholds
The first approach is based on determining effort overhead thresholds for a project. The thresholds delimit effort overhead intervals, which are judged more or less risky. Consequently, these intervals can be regarded as risk levels. We explained

the idea of setting up risk thresholds in the previous paragraph and illustrated it in Fig. 7.4. Using this information, we can determine the risk level for the project.

The risk level for a project is defined as the interval into which its mean effort overhead falls with the mean effort overhead being calculated from the relative frequency distribution produced by the CoBRA model in a Monte Carlo simulation. Figure 7.4 illustrates two example thresholds T_1 and T_2. Based on these thresholds and on the project's mean effort overhead (EO), we can assess the risk of the project relative to already completed successful projects. We do this in the following way:

- If $EO < T_1$, the project falls into the group of low-risk projects.
- If $T_1 \leq EO \leq T_2$, the project falls into the group of moderate-risk projects.
- If $EO > T_2$, the project's falls into the group of high-risk projects.

Since the mean effort overhead of the example project in Fig. 7.4 falls between T_1 and T_2, it would be regarded as being of moderate risk. After the risk probability level for the project is determined, the preventive/corrective actions associated with that risk level are performed.

In CoBRA, we would typically set up the effort overhead thresholds T_1 and T_2 based upon the 50th and 75th percentiles,[2] respectively, from a sample of successful historical projects. In this case, half of the considered historical projects would have a mean effort overhead lower than T_1 (the 50th percentile), and 75 % of the historical projects would have an effort overhead that is lower than T_2 (the 75th percentile).[3] For reasons of convenience, we refer to these thresholds as representing the "typical" projects and the "majority" of the projects, respectively. These two thresholds define three risk levels: low, moderate, and high risk.

In general, we may define any reasonable number n of thresholds as *percentiles* upon the distribution of mean effort overhead of successful historical projects. A reasonable number would be between 1 and 5. When n thresholds are selected, then $n + 1$ risk levels have to be managed in the sense that for each risk level, specific actions have to be specified. In practice, the number and percentile values of the thresholds should be determined by experienced project managers in conjunction with quality assurance staff. The thresholds should be updated regularly as new and different types of projects are completed and as experience is gained in their use. A specific set of actions should be associated with each interval, except for the lowest one. The higher the risk probability level, the more consequential and costly these actions are likely to be due to the higher number and greater complexity of the software development processes that need to be addressed.

Figure 7.5 shows the two example thresholds derived from a sample of past projects and the curves of the cumulative effort overhead distribution for three

---

[2] The 25th, 50th, and 75th percentiles are referred to as lower, middle, and upper quartile. The middle quartile represents the median.

[3] These percentages may seem high, but it should be remembered that nominal projects never occur in practice and would consume very low and, at any rate, unrealistic effort, hence the large effort overhead percentages.

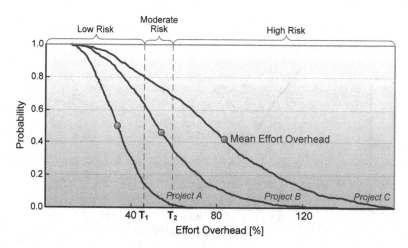

Fig. 7.5   Example risk assessment based on risk threshold

hypothetical projects. For this example, the mean value of the effort overhead for *Project C* falls into the high-risk projects. Moreover, it has a probability of about 0.7 of exceeding T_2, that is, the effort overhead of the majority of the projects. *Project A*, on the other hand, is located in the low-risk class of projects and has a probability of merely 0.15 of exceeding T_1, which is the effort overhead of typical projects. Finally, *Project B* can be considered as a moderate-risk project compared to the already completed projects upon which the risk baseline (using thresholds) is based.

Risk Assessment Based on Acceptable Risk Probability

The aforementioned simple, threshold-based approach is appealing because of its simplicity. However, it does not take into account the probability of the project's overhead falling into a different risk level. For example, if the mean effort overhead for a project falls in between T_1 and T_2—as *Project B* in Fig. 7.5—the project may still have a high probability of having an effort overhead exceeding T_2. Using the simple approach in our example, we would have designated *Project B* as having moderate risk, when in fact it still has a high probability (~0.35) of falling into the class of highly risky projects, as illustrated in Fig. 7.6. This means that the project manager performs the risk reduction actions for a moderate-risk project, whereas she/he should rather consider performing the risk reduction actions for a high-risk project.

To address this shortcoming, we must first define the concept of *Acceptable Risk Probability Level* (*ARP*). To continue from the example above, the acceptable risk probability answers the question of "how high does the probability of the effort overhead exceeding the 'majority' threshold have to be before we consider the project at high risk (instead of moderate risk)?" Therefore, we define acceptable risk probability as the maximum risk that the organization is willing to tolerate without taking actions to manage and reduce it.

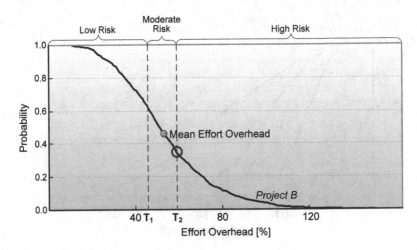

Fig. 7.6 Threat of threshold-based risk assessment

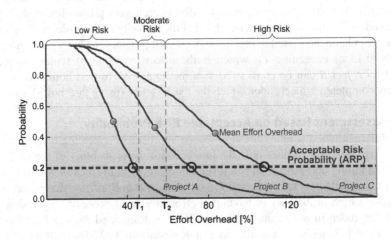

Fig. 7.7 Example of risk assessment based on acceptable risk level

One way to specify acceptable risk is to set up a probability value that indicates the probability above which actions should be triggered. Continuing our example, in Fig. 7.7 we selected the value of $ARP = 0.2$ as the acceptable risk probability value for both the typical (T_1) and the majority (T_2) thresholds.

For the project for which risk assessment is to be performed, we run the effort overhead estimation model and generate the cumulative probability curve, like the curves for projects A, B, and C in Fig. 7.7. In order to determine the risk level for a given project, we follow the effort overhead curve from left to right until we reach the intersection with the acceptable risk probability value that was chosen (bold dashed line at probability level 0.2 in Fig. 7.7). This intersection falls into one of the risk levels, and this is the risk level assigned to the project. In the example illustrated in Fig. 7.7, we show the cumulative effort overhead probability functions for three hypothetical projects, each of them belonging to one of the three risk levels defined by the two thresholds and the acceptable risk probability value. It can be seen that *Project A* has a probability of less than 0.2 of having an effort overhead equal to or exceeding that of the "typical" and "majority" thresholds. Therefore, it is considered as being of low risk. On the other hand, *Project B* and *Project C* have a probability greater than 0.2 of exceeding the effort overhead for the typical projects and the majority of projects. Therefore, they are considered to be of high risk.

Note that the value of the acceptable risk level should again be determined by the most experienced project managers in conjunction with the quality assurance staff. It will be revised as more experience with the use of the model for risk assessment is gained. It should be remembered that acceptable risk is a business decision and should reflect the objectives and strategies of the organization as a whole.

Risk Assessment Based on Acceptable Risk Exposure

In the example presented in Fig. 7.7, the acceptable risk probability value was fixed as a common value across all risk levels and independent of potential "loss" in terms of effort overhead, meaning additional effort that needs to be spent in the project. This would mean that we are willing to accept higher exposure[4] to risk for the project with larger effort overhead. In order to maintain acceptable exposure to risk at the same level, we would define the acceptable risk probability value for high-risk projects (with large effort overhead) to be lower than the acceptable risk probability value for low-risk projects (with small effort overhead).

To address this issue, we will define acceptable risk in terms of *Acceptable Risk Exposure* (*ARE*) as opposed to a simple acceptable risk probability in terms of a fixed likelihood of exceeding a certain effort overhead value. Acceptable risk exposure is defined (7.2) as the product of acceptable risk probability (ARP) and effort overhead threshold (EO$_T$)

$$ARE = ARP \cdot EO_T \tag{7.2}$$

Please note that in order to explicitly distinguish between simple risk probability and the product of risk probability and potential loss, we introduce the term "risk exposure." Yet, in project risk management terminology, risk as such is defined as the product of an event's probability and potential loss (in contrast to simple event probability).

---

[4] We define risk exposure as the product of the probability of an undesired event and the potential loss if this event occurs. In our case, the undesired event is a project exceeding a certain effort overhead, and potential loss is the effort overhead.

Risk Versus Risk Probability Versus Risk Exposure.
In risk management, there are many different definitions of risk, which often leads to confusion. In the context of software project management, risk is defined as the product of an undesired event and the potential loss if the event occurs:

$$Risk\ (undesired\ event) = Probability\ (event\ occurring) \times Expected\ loss$$
$$(after\ event)$$

In order to explicitly differentiate between the simple probability of an undesired event and risk, we introduced two terms: risk probability and risk exposure. However, risk exposure actually corresponds to what is commonly referred to as risk.

In the ARE formula (7.2), acceptable risk probability (ARP) represents the probability of an undesired event and the effort overhead threshold (EO_T) represents the potential loss.

Let us illustrate the idea of risk exposure using the example we have been considering to explain previous risk assessment approaches earlier in this section. In Fig. 7.8, the acceptable risk exposure level for the threshold $T_1 = 45$ % and the acceptable risk probability level 0.2 is equal to 0.2×45 %, which is approximately $ARE_1 = 9$ %. Acceptable risk exposure for the threshold $T_2 = 57$ % and the 0.2 probability is equal to $ARE_2 = 11.4$ %. As we can see, the maximum acceptable risk exposure level is not constant across levels. Counterintuitively, for obviously high-risk projects (with large effort overhead) we are allowing greater risk exposure than for moderate-risk projects (moderate effort overhead) at the moderate-risk level before triggering risk management actions.

We may address this issue by setting acceptable risk exposure to be maintained constant across all risk classes determined by the effort overhead threshold (in our case three risk classes determined by the thresholds T_1 and T_2). Next, we would use a constant risk exposure level for recomputing the initially set acceptable risk probability level. Let us assume that we want to set risk exposure to the level of moderate-risk projects, $ARE_1 = 9$ %. The acceptable risk level for high-risk projects should then be set to $ARP_1 = ARE_1/T_2 = 0.16$ instead of 0.2, as it remains for the class of moderate-risk projects determined by threshold T_1. After modifying the acceptable risk probability level for T_2, the risk exposure for both T_1 and T_2 will be the same and equal to $ARE_1 = ARE_2 = 9$ %.

To determine the risk level using this approach, we follow the effort overhead curve just as in the approach based on acceptable risk level. We check in which risk interval (class) the curve crosses the acceptable risk probability or exposure level. Since these levels may differ across risk intervals, it is possible that the effort overhead curve intersects the risk probability or exposure levels in two or more different intervals. In such a case, we should classify the project into the highest risk class.

Figure 7.8 presents the analysis of a project's risk based on risk exposure for the three example projects: A, B, and C. If we consider the threshold-specific acceptable risk exposure levels ARE_1 and ARE_2, *Project A* will be classified as moderate risk,

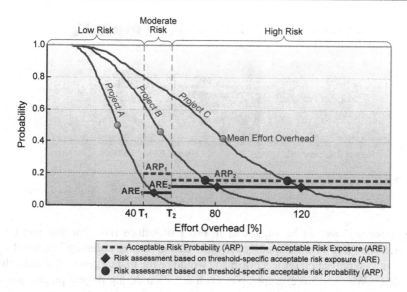

Fig. 7.8 Example of risk assessment based on acceptable risk exposure level

whereas *Project B* and *Project C* will be classified as high risk. Now, if we take ARE_1 as the baseline acceptable risk exposure for all project risk classes, the acceptable risk probability level will be equal to $ARP_2 = 0.16$ for high-risk projects and remain at the initial level $ARP_1 = 0.2$ for moderate-risk projects. With respect to the threshold-specific acceptable risk levels ARP_1 and ARP_2, *Project A* would remain a low-risk project, whereas *Project B* and *Project C* would remain high-risk projects.

Note that the value of the acceptable risk level should again be determined by the most experienced project managers in conjunction with the quality assurance staff. This value will be revised to reflect experiences gained as well as changes in the business objectives and environment of the software organization applying the CoBRA method.

7.2.3 Risk Reduction

Once we have determined the risk level by applying one of the methods presented above, we may wish to identify those factors that have the strongest association with effort overhead in order to reduce risk. This information can be obtained through a so-called sensitivity analysis. This is an analysis of the actual contribution of the considered effort drivers to the effort overhead of a specific project. Figure 7.9 shows an example output of a sensitivity analysis. The contribution of the five most relevant effort drivers to the effort overhead for a specific project can then be used to drive risk reduction activities. For each of these factors, specific preventive and

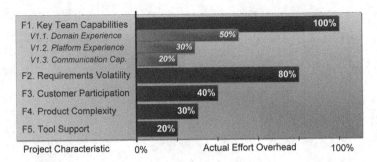

Fig. 7.9 Example output of a CoBRA sensitivity analysis

corrective actions can be suggested in order to reduce risk. For this particular project, the *"Key Team Capabilities"* and *"Requirements Volatility"* factors have the strongest impact on project effort and would be the first targets of risk reduction activities. We may, for example, pay extra attention during project preparation to the capabilities of the project team and ensure that at least the key team members have necessary expertise and experience. In particular, we should consider the aspect of *"Domain Experience,"* as the sensitivity analysis indicated the corresponding effort variable as being responsible for the greatest portion of effort overhead associated with the *"Key Team Capabilities"* effort factor.

Summarizing, we can say that in order to systematize the process of risk assessment and reduction outlined above, a set of guidelines for managing risks should be developed. These guidelines should consist of actions intended to reduce the impact of the identified effort drivers on each risk level. They should include typical types of responses to project risk (PMI 2007, Ch. 11) such as avoiding, transferring, mitigating, and accepting risk. Figure 7.10 presents the general steps of a simple effort-driven risk management approach.

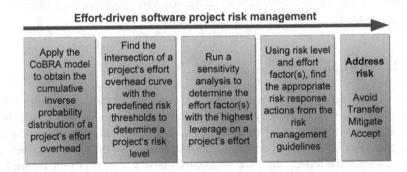

Fig. 7.10 Simple risk management process

Avoid Risk

Avoiding risk refers to actions the project manager should attempt to perform in order to entirely eliminate the negative impact of a certain effort factor on project effort.

Mitigate Risk

Mitigating risk refers to actions the project manager should attempt to perform in order to reduce the probability and/or magnitude of the negative impact of a certain effort factor on project effort.

Avoidance and mitigation strategies use similar actions for addressing risk. In the context of effort estimation, risk avoidance would focus more on actions before project starts (thus offering a greater chance of entirely eliminating risk), whereas risk mitigation would focus on actions during the project. Typical actions include adjustments of the organization's processes or context characteristics. Globally, preventive actions are typically based on the impact of a certain effort factor over multiple projects. Recurrence of a certain factor with a negative impact on development effort may call for preventive actions to avoid it in the future. In this case, preventive actions focus on improving processes and environmental characteristics on the organizational level (organization-wide). Global changes make sense only when a specific process or context characteristic has been observed to consistently have a negative impact on project performance over all projects, independent of other project aspects. Locally, preventive actions are based on the expected negative impact of certain effort factors in the context of a specific project. Local actions typically make sense when a certain effort factor has a negative impact on project effort only in specific project conditions, for example, in conjunction with certain values of other effort factors.

Example 7.1 Mitigating Project Risk Through Local Preventive Actions.

Let us consider an example in which the project manager mitigates the risk of exceeding the acceptable project budget. The project manager mitigates this risk by improving those project characteristics the CoBRA estimation indicated as having the greatest negative impact on project effort.

The task of the project manager is to plan a new project so that it can be successfully completed within an *acceptable effort budget of 1,000 person-days*. The *acceptable risk level* was set at *Probability = 0.2* of exceeding the acceptable effort limit. The CoBRA effort estimation model used in the project considers five effort factors, of which two are indirect factors and one is a composite factor. Figure 7.11 shows the effort overhead model of the CoBRA model used for estimating a new software project.

At the start of the project, the project manager assesses the values of the effort factors using their definitions and quantifications specified in the CoBRA model. Table 7.1 summarizes the definitions of the effort factors and their measured (assessed) levels for the new project.

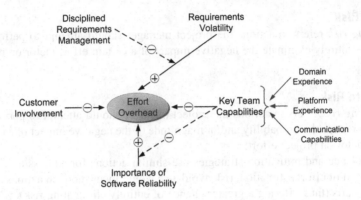

Fig. 7.11 Example: effort overhead model

Table 7.1 Example: effort factor data for estimated project

Effort factor	Definition	Value
Key team capabilities	The extent to which the software development team possesses the skills and experiences necessary for the successful and efficient completion of the project (i.e., delivering software products of required functionality and quality within specified budget and time).	–
Domain experience	The extent of the project team's familiarity and comprehension of the target domain in which the developed software system is to be applied.	*3*
Platform experience	The extent of the project team's familiarity and comprehension of the platform for which the developed software system is intended.	1
Communication capabilities	The ability of the project team to communicate easily and clearly within the team (with other team members).	1
Requirements volatility	The extent to which the requirements are expected to change over time, after the requirements freeze.	2
Disciplined requirements management	The extent to which requirements are explicitly defined, tracked, and traced. This also includes the extent to which changes to requirements after their freeze are systematically managed (e.g., supported by the use of change management methods and tools).	0
Customer involvement	The extent to which the user/customer is involved in the project, providing necessary/useful information, reviewing requirements documents, performing some of the analyses themselves, and taking part in acceptance testing.	1
Importance of software reliability	The amount of attention that needs to be given to minimizing failures and ensuring that any failures will not result in safety, economic, security, and/or environmental damage, achieved through actions such as formal validation and testing, fault tolerant design, and formal specifications.	1

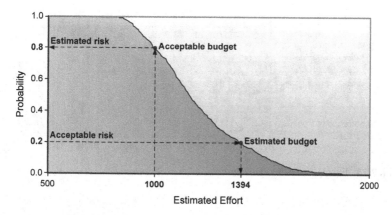

Fig. 7.12 Example: distribution of initial effort estimate

Next, the project manager applies CoBRA model upon the data to obtain project estimates. Figure 7.12 presents the distribution of the initially estimated project effort. An analysis of the distribution indicates high risk (*Probability = 0.80*) of exceeding the acceptable project budget.

Mitigating the risk would require that the project manager either increases the project budget or the project's performance by improving those project characteristics that contribute to increased project effort. In order to stay within the acceptable probability (0.2) of exceeding the project budget, the budget would have to be increased to 1,394 person-days, which is almost 40 % more than the acceptable 1,000 person-days. Since increasing the project budget is not acceptable, the project manager has to mitigate the risk by increasing the project's performance.

In order to increase project performance and decrease its effort, the project manager looks at those project characteristics that contribute the most to increased project effort. For this purpose, the project manager runs a sensitivity analysis upon the CoBRA estimates and checks which of the effort factors considered in CoBRA model contribute the most to the project's effort overhead.

Since increasing the project budget is not possible, the project manager needs to identify the most promising improvement potentials with respect to the factors contributing to increased project effort. For this purpose, the project manager runs a sensitivity analysis upon the project data in order to check which effort factors considered in the CoBRA model actually have the greatest negative impact on the project effort. Figure 7.13 illustrates the results of the sensitivity analysis.

The results of the sensitivity analysis clearly indicate the dominant role of the project team's capabilities for successful project performance. From among the

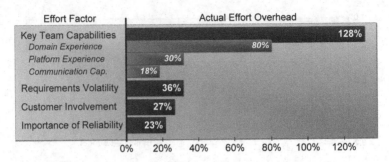

Fig. 7.13 Example: sensitivity analysis

considered detailed capabilities, domain experience and platform experience have the greatest impact on project effort. These factors are first candidates for improvement; not only because they have the greatest impact on effort but also because the next most influential factors ("*Requirements Volatility*" and "*Customer Involvement*") depend on the customer and thus are rather difficult to improve.

The project manager decides to address this high project risk by first improving the domain experience of the key members of the project team. He achieves this objective by involving the domain experts in the key positions in the project and by providing domain training to the remaining team members. With the help of these means, the domain experience of the team improves dramatically from the worst level (factor value $= 3$) to the best level (factor value $= 0$). After improving the team's domain experience, the risk of exceeding the project budget deceases to *Probability $= 0.42$*. Still, this is more than acceptable level of 0.2. Figure 7.14 illustrates this improvement.

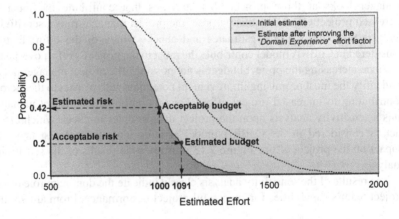

Fig. 7.14 Example: estimated effort after improving domain experience

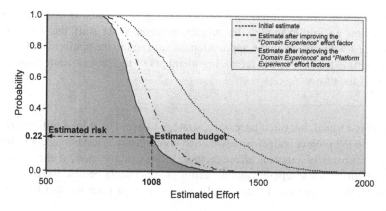

Fig. 7.15 Example: estimated effort after improving domain and platform experience

If the project manager wants to keep the acceptable risk threshold, the project budget would need to be increased to 1,091 units, which is about 10 % over the acceptable project budget of 1,000 person-days. This is still an unacceptable solution. Therefore, the project manager decides to increase the project's perfor-mance by improving another project aspect represented by an effort factor in the CoBRA model. The project manager notices that the domain experts who are involved in the project to improve the domain experience of the team also have high platform experience. The only thing needed to increase the entire team's platform experience to the best level is appropriate training for the remaining team members. The project manager decides to include training in the project preparation phases. This way the level of the *"Platform Experience"* effort factor improves from 1 to 0.

As a result of improving both the *"Domain Experience"* and *"Platform Experience"* effort factors in the project, the risk of exceeding the acceptable project budget of 100 person-hours drops to *Probability = 0.22* (Fig. 7.15). The actual risk level is just a little higher than the acceptable risk threshold of 0.2. In practice, the project could already be accepted. Although the project manager wants to meet the acceptable risk threshold by increasing the project budget, this would require increasing the budget by less than 1 % to 1,008 person-days. In practice, such an increase would probably also be acceptable.

Summarizing, it can be seen that the CoBRA method supports the project manager not only in identifying potential project risk but also helps him to reduce this risk by identifying the most important sources of risk and, related to that, the most promising means of risk mitigation. In practice, besides looking at the results of the sensitivity analysis, a project manager can simply play with the values of the effort factors he thinks he may improve and look at the outcomes of the estimation. In this trial and error way, the project manager can come up with a set of effort factor values that are necessary to meet the project's risk requirements. The discrepancy between expected and necessary factor values will then serve as a basis for the project planning and preparation activities. In our example, the project manager must staff the key project positions with experts in the application domain and in the platform and provide appropriate training to the remaining members of the project team prior to the start of the project.   ∎

Finally, a trivial, but often necessary, strategy to avoid or at least mitigate risk is to increase the project budget by a so-called contingency reserve to account for all negative impacts of relevant effort factors. In an extreme case, if the estimated project effort is not acceptable and the effort factors cannot be affected to decrease the effort, the project can be canceled, either before or after its start (preferably before).

Transfer Risk

Transferring risk refers to actions that aim at shifting some or all of the negative impact of a certain effort factor outside the project or the organization. In the context of CoBRA effort estimation, one possible action would be to shift responsibility for improving customer-specific factors to the customer. For example, if customer involvement in the project is a critical effort factor, the customer should bear the consequences of his insufficient involvement in terms of increased project effort. Another possibility of transferring risk is to outsource risky project activities to a third-party organization. For example, if quality of testing is a critical effort factor and if the organization does not have sufficient expertise in testing, the testing activity can be entrusted to an independent company (this approach is known as independent verification and validation, IV&V). In this case, the IV&V organization takes over the risk of the testing activity, including the risk of keeping within the testing budget.

Accept Risk

Accepting risk refers to a situation where none of the aforementioned three strategies can be used and accepting the risk "as is" is the only possibility left.

7.3   Project Scope Negotiation

Experiences we gained in industrial contexts indicate that customer involvement in software development is one of the factors that contribute significantly to overall development effort. Yet since software organizations typically have limited ability to affect this aspect, it is quite difficult to reduce the impact of this effort factor on project effort through internal improvement activities only. In practice, software project managers often face the situation where much of the project success depends on factors that are largely dependent on external parties. In this case, traditional risk mitigation and process improvement activities might not be effective because we have limited ability to influence the characteristics of an external entity involved in the project. At that point, we may consider two ways to prevent a project running into troubles:

- *Improvement of internal processes* (we discuss this aspect in Sect. 7.5). In this approach, we look for internal processes that may moderate the negative impact of the external party's characteristics on the project. In an effort model, this would be represented by interacting factors. Negative impact of insufficient customer involvement in the project may potentially be made less severe by improving the communication capabilities of the development team.
- *Negotiate project scope*. In this approach, we focus on those effort factors that refer to characteristics of external parties such as customers or external product/service providers. If one or more of these effort factors happen to be the source of large effort overhead, we can use this fact as an argument while negotiating the project conditions. For example, a software development company may require customer involvement in the project if finishing the project within the effort fixed by the customer largely depends on such involvement.

7.4 Project Benchmarking

The objective of project benchmarking in CoBRA is to compare software projects with respect to effort-related risks. In essence, in order to benchmark projects, we may use one of the risk analysis methods we presented for analyzing effort-driven project risks (Sect. 7.2). As a baseline for performing the benchmark, we take the risk thresholds we defined as percentiles upon the mean effort overhead of already completed successful projects. After setting up the thresholds, we can take one of the following benchmarking approaches:

1. Based on effort overhead thresholds: Comparing risk levels with respect to the mean effort overheads of benchmarked projects (Fig. 7.5).
2. Based on acceptable risk probability: Comparing risk levels with respect to the acceptable risk level assigned by an expert, for example, a quality engineer or project manager who is experienced in risk management (Fig. 7.7).
3. Based on acceptable risk exposure: Comparing risk levels with respect to risk exposure levels assigned by an expert (Fig. 7.8).

Figure 7.16 presents an example that illustrates the differences in the aforementioned three benchmarking strategies.

As we can see, depending on the risk assessment approach, projects may be assigned to different risk classes. Table 7.2 summarizes the classification of the three example projects with respect to the different risk assessment approaches.

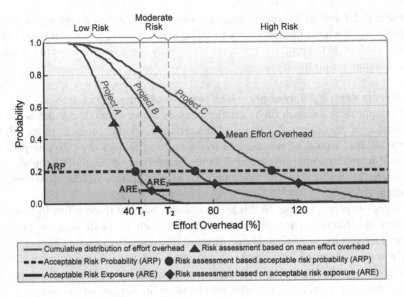

Fig. 7.16 Comparison of various benchmarking strategies

Table 7.2 Example benchmark with respect to project risk

Risk assessment approach	Risk class		
	Project A	Project B	Project C
Mean effort overhead	Low	Moderate	High
Acceptable risk probability	Low	High	High
Acceptable risk exposure	Moderate	High	High

7.5   Process and Productivity Improvement

In principle, the goal of CoBRA modeling is to identify the most relevant effort dependencies. In other words, we look for project characteristics and their interactions that have the greatest impact on software development productivity[5] and effort. Running a sensitivity analysis on the effort model quantified for a specific project allows identifying those effort factors that actually have the greatest impact on the productivity and effort of this very specific project. In the short-term perspective, this information can be used locally, within the project, to avoid or mitigate project risks. When collected over multiple projects, this information can, in the long-term perspective, be used to drive process improvement activities. In this approach, we first identify processes that are indicated by effort factors that

---

[5] In practice, CoBRA can also be applied to model the effort of service-oriented software projects. In contrast to product development (product-oriented) projects, we would then refer to service efficiency instead of development productivity.

contributed the most to effort overhead across multiple projects. Next, we improve these processes in order to avoid large effort overheads in future projects.

Example 7.2 Effort-Driven Software Process Improvement.

Let us consider the example CoBRA effort overhead model in Fig. 7.17 and synthesized the results of the sensitivity analysis over the multiple historical projects in Fig. 7.18. We can see, for example, that the *"Key Team Capabilities"* make a consistent, significant contribution to the project costs. The sensitivity analysis indicates that, on average, 125 % of the project overhead is spent on overcoming the insufficient capabilities of key members of the project team. In order to decrease this additional effort and improve development productivity, an improvement of the organization's processes related to team capabilities is required.

In order to focus improvement actions, a detailed analysis of which team member and which capabilities exactly contribute most is required. In our example, definition of the factor provides first indication of the improvement area. Three specific key capabilities are considered here, of which the *"Domain Experience"* and *"Platform Experience"* factors have the greatest impact on effort. Next, the roles and activities in which these two capabilities are affecting

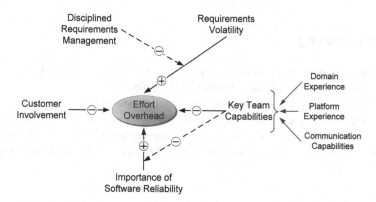

Fig. 7.17 Example CoBRA effort causal model

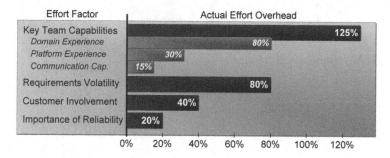

Fig. 7.18 Example results of a CoBRA sensitivity analysis

development productivity the most should be identified, and related processes should be analyzed for possible improvements.

The second most influential factor is *"Requirements Volatility."* Here, the project manager may look for processes that are a potential source of volatile requirements and undertake appropriate improvement steps. Knowing, for example, that requirements specification is performed in a chaotic manner, the process group may decide about introducing systematic requirements specification processes. At the project level, the project manager can pay extra attention to this process and request extra provisions in the contract that the client commit to this process.

The project manager may, however, have little or no direct control over the sources of volatile requirements to reduce related effort overhead. In such a case, the effort overhead model suggests another solution. The manager may focus on improving *"Disciplined Requirements Management,"* which alleviates the negative impact of volatile requirements on project effort. In principle, even though the effort model does not explicitly identify any useful factor interactions, the project manager can still identify indirect processes that moderate the negative impact of direct factors on project effort.   ∎

Further Reading

- *A Guide to the Project Management Body of Knowledge—PMBOK Guide*, 4th Edition. Project Management Institute, Inc., 2008.

  PMBOK presents synthesized best-practice knowledge regarding project management. In particular, Chap. 11 of PMBOK summarizes basic approaches for managing project risks. The presented approaches may be used as a starting point for creating guidelines for managing effort-driven risks identified using the CoBRA method.

Part III

Industrial Applications

Example is the school of mankind, and they will learn at no other.

Edmund Burke

The use of the CoBRA method is not limited to any particular software development environment. The method can, in principle, be applied in any software development context in which the minimal prerequisites of using the CoBRA method are fulfilled. The CoBRA model development and application processes can be adjusted to a certain extent depending on the capabilities of the specific software development organization in which CoBRA is applied.

In this part of the book, we present example applications of the CoBRA method in real-world industrial contexts. We illustrate the example implementations of the CoBRA method in the context of five organizations with different profiles, namely:

- Chapter 8 presents the application of the CoBRA method at *software design & management AG (sd&m)*, Germany.
- Chapter 9 presents the application of the CoBRA method at *Allette Systems Pty. Ltd*, Australia.
- Chapter 10 presents the application of the CoBRA method at *Oki Electric, Ltd*, Japan.
- Chapter 11 presents the application of the CoBRA method at *Siemens Information Systems, Ltd*, India.
- Chapter 12 presents the application of the CoBRA method at *Japan Manned Space Systems Corporation (JAMSS)*, Japan.

All chapters are structured in the same way and provide the following information: basis characteristics of estimation context, goals of effort estimation, context-specific adaptions of the CoBRA model development process, benefits and costs of applying the CoBRA method.

Please note that due to confidentiality reasons, some results of the CoBRA application are presented in an anonymized form or have been completely excluded.

Software Design and Management, Germany

8

This chapter summarizes the application of the CoBRA method in the context of *software design & management AG*, Germany (*sd&m*). In the sd&m case, we considered multiple indirect influences on project effort, which resulted in a relatively complex effort overhead model. In the subsequent industrial applications, we walked away from modeling multiple indirect influences on project effort. We observed that modeling complex indirect influences typically costs much effort and brings little benefit in terms of improved estimates.

The sd&m case is worth studying to learn an alternative implementation of the general CoBRA modeling process we present in this book. The reader can also learn potential issues of building a CoBRA model in practice and how to deal with such issues. Finally, one can analyze the use of the CoBRA method in the domain of management and information systems.

8.1   Context Characteristics

In 1997, the CoBRA method was applied in a midsize German software development company, *software design & management AG (sd&m)*, currently *Capgemini Deutschland Holding GmbH*.[1] Table 8.1 summarizes the basic characteristics of the context of sd&m in which we applied CoBRA. The technology transfer was led by two external CoBRA experts (analysts).

In the next two paragraphs, we take a closer look at two aspects of the sd&m context that were particularly important for using CoBRA, namely, the available measurement data and the domain experts.

---

[1] In 2011, sd&m AG changed its name to Capgemini Deutschland Holding GmbH.

A. Trendowicz, *Software Cost Estimation, Benchmarking, and Risk Assessment*,
The Fraunhofer IESE Series on Software and Systems Engineering,
DOI 10.1007/978-3-642-30764-5_8, © Springer-Verlag Berlin Heidelberg 2013

Table 8.1 sd&m: characteristics of the CoBRA application context

Context factor	Value
Organization	Software design and management AG, Germany
Maturity	Unknown (no formal certificate available)
Domain	Management information systems (MIS)
Development type	New development
Life cycle model	Waterfall
Programming language	C/C++

8.1.1 Measurement Data

Available project data included size and effort measurements collected for nine already completed projects. Size was measured in terms of non-commented lines of source code (LOC), excluding code produced by code generators. Project effort was measured in person-hours (PH). Figure 8.1 illustrates the distribution of actual development productivity across the initially considered projects. We normalized the productivity values because of confidentiality reasons.

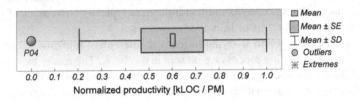

Fig. 8.1 sd&m: initial project measurement data

After validating the available project measurement data in more detail, the analysts excluded four projects from further study. The reasons were incomplete size and/or effort measurements and inconsistent project context. For instance, some of the projects were maintenance projects, for which a large part of the measured code had been generated automatically. Since it was difficult to determine what part of the measured software size corresponds to manually developed code and which to generated code, the analysts decided to exclude these projects from consideration. Other projects used a second programming language for which size measurements were missing. Therefore, it was decided to exclude these projects, too. At the end, only six historical projects were used as a basis for building and validating the CoBRA effort estimation model.

8.1.2 Domain Experts

Initially, 11 sd&m project managers, representing different levels of experience, were involved in the CoBRA application.

During the selection of the most relevant factors influencing software development effort, the analysts observed significant disagreement among the domain experts with respect to the relative importance of the considered effort factors. The ranks individual experts assigned to the same effort factors deviated from the central tendency—measured by means of the statistical median—proportionally to the experience of the involved experts. Therefore, the analysts decided to exclude from the study the four least experienced experts. The remaining seven domain experts provided the input for the CoBRA modeling.

8.2   Estimation Objectives

The general objective of the CoBRA application at the sd&m was to build an explicit context-specific model for reliably estimating the effort of future projects. In particular, the achievement of the following objectives was to be supported by the CoBRA method:

- *Project effort estimation*: Provide less experienced project managers with comprehensive support for making reliable and repeatable estimates.
- *Project control*: Provide project managers with comprehensive support for tracing projects against the estimates in order to detect potential deviations early and to identify the causes of observed deviations.
- *Project risk management*: Support project managers in assessing and reducing (mitigating) project risks at the start of a project.
- *Justifying and negotiating project costs*: Provide project managers with reliable information for justifying and negotiating planned software cost and its scope in terms of its functional and nonfunctional characteristics.
- *Productivity baselining and benchmark*: Provide project decision makers with a baseline development productivity and a reliable means for benchmarking projects with respect to development productivity, including support for identifying potential sources of productivity variance.
- *Reduction of software management overhead*: Relieve seasoned human experts (e.g., experienced project managers) of the burden of being involved too frequently in effort estimations.
- *Process improvement*: Support software process improvement. In the long perspective, factors identified as having a significant negative impact on development productivity across past projects should be used to focus improvement activities on appropriate development processes.

Moreover, introducing the CoBRA method was expected to launch the establishment of a goal-oriented measurement for the purpose of effort and productivity management. Collecting measurement data could then, in the future, be used to gain higher confidence in effort predictions since subjective data based on expert judgment was excluded. In particular, the following objectives ware defined:

- Identify the most relevant factors influencing development productivity and effort
- Provide precise, suitable, and unambiguous definitions for all factors identified
- Define measurement scales for the factors in order to collect past project data and quantify each factor's impact on productivity and effort
- Set up a measurement repository and collect project data

8.3   Model Development

Transferring the CoBRA method to the context of sd&m consisted of a pilot application of the method where an effort model was built and validated using the available project data. The general CoBRA process was adjusted to the specific characteristics of the application context summarized in Sect. 8.1. Figure 8.2 illustrates the major steps of the CoBRA modeling process used in the context of sd&m.

8.3.1   Step 1: Preparation and Planning

In the first step, the external analysts provided a detailed CoBRA method tutorial to the internal analysts, that is, the company representatives who were to be responsible for maintaining the CoBRA method and models within the whole organization. Next, the analysts determined the objectives of the study and characterized the context of the CoBRA application. The context referred to the part of the sd&m organization for which the CoBRA model was to be created and used for estimating software development projects. Finally, the analysts planned the individual activities of the CoBRA effort modeling. In addition, the analysts created a reference list of typical factors influencing software development effort. They based this list on the analysis of domain literature, such as the factors used in the COCOMO model (Boehm et al. 2000).

8.3.2   Step 2: Identifying and Defining Relevant Effort Factors

In this step, the first brainstorming group session with 11 sd&m domain experts took place. During the session, the domain experts reviewed the reference list of potential productivity factors and analyzed each factor to see whether they understood it consistently and whether it was relevant in the context of their organization, that is, within the specified scope of the CoBRA application. During the meeting, the domain experts could remove, modify (redefine), add, or decompose/join effort factors depending on whether they were deemed relevant, complete, and well defined. At the end of the brainstorming session, the analysts asked each domain expert to rank the factors—beginning from the most relevant one—they had defined within each category: product, process, project, and personnel.

After the brainstorming session, the analysts first analyzed the ranking results with respect to their consistency across multiple domain experts. For this purpose, they used two measures:

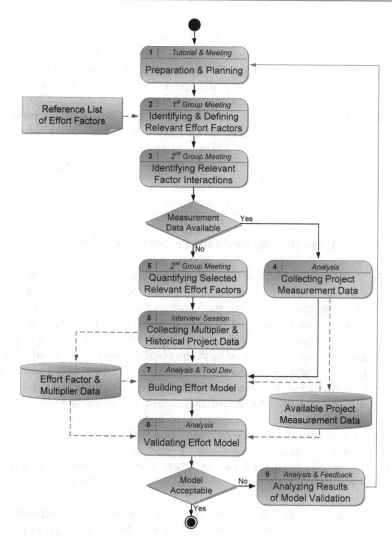

Fig. 8.2   sd&m: CoBRA model development procedure

- *Kendall's coefficient of concordance.* The analysts employed this measure for investigating the level of agreement among the rankings provided by all experts.
- *Ranking error.* The analysts computed ranking error as the deviation of an individual rank from the average rank across all experts. They used this measure to investigate whether the deviation of individual domain experts was related to their experience.

The investigation of the factor rankings showed significant agreement among the domain experts. Kendall's coefficient of concordance was equal to 0.38 and significant with an alpha level 0.1. At the same time, the analysts observed a significant negative correlation between the deviation of individual ranks and the experience of the domain experts. Spearman's correlation between expert's experience and ranking error was equal to -0.48 and significant with an alpha level of 0.1. This negative correlation indicated that as project management experience—and thus estimation experience—increases, ranking error decreases. Therefore, the analysts decided to remove the rankings of the least experienced experts and to revise the ranking statistics. They then observed increased ranking agreement in terms of Kendall's concordance, which went up to 0.54.

Finally, the analysts used the integrated ranking results to preselect the 12 highest-ranked effort factors.

8.3.3 Step 3: Identifying Relevant Factor Interactions

This step involved a second group meeting, which the analysts started by presenting the results of the ranking analysis to the domain experts. The subsequent group discussion revealed that some of the inconsistencies in factors' ranks were caused by an inconsistent understanding of the factors' definitions. The definitions of the factors were thus refined so that they were precisely formulated (using appropriate wording) and consistently understood by the involved domain experts. Finally, based on the results of the ranking and the group discussion, the experts decided about the final set of twelve factors and seven variables to be considered in the effort model.

Table 8.2 presents the final list of factors selected based upon the ranking provided by the most experienced experts. In addition, factors that represented complex (multidimensional) concepts were split into their component aspects, so-called variables. For example, the factor "*Team capabilities*" was split into the specific capabilities of particular team members, such as "*Familiarity with application domain*", "*Familiarity with application domain*", or "*Team communication skills.*"

Next, the analysts asked the domain experts to identify potential dependencies between selected effort factors and specify how each factor affects project effort. Potential impacts included:

- *Positive impact*: Increase of the effort factor's value contributes to increased development effort.
- *Negative impact*: Increase of the effort factor's value contributes to decreased development effort.

Based on the identified most relevant effort factors and their interactions, the analysts created an initial effort overhead model. Figure 8.3 illustrates the structure of the final causal dependencies between the identified factors.

Table 8.2 sd&m: the most relevant effort factors

Effort factor	Factor definition
Understanding and consistency of business objectives for the project and product	The extent to which the project and product objectives are clearly defined and the customer(s) and the project team are consistent in their understanding of these objectives, meaning there are no conflicts in their interpretation of the objectives.
Number of user departments involved	The number of different departments (business units) on the customer side that are involved in the development project.
Development schedule constraints	The extent to which a reasonable project schedule is compressed without changing any of the stated requirements.
Meeting reliability requirements	The amount of extra attention beyond what is stipulated in the organization's common practices that is necessary to meet the reliability requirements for the developed software system. The higher the reliability requirements, the more extra attention is needed to meet these requirements.
Key project team capabilities	The knowledge of key people on the project team about the application domain for the project, the process and documentation standards and common practices to be used on the project, the development platform and environment, and dealing with people.
• Knowledge of application domain	Familiarity with and comprehension of the application domain.
• Knowledge of application platform	Familiarity with and comprehension of the platform to be used, where platform refers to aspects such as programming languages, operating system, and database management systems.
• Knowledge of software system architecture	Familiarity with the type of system architecture used. Example architecture types include client–server and Internet Java applications.
• Knowledge of development environment	Familiarity with and comprehension of the software development environment. Example elements of the development environment include compiler, code generator, and CASE tools.
• Communication skills	The ability to communicate easily and clearly with the customer. This factor includes such aspects as interviewing skills or skills in other information gathering techniques, verbal communication skills, and ability to lead people.
• Knowledge of software development processes and techniques	The knowledge and experience of the software development process and techniques to be used during the project. Example processes and techniques include functional and/or object modeling techniques and cost/benefits analysis.
• Knowledge of documentation standards	The knowledge and experience of the documentation standards to be used during the project. Example knowledge includes modeling notations or structure and content of requirements documents.

(continued)

Table 8.2 (continued)

Effort factor	Factor definition
Meeting performance requirements	The amount of extra attention beyond what is stipulated in the organization's common practices that is necessary to meet the performance requirements for the developed software system. Software system performance includes such aspects as response time, execution time, and memory usage.
Meeting usability requirements	The amount of extra attention beyond what is stipulated in the organization's common practices that is necessary to meet the usability requirements for the developed software system. Usability is understood as the ease with which users can understand, learn, and operate the software.
Customer participation	The extent to which the users efficiently and promptly perform some of the development activities themselves, providing information, reviewing project documents, and taking part in acceptance testing.
Customer competence	The level of adequacy and the quality of the information provided by the customer during the project, for example, during interviews, when given questionnaires by the project staff, when presented with a "system walk-through," and/or when asked to provide feedback on a prototype.
Mixed project teams	The extent to which customers are actively involved in the project as members of a mixed project team.
Requirements volatility	The extent to which the agreed upon requirements are expected to change over time during the project.
Disciplined requirements management	The extent to which disciplined requirements management activities are performed in the project, that is, whether requirements are explicitly defined, tracked, and traced to design, code, and validation testing.

8.3.4 Step 4: Collecting Project Measurement Data

In this step, the analysts investigated the availability of project measurement data for the factors included in the effort overhead model. If such data were found, the analysts could adopt the scale defined by the corresponding measure for quantifying the associated effort factor and use the available historical project measurement data for building the effort model. Unfortunately, they could not find any historical project measurement data for the factors considered in the effort overhead model. In consequence, they had to define measures for all factors from scratch (Step 5) and collect project data for the considered historical projects using expert judgment (Step 6).

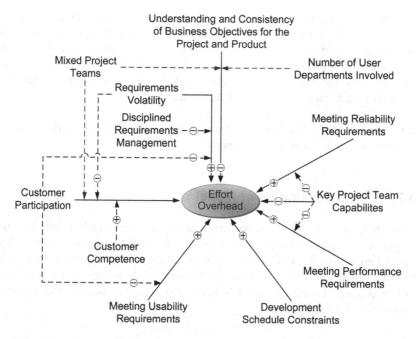

Fig. 8.3   sd&m: final causal effort model

8.3.5   Step 5: Quantifying Selected Relevant Effort Factors

In order to quantitatively measure all the factors, a measurable scale needed to be defined for each effort factor. This step did not typically concern factors for which measurement data were already available. Yet, in the context of sd&m, none of the factors considered in the causal effort model had been subject to measurement. Therefore, the analysts needed to define scales for all selected effort factors. They defined factor scales together with the domain experts at the end of the second group meeting. For the sake of simplicity, each factor was quantified using a 4-point approximately ratio scale. For each level, the analysts and the domain experts used the judgment of the involved experts to define an unambiguous specification in order to ensure consistency of the data collected later on (Step 6).

8.3.6   Step 6: Collecting Multiplier and Historical Project Data

Based on the final effort overhead model and the scales defined for the factors included in the model, the analysts collected the input data for building the CoBRA effort model:

- *Multiplier data*: The domain experts provided the effort overhead for each individual factor.

- *Project data*: The domain experts judged the value of each effort factor for six already completed projects considered in the study. Moreover, as software size and project effort data were not available, the analysts needed to collect them retroactively. Software size was collected by measuring the software code delivered by the considered projects. Project effort was acquired from the domain experts together with effort factor data.

The analysts collected both effort multiplier and effort factor data during interviews with individual domain experts.

8.3.7   Step 7: Building Effort Model

In this step, the analysts combined the quantified effort overhead model, the multiplier data, and the past project data within a CoBRA simulation tool. Using the tool, they computed nominal productivities across historical projects as a basis for estimating new projects. Because the nominal productivities obtained for the historical projects still varied, the analysts decided to use the median value as input for estimating future projects.

8.3.8   Step 8: Validating Effort Model

In the final step, the analysts validated the effort model by applying it to the data from successful past sd&m projects. They used the model for each past project in order to estimate its effort. The obtained distribution of the estimated effort was compared to the project's actual effort value. The model provided estimates with an average estimation error of less than 10 %.

8.3.9   Step 9: Analyzing Results of Model Validation

sd&m was satisfied with the predictive performance of the CoBRA effort model when applied to the six already completed projects. Therefore, there was no need for detailed analysis of the model validation results and for additional iterations to refine the model.

8.4   Benefits and Costs

The major output of the pilot application of the CoBRA method was an estimation model for predicting future development projects. Its application on the data from already completed projects provided valuable information for the purpose of managing development productivity and effort. The average nominal productivity computed across historical projects was proposed as an initial baseline for controlling the productivity of future development projects.

As an additional result from the investigations general, process improvements with respect to effort reduction—and productivity improvement—were suggested. The results from the risk analysis of the available past projects indicated some factors[2] that made a substantial contribution to total effort overhead. For instance, the sensitivity analysis showed that "requirements were not well understood by all parties (developers and customers) at the beginning of the project." In terms of the example sd&m project, low understandability of the requirements led to a 22 % effort overhead and, consequently, approximately five additional man-months in terms of project duration. The outputs of the risk analysis formed the basis for increasing development productivity through improved management of the factors identified as having the most significant negative impact.

Summarizing, the pilot application of the CoBRA method has shown its significant contribution to the achievement of the organization's objectives. Already during the validation of the pilot effort model, CoBRA provided the following benefits:

- *Project effort estimation*: The application of the CoBRA method provided a reliable basis for accurate software effort estimation.
- *Project control*: Project managers, especially those with relatively little experience, gained comprehensive support for planning and tracing projects against the plan.
- *Project risk management*: The transparent, context-specific effort overhead model provided information on the most critical threats to project success. Information on factors having the largest impact on productivity and effort allowed for reducing project risks early in the development process and, in the long-term perspective, focused improvement activities on appropriate process areas.
- *Justifying and negotiating project costs*: Explicit information on customer-dependent factors influencing development effort formed the basis for negotiating with the customer about the planned software cost and scope.
- *Productivity baselining and benchmark*: CoBRA provided the project managers with a reliable basis for benchmarking projects with respect to development productivity. In particular, the unified measure of nominal productivity and project-specific effort overhead measures allowed for meaningful comparisons between different projects.
- *Reduction of software management overhead*: The project managers obtained an effort model that is easy to use for estimating multiple projects. This allowed for reducing estimation overhead compared to tedious estimation based on expert judgment.

---

[2] Due to confidentiality reasons, we are not allowed to name all these factors.

Table 8.3 sd&m: approximate costs of introducing the CoBRA method

Cost aspect	Cost
Involved personnel	14 persons: • 2 external analysts • 1 internal analyst • 11 domain experts
Total duration	8 months
Effort per sd&m team member	16 person-hours
Total effort	3 person-months

- *Process improvement*: The identified deficiencies of defined size and effort metrics allowed for improving the corresponding measurement processes. Moreover, effort factors that showed to have a significant impact on development productivity and effort over multiple projects indicated processes that should be included in long-term process improvement initiatives.

Table 8.3 summarizes the approximate costs of developing the CoBRA model at sd&m. Note that the future cost of the initial model's application and maintenance would only be a fraction of the cost needed for developing the initial model. The two factors that contributed to the relatively high costs of building an initial CoBRA model were (1) learning the CoBRA method and (2) building a completely new model from scratch.

Further Reading

- L. C. Briand, K. El Emam, and F. Bomarius, "COBRA: a hybrid method for software cost estimation, benchmarking, and risk assessment," in *Proceedings of the 20th International Conference on Software Engineering*, pp. 390–399. 1998.

  This conference paper briefly describes the very first version of the CoBRA method and reports on its application at sd&m. The reader might be interested in additional details of the sd&m case, including how particular modeling and validation activities were implemented, and in the experiences gained. Yet, the technical details about the CoBRA method presented in this paper should not be considered because the method presented in the paper differs from its improved version specified in this book.

Allette Systems, Australia

9

This chapter summarizes the CoBRA application in the context of Allette Systems Pty. Ltd., Australia (Allette). In the context of Allette, we developed a very simple effort model. Based on the experiences from the previous applications and the small size of the Allette company, we aimed at building a simple effort model. In particular, we avoided modeling indirect influences on effort.

The Allette case is worth studying in order to learn an alternative implementation of the general CoBRA modeling process presented in this book. The reader can also learn potential issues of building a CoBRA model in practice and how to deal with such issues. Finally, one can analyze the use of the CoBRA method in the domain of web applications.

9.1 Context Characteristics

In 2002, the CoBRA method was applied in a small (~20 employees) Australian software company, Allette Systems Pty. Ltd. Table 9.1 summarizes the basic characteristics of the context of Allette in which CoBRA was applied. The technology transfer was led by two external CoBRA experts (analysts).

Table 9.1 Allette: characteristics of the CoBRA application context

Context factor	Value
Organization	Allette Systems Pty. Ltd., Australia
Maturity	Unknown (no certificate available)
Domain	Web applications (i.e., web application, web service, and web interface projects)
Development type	New development, redevelopment, enhancement
Life cycle model	Not specified
Programming language	Java

A. Trendowicz, *Software Cost Estimation, Benchmarking, and Risk Assessment*,
The Fraunhofer IESE Series on Software and Systems Engineering,
DOI 10.1007/978-3-642-30764-5_9, © Springer-Verlag Berlin Heidelberg 2013

In the next two paragraphs, we take a closer look at two aspects of the Allette context that were particularly important for using CoBRA, namely, the available measurement data and the domain experts.

9.1.1   Measurement Data

Available measurement data was collected from 14 projects completed between 1998 and 2002. All considered projects were web application projects and were similar with respect to functionality, target platform, and complexity. They encompassed financial/trading, business-to-business, and intranet applications. They included new development, redevelopment, and enhancement projects. There were no size data available at the time of the CoBRA application. Project effort, measured in terms of person-hours (PH), had been collected at Allette for all projects on a daily basis and stored in a time-tracking repository. Yet, Allette had not collected software size data across their projects.

Initially, 119 already completed web projects were identified. The number of considered projects was reduced after Allette limited the scope of the CoBRA estimation to a particular type, namely, web application, web interface, and web service. Table 9.2 provides a definition of these application types taken from Ruhe (2001).

Table 9.2 Allette: application types considered in the study

Application type	Definition
Web application	A web-based application provides full user functionality of a software application and broad and remote access through a web browser. They are implemented by HTML-based forms, embedded scripts, and dynamically generated HTML pages for entry and display of data and servers for performing the application's processing. The web is used as a standard interface in which to wrap an independent application (JAVA applet).
Web interface	Web interfaces to existing applications extending existing applications through the addition of a web interface. They provide remote and broad access to an existing application with the same or similar functionality. Web interfaces are usually implemented using HTML-based forms, embedded scripts, and dynamically generated HTML pages that communicate with the existing application.
Web service	Web services provide intelligent web-based interapplication communication that is independent of both the programming language and the protocol. Web service components can be recombined by other companies to meet the needs of their own software applications or business processes.

For these application areas, 14 already completed projects were identified. For these projects, the Web Objects size measure was defined to collect software size data. Two projects were excluded from further consideration because documentation required to measure Web Objects was not available. At the end, 12 already completed projects were used to develop the CoBRA effort estimation model. Nine

Table 9.3 Allette: characteristics of the available measurement data

Measure	Min	Max	Mean	Std. dev.
Effort [person-hours]	267	2,504	883	710
Size [Web objects]	67	792	284	227
Max team size [persons]	2	6	3	1.5

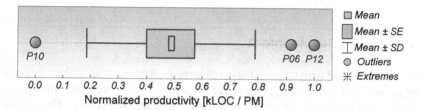

Fig. 9.1 Allette: initial project measurement data

projects were new developments, one was an enhancement, and two were redevelopment projects. Table 9.3 provides the basic statistics for the final 12 projects considered in the Allette context.

Figure 9.1 illustrates the distribution of the actual development productivity across the initially considered projects. We normalized the productivity values because of confidentiality reasons.

9.1.2 Domain Experts

At Allette Systems, only five project managers were available who had working experience in the area of web development. Their experience in this area ranged from 2 years to several years.

9.2 Estimation Objectives

The general objective of the CoBRA application at Allette was to move from ad hoc subjective estimates based on human judgment in favor of systematic method based on quantitative project data. In particular, the achievement of the following objectives was to be supported by the CoBRA method:

- *Project planning*: Provide less experienced project managers with a systematic, context-specific method for estimating development effort at the beginning of a new project.
- *Change management*: Provide project managers with efficient support for replanning a software project in case of change in the project scope (at Allette, tasks often needed to be added later on in the project, which resulted in overruns of the initial project budget).

- *Project risk management and process improvement*: Provide project managers with comprehensive support for investigating the potential sources of a project's deviations from the estimates for the purpose of project risk management (short-term perspective) and process improvement (long-term perspective).
- *Reduction of project management overhead*: Provide project managers with an estimation method that is neither complex nor requires too much project time while being applied.

9.3   Model Development

Similar to other industrial cases, transferring the CoBRA method in the context of Allette consisted of a pilot application of the method where the effort model was built and validated using the available context-specific project data. The general CoBRA process was adjusted to the specific characteristics of the application context summarized in Sect. 9.1. Figure 9.2 illustrates the major steps of the CoBRA modeling process used in the context of Allette. In the next paragraphs, we briefly describe the content of each step.

9.3.1   Step 1: Preparation and Planning

The transfer of the CoBRA method to Allette Systems began with the study setup phase. In that phase, the CoBRA method was first presented in detail to company representatives who, in the future, will be responsible for transferring the knowledge within the whole organization.

Next, the availability of the resources required for the pilot application of the CoBRA method was clarified with representatives of Allette. This included identification of the quantity and type of the measurement data collected from already completed projects (so-called historical data), which could be used as input for building the initial effort model. During the initial analysis of existing historical project data, very small projects for which project effort was less than 50 person-hours were excluded because they are easy to manage and estimate. One hundred nineteen projects remained for which effort was greater than 50 PH. Moreover, the availability of the domain experts who could provide input for effort modeling wherever measurement data were missing was identified. Multiple experts are typically required because they can provide the most valuable—that is, reliable and consistent—input for effort modeling. In the Allette context, five project managers who were experienced in the selected context were supposed to participate. Their experience in the area of web development ranged from 2 to several years.

Next, the detailed scope of the CoBRA pilot application was specified. For that purpose, the initially filtered 119 historical projects were now analyzed with respect to their exact type using a questionnaire designed together with the involved Allette project managers. Example project characteristics considered included web-based

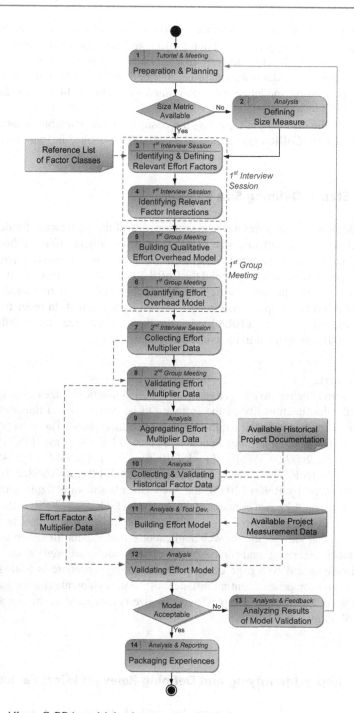

Fig. 9.2 Allette: CoBRA model development procedure

application, web interface, web service, static website, dynamic website, integration project, design project, conversion project, and database management. Those characteristics were then used to perform a brief interview session where the project managers selected similar historical projects. Based on the results of the survey, the scope of pilot effort modeling was determined—it included 14 web application, web service, and web interface projects.

Based on the information regarding the context and the available resources, an initial plan for the CoBRA pilot application (activities and schedule) was developed.

9.3.2   Step 2: Defining Size Measure

The CoBRA method requires a size measure as one of the main inputs for developing an effort model; software size is a key driver of project effort. Although no specific size metric is required, it needs to be consistently measured across the historical projects considered to build the CoBRA effort model. Since in the context of Allette, no specific size metric had been either defined or measured across historical projects, an appropriate metric needed to be defined. In order to assure early applicability of the CoBRA model, the *Web Objects* size metric defined by Reifer (2000) was adapted to the context of Allette.

Web Objects
Web Objects belong to a larger group of so-called functional size metrics that quantify the functionality of the software to be delivered and thus can be applied already during the requirements specification phase. The most popular functional metrics are Function Points (FP), such as IFPUG FP (ISO20926, 2009), COSMIC FP (ISO19761, 2003), NESMA FP (24570, 2005), FiSMA FP (ISO29881, 2008), and MARK II FP (ISO20968, 2002).

Introduced by Reifer (2000), the Web Objects software sizing method extends the well-known Function Point Analysis (ISO-20926 2009) in that, in addition to the five elements already considered in FPA, it counts four elements that are specific for web applications: multimedia files, web building blocks, scripts, and links. Web Objects are measured upon user requirements and web page designs. The counting procedure is analogical to FPA and comprises counting instances of the nine elements and weighting them according to their complexity. Total size is computed as the weighted sum of all individual counts.

9.3.3   Step 3: Identifying and Defining Relevant Effort Factors

Since there was hardly any reference list available that provided typical factors influencing software development productivity and effort in the context of web development, the factors needed to be elicited from scratch through personal interviews with five of the involved domain experts. As input, the experts received high-level definitions of predefined factor classes they should consider while determining particular factors. These classes included product-, personnel-, project-, and process-related factors. The domain experts were provided with detailed definitions of the factor groups by e-mail 3 days before the factor identification interview session in order to have enough time for preparation.

During the interviews, the purpose of the interview was first explained to the experts. Next, the experts were asked open questions to identify and describe context-specific factors influencing development productivity and effort for each of the four predefined factor groups. In order to avoid bias in the answers given by the experts, we did not provide them with any reference list of effort factors. Instead, we asked the experts to report factors based on their individual knowledge and experience.

Each interview was performed by two CoBRA experts (analysts), one interviewing a domain expert and one carefully recording the interview outputs. The interviews took between 25 and 50 min. One interview took 50 min because the interviewee had not prepared beforehand. The remaining interviews took between 25 and 35 min. As a result, the analysts identified 35 potential effort factors that were specific to web development at Allette.

At the end of the group meeting, the analysts asked each domain expert to rank the factors initially identified. In particular, they asked the experts to rank the factors within each of the four factor groups independently, beginning from the most relevant factor.

After that, the analysts analyzed the ranking results with respect to their consistency—that is, the agreement between the ranks provided by the individual experts—and integrated them in order to select a subset of the most relevant productivity factors.

9.3.4 Step 4: Identifying Relevant Factor Interactions

Already during the first interview session, the analysts asked the domain experts to initially identify the most relevant dependencies between the effort factors they had identified so far. These dependencies were going to be the input for discussing the final effort overhead model during the subsequent group meeting (Step 5).

9.3.5 Step 5/6: Building Qualitative Effort Overhead Model & Quantifying the Model

At Allette, building the qualitative effort overhead model and quantifying the model (Steps 5 and 6) were actually performed during one group meeting. The reason for merging the two steps was that no factor interactions were modeled. As a consequence, it was rather easy to build a qualitative causal effort model and quantify it during a single group meeting.

In general, modeling interactions among effort factors—that is, indirect influences on effort—increases the complexity of the model and requires ensuring a common understanding among the experts regarding such interaction. Therefore, we recommend considering only the most relevant interactions that are expected to contribute to significant improvement of the model's performance.[1]

In the Allette case, the analysts documented and analyzed the dependencies between the effort factors identified by the experts during the factor identification interviews. In particular, they were interested in how to avoid modeling indirect influences in the effort overhead model. Ultimately, the analysts needed to resolve three factor dependencies that were reported by more than two domain experts:

- *"Novelty of Requirements"* ↔ *"Novelty of Technology"*: In the discussion with the experts, it was found that the dependency was caused by the misinterpretation of the factor definitions. A clear distinction between new functional requirements and new requirements in terms of technological novelty needed to be made.
- *"Quality Project Management"* ↔ *"Team Communication Skills"*: Communication skills have a positive influence on project management in the sense that good communication skills facilitate project management. Therefore, the definition of the "Communications Skills" factor was limited to the developers only, instead of the whole project team.
- *"Customer Participation"* ↔ *"Requirements Volatility"*: The domain experts considered the degree of customer participation during the project as having an influence on requirements volatility. In order to make the two factors orthogonal to each other, the definition of *"Customer Participation"* was changed to *"Customer Input and Motivation,"* which focuses especially on the participation of the customer at the beginning of the project. *"Requirements volatility,"* on the other hand, is a factor that becomes important later on in the project.

In order to achieve maximum independence between the effort factors, the identified dependencies were removed by adjusting the appropriate factor definitions.

During the group meeting, the analysts first presented the results of the ranking aggregation and the changes in the factor definitions to the experts, who then discussed the proposed changes. Finally, the experts accepted the nine independent factors suggested by the analysts. Table 9.4 list the factors accepted for inclusion in the effort overhead model.

Figure 9.3 presents the qualitative causal effort model, which was constructed based upon the assumption that the nine selected factors have only direct impact on effort.

---

[1] The experiences we gained across several applications of the CoBRA method indicate that the additional effort required for modeling all factor interactions proposed by the domain experts typically does not pay off with any significant improvement in the predictive performance of the CoBRA effort model.

Table 9.4 Allette: the most relevant factor influencing development productivity

Effort factor	Factor definition
Novelty of requirements	The extent of new functionality required for the current project compared to past well-known projects, ranging from novel project of a type never attempted before to conversion or functional repetition of a well-known software product.
Novelty of technology	The extent of new technology and tools required for use in the current project, for example, new databases, languages, and "strategic technologies" such as XML and JAVA.
Requirements volatility	The extent to which requirements are expected to change over time, to be unclear, incomplete, or inconsistent. Requirements may be internal or external.
Customer input and motivation	The extent to which the customer is willing to cooperate and his understanding of the project as well as his motivation to provide input for the project in terms of clear requirements. For example, the customer may provide ideas about the web design or the functionality provided by the web application.
Quality of specification and documentation methods	The extent to which documentation is facilitated and the specification is clear for all the developers and kept up-to-date.
Team communication skills	The communication capabilities of the project team members. Capability is meant to be the ability to communicate properly, efficiently, and sufficiently within the team, as well as the ability to adequately communicate with the customer on the phone, via e-mail, or personally.
Developers' technical capabilities	The analysis, design, and programming capabilities of the developers. Capability is meant to be the general ability to work efficiently and thoroughly. For example, efficient and thorough work excludes such work approaches as experimenting.
Quality of project management	The extent of efficiently managing resources, tasks, milestones, and project delivery dates, and the level of quality in organizing the project, including the extent of agreement on project goals, methods, schedules, or the clarity of project team roles and responsibilities.
Importance of software maintenance	The extent to which code is required to be easily maintainable from a developer's as well as a customer's point of view. The code needs to be easy to understand, modify, extend, and maintain by the customer. From the developer's or Allette's point of view, it is the extent to which code will be reused for developing software in the current or future projects.

9.3.6 Step 7: Collecting Effort Multiplier Data

Based on the specified effort overhead model and the scales defined for the considered factors, effort multiplier data were collected during individual interviews with the domain experts. The interviews were performed by two analysts, one who interviewed a domain expert and one who observed the interview and documented the interview outcomes. At the beginning of each interview,

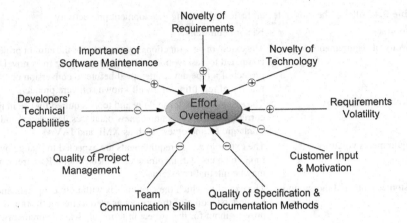

Fig. 9.3 Allette: final causal effort model

the interviewing analyst introduced to the interviewed expert the concepts of an effort overhead model and of an effort multiplier. Afterwards, each expert was asked to estimate the minimal, maximal, and most likely values of the effort multipliers for each considered factor given its worst case—that is, the case when it has the largest negative impact on effort. The duration of the interviews varied between 30 and 90 min.

9.3.7 Step 8: Validating Effort Multiplier Data

Unlike in the sd&m case discussed in Sect. 8.3, in the Allette case no systematic outlier analysis was performed to exclude exceptional effort multiplier data. Instead, the analysts computed simple standard deviations on the minimal, maximal, and most likely effort overheads provided by the experts to assess the magnitude of the experts' disagreement and to identify boundary values of effort overhead. The results of the analysis were then presented to the experts and discussed in a group meeting. During the meeting, the domain experts presented the collected multipliers and discussed inconsistencies between individual estimates. The analysts started the meeting with an explanation of the idea of an effort multiplier. Next, for each factor, the analysts gave its definition and the specification of its worst case. The factors for which the estimated multipliers were characterized by the largest inconsistency (in terms of statistical variance) were discussed first because they seemed to be most difficult to estimate. A person whose multipliers were most different from the others was chosen to start the discussion. The expert provided his understanding of the factor and justified the multiplier values he had estimated.

The group meeting lasted for 2 h and was perceived by both the analysts and the domain experts as a very valuable step of the CoBRA model development.

9.3.8 Step 9: Aggregating Effort Multiplier Data

In the CoBRA method, effort multipliers provided for a single factor by multiple domain experts are typically aggregated by means of simulation. For each factor, multiplier data provided by a randomly selected expert is used in a single simulation run. Throughout multiple simulation runs, each expert has the same probability of being sampled. In the Allette case, a median measure of central tendency was employed instead.[2] For each factor, the effort multiplier data was computed as the median across the values provided by multiple experts. In principle, weights could have been further used while computing the median in order to take into account the different degrees of experience of the experts. However, this was not necessary in the Allette case because the experts were characterized by very similar experience.

9.3.9 Step 10: Collecting and Validating Historical Project Data

In this phase, 14 already completed web projects were considered for collecting project data upon which to base the CoBRA model. The actual project data were collected for 12 projects. The project data encompassed software size, project effort, and the effort factors included in the CoBRA effort overhead model.

Before the start of the data collection process, the projects were scanned for available documents and files that could potentially support the acquisition of the required project data. For two projects, neither documents about the developed software application nor the delivered software product itself was available. Moreover, the personal memory of neither the project managers nor the developers was sufficient to provide reliable project data. Therefore, the two projects were excluded from further consideration. Of the remaining projects, nine were new development, two were redevelopment, and one was an enhancement one.

The past project data on the effort factors were provided by the project manager of each of the considered projects. In case of uncertainty regarding an effort factor, the project manager could give two answers that seemed most likely. Later on, the average of these two answers was used as the final value.

For the purpose of collecting the effort data, the timesheet system of Allette was used to determine the actual effort spent in each project. In order to ensure the validity and completeness of the data, one of the analysts (CoBRA experts) was involved throughout the whole data collection process. The size of the software produced in the considered projects was measured by the analyst alone.

Figure 9.4 illustrates the size and effort data[3] for the 12 projects considered for creating CoBRA effort estimation model.

---

[2] The median is more robust against data outliers than simple measures, such as the mean (average).

[3] For confidentiality reasons, we do not specify exact values on the size and effort axes in the figure.

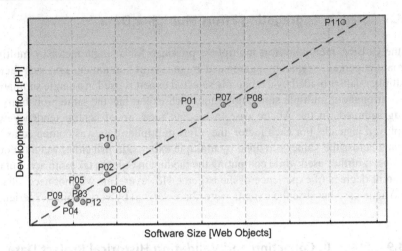

Fig. 9.4 Allette: software size and effort data

A few interesting observations were made by looking at the project size and effort data:

- Most of the considered projects are relatively small in terms of Web Objects. Three projects (P01, P07, and P08) are large ones and one (P11) is extremely large (an outlier).
- Three projects of almost the same size (P02, P06, and P10) are characterized by almost the same development effort.
- Three projects of different size (P01, P07, and P08) are characterized by almost the same development effort.

In practice, we would expect that the CoBRA effort overhead model will explain the causes of the observed productivity variances and that the effort overhead model delivered for each project will account for the project's productivity deviation caused by its particular characteristics.

9.3.10 Step 11: Building Effort Model

In this step, the quantified causal effort model, the multiplier data, and the past project data were integrated using simulation in order to obtain a final effort model. In the Allette case, unlike typical cases, software size was modeled as an uncertain variable represented by a triangular distribution. This decision was made because (1) Web Object counting is a subjective way of measuring software size, (2) the CoBRA expert who counted the Web Objects at Allette had no counting experience, and (3) the applied Web Objects metric was tailored to the Allette context and, as such, had not been empirically validated before. For this reason, an uncertainty level of 5 % was used. The most likely value of size was the actual counted number of Web Objects, where the minimum and the maximum values of the size were calculated as 95 % and 105 % of the actual counted number values, respectively.

9.3.11 Step 12: Validating Effort Model

In the final step, the analysts validated the effort model by applying it to the data from the 12 already completed web development projects. The model was run for each past project, and the obtained distribution of the estimated effort was compared to the project's actual effort.

There was no need for improving the model because the initial model already provided acceptable estimates; that is, estimation error did not exceed 20 %.

9.3.12 Step 13: Analyzing Results of Model Validation

The analysis of the estimated project effort revealed several projects for which prediction error exceeded 25 %. A closer look at those projects revealed that they differed from the main body of the projects considered in the following terms:

- *Old project (29 % overestimation)*: The project was actually the oldest one considered (finished in 1998). Due to the lack of project documentation, the collected data was based solely on the project manager's memory. Moreover, the developed application had been enhanced and redeveloped since its first version. In addition, it was not possible to identify which parts of the current version of the application had been developed in the initial project because the initial web application was not accessible anymore.
- *Borderline project (35 % underestimation)*: The project was by definition a borderline one because it was actually a software application with only a small web interface. Although it fulfilled both the definition of a traditional software application and the definition of a web application, it was decided to consider it because it was compliant with the defined context characteristics. Moreover, the technologies used in the development process of this project were different than those used for the other 11 projects.
- *Enhancement project (32 % overestimation)*: The project differed from the remaining 11 projects in that it was the only enhancement project.

Despite these outcomes of the analysis, no formal model improvement iteration was performed. The analysts and the domain experts decided to simply exclude from the model two of the outlying projects, namely, the borderline and the enhancement project. This resulted in a reduced estimation error of 14 %.

9.3.13 Step 14: Packaging Experiences

In the final phase, the analysts documented the experiences from the CoBRA model development and identified the model's weaknesses in order to guide its future improvements and to support the development of new CoBRA models in other contexts within Allette, for example, for other application types.

9.4   Benefits and Costs

The pilot application of the CoBRA method showed its significant contribution to the achievement of the estimation objectives specified by Allette. In particular, the following benefits were achieved:

- *Improved estimation accuracy*: Compared to the subjective estimation based on human judgment applied before (37 % error), the application of the CoBRA method reduced estimation error by about half (14 %).
- *Support for change and process improvement*: The method supported the management of project changes since it was easy to apply throughout the whole software development lifecycle, starting at early stages such as requirements specification. The method supported the investigation of context-specific sources of effort and productivity deviations by providing a transparent and intuitive model of causal dependencies between the most relevant factors influencing development productivity and effort. For example, it was observed that for three projects that delivered software of almost the same size but required significantly different amount of effort (projects P02, P06, and P10 in Fig. 9.4), *"Requirements Volatility"* and *"Quality of Project Management"* were identified as the most relevant factors influencing effort. On the other hand, three other projects required similar effort, but the software they delivered differs significantly with respect to size (projects P01, P06, and P08 in Fig. 9.4). In this case, the most relevant factors influencing effort were again *"Requirements Volatility,"* *"Quality of Project Management,"* as well as *"Novelty of Requirements"* and *"Novelty of Technology."*
- *Support for knowledge management*: The method supported the organization's knowledge management by providing means for explicit modeling (in the form of a quantitative causal model) expert knowledge for future reuse.
- *Reduced cost of project planning*: The method reduced the cost of project planning and management. On the one hand, it delivered a comprehensible, reliable effort estimation model based on the combination of human expertise and measurement data. On the other hand, it provided a reusable effort estimation model and relieved the domain experts of expensive judgment-based estimation, which needed to be repeated each time project estimates were required.
- *Building up measurement practices*: In addition, the process of early size measurement was initiated by introducing the Web Objects metric. The original metric defined by Reifer (2000) was adjusted to the context of Allette, and a counting manual was developed (including detailed instructions and counting examples).

Table 9.5 Allette: approximate costs of introducing the CoBRA method

Cost aspect	Cost
Involved personnel	8 persons: • 2 external analysts • 1 internal analyst • 5 domain experts
Total duration	6 months: • Setup phase (preparation, context characterization, identification of relevant effort factors, definition of required metrics, etc.): 8 weeks • Development of causal effort model: 2 weeks • Data collection and preparation: 9.5 weeks • Effort model development and validation: 5 weeks
Total effort	2.7 person-months

After the completion of the study, a survey on the acceptance[4] of the CoBRA method was performed among the involved Allette domain experts. The survey results showed the high appropriateness of CoBRA in the context of Allette. The method was perceived as highly useful (81 %) and easy to use (86 %). Moreover, the experts predicted a high level of usage for the method in the future (91 %).

Achieving these long-term benefits required certain initial investments at Allette, mainly to learn the CoBRA method and to develop the CoBRA effort model. Table 9.5 summarizes the costs of the pilot application of the CoBRA model and of the building of the initial effort model.

Further Reading

• M. Ruhe, R. Jeffery, and I. Wieczorek, "Cost estimation for web applications," in *Proceedings of the 25th International Conference on Software Engineering*, 3–10 May 2003, pp. 285–294

  This conference paper provides a brief overview of the CoBRA application at Allette Systems. In addition to what we presented in this book, the paper presents the results of the multiplier analysis (Step 8). Moreover, the authors compare the predictive power of the CoBRA method to two alternative approaches: expert judgment and simple statistical regression.

• M. Ruhe, R. Jeffery, and I. Wieczorek, "Using Web Objects for Estimating Software Development Effort for Web Applications," in *Proceedings of the 9th International Symposium on Software Metrics*, 2003, pp. 30–37

  This conference paper investigates the use of alternative software sizing methods for the purpose of project effort estimation in the context of Allette

---

[4] The survey was performed using the Technology Acceptance Method (TAM) defined by Davis (1989).

Systems. The authors compare the predictive performance of ordinary least squares regression when applied with two alternative software sizing methods, Web Objects and Function Points, to estimation based on expert judgment.

- M. Ruhe, *The Accurate and Early Effort Estimation of Web Applications*, Master Thesis, University of Kaiserslautern, Kaiserslautern, Germany, August 2002. Supervisors: I. Wieczorek, D. Rombach, and R. Jeffery.

  This master thesis documents the detailed process of the application of CoBRA at Allette Systems. For each model development step, the author provides an in-depth insight into the analyses she performed and the results she obtained. Moreover, the appendices list the tools used for developing the CoBRA model and the outcomes of the individual modeling steps.

Oki Electric, Japan

10

This chapter summarizes the CoBRA application in the context of Oki Electric Industry, Ltd., Japan (Oki). In this chapter, we will show how to adapt the baseline CoBRA model development process to the needs and constraints of a particular organization in the management and information systems domain. Moreover, we report on experience regarding the development of the CoBRA model throughout multiple refinement iterations. In particular, we show how to analyze the performance of the CoBRA model, where to look for potential causes of observed deficits of the model and how to appropriately improve the model.

10.1 Context Characteristics

In 2005/2006, the CoBRA method was applied in the context of the medium-size software development branch of Oki Electric Industry Co. Ltd., Japan (Oki), an international provider of software systems. Table 10.1 summarizes the detailed characteristics of the case study context. The technology transfer was led by two external CoBRA experts (analysts) supported by an Oki analyst who was supposed to learn the CoBRA method.

Table 10.1 Oki: characteristics of the CoBRA application context

Context factor	Value
Organization	Oki Electric Industry Co. Ltd., Japan
Maturity	ISO 9000
Domain	Management information systems
Development type	New development, enhancement
Life cycle model	Waterfall
Programming language	Java, C++

A. Trendowicz, *Software Cost Estimation, Benchmarking, and Risk Assessment*,
The Fraunhofer IESE Series on Software and Systems Engineering,
DOI 10.1007/978-3-642-30764-5_10, © Springer-Verlag Berlin Heidelberg 2013

10.1.1 Measurement Data

For the purpose of size measurement, we adapted the lines of code (LOC) size metric already defined at Oki as the number of newly developed lines of code excluding comments. Effort comprised total development effort in person-hours.

The data on size and effort from 16 already completed projects in a specified context were available for the purposes of the CoBRA model development. In addition to size and effort, 30 further characteristics of the software development environment concerning projects, products, processes, and resources were measured. The data set we initially acquired suffered from minor incompleteness—2.7 % of the overall measurement data were missing. The actual development productivity was computed according to the classical definition of production rate, that is, size of product divided by the effort required to produce it (IEEE-1045 1993). Figure 10.1 illustrates the distribution of the development productivity across the 16 already completed projects initially considered (we normalized productivity data due to confidentiality reasons).

The validation of the initial project data performed across several model development iterations revealed several inconsistencies. Project P16, an outlier with respect to productivity, was actually recognized as deviating from the context of the study. The project was excluded from the data in the second iteration of the model development. Figure 10.2 illustrates the distribution of development productivity across the already completed projects after excluding the outlier project P16.

In the subsequent model development iterations, a few more issues regarding the project measurement data were revealed. The effort data covered inconsistent project scope, that is, various phases of the development life cycle. This

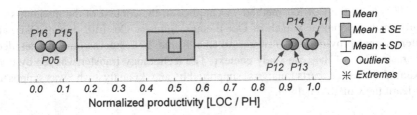

Fig. 10.1   Oki: initial project measurement data

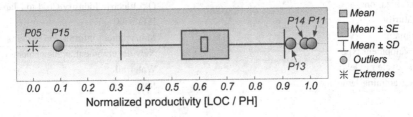

Fig. 10.2   Oki: project measurement data after exclusion of outlier project P16

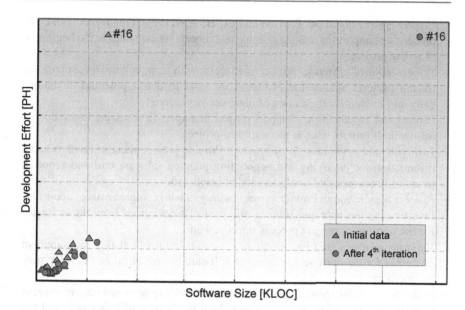

Fig. 10.3 Oki: initial versus final project effort and size data

inconsistency was resolved by adjusting the effort so that a consistent project scope was covered for all projects considered in the study. Finally, the size metric initially defined at Oki was found not to cover all significant aspects of the software volume. This problem was solved by updating the definition of the existing size metric and adjusting (re-collecting) the historical project data. Figure 10.3 illustrates the distribution of development productivity of the project data, re-including outlier project P16, after all these validation and preprocessing steps.

10.1.2 Domain Experts

Initially, there were 12 domain experts involved in the model development: 9 project managers, a quality engineer, a business planner, and a group leader. Their overall professional experiences ranged between 15 and 33 years, whereas experience in the current role ranged between 1 and 20 years. During the subsequent model refinement steps, the number of involved experts was reduced down to eight.

10.2   Estimation Objectives

Oki expected the introduction of the CoBRA method to contribute to the following objectives of the organization:

- *Project effort estimation*: Provide less experienced project managers with comprehensive support for making <u>reliable</u> and <u>repeatable</u> estimates at the beginning of a new project.
- *Project control*: Provide project managers with comprehensive support for tracing projects against the estimates in order to detect potential deviations early and to identify the causes of observed deviations.
- *Project risk management*: Support project managers in assessing and reducing (mitigating) project risks at the start of a project.
- *Justifying and negotiating project costs*: Provide project managers with reliable information for justifying and negotiating planned software cost and scope in terms of functional and nonfunctional characteristics.
- *Process improvement*: Provide project managers with comprehensive support for investigating the potential sources of a project's deviations from the estimates for the purpose of project process improvement.
- *Build up goal-oriented measurement program*: Improve existing measurement processes for the purpose of managing software project effort and development productivity.
- *Reduction of software management overhead*: Relieve seasoned human experts, such as experienced project managers, from the burden of being involved too frequently in effort estimations.

10.3   Model Development

In the Oki case, the CoBRA effort estimation model was developed in five iterations. Figure 10.4 illustrates the major phases of the CoBRA model development at Oki. Table 10.2 presents an overview of the model development iterations and the major refinement activities performed in each iteration.

10.3.1 Iteration 1: Initial Modeling

I1. Step 1: Preparation and Planning
The transfer of the CoBRA method to Oki started with a 1-day tutorial where the external analysts provided the detailed theoretical background for the CoBRA method to the Oki personnel, in particular to the analyst who was going to take over the responsibility for transferring the CoBRA expertise internally; additionally, several Oki effort estimators participated in the tutorial. The practical part of the technology transfer consisted of the pilot application of CoBRA at Oki following the introductory part.

The actual method application started with a kick-off meeting. During the meeting, the external analysts and the Oki analyst determined the scope of the CoBRA application and the detailed objectives of the effort estimation. Moreover, they identified relevant characteristics of the context in which CoBRA was to be applied. These characteristics served to determine the available sources of

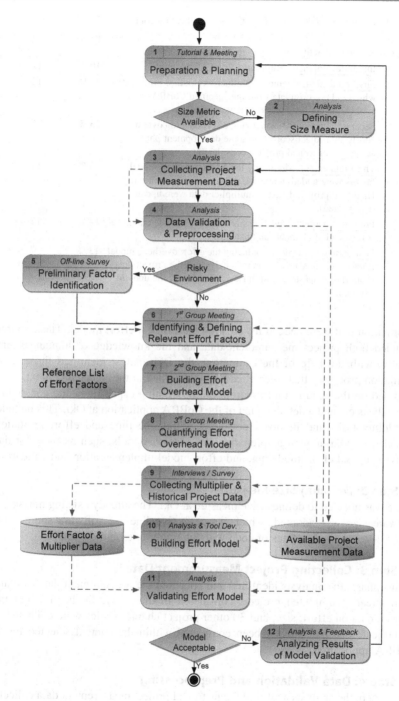

Fig. 10.4 Oki: CoBRA model development procedure

Table 10.2 Oki: characteristics of the CoBRA application context

Iteration	Refinement activities	Estimation error	Number of factors
I1	Initial development: Building a first CoBRA model.	107 %	12
I2	First refinement: Excluding productivity outlier project P16, which did not originate from the specified CoBRA application context (platform development project).	32 %	12
I3	Second refinement: Normalizing effort data to cover a consistent project scope (the same development phases) across the historical projects considered.	23 %	17
I4	Third refinement: Modifying the effort overhead model: factors were added, removed, and modified (definition). Historical project data and multiplier data were updated (recollected).	23 %	17
I5	Fourth refinement: Updating size metric to include the size of software GUI elements and batches.	14 %	17
I6	Postmortem refinement: Reducing the effort overhead model (factors removed) based on the analysis of the project data (both those measured and those acquired from the domain experts).	13 %	7

information that were needed for creating the CoBRA effort model. These sources included both project measurement data and the knowledge of human experts. Finally, with the help of the estimators, the Oki analyst identified those effort estimation processes that were already implemented in the selected context.

Based on the acquired information on the existing capabilities and constraints, the analysts created a detailed plan of the CoBRA application at Oki. This included scheduling tasks and involved personnel within the time and effort limitations provided by Oki as well as preparing the necessary tools, such as tools for data analysis, causal effort modeling, and effort model implementation and validation.

I1. Step 2: Defining Size Measure

There was no need to define a size measure at Oki. The already existing measure of software size was adopted, which was effective lines of software source code (eLOC)—measured as lines of code without empty lines and comments.

I1. Step 3: Collecting Project Measurement Data

In this phase, the analysts identified and collected the measurement data available from already completed projects considered in the study. In the first iteration project, data on effort, size, and 30 other project characteristics were collected for 16 projects that had already been completed within the context selected for the CoBRA application.

I1. Step 4: Data Validation and Preprocessing

In this step, the analysts analyzed the historical project measurement data collected in the previous step (Step 3) with respect to consistency and prepared the data for use in the CoBRA model development. The analysis of the input data in the first modeling iteration revealed several issues that needed to be considered during the development of the CoBRA model. The investigation of the software production line illustrated in Fig. 10.3 indicated several projects that lay outside the main body of data. The outlier projects included project #16 and the group of projects #11 to #14. The analysts stored the productivity variances observed across the historical projects as input for driving the effort overhead modeling activities; the major objective of later modeling was to explain these variances through an appropriate effort overhead model.

I1. Step 5: Preliminary Factor Identification

Due to the significant time limitations on performing on-site meetings and interviews as well as due to the cultural and language barrier, the project was burdened with relatively high risks. In order to mitigate them while building an initial effort model (in the first iteration), the analysts decided to perform a preliminary survey among the Oki experts to obtain an initial definition of relevant factors influencing development effort in the Oki context, their rankings, and potential dependencies. The results of the survey allowed the analysts to prepare appropriately for the face-to-face meetings and interviews performed in the subsequent steps and iterations of the CoBRA model development.

I1. Step 6: Identifying and Defining Relevant Effort Factors

The objective of this phase was to identify the factors with the most significant impact on development effort. For this purpose, the analysts used the expertise of the involved domain experts and the analysis of the available historical project measurement data—if appropriate, data were available. In this step, the analysts organized a group meeting during which the invited domain experts provided their expertise regarding the most relevant factors influencing development effort in the Oki context. The analysts facilitated discussions during the meeting by presenting the results of the analysis of the available project measurement data they had performed before the meeting.

In the first part of the meeting, the analysts asked the involved domain experts to perform a brainstorming session in which they reviewed the initial list of factors provided in Step 5 and discussed their individual experiences regarding relevant factors influencing development effort. At this stage, factors could be removed, modified (redefined), and added, depending on whether they were deemed relevant, complete, and well defined.

Since the brainstorming session ended with a total number of factors that was too high to be used for building a reasonable model under the given time constraints, the analysts had to reduce the set of factors to be considered in the further modeling steps. They needed to confine the list of factors to those that were considered to have the highest impact on effort while disregarding the others. They achieved this by asking the experts to rank all factors according to their relative impact on effort. The analysts grouped the identified effort factors into four categories—personnel, product, process, and project factors—and asked the domain experts to rank the individual factors in each category independently.

After the group meeting, the analysts integrated the rank orders provided by the individual domain experts for each of the predefined four categories in order to identify the most important factors in each category. It was important at this stage that the ranking was the result of a consensus between all managers interviewed in order to take into account the variety of experiences available at Oki. The outcomes of this analysis, including preselection of top-ranked factors, served as the input for building the effort overhead model (Step 7).

I1. Step 7: Building Effort Overhead Model

In this phase, a group meeting took place, with two objectives: (1) reviewing the results of the factor ranking and selecting the most relevant effort factors, and (2) identifying potential factor dependencies and building the structure of an effort overhead model.

In the first part of the meeting, the experts reviewed the results of the factor ranking and, based on those results, chose the most significant effort factors. A simplistic approach in that situation would be to choose a certain number of top-ranked factors from each category. Yet, it could occur that in reality, the experts would prefer factors from one category over the others. Therefore, the experts were asked to decide how many top-ranked factors from each separate category should be included in the effort model.

During the meeting, some experts suggested that the "importance of software reliability" factor might not be relevant and thus could possibly be excluded from the causal model. Yet, this change was not implemented because the majority of the experts voted against excluding this factor from the model.

In the second part of the meeting, the experts were asked to identify the causal relationships between the effort factors. This included identification of the direct influences of the effort factors on effort overhead as well as (if relevant) indirect relationships (i.e., some factor may weaken or strengthen the direct influence of another factor on effort overhead). From the meeting results, a causal effort model was built, i.e., a model of the causal relationships between effort factors and effort overhead.

I1. Step 8: Quantifying Effort Overhead Model

After building the qualitative causal model, two issues had to be tackled: (1) many of the factors selected represented complex concepts that needed to be split into their component aspects, and (2) the factors and variables included in the causal model had to be quantified. The aforementioned issues were addressed during the third group meeting.

In the first part of the meeting, for those factors that represent complex (n-dimensional) concepts, these component aspects were identified and defined precisely. Each complex factor was decomposed into its component aspects called variables. The domain experts decomposed several effort factors identified in the previous step into specific aspects. For example, the "Level of experience and *knowledge*" factor was decomposed into the two most relevant aspects, namely, "*Application domain experience*" and "*Platform experience.*"

Next, quantification of the refined causal model took place. In order to quantitatively measure all variables, a measurable scale had to be defined for each factor and variable. As none of the identified factors and variables had been measured yet at Oki, quantitative scales for all of them had to be defined. For those factors, a 4-point approximately ratio scale was defined. Each level on the 4-grade scale was precisely defined so that the experts would have a consistent understanding and could provide consistent project data. Table 10.3 provides the definitions of the effort factors included in the final effort model at Oki.

I1. Step 9: Collecting Multiplier and Historical Project Data

The purpose of this step was to collect effort multiplier and historical project data for the modeled effort factors. *Effort multipliers* quantify the impact of the effort factors considered in the effort overhead model on effort. *Historical project data* quantify the actual values of the effort factors in each already completed project considered in the Oki context. In case of complex factors, only the data for a factor's composite variables needed to be collected.

The analysts collected multiplier and project data during individual interviews with the domain experts. In practice, the data for each effort multiplier should be provided by all involved experts, whereas the project data for each historical project should be provided by at least two experts who are familiar with the project. This allows identifying inconsistencies between related information provided by different experts and, in turn, allows preventing potentially invalid input to the CoBRA modeling. Due to the time constraints and limited availability of appropriate domain experts, the analysts could collect such "redundant" information only for effort multipliers.

Effort Multipliers During multiplier data collection, the analysts asked the interviewed experts to relate to their real project experiences, that is, to consider all projects they had participated in or select up-front one representative project and stick to it during the whole interview as a point of reference. For each effort factor (or variable), the experts were asked to quantitatively assess the percentage impact the factor had or would have on effort in the respective reference projects, assuming it had the worst-case value.

During the interviews, the domain experts indicated that it was very difficult to imagine the effects each factor may cause in isolation from all others when collecting multiplier data, which is absolutely necessary for getting the effort overhead values for each effort factor.

For each effort factor, the analysts collected multiplier data from 12 experts. The analysis of the experts' judgment revealed that three experts provided multipliers that differed significantly from those of the other experts. In practice, such inconsistencies are normal because they reflect individual experiences of the experts, gained in numerous projects. We cannot expect that different experts have experienced all possible project situations, and thus they are not always able to provide accurate multipliers for all effort factors. One way to deal with outlier multiplier data in the CoBRA method is to remove them from further analysis, especially if the outlier data are provided by the least experienced domain experts. Yet, before excluding outlier data, we should first clarify the potential causes of the differences in the data, and we should make sure that excluding the data is justified and leads to the improved model quality. In the Oki case, the analysts decided to retain all multiplier data because the differences in the experts' experience were not significant and because they wanted to include the whole range of experiences represented by all domain experts in the CoBRA model.

Historical Project Data Due to the time constraints of the Oki study, only one expert provided effort factor data for each historical project considered in the study. As a consequence, the analysts could not mitigate the risk of invalid project data by comparing information acquired from multiple experts. Doubts regarding the validity of the project data provided by a single expert were additionally supported by a contradiction observed between the project measurement data on software size and the expert evaluations of the *"Software complexity"* effort factor. In particular, compared to the very large project #16, the experts considered several much smaller projects as having equal or even higher complexity. In principle, such a situation may occur in reality, but it is very unlikely for the projects considered in the Oki context. First, the definition of the *"Software complexity"* factor actually included the aspect of the volume of the software delivered as output of the project. Second, the difference in measured size between project #16 and the other projects was very large.

I1. Step 10: Building Effort Model
In this step, the analysts combined the quantified effort overhead model, the multiplier data, and the past project data within a CoBRA simulation tool. Using the tool, they computed the nominal productivities across the historical projects as a basis for estimating new projects. Because the nominal productivities obtained for the historical projects still varied, the analysts decided to use the median value as input for estimating future projects.

I1. Step 11: Validating Effort Model
In order to initially validate the predictive performance of the CoBRA model created in the first iteration, the analysts applied it to the historical projects using a leave-one-out strategy. In this strategy, the effort of each historical project is estimated using the actual data of this project and the median nominal productivity computed across the remaining historical projects. Afterwards, the analysts compared the estimated effort to the actual effort documented for the project and quantified estimation error by means of magnitude of relative error (MRE). Oki used the mean magnitude of relative estimation error (MMRE) as a criterion for accepting or rejecting the CoBRA model.

The initial CoBRA model presented MMRE = 107 %, which was an unacceptably low predictive performance for Oki. Therefore, they decided to perform a model refinement iteration with the objective of improving its predictive performance, meaning reducing its estimation error.

I1. Step 12: Analyzing Results of Model Validation

An analysis of the distribution of estimation error across individual historical projects revealed several projects that had extremely large estimation error as compared to other projects. These were project #16 and the group of projects #11 to 14#. The analysts discovered that these were the same projects that were outlying with respect to development productivity. The first conclusion drawn was that the CoBRA model is not able to explain productivity variance among the projects considered in the selected estimation context. The analysts considered several potential reasons for this poor performance of the model. On the one hand, the effort overhead model might have missed relevant effort factors that are responsible for the observed variances in the projects' development productivities while considering irrelevant and misleading factors. On the other hand, the multiplier and project data the domain experts provided for the model might have differed from the actual values (Fig. 10.5).

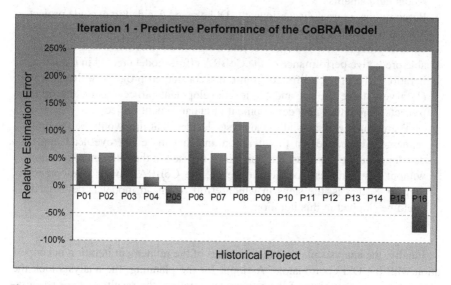

Fig. 10.5   Oki: estimation error of the initial CoBRA model (first iteration)

The analysts presented the results of the first model development iteration during a feedback session with the Oki staff involved in the study. After the meeting, Oki decided to go through an additional model refinement iteration with the objective of improving its predictive performance. The analysts and the domain experts took observations from the model validation and analysis step as the entry point for improving the model in the refinement iteration. The Oki domain experts committed to investigating internally (off-line) the historical projects considered in the study and the data they had provided in order to find potential reasons for the poor performance of the model. In particular, they were to look closer at the outlier project #16 and the group of projects #11 to #14.

10.3.2 Iteration 2: Model Refinement

I2. Step 1: Preparation and Planning

During the preparation for the refinement iteration, both the external analysts and the Oki experts individually investigated the outcomes of the initial model development. In particular, they looked for possible reasons for the poor performance of the model and for appropriate improvement potentials. The results of the internal analysis and potential model improvements were discussed during a group meeting. At the end of the meeting, the analysts and the domain experts decided on the exact refinement that would be the subject of this iteration.

Model Refinements

Based on the internal discussions, the Oki experts decided to exclude project #16 from the input project data, which was an outlier with respect to development productivity. This project had a significant impact on the unacceptable predictive performance of the CoBRA effort model created in the initial iteration. The project differed from other considered projects in that it was (1) a very large project and (2) a redevelopment project, while the other projects were either new development or enhancement projects.

The domain experts and the analysts decided that this would be the only refinement introduced in this iteration and that the effort overhead model developed in the previous iteration would be used in the refinement iteration without any changes. As a consequence, the CoBRA model development Steps 5–8, that is, the steps in which effort overhead model is developed, could be skipped in this iteration.

Finally, the analysts planned the activities of the refinement iteration in cooperation with the Oki coordinators. As input for the planning, the analysts took the objectives and constraints of the refinement iteration, the results of the first iteration, and the experiences they had gained in the previous iterations concerning the resources that are actually needed for performing particular activities. Planning consisted of specifying the exact model refinements, identifying existing information sources, and planning the iteration steps within available time, budget, and personnel resources.

I2. Step 2: Defining Size Measure

In this iteration, the analysts used the size measure they already employed in the first iteration (I1) without changes.

I2. Step 3: Collecting Project Measurement Data

In this step, the analysts removed the data for the historical project #16 from the project data set used for developing and validating the CoBRA model.

I2. Step 4: Data Validation and Preprocessing

In this step, the analysts scrutinized the historical project data that remained after excluding outlier project #16. In particular, they looked at the project's development productivity computed as the size of the delivered software divided by the effort consumed. The analysis revealed a lot more significant relationships between size and effort, meaning less variance between projects with respect to their productivity. Yet, the outlier group of projects #11 to #14 remained an issue to address.

I2. Step 5: Preliminary Factor Identification

The analysts introduced this step in the first modeling iteration in which the initial CoBRA model was to be developed from scratch. The purpose of this step was to reduce the time required for the group meeting during which the domain experts defined an initial list of relevant effort factors. In the Oki context, there was a high risk of exceeding the available time due to expected additional overhead required to overcome culture and language differences. In order to mitigate this risk and to meet the time constraints specified by Oki, the analysts performed an off-line survey in which the domain experts could individually identify the effort factors they perceived as relevant in the considered estimation context. Having an initial list of relevant effort factors already defined allowed for reducing the time required for performing the factor identification and definition meeting (Step 6 in the CoBRA model development process).

Yet, this step can typically be excluded in subsequent modeling (refinement) iterations because the previous iteration already delivers a set of the effort factors included into the effort overhead model.

I2. Step 6: Identifying and Defining Relevant Effort Factors

The domain experts did not introduce any changes to the set of effort factors identified in the first iteration. Consequently, there was also no need to repeat the factor ranking.

I2. Step 7: Building Effort Overhead Model

The domain experts did not introduce any changes to the effort overhead model. This refinement iteration simply took over the initial set of effort factors and their iterations, which had already been defined in the first iteration.

I2. Step 8: Quantifying Effort Overhead Model

Domain experts did also not change quantification of the effort factors in the effort overhead model. This refinement iteration used factor quantifications that were already defined in the first iteration.

I2. Step 9: Collecting Multiplier and Historical Project Data

There was no need to collect effort multiplier data in this refinement iteration because (1) the effort overhead model was not changed and (2) the multiplier data collected in the previous iteration were considered as valid.

I2. Step 10: Building Effort Model

In this step, the analysts combined the quantified effort overhead model, the multiplier data, and the past project data within a CoBRA simulation tool. Using the tool, they computed the nominal productivities across the historical projects as a basis for estimating new projects. Because the nominal productivities obtained for the historical projects still varied, the analysts decided to use median value as basis for estimating future projects—this time excluding project #16.

I2. Step 11: Validating Effort Model

Finally, the analysts validated the predictive performance of the refined model on the set of historical projects they had considered in this iteration. The model showed a significantly reduced average estimation error of 32 % compared to the 107 % of the initial model developed in the first iteration. Moreover, the nominal productivity computed using the CoBRA model across the historical projects was less dependent on software size only. The reduced estimation error and the lower dependency on size indicated that the model was now better able to account for variances in development productivity in the historical projects.

I2. Step 12: Analyzing Results of Model Validation

An analysis of the estimation error for the individual projects and their actual development productivity data indicated that the group of projects #11 to #14 clearly differed from the other projects. Again, these were the same projects that were outlying with respect to development productivity, confirming the observation that the CoBRA model is not able to account for their productivity variance (Fig. 10.6).

After a closer look at the detailed project data, in particular the effort spent per individual development phase, the analysts discovered that the total project effort reported for different historical projects actually included different development phases. Such an inconsistency typically challenges the validity of any effort estimation model based on project size and effort measurement data. Therefore, the analysts recommended to Oki that the project data should be corrected and the CoBRA model should be rebuilt upon it, before releasing the model for estimating future projects.

The analysts presented these results to the Oki experts in a feedback session. After the meeting, Oki decided to perform a refinement iteration through the model with the objective of correcting the historical project data and further improving the model's predictive performance. The Oki domain experts committed to investigating the historical projects considered in the study internally (off-line) and check how to resolve the issue of inconsistent effort measurements.

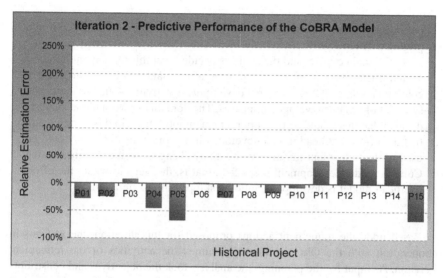

Fig. 10.6 Oki: estimation error of the refined CoBRA model (second iteration)

10.3.3 Iteration 3: Model Refinement

I3. Step 1: Preparation and Planning

In the preparation for the refinement iteration, both the external analysts and the Oki experts individually investigated the outcomes of the model validation in the second iteration. In particular, the Oki experts looked for possible solutions to correct the historical project effort data. The results of the internal analysis and potential model improvements were discussed during a group meeting. At the end of the meeting, the analysts and the domain experts decided on the exact refinement that was to be the subject of this iteration.

Model Refinements

Following an internal analysis of the historical project effort data, the Oki experts came to the conclusion that the total effort of the different projects did, in fact, include distinct development phases. According to Oki's data collection process, effort data was collected correctly for each development phase. Yet, for some projects, the effort spent on requirements specification and/or system testing was not available and, therefore, was not included in the total effort data. A typical cause of missing effort measurement was that the affected development phase had been performed outside Oki. One example situation was when requirements were specified by customers and utilized by Oki "as-is." Another situation was when certain testing activities were performed by the customers. In these cases, the effort for the externally

(continued)

performed phases was not known to Oki and thus not accounted for in the project data repository.

The domain experts and the analysts decided that this refinement iteration should focus on correcting the project effort data so that it included a consistent scope of the software development activities—in this case, the same set of project development phases. The domain experts and the analysts decided that this would be the only refinement introduced in this iteration and that the effort overhead model developed in the previous iteration would be used in the refinement iteration without any changes. As a consequence, the CoBRA model development Steps 5–8, that is, the steps in which the effort overhead model is developed, could be skipped in this iteration.

Based upon the refinement actions proposed for this iteration, the analysts in cooperation with the Oki coordinators planned the activities of the refinement iteration. As input for the planning, the analysts took the objectives and constraints of the refinement iteration, the results of the first iteration, and the experiences they had gained in the previous iterations concerning the resources actually needed for performing particular activities. Planning consisted of specifying the exact model refinements, identifying existing information sources, and planning the iteration steps with the available time, budget, and personnel resources.

I3. Step 2: Defining Size Measure
In this iteration, the analysts used the size measure they already employed in the first iteration (I1) without changes.

I3. Step 3: Collecting Project Measurement Data
The objective of this phase was to find a way of correcting the effort data for the 15 historical projects considered in the study so that it encompassed a consistent range of development phases. In principle, the Oki experts considered two ways of achieving this objective:

1. *Approximate missing effort measurements*: In this case, the effort data of the missing development phases would be approximated using the information on phase-wise effort distribution observed in the projects where all phases were performed by Oki and corresponding effort data was available. In other words, the missing historical effort data would be approximated using a simple method of proportions. This option would require that at least some historical projects at Oki included all development phases and that corresponding effort data were available.
2. *Reduce scope of effort measurement*: In this case, the "total" project effort would only include those development phases for which effort was consistently measured throughout all historical projects considered in the study. In this option, the effort estimation model would be based upon the effort data for

a certain excerpt from the complete development life cycle; thus it would account only for a subset of the development activities. In consequence, the model would allow for estimating the corresponding part of total project effort. The remaining part would need to be approximated, for example, using the method of proportions.

3. *Reduce set of historical projects*: In this case, the set of historical projects would be reduced to those projects for which the effort data covers all development phases. In this option, there was a risk that too few historical projects would remain to build a reliable effort estimation model (CoBRA requires about ten projects).

4. *Estimate effort per phase*: In this case, separate effort estimation models would be created for each development phase using only those historical projects for which the effort of the appropriate phase was available. This option would lead to relatively large costs for developing multiple estimation models. Moreover, there would be a risk that for certain development phases, too few historical projects would report actual effort data for building a reliable effort estimation model (CoBRA requires about ten projects).

After some deliberation, the Oki experts decided to go with the first option, approximating missing effort data based on the phase-wise effort data of other projects and the knowledge of the experts who had been involved in particular projects.

I3. Step 4: Data Validation and Preprocessing

An analysis of the historical project data, including the modified effort entries, did not reveal further issues. The updated data revealed an improved (higher) correlation between size and effort. However, although projects #11 to #14 were not outliers anymore, they still formed a visually outstanding cloud of data. If they would continue to stand out with respect to estimation error after the validation, the next potential refinement iteration should probably concentrate on explaining what distinguished these projects from the others.

I3. Step 5: Preliminary Factor Identification

This step could be excluded in this iteration because the previous iteration had already delivered an input set of the effort factors included in the effort overhead model.

I3. Step 6: Identifying and Defining Relevant Effort Factors

The domain experts did not change the set of effort factors identified in the previous iteration. Consequently, there was also no need to repeat the ranking of the effort factors.

I3. Step 7: Building Effort Overhead Model

The domain experts did not introduce any changes to the effort overhead model. This refinement iteration simply took over the initial set of effort factors and their iterations, which were already defined in the first iteration.

I3. Step 8: Quantifying Effort Overhead Model

The domain experts did not change the quantification of the effort factors in the effort overhead model either. This refinement iteration used factor quantifications that had already been defined in the first iteration.

I3. Step 9: Collecting Multiplier and Historical Project Data

There was no need to collect effort multiplier data in this refinement iteration because (1) the effort overhead model was not changed and (2) the multiplier data collected in the previous iteration were considered as valid.

I3. Step 10: Building Effort Model

In this step, the analysts combined the quantified effort overhead model, the multiplier data, and the past project data within a CoBRA simulation tool. Using the tool, they computed the nominal productivities across the historical projects as a basis for estimating new projects. Because the nominal productivities obtained for the historical projects still varied, the analysts decided to use the median value across the 15 historical projects considered in this iteration as a basis for estimating future projects.

I3. Step 11: Validating Effort Model

An analysis of the predictive performance of the refined model showed further improvement. The average estimation error on the 15 historical projects was reduced down to 23 %. The improvement observed in the model's performance indicated that the ambiguous data collection processes identified in the previous iteration had a significant impact on the quality of the estimation model. Yet, several issues, such as the group of outstanding projects #11 to #14, remained unresolved.

I3. Step 12: Analyzing Results of Model Validation

An analysis of the estimation error for individual projects and their actual development productivity data indicated that the group of projects #11 to #14 still differed from the other projects. Another issue that needed clarification was the highly underestimated projects #05 and #15 (Fig. 10.7).

A closer look at the historical project data revealed two major issues. First, an analysis of the project data for the effort factors incorporated into the effort overhead model indicated several cases where the domain experts provided significantly inconsistent assessments—although they provided data for the same effort factor in the same already completed project. Second, after a closer look at the measured project characteristics, the analysts discovered that projects #11 to #14 had actually been partly developed in C, while the other projects had been developed completely in Java. Since the current model did not include a cost factor that deals with the programming language, the analysts considered the appropriate enhancement of the effort overhead model as one of the possible improvement potentials for the next model refinement iteration. Based on the analysis of the

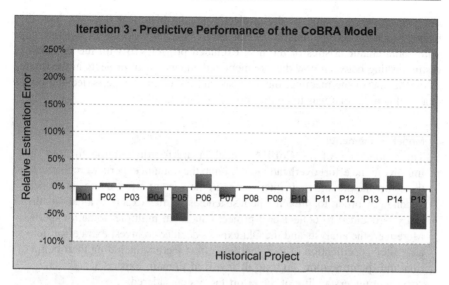

Fig. 10.7 Oki: estimation error of the refined CoBRA model (third iteration)

model's performance and the improvement potentials discovered, Oki decided to run an additional refinement iteration on the CoBRA effort estimation model.

10.3.4 Iteration 4: Model Refinement

I4. Step 1: Preparation and Planning

In the preparation for the refinement iteration, both the external analysts and the Oki experts individually investigated the outcomes of the initial model development. In particular, they looked for possible reasons for the poor performance of the model and for appropriate improvement potentials. The results of the internal analysis and the potential model improvements were discussed during a group meeting.

After the internal discussions, the domain experts and the Oki analysts concluded that the effort overhead model was missing several important cost factors that make project #16 and projects #11 to #14 productivity outliers compared to other projects. According to the Oki experts, this includes "*Support from project-external technical people*" and makes projects #11 to #14 different from all other projects considered in the study. "*Use of a second programming language*," identified during the analysis of the measurement data as potentially distinguishing projects #11 to #14 from other projects, was actually not considered as a crucial effort factor. As far as project #16 is concerned, the experts admitted that its context differs significantly from the other projects considered. As already noticed, in the first iteration, project #16 was a redevelopment project building a whole software platform, whereas all other projects were newly developed projects or software enhancement projects based on that very platform. Therefore, the experts confirmed once again the exclusion of this project from the historical data set. Yet, they decided to additionally include several new cost factors in the model that cope with some characteristics of the now excluded project #16 with the intention of distinguishing between new development and enhancement projects in the future.

At the end of the meeting, the analysts and the domain experts decided on the exact refinement that was to be the subject of this iteration.

Model Refinements
The refinements of the CoBRA model in the fourth iteration focused on improving the effort overhead model. First, the domain experts were to revise the effort factors and their interactions in the current effort overhead model. Second, in order to prevent inconsistencies in the expert evaluation, the analysts decided to collect past project data from multiple domain experts. Moreover, the analysts and the Oki experts decided to invest extra effort into a detailed specification of the identified effort factors, including their definition and quantification, so that all involved domain experts would have a consistent understanding of the effort factors considered.

Finally, the analysts planned the activities of the refinement iteration in cooperation with the Oki coordinators. As input for the planning, the analysts took the objectives and constraints of the refinement iteration, the results of the first iteration, and the experiences they had gained in the previous iterations concerning resources actually needed for performing particular activities. Planning consisted of specifying the exact model refinements, identifying existing information sources, and planning the iteration steps with the available time, budget, and personnel resources.

I4. Step 2: Defining Size Measure
In this iteration, the analysts used the size measure they had already employed in the first iteration (I1) without changes.

I4. Step 3: Collecting Project Measurement Data
In this iteration, there was also no need to (re-)collect any historical project measurement data—meaning software size and development effort data.

I4. Step 4: Data Validation and Preprocessing
Since the project measurement data did not change in this iteration, there was also no need to repeat the validation and preprocessing step.

I4. Step 5: Preliminary Factor Identification
This step could be excluded in this iteration because the previous iteration had already delivered an input set of the effort factors included in the effort overhead model.

I4. Step 6: Identifying and Defining Relevant Effort Factors

In this iteration, the analysts and the domain experts performed a joint meeting during which the experts revised the effort overhead model created during previous iterations. The domain experts removed or modified (redefined) effort factors that were already included in the effort overhead model, and added several new factors to the model.

Motivated by the outlier project #16, which was a major redevelopment project, the domain experts introduced the *"Degree of product enhancement"* factor to the model. They wanted the effort model to distinguish between new development and enhancement projects in the future. This way, the experts wanted to ensure that both types of projects were estimated equally well using the same CoBRA model.

Interestingly, although analysis of the project data indicated the use of a second programming language as a potential reason for the poor performance of the model for the selected projects, the domain experts did not decide to modify the model to account for this issue. Instead, they decided that in this case, a more important factor was the involvement of a technology support team external to the project. In order to reflect this aspect, the experts added the *"Support by project-external technical experts"* factor to the effort overhead model.

Moreover, after some deliberation regarding the relevance of the *"Importance of software reliability"* factor, the domain experts decided to retain it in the model. Figure 10.8 presents the improved causal model as the result of the expert meeting. The underlined factors (or the underlined parts of factor's names) are those that were added to the initial model.

Finally, the analysts asked the domain experts to decompose those effort factors into appropriate variables that represented complex concepts. For example, the experts redefined existing variables associated to the *"Level of experience and knowledge"* factor and added one more variable to it.

Since the domain experts introduced changes to the effort factors by directly modifying the effort overhead model, there was no need to repeat the ranking procedure as they had done in the initial modeling iteration. The experts simply included in the model those effort factors they considered as the most relevant ones and removed the irrelevant factors. Table 10.3 summarizes the effort factors defined in this iteration, which were actually the final set of factors defined at Oki.

I4. Step 7: Building Effort Overhead Model

This step took place at the end of a group meeting during which the domain experts revised the effort factors in the effort overhead model (Step 6). The analysts asked the experts to revise the interactions between the effort factors they incorporated into in the effort overhead model. Figure 10.8 presents the effort overhead model created in this iteration. The model elements marked with underlined font are those that changed in this iteration; the remaining elements resulted from previous iterations—mainly the first iteration where the initial CoBRA model was created. This model is actually the final model created jointly with the Oki domain experts.

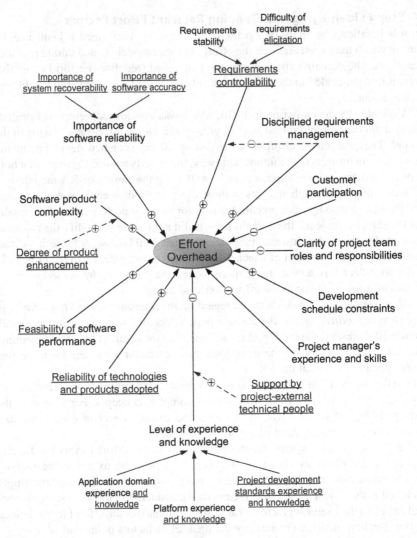

Fig. 10.8 Oki: final effort overhead model (the underlined elements were defined in the fourth iteration)

I4. Step 8: Quantifying Effort Overhead Model

In this step, the domain expert and the analysts defined the quantitative scales for the effort factors included in the effort overhead model. During a joint meeting, the domain experts revised the scales of all effort factors.

In order to ensure the same understanding of the subjective scales defined to quantify each factor, the analysts and the domain experts invested extra effort into giving a detailed definition of the project situation related to a specific factor value and also deliberated the scales in a group discussion involving all experts.

Table 10.3 Oki: the most relevant factors influencing development productivity

Effort factor	Factor definition
Personnel-related factors	These factors encompass the characteristics of the personnel involved in the software development.
Level of experience and knowledge	The experience and knowledge of people in the project team regarding the application domain of the project, the process and documentation standards and common practices (which are not documented in the process, but usually applied), the development platform, and the environment at the start of the project.
• Application domain experience and knowledge	The experience and knowledge of the people in the project team regarding the customer's business and system characteristics at the start of the project.
• Platform experience and knowledge	The experience and knowledge of people in the project team regarding the development platform and/or framework (OS, hardware, middleware, programming language) at the start of the project.
• Project development standards experience and knowledge	The experience and knowledge of people in the project team regarding the process and documentation standards and common practices (which are not documented in the process, but usually applied) at the start of the project.
Project manager's experience and skills	The level of experience and skills of the project manager of the team in managing a project (ranging from having implemented many priority projects to never having managed a project before) at the start of the project.
Support by project-external technical experts	The level of support provided by technical experts (e.g., for a common framework) external to the project during the lifetime of the project.
Product-related factors	These factors encompass the characteristics of the artifacts delivered during software development, commonly referred to as software development products.
Importance of software reliability	The amount of attention given to minimizing failures and ensuring that any failures will not result in safety, economic, security, and/or environmental damage, achieved through actions such as validation and testing, fault-tolerant design, and formal specifications.
• Importance of software accuracy	The extent to which accuracy of the functionality is strictly required to avoid the social effects a failure may cause (economic damage, financial loss, or inconvenience).
• Importance of system recoverability	The capability of the software product to reestablish a specified level of performance and recover the data directly affected in case of a failure and the capability of being replaced by an alternative procedure resuming its functionality.
Requirements controllability	The extent to which the requirements are controllable over the project's lifetime (includes tendency of different customers).
• Difficulty of requirements elicitation	The number of stakeholders (e.g., customers, departments) involved in requirements elicitation and how easily agreement can be reached with regard to the defined requirements.

(continued)

Table 10.3   (continued)

Effort factor	Factor definition
• Requirements stability	The extent to which customers change their mind about the requirements during the project's lifetime after the definition of the initial requirements (defined at the beginning of the project).
Software product complexity	The extent to which some aspects of the software product (e.g., interface, architecture, database, algorithms, or relation to other systems) are expected to be complex or relatively large.
Feasibility of software performance	The feasibility of implementing the performance required (e.g., execution time, download time).
Degree of product enhancement	The degree to which the created software product is based on parts of an already existing software system that has to be understood and must be included in testing.
Evidence of technologies and products adopted	The amount of evidence that is provided for the industrial application of technologies and products adopted in the project (e.g., OS, middleware, or protocols).
Process-related factors	These factors encompass the characteristics of software development processes.
Disciplined requirements management	The extent of disciplined requirements management—whether requirements are explicitly defined, tracked, and traced to design, code, and validation testing.
Customer participation	The extent of user/customer participation—whether the users are providing information, reviewing requirements documents, performing some of the analyses themselves, and taking part in acceptance testing.
Project-related factors	These factors encompass the characteristics of a software development project, such as project organization and constraints.
Clarity of project team roles and responsibilities	The extent to which project team roles and related project responsibilities are clearly defined and well-understood (and committed to) by the team members.
Development schedule constraints	The extent to which the planned project schedule is reasonable to attain a system that meets all of the requirements. The extent to which the schedule is shortened assuming that the optimal one is 100 %.

14. Step 9: Collecting Multiplier and Historical Project Data

In this step, the analysts acquired the multiplier data for all effort factors in the effort overhead model. In order to prevent inconsistencies in the expert evaluation, the analysts decided to collect past project data from multiple experts, at least from three. Since all domain experts already knew the data acquisition procedure, they could provide their assessments in an off-line survey. This allowed for reducing the effort required from the domain experts, compared to performing individual data acquisition interviews with all experts—as was the case in the first iteration. The effort saved could then be invested into acquiring the same project data from more than one domain expert. Later on, this allowed analyzing potential inconsistencies between the data provided by multiple domain experts and increasing the reliability of the data.

In fact, the acquired project data showed significant inconsistencies. In several cases, the experts gave extremely different evaluations of the same factor in the same project. The problem was solved by a joint experts' meeting where the involved experts discussed the data inconsistencies and came up with a common factor rating. Interestingly, even though all experts participated and contributed to the detailed definition of the scales for each factor, there were still inconsistencies in interpreting the scales and related project situations.

I4. Step 10: Building Effort Model

In this step, the analysts combined the quantified effort overhead model, the multiplier data, and the past project data within a CoBRA simulation tool. Using the tool, they computed the nominal productivities across the historical projects as a basis for estimating new projects. Because the nominal productivities obtained for the historical projects still varied, the analysts decided to use the median value across the 15 historical projects considered in this iteration as a basis for estimating future projects.

I4. Step 11: Validating Effort Model

The model validation showed a slight improvement in estimation accuracy. The average estimation error could be reduced down to 23 %. However, the variance of estimation error across the historical projects could not be reduced much. For example (Fig. 10.9), a few projects were underestimated to a rather large degree.

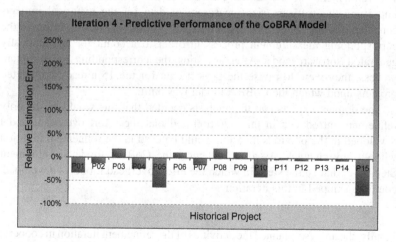

Fig. 10.9 Oki: estimation error of the refined CoBRA model (fourth iteration)

I4. Step 12: Analyzing Results of Model Validation

A deeper analysis of the past project characteristics revealed that the outlying projects had a very large number of GUI (graphical user interface) elements and batches implemented.

After discussing this issue with the domain experts, it turned out that the currently used size metric reflected only code directly implemented by software developers and did not include other elements of software size, such as the code generated for the GUI and batches. The experts agreed that—from the perspective of effort estimation—even if some parts of the software are generated, they still contribute to the overall project effort. For example, such parts of the software at least require effort for designing and testing. Considering this fact, the analysts and the estimators decided to modify the current size measure by counting automatically generated code for GUI and batch elements.

Based on these observations, the Oki expert decided on performing another refinement iteration, in which they revised the software size measurement in order to address generated code.

10.3.5 Iteration 5: Model Refinement

I5. Step 1: Preparation and Planning

In the preparation for this refinement iteration, both the external analysts and the Oki experts individually investigated the outcomes of the initial model development. In particular, they looked for possible reasons for the poor performance of the model and for appropriate improvement potentials.

> **Model Refinements**
> The refinements of the CoBRA model in the fifth iteration focused on improving the software size measurement data for the historical projects considered in the study. The domain experts considered how to improve the corresponding measurement process in order to account for automatically generated software code. After adjusting the corresponding measurement process, they were to revise the project data for the 15 already completed projects upon which the CoBRA model was built.
>
> The domain experts and the analysts decided that this would be the only refinement introduced in this iteration and that the effort overhead model developed in the previous iteration would be used in the refinement iteration without any changes. As a consequence, the CoBRA model development Steps 5–8, that is, the steps in which the effort overhead model is developed, could be skipped in this iteration.

Finally, the analysts planned the activities of the refinement iteration in cooperation with the Oki coordinators. As input for the planning, the analysts took the objectives and constraints of the refinement iteration, the results of the first iteration, and the experiences they had gained in the previous iterations concerning resources actually needed for performing particular activities. Planning consisted of specifying the exact model refinements, identifying existing information sources, and planning the iteration steps with the available time, budget, and personnel resources.

I5. Step 2: Defining Size Measure
In the previous iteration (I4), a detailed analysis of the project measurement data showed that the collected size data did not include generated code for elements of graphical user interface (GUI) and for batches. After some discussions and analysis, the Oki estimators and the domain experts decided that those parts of the software make an important contribution to project effort and, therefore, need to be included in the size measure. After that, the Oki size measurement process was refined appropriately to consider generated code, and the existing measurement data was updated according to this process.

I5. Step 3: Collecting Project Measurement Data
After modifying the size measure for the project data used for building the CoBRA model, the domain experts revised the size measurement data for the 15 historical projects considered in the CoBRA application at Oki accordingly.

I5. Step 4: Data Validation and Preprocessing
The validation of the revised historical project data did not indicate any other critical issues that would have required an additional refinement iteration.

I5. Step 5: Preliminary Factor Identification
This step could be excluded in this iteration because the previous iteration had already delivered an input set of the effort factors included in the effort overhead model.

I5. Step 6: Identifying and Defining Relevant Effort Factors
The domain experts did not change the set of effort factors identified in the previous iteration. Consequently, there was also no need to repeat the ranking of the effort factors.

I5. Step 7: Building Effort Overhead Model
The domain experts did not introduce any changes to the effort overhead model. This refinement iteration simply took the initial set of effort factors and their iterations, which had already been defined in the first iteration. Figure 10.8 presents the final structure of the causal effort model built in the context of the pilot application of CoBRA at Oki.

I5. Step 8: Quantifying Effort Overhead Model
The domain experts also did not change the quantification of the effort factors in the effort overhead model. This refinement iteration used the factor quantifications that had already been defined in the first iteration.

I5. Step 9: Collecting Multiplier and Historical Project Data

There was no need to collect effort multiplier data in this refinement iteration because (1) the effort overhead model was not changed and (2) the multiplier data collected in the previous iteration were considered as valid.

I5. Step 10: Building Effort Model

In this step, the analysts combined the quantified effort overhead model, the multiplier data, and the past project data within a CoBRA simulation tool. Using the tool, they computed the nominal productivities across the historical projects as a basis for estimating new projects. Because the nominal productivities obtained for the historical projects still varied, the analysts decided to use the median value across the 15 historical projects considered in this iteration as a basis for estimating future projects.

I5. Step 11/12: Validating Effort Model and Analyzing Results of Model Validation

The validation results showed a significant improvement in the model's predictive power. Compared to the previous iteration, the average estimation error was reduced from 23 % down to 14 %. Moreover, the estimation error was relatively stable across the historical projects, as illustrated in Fig. 10.10. This allowed concluding that the CoBRA estimation model explained the productivity variances across the considered types of projects well and that it is very likely that it will estimate future projects within the observed estimation error margin.

Yet, there was still room for improvement. On the one hand, the model still did not fully explain the productivity variance across the considered historical projects, which resulted in considerable estimation error (>5 %). On the other hand, the resulting CoBRA model was relatively large and complex, containing a number of effort factors and their interactions. Maintaining such a model—and the

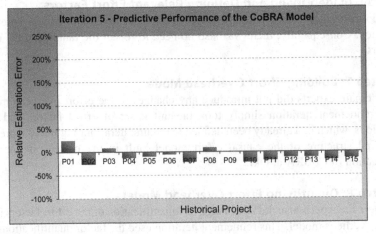

Fig. 10.10 Oki: estimation error of the refined CoBRA model (fifth iteration)

associated measurement data—might involve substantial cost. The question that was left open was whether all the effort factors included in the CoBRA model really had a relevant impact on variance in development productivity and were thus necessary for accurately estimating project effort. Since reducing the costs of effort estimation was among the objectives of the CoBRA application at Oki, the company was to investigate the possibilities of simplifying the CoBRA model while refining it in the future.

In order to leave some guidelines regarding potential directions for further model improvements, the analysts decided to attempt to reduce the model based solely upon the quantitative analysis of the project data collected during the Oki study. This was the subject of a postmortem model refinement, which will be described briefly in the next section.

10.3.6 Iteration 6: Postmortem Refinement

In this iteration, the analysts performed a simple quantitative analysis of the historical project data collected during the pilot application of the CoBRA method at Oki. The objective of the analysis was to investigate the effort factors incorporated in the final CoBRA model created at Oki with respect to their contribution to the productivity variances observed across the historical projects used for creating the model.

Problem
One of the estimation objectives defined at Oki was reduction of the project overhead imposed by effort estimation. In general, the CoBRA method proved to significantly reduce the cost of effort estimation compared to estimation based on human judgment. Once developed, an effort model can be simply reused multiple times within a project—across development phases—and across various projects. Yet, since the Oki model contained a large number of effort factors, the suspicion arose that not all of them might be relevant. If this was true, potentially irrelevant effort factors would contribute to increased costs for collecting related project data and maintaining the effort model without appropriate payoff in terms of increased performance of the model.

Idea
In order to check the relevancy of the effort factors incorporated in the Oki effort model, the analysts investigated the project data collected after the model's last refinement iteration (I5). They considered the historical project data obtained through measurement and those acquired from the domain experts. The purpose of the analysis was to determine which of the considered factors actually had the greatest impact on the variance of development productivity observed across the already completed software projects considered at Oki. The analysts wanted to

employ the RReliefF[1] factor weighting technique (Robnik-Sikonja and Kononenko 2003) on the project data delivered by the domain experts to identify those effort factors that RReliefF indicates as having a significant impact on the variance of development productivity. Next, they wanted to remove from the CoBRA model all effort factors that were not chosen by RReliefF and validate the predictive power of the reduced model using Oki's historical project data.

Solution

The analysts used the implementation of RReliefF in the Weka tool (Hall et al. 2009). They set the number of nearest neighbors to $k = 2$ and used the default settings for the remaining parameters required by the tool. On the output, RReliefF provided a set of numerical weights assigned to each of the considered effort factors. Table 10.4 presents the weights provided by RReliefF. Factors that were

Table 10.4 Oki: analytical weighting of effort factors' impact on development productivity

Effort factor	Factor weight	Inclusion
Personnel-related factors		
Level of experience and knowledge	–	×
• Application domain experience and knowledge	0.0994	√
• Platform experience and knowledge	0.1567	√
• Project development standards experience and knowledge	−0.0836	×
Project manager's experience and skills	0	×
Support by project-external technical experts	−0.0332	×
Product-related factors		
Importance of software reliability	–	×
• Importance of software accuracy	−0.0697	×
• Importance of system recoverability	0.1008	√
Requirements controllability	–	×
• Difficulty of requirements elicitation	0.0978	√
• Requirements stability	0.0865	√
Software product complexity	0.1997	√
Feasibility of software performance	−0.0516	×
Degree of product enhancement	0.0814	√
Evidence of technologies and products adopted	0	×
Process-related factors		
Disciplined requirements management	0	×
Customer participation	0	×
Project-related factors		
Clarity of project team roles and responsibilities	0	×
Development schedule constraints	0	×

---

[1] In Sect. 5.6.1. (Example 5.4.), we illustrate how to use the RReliefF technique for the purpose of quantifying the importance of potential effort factors covered by historical project measurement data.

assigned weights greater than zero are considered to have an impact on the variance of development productivity.

The analysts decided to reduce the CoBRA effort model to these factors, that is, remove from the model all factors that were assigned a weight that was lower than or equal to zero. Figure 10.11 illustrates the reduction of the CoBRA model created at Oki. The effort factors that were removed from the model are marked in gray. The underlined factors are those modified in the fourth model refinement iteration (Fig. 10.8).

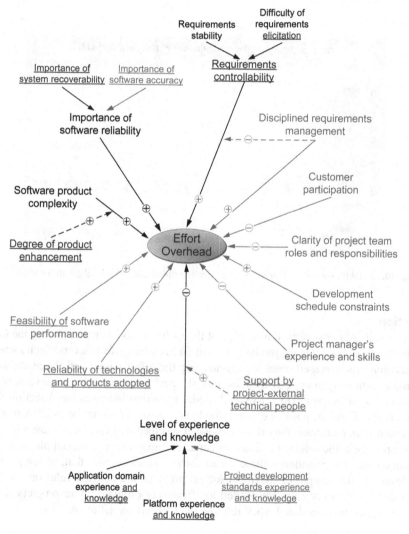

Fig. 10.11   Oki: reduced effort overhead model (removed elements marked in gray)

Benefit

During the validation, the reduced model showed more or less unchanged predictive performance compared to the full model. In fact, the average estimation error dropped from 14 % for the full model down to 12 % for the reduced model. Figure 10.2 illustrates the exact distribution of the relative estimation error among the 15 historical projects considered in the Oki study on which the analysts validated the full and the reduced CoBRA models (Fig. 10.12).

The validation result shows that not all effort factors considered by the Oki CoBRA model are necessary to explain the productivity variance of the historical projects considered and to effectively estimate these projects.

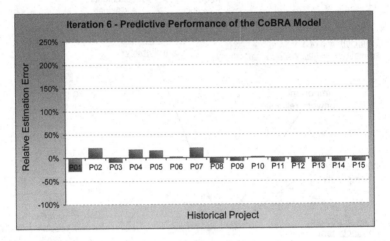

Fig. 10.12 Oki: estimation error of the analytically refined CoBRA model (sixth iteration)

Action

The results of the analytical reduction of the CoBRA model created during the Oki pilot study suggest that the model may contain irrelevant effort factors. Such factors contribute to increased costs for maintaining the effort model and the associated project data without any payoff in the model's performance and the achievement of estimation objectives. This analytical model reduction indicates the direction the Oki analysts and the domain experts should take when adjusting the CoBRA model internally. In particular, they should consider whether all effort factors are relevant for projects in the selected estimation context. It may occur, for example, that the domain experts considered these effort factors in the model that, although not relevant in the sample of the 15 historical projects, are actually relevant for the selected context and thus are needed to effectively estimate future projects. This issue should be considered when refining the CoBRA model at Oki.

10.4 Benefits and Costs

The pilot application of the CoBRA method showed its significant contribution to the achievement of the estimation objectives specified by Oki. During each iteration of the CoBRA model improvement, the weaknesses of the estimation model were discussed with respect to data validity and consistency as well as cost factors of the causal model. The related data collection processes were improved, and the model was enhanced accordingly. The causal model obtained at the end reflected the main factors that influence costs and productivity for the company according to the experts involved. Moreover, the sensitivity analysis allowed Oki to exclusively focus risk management and process activities on selected factors with the greatest influence on productivity.

Figures 10.13 and 10.14 graphically summarize the improvement of the CoBRA model's predictive performance achieved through the refinement iterations in the context of Oki. Figure 10.13 shows the mean magnitude of estimation error, whereas Fig. 10.14 shows the percentage of the historical projects for which estimation error was lower than or equal to 25 %.

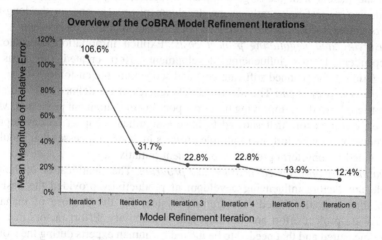

Fig. 10.13 Oki: mean magnitude of estimation error across modeling iterations

Summarizing, the pilot application of the CoBRA method at Oki provided the following benefits:

- *Project effort estimation*: The pilot CoBRA model provided accurate and repeatable estimates. The average error of estimates was 14 %, with 93 % of the estimates being below 25 %. Moreover, the postmortem analysis of the effort model indicated further improvement potentials in terms of estimation error.
- *Project control*: The project managers, especially those relatively inexperienced, got comprehensive support for planning and tracing projects against the plan.
- *Project risk management*: The transparent, context-specific effort overhead model provided information on the most critical threats to project success. Information

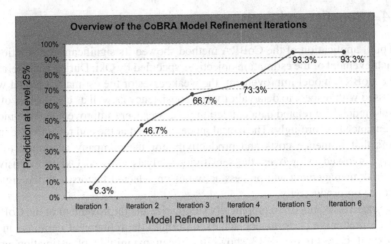

Fig. 10.14 Oki: prediction at level 25 % across modeling iterations

on the factors with the largest impact on productivity and effort allowed for reducing project risks early in the development process and, in the long-term perspective, focused improvement activities on appropriate process areas.

- *Justifying and negotiating project costs*: Explicit information on customer-dependent factors influencing development effort created the basis for negotiating the planned software cost and scope with the customer.
- *Process improvement*: The identified deficiencies of the defined size and effort metrics allowed for improving the corresponding measurement processes. Moreover, effort factors that showed to have a significant impact on development productivity and effort over multiple projects indicated processes that should be included in long-term process improvement initiatives.
- *Buildup of goal-oriented measurement program*: The identification of the most relevant factors influencing development productivity provided the basis for building a goal-oriented measurement system for the purpose of managing software project effort and development productivity. Effort factors that were not measured and that needed to be judged by human experts during the CoBRA model development could then be included in the measurement program to gain a quantitative basis for estimates in the future.
- *Reduction of software management overhead*: Finally, the reusable CoBRA model allowed for reducing estimation overhead in the future, compared to the estimation based on expert judgment applied so far. Moreover, as shown by the postmortem analysis of the CoBRA model (Iteration I6), the model can be potentially reduced without loss of its predictive performance. This would allow to further decrease the overall costs of effort estimation by reducing the overhead required to maintain the CoBRA model and the associated measurement data.

Table 10.5 summarizes the cost of the pilot application of the CoBRA model and of building an initial effort model.

Table 10.5 Oki:
approximate costs
of introducing the
CoBRA method

Cost aspect	Cost
Involved personnel	15 persons: • 2 external analysts • 1 internal analyst • 12 domain experts (reduced down to 8)
Total duration	4 months
Effort per Oki team member	26 person-hours
Total effort	3.5 person-months

Further Reading

- A. Trendowicz, J. Heidrich, J. Münch, Y. Ishigai, K. Yokoyama, and N. Kikuchi, "Development of a hybrid cost estimation model in an iterative manner," *Proceedings of the 28th international Conference on Software Engineering,* pp. 331–340. 2006.

  This paper briefly describes the CoBRA pilot application in the context of the Oki company described in this chapter. Yet, in addition to this chapter, the article reports the results of a comparison between CoBRA and simple data-driven effort estimation with ordinary least squares regression (OLS). Compared to CoBRA, OLS method, which is popular in the software industry, showed lower predictive performance in terms of estimation error. Moreover, OLS did not contribute to the achievement of the other estimation objectives, such as managing project risks or justifying estimates. Finally, the paper reports several lessons learned during the pilot application of CoBRA at Oki.

- A. Trendowicz, J. Heidrich, J. Münch, Y. Ishigai, K. Yokoyama, N. Kikuchi, "Development of a Hybrid Cost Estimation Model in an Iterative Manner," (in Japanese), *Software Engineering Center Journal,* no. 7. September 2006, Tokyo, Japan, ISSN 1349–8622.

  This paper reports on the pilot application of the CoBRA method at the Oki company in Japan. The content of this paper is approximately the same as that of the publication "Development of a hybrid cost estimation model in an iterative manner" we cited above.

Siemens Information Systems, India

11

This chapter summarizes the CoBRA application in the context of Siemens Information Systems, Ltd, India (SISL). In this chapter, we will present how to adapt the baseline CoBRA model development process to the needs and constraints of a particular organization in the embedded software systems domain. Moreover, we report on experience regarding the development of the CoBRA model throughout multiple refinement iterations. In particular, we will show how to analyze the performance of the CoBRA model, where to look for potential causes of observed deficits of the model, and how to appropriately improve the model. Finally, the SISL context shows how important the appropriateness and quality of the data used for estimation are for the successful estimation. We will provide examples of common deficits of measurement data and simple ways to identify and solve these deficits. In particular, we demonstrate how to define an appropriate size measurement approach for enhancement projects.

11.1 Context Characteristics

In 2008, the CoBRA method was applied in the context of the large-size software development organization Siemens Information Systems Ltd, India (SISL), a software development branch of a large international provider of software systems. Table 11.1 summarizes the detailed characteristics of the case study context. The technology transfer was led by one external CoBRA expert (analyst).

11.1.1 Measurement Data

For the purpose of size measurement, the size measure already defined at SISL was adopted. Software size was measured on software source code and used "Enhancement lines of code" (LOC_{Enh}) as presented in (11.1), where LOC_{Add}, LOC_{Mod}, and LOC_{Del} refer to added, modified, and deleted lines of code, respectively.

A. Trendowicz, *Software Cost Estimation, Benchmarking, and Risk Assessment*,
The Fraunhofer IESE Series on Software and Systems Engineering,
DOI 10.1007/978-3-642-30764-5_11, © Springer-Verlag Berlin Heidelberg 2013

Table 11.1 SISL: characteristics of the CoBRA application context

Context factor	Value
Organization	Siemens Information Systems, Ltd (SISL), India
Maturity	Certified at level 3 of the CMMI (v.1.1) model
Domain	Embedded software systems, medical systems
Development type	Enhancement
Life cycle model	Waterfall
Programming language	C++

$$LOC_{Enh} = LOC_{Add} + LOC_{Mod} + LOC_{Del} \qquad (11.1)$$

Project effort was measured in person-hours. Yet, similar to the Oki case (Chap. 10), in the context of SISL, the project effort for historical projects also included different project activities. In the SISL case, the reported project effort not only included different project phases but, for some cases, also included project management activities, while in other case, it did not. In order to address this issue and come up with consistent effort data for estimation purposes, the analysts decided to limit the scope effort measurements to engineering effort until integration testing. In other words, the historical project effort data used for the CoBRA model development included only engineering activities and covered the development phases from requirements specification via design, coding, and unit testing to integration testing. The effort measurements did not include project management activities such as configuration management.

The size and effort data for 13 already completed projects in a selected CoBRA modeling context were available. In addition to size and effort, the available project measurement data covered 62 additional attributes of the software development environment, including characteristics of the project, products, processes, and resources.

The actual development productivity was computed according to the classical definition of production rate defined in the IEEE-1045 (1993), that is, size of product divided by the effort required to produce it. Figure 11.1 presents the distribution of development productivity across those projects. We normalized the data for confidentiality reasons.

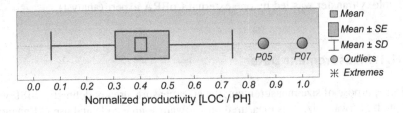

Fig. 11.1 SISL: initial project measurement data

The initial project data set suffered from major incompleteness. In total, 18.2 % of the project data entries were missing. Moreover, throughout the model development iterations, the analysts and the domain experts identified and eliminated several inconsistencies in the project data. Some of the identified data deficits reduced the data set by excluding from the study either complete project characteristics or complete projects. Finally, after the third iteration, the historical data set considered in the study incorporated 10 historical projects for which 15 characteristics were measured. Table 11.2 summarizes the changes to the SISL historical project data made during the course of CoBRA model development iterations.

Table 11.2 SISL: characteristics of the CoBRA application context

Measure	Initial data set	After iteration 1	Final data set
Number of projects available	13	11	10
Number of measures collected	62	15	15
Total ratio of missing data [%]	18.2 %	16.4 %	15.3 %

11.1.2 Domain Experts

CoBRA modeling at SISL involved three project managers with 10, 9, and 3 years of domain experience, respectively.

11.1.3 Additional Constraints

During the pilot application of the CoBRA method at SISL, two particular constraints needed to be considered:

- *Time resources*: Only a limited number of model development iterations and analyses within each iteration could be performed due to the fixed study schedule.
- *Business objectives*: The focus on achievement of the organization's objectives partially collided with the research objectives. Exclusion of experts was not possible, as the domain experts should get familiar with the CoBRA process (technology transfer objective). Moreover, as the process improvement and organizational learning objectives were the focus, we decided on informal integration of the results of the analytical and expert-based causal effort modeling.

11.2 Estimation Objectives

SISL expected the introduction of the CoBRA method to contribute to the following objectives of the organization:

- *Accurate project resource planning*: Effort estimation should provide accurate predictions of the effort required to complete software development project.

- *Effective project risk management*: Effort estimation should support project managers in identifying, analyzing, and managing potential project risks, that is, threats to successful project completion.
- *Effective productivity improvement*: Effort estimation should support project decision makers in selecting effective means to improve development productivity.
- *Effective process improvement*: Effort estimation should support the identification of process areas that potentially need improvement from the project management perspective.

11.3   Model Development

In order to minimize the overhead required for developing an effort model, incremental model development was applied in the SISL context. Figure 11.2 illustrates the procedure of the model development, which represents an adaptation based on the CoBRA modeling process described in Chap. 5.

In each development iteration, only a limited number of elements (factors and factor dependencies) that contributed to an improvement of the model's performance were changed (added, removed, or modified) in the causal effort model. Table 11.3 summarizes the model development iterations and the major refinement activities performed in each iteration. In Sects. 11.3.1–11.3.4, we briefly describe the content of the model development steps in each refinement iteration.

11.3.1 Iteration 1: Initial Modeling

I1. Step 1: Preparation and Planning
The transfer of the CoBRA method started with a 2-day tutorial where the external analysts provided the detailed theoretical background for the CoBRA method to one SISL internal analyst. Next, the internal analyst conveyed the theoretical CoBRA background to the SISL personnel who would later be involved in the pilot application of the CoBRA method at SISL. They included members of the corporate technology excellence team responsible for estimation technologies and project estimators—mainly project managers.

The pilot application started with a joint kick-off meeting where the external and internal analysts defined the detailed objectives of effort estimation at SISL. Moreover, they determined the organization's scope of the CoBRA application and specified the characteristics of the context in which CoBRA was to be applied. In particular, the analysts identified the available information sources—that is, measurement data and domain experts—and current estimation practices. The context information served as the input for the detailed planning of the CoBRA model development and validation. Planning included scheduling work activities and meetings with the involved SISL personnel (especially domain experts), collecting information regarding sources of available measurement data, and

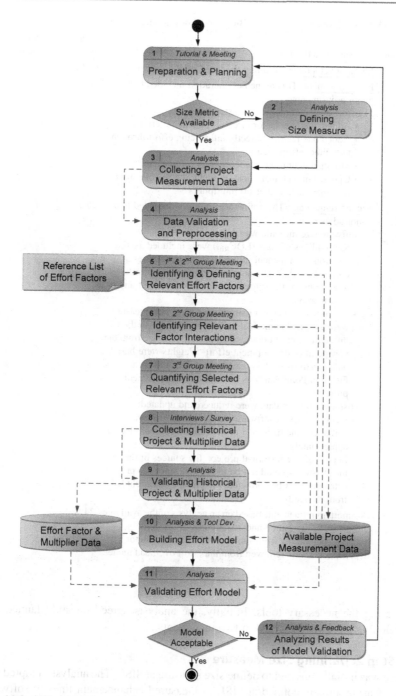

Fig. 11.2 SISL: CoBRA model development procedure

Table 11.3 SISL: overview of the CoBRA model development iterations

Iteration	Refinement activities	Estimation error	Number of factors
I1	Initial development: Building the first CoBRA model	65 %	5
I2	First refinement: This refinement iteration included two major adjustments: 1) Effort overhead model was extended: • Added one new factor directly influencing effort • Added one factor indirectly influencing effort through two direct effort factors • Modified definition of one existing effort factor • Updated model quantification including re-collection of project data and effort multipliers	56 %	7
I3	Second refinement: This refinement iteration included two major adjustments: 1) Software size measure was adjusted: • Reused lines of code (LOC_{Rus}) were included as an additional component in the "Enhancement lines of code" (LOC_{Enh}) size measure used at SISL in order to account for the software code reused without any modifications. • All components comprising the LOC_{Enh} size measure were assigned numerical weights to distinguish their different contributions to the total software size from the viewpoint of development effort. Weights were based on an analysis of the measurement data and on a Function Point Analysis for software enhancement projects. 2) Historical project data were reduced and updated: • Inconsistency in software size measurements was corrected, and historical project data were re-collected appropriately. • In case of one historical project, the sources of the inconsistency could not be identified. Since the project data could not be corrected, the project was excluded from the study.	26 %	7
I4	Postmortem refinement: Based on an analysis of the available project data—measured and acquired from the domain experts—potentially irrelevant effort factors and factor dependencies were removed from the effort overhead model.	24 %	4

preparing the necessary tools. Initially, the analysts agreed on and planned for developing the CoBRA model in two increments.

I1. Step 2: Defining Size Measure

There was initially no need to define size measure at SISL. The analysts adopted the size measure already defined at SISL. It measured enhancement lines of software source code and was defined as the sum of added, removed, and modified lines of software source code (11.4).

$$LOC_{Enh} = LOC_{Add} + LOC_{Mod} + LOC_{Del} \qquad (11.2)$$

I1. Step 3: Collecting Project Measurement Data

In this phase, the SISL analysts identified and collected the available measurement data for already completed projects within the context considered in the study together with the appropriate project managers. In the first iteration, project data on 62 project characteristics for 13 already completed projects were collected.

I1. Step 4: Data Validation and Preprocessing

Data Validation The measurement data collected from already completed projects initially required extensive preprocessing. Typical problems were a high rate of missing data and inconsistency of the collected measurements.

During initial data preprocessing, the analysts resolved the identified inconsistencies by consulting the managers of the considered projects. Moreover, the analysts compared the measurement data provided by individual project managers to the data extracted from the organization-wide central measurement database. As a result, they identified two outlier projects that differed significantly from the remaining 11 projects considered initially. These projects actually fell beyond the specified scope of the CoBRA application and as such were excluded from further consideration.

Data Preprocessing Next, the analysts looked closely at the 62 characteristics measured for the remaining 11 projects. Their objective was to prepare the data for automatic analysis. The analysts wanted to apply analytical techniques for identifying relevant factors influencing development productivity—meaning factors that should be considered in the CoBRA effort overhead model.

First, the analysts excluded all project characteristics that somehow related to software size or project effort and thus were obviously correlated to development productivity. For the remaining data, the analysts detected a few significant inconsistencies. For instance, they observed in the project data sheet inconsistent usage of empty cells—either "0" or "n/a"—for coding a zero value, a missing value, and "not applicable" for certain measures. Since these three values are semantically very different, analyzing such data may lead to wrong conclusions. This issue was resolved by revising the measurement data and consistently coding the respective measurements.

Another inconsistency was that the *number of hazardous requirements* was greater than the *total number of requirements*. The analysts resolved the inconsistencies they detected after consultation with the managers of the affected projects. For example, the inconsistency between the number of hazardous requirements and the total number of requirements was caused by different levels of detail of the associated measurement processes. Unlike the total requirements count, the hazardous requirements were considered on the level of sub-requirements. As a consequence, more than one hazardous sub-requirement could be counted for a single requirement.

An additional issue was the amount of useful information conveyed by the measurement data. On the one hand, for many project characteristics in the measurement data set, only a few data entries were actually provided. On the other hand, many characteristics had the same value over all considered historical projects. In both these cases, the available information was insufficient to draw reliable conclusions about the impact of a given characteristic on the productivity variance observed across the historical projects. Therefore, the analysts decided to exclude from the analysis those project characteristics that either had the same value for the historical projects considered or had more than 70 % of the data entries missing.

The analysts prepared the remaining measurement data for automatic analysis. For example, they converted the data format so that it was acceptable for particular analysis tools, and they removed special characters that might be misinterpreted by these tools. After preprocessing, the final data set consisted of 11 projects, for which 15 characteristics were measured with 16.4 % missing data.

I1. Step 5: Identifying and Defining Relevant Effort Factors

In this step, the analysts and the domain experts performed the first brainstorming session during which the involved domain experts identified those factors that, according to their experience, have a significant impact on development productivity in the considered context. Next, the analysts asked the domain experts to individually rate each identified effort factor with respect to three criteria:

- *Impact*: The strength of influence a given factor has on development productivity and effort (in the SISL context, we referred to this aspect as *importance*).
- *Measurability*: The difficulty (overhead) of collecting factor-related project data. This includes the ease of defining a quantitative measure and collecting the respective quantitative data.
- *Controllability*: The extent to which a software organization can influence/control the factor's value. For example, internal characteristics of an external customer organization are typically hard to control.

To assign values to each criterion, the domain experts used a 4-point approximately ratio scale, where rate 1 referred to the criterion's best value (e.g., the highest measurability) and rate 4 to the criterion's worst value. The analysts synthesized the rating outcomes and presented them to the domain experts during the next group meeting. During this meeting, the domain experts discussed the discrepancies between their individual ratings. However, only minor differences were identified. Afterwards, the analysts aggregated the ratings of the individual experts for each criterion using a simple arithmetic mean. Finally, the most relevant productivity factors were selected based on the aggregated impact and the measurability ratings. At that time, the controllability criterion was excluded as having

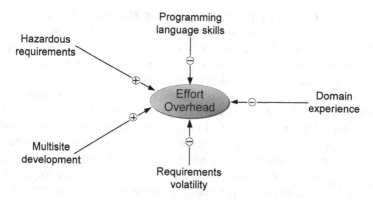

Fig. 11.3   SISL: initial effort overhead model

minor importance for the purpose of effort estimation. Yet, it was to be considered later on when applying the effort estimation model for negotiating project costs with external parties.

Based on the discussions, the domain experts decided to include five effort factors in the initial CoBRA model: *Programming language skills*, *Domain Experience*, *Requirements volatility*, *Hazardous requirements*, and *Multisite development*.

I1. Step 6: Identifying Relevant Factor Interactions
During the second group meeting, after selecting the most relevant effort factors, the analysts asked the domain experts to identify potential interactions between the effort factors included in the effort overhead. The analysts explicitly stressed the need to focus only on those factor interactions that may have a significant influence on each factor's impact on effort. After a joint discussion, the domain experts decided that there were no significant interactions between the effort factors considered in the effort overhead model (Fig. 11.3).

I1. Step 7: Quantifying Selected Relevant Effort Factors
The qualitative effort overhead model was then quantified in the next group meeting. During the meeting, the analysts asked the domain experts to define quantitative scales for those effort factors in the effort overhead model for which no measurement data were available yet. Since none of the considered effort factors had already been measured, the experts quantified all of them. The experts were asked to quantify each effort factor using a 4-grade approximately ratio scale, where 0 corresponded to the best-case and 3 to the worst-case value of the factor. For each value, the experts defined an unambiguous description of the project situation this value represented. Since the domain experts were supposed to provide the project data for respective factors, it was crucial that each expert interpreted the defined factor's values in exactly the same way.

I1. Step 8: Collecting Historical Project and Multiplier Data

After quantifying the effort factors included in the model, the analysts performed an interview session with all involved domain experts in order to acquire the project and effort multiplier data for all five effort factors in the effort overhead model.

Project data: First, the analysts asked each domain expert to provide the effort factor data for these projects that were known to the expert—for example, because the expert was directly involved in these projects. The involved domain experts were able to provide historical factor data for all 11 projects considered in the CoBRA modeling process. For some projects, more than one domain expert could provide factor data. This allowed comparing the experts' judgments and detecting potential inconsistencies.

Effort multipliers: Next, each expert was asked to quantify the impact of each factor on effort in terms of the percentage increase in effort caused by the factor, given it had its worst-case value and all other factors had their best-case values. In order to cover the experts' uncertainty, the analysts asked the domain experts to provide three multiplier values for each effort factor: the minimal (min), maximal (max), and most likely (ML) percentage increase in effort caused by the factor.

I1. Step 9: Validating Historical Project and Multiplier Data

After collecting the historical project and multiplier data, the analysts investigated the data with regard to potential inconsistencies.

Project data: The analysts used two strategies for validating the consistency of the provided historical project data:

- *Consistency against measurement data*: The analysts looked through the available measurement data to find project characteristics that were related to the effort factors quantified by the domain experts. If the analysts found corresponding measurement data, they compared them to the expert judgments.
- *Consistency between experts*: The analysts looked at the effort data that were provided by more than one expert and compared them to each other.

Effort multipliers: The analysts used two strategies for validating the consistency of the provided effort multiplier data:
- *Consistency between experts*: In order to identify potential inconsistencies, the analysts looked at the corresponding multipliers provided by different experts.
- *Consistency between factor ratings*: The percentage impact on effort was compared to the initial factors' ratings on the impact criterion given by the experts in the "*Identifying and Defining Relevant Effort Factors*" step (Step 5). An example inconsistency was that a given expert rated several effort factors as having clearly different levels of importance, but then the expert assigned very similar effort multipliers to these factors, which would suggest that they actually had a similar importance.

The analysts discussed and clarified the inconsistencies they detected with the corresponding domain experts. Based on these discussions, they made appropriate adjustments to the data.

I1. Step 10: Building Effort Model

In this step, the analysts combined the quantified effort overhead model, the multiplier data, and the past project data within a CoBRA simulation tool. Using the tool, they computed the nominal productivities across the historical projects as a basis for estimating new projects. Because the nominal productivities obtained for the historical projects still varied, the analysts decided to use the median value across the 11 historical projects considered in this iteration as a basis for estimating future projects.

I1. Step 11: Validating Effort Model

For the purpose of validation, the developed effort model was run on the available past project data. The performance of the initial effort model was not satisfactory. When validated on the historical projects, the model provided highly unstable estimates with an average error of 65 %. The planned second model development iteration aimed to improve the model's performance.

I1. Step 12: Analyzing Results of Model Validation

Before the model improvement iteration could start, the analysts needed to find the potential causes of the model's poor performance. The analysts investigated several issues.

Effort factors: In the first iteration, the domain experts had decided to include an effort factor "Hazardous requirements" although it was not the highest ranked one. In the validation phase, the analysts wanted to evaluate the impact of this very factor on the estimation performance of the CoBRA effort model. For this purpose, they excluded this factor from the model and validated it again on the historical project data. After excluding this effort factors, the model's performance was only slightly worse than the performance of the complete model including the factor. This result suggested that the considered effort factor did not have much impact on the performance of the CoBRA model and could potentially be excluded from the model.

Development productivity: The analysts looked at the model's ability to explain the variance of the actual development productivity across the considered historical projects. On the one hand, they checked how well the CoBRA model met the assumption of linear dependency between project effort and size (so-called production function). On the other hand, they looked at the distribution of nominal productivity provided by the model and compared it to the actual development productivity. The analysts noticed that the CoBRA model did not contribute to improve the linearity of the production function.

Effort overhead: Finally, the analysts looked at how the effort overhead related to the actual development productivity. According to the assumption of the CoBRA model, productivity should decrease with increasing effort overhead, in a nonlinear manner. Yet, the CoBRA model obtained after the first iteration did not show any clear trend between the effort overhead delivered by the model and the actual development productivity across the historical projects considered.

Table 11.4 SISL: improvement potentials after iteration I1

Issue	Improvement action	I2
Current measurement data indicated much lower development productivity for project P07 than expected by the domain expert who knew the project.	The measurement data for historical project P07 needed to be revised.	×
The domain experts realized that some of the relevant effort factors may be missing in the model.	Potentially missing effort factors that might explain the remaining productivity variance across the historical projects needed to be considered and added to the model.	√

The analysts presented the results of this analysis during a joint feedback session. During this session, the analysts and the domain experts discussed possible causes of the model's poor performance. In the end, the analysts and the domain experts came up with a list of two issues and corresponding improvements that should potentially be the subject of the next model refinement iteration. Table 11.4 summarizes the identified issues and the proposed improvement actions. The analysts and the domain experts agreed to address both issues in the next modeling iteration.

11.3.2 Iteration 2: Model Refinement

I2. Step 1: Preparation and Planning

During the preparation for the second iteration, both the SISL domain experts and the internal analysts individually investigated the outcomes of the initial model development iteration. They looked for possible reasons of the model's poor performance, in addition to those already discussed during the feedback session at the closure of the first modeling iteration. In particular, they investigated size and effort measurement for the historical projects considered in the study. Based on the outcomes of the feedback session in the first iteration and internal SISL investigations, the analysts and the domain experts decided on the exact model refinements.

> **Model Refinements**
> Based on the analysis of the model's performance and on discussions with the domain experts, the analysts decided that the second iteration should focus on revising the effort overhead model.

Finally, the external and internal analysts planned the activities of the refinement iteration. As input for the planning, the analysts took the objectives and constraints of the refinement iteration, the results of the first iteration, and the experiences they had gained in the previous iterations concerning the resources actually needed for performing particular activities. Planning consisted of specifying the exact model refinements, identifying existing information sources, and planning the iteration steps with the available time, budget, and personnel resources.

I2. Step 2: Defining Size Measure

In this iteration, the analysts used the size measure they had already employed in the first iteration (I1) without changes.

I2. Step 3: Collecting Project Measurement Data

In this step, the SISL domain experts and internal analysts reviewed the measurement data of the 11 historical projects considered in the study. The data from the first modeling iteration were taken without changes.

I2. Step 4: Data Validation and Preprocessing

The investigation of the project measurement data confirmed the results of the previous iteration in that project P07 was an outlier with respect to development productivity. In addition, the productivity of two more projects differed significantly from the other projects. The observed discrepancies in the projects' development productivity were to be addressed during the revision of the effort overhead model; the domain experts were to think about factors that made the productivity of these three projects differ from that of the others.

I2. Step 5: Identifying and Defining Relevant Effort Factors

The objective of this step was to revise the effort overhead model with respect to the most important factors influencing development productivity. In particular, the investigation focused on those factors that were responsible for the productivity variance across the 11 historical projects considered in the study.

In the second iteration, the analysts used analytical methods to support the domain experts in identifying the most relevant effort factors. The analysts employed factor selection techniques on whatever measurement data were available in order to identify those project characteristics that contribute most to the observed variance in productivity. Development productivity was defined according to IEEE-1045 (1993) as software size divided by development effort. Specifically, they used factor weighting technique called RReliefF[1] which was proposed by Robnik and Kononenko (2003) and implemented in the Weka[2] software tool (Hall et al. 2009). Factor weighting identified seven measured project characteristics that had a nonzero contribution to the variance in actual development productivity across the historical projects.

---

[1] In Sect. 5.6.1 (Example 5.4), we illustrate how to use the RReliefF technique for the purpose of quantifying the importance of potential effort factors covered by historical project measurement data.

[2] In the Weka implementation of the RReliefF technique, the analysts used the following settings: Attribute Selection Mode = "Cross-validation," numNeighbours = 2. All other settings were used with their default values.

In addition, the analysts integrated the rating of the factors' importance provided by the domain experts in the first modeling iteration with the analytical weights delivered by RReliefF. For this purpose, they computed an average weight over the normalized values of importance rates and weights. The combined results indicated "*Personnel turnover*" as having the greatest impact on productivity variance. Other important factors were "*Platform experience*" and "*Programming language experience*," with the latter factor already considered in the CoBRA model as "*Programming language skills.*"

Finally, the analysts presented the results of the analytical factor selection to the domain experts during a group session where the experts discussed these results. The main objective of this session was to refine the model so that it explained the variance in development productivity across the considered historical projects better. In particular, the distribution of nominal productivity showed two outlier projects. Project P05 was characterized by very high and project P08 by very low nominal productivity relative to the remaining projects. Therefore, the analysts asked the domain experts to look at the current model and at the distribution of development productivity across the considered historical projects and to think about how the model could be improved in order to better account for the observed productivity deviations.

After some discussion, the domain experts concluded that the model was missing two factors that, according to their project experience, have a significant impact on development productivity, namely, "*Platform experience*" and "*Number of key persons.*" After some deliberation, the group decided to add the "*Platform experience*" to the model as an effort factor directly contributing to project effort overhead and "*number of key persons*" as an indirect effort factor. According to the experts, the impact of the team's "*Domain experience*" and "*Platform experience*" depends on the "*Number of key persons*" in the team. Consequently, the new factor "*Number of key persons*" was added to the model as indirectly influencing project effort through the "*Domain experience*" and "*Platform experience*" factors.

Moreover, the definition of the *Domain experience* factor was refined, after it was revealed that it had been interpreted inconsistently by the involved domain experts. The revised factor was renamed to "*Domain/product experience.*"

Finally, the experts decided to retain the "*Hazardous requirements*" factor in the model although the model's validation in the previous iteration (I1) has shown a rather insignificant impact of the factor on the project effort. The experts' motivation was that although the factor might seem to have little impact on the effort of the considered historical projects, it principally had a significant impact on the effort of other projects they had worked in, but which were not considered in the development of the CoBRA model.

Table 11.5 summarizes effort factors defined in this iteration, which were actually the final set of factors defined at SISL.

I2. Step 6: Identifying Relevant Factor Interactions

The domain experts decided to add the "*Number of key persons*" factor as an indirect one. It has an indirect influence on two other factors, meaning two indirect

Table 11.5 SISL: the most relevant factors influencing development productivity

Effort factor	Factor definition
Programming language skills	Team experience regarding the programming language employed in the projects at the beginning of the development life cycle, that is, at the beginning of a project.
Domain/product experience	Experience in the project domain of the people who are expected to have such experience. In the context of SISL, the domain referred to medical applications and medical information systems.
Requirements volatility	Percentage of requirements that were changed after requirements freeze. The percentage of changes is considered in terms of the required rework effort rather than in terms of functional software size.
Multisite development	Number of separate development sites involved in a software development project.
Hazardous requirements	Percentage of hazardous requirements—relative to the total number of requirements – defined in a software development project.
Platform experience	Team experience regarding the application platform at the beginning of a project.
Number of key people	Number of people in a project whose experience and involvement are crucial for the success of a project.

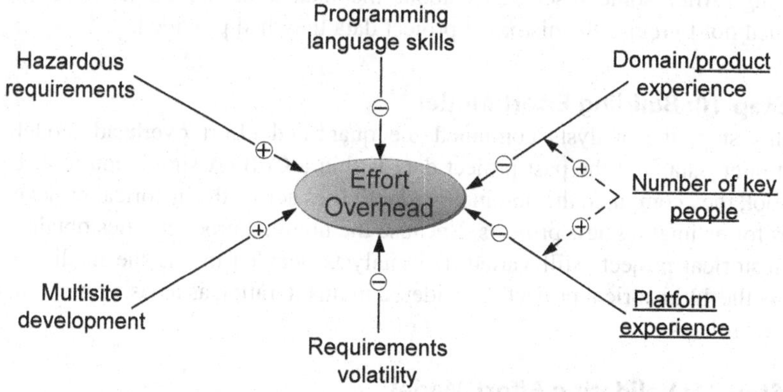

Fig. 11.4 SISL: effort overhead model (underlined elements were defined in the second iteration)

influences were added to the effort overhead model. Figure 11.4 illustrates the effort overhead model after the second modeling iteration.

l2. Step 7: Quantifying Selected Relevant Effort Factors

The objective of this step was to revise the quantitative measurement scales defined for the effort factors according to the most recent changes in the effort overhead model. During a group meeting, the domain experts defined quantitative scales for the newly added effort factors and revised the scales for the modified factors.

I2. Step 8: Collecting Historical Project and Multiplier Data

In this step, the analysts collected the effort factor data for the historical projects and the effort multipliers for the recently revised effort overhead model. Because the domain experts were already familiar with the data collection procedure, it could be performed off-line. Instead of interview sessions, the domain experts provided the data through an e-mail survey in which they filled out an appropriate questionnaire prepared by the analysts.

I2. Step 9: Validating Historical Project and Multiplier Data

In this step, the analysts applied an analytical factor weighting technique (RReliefF) on the factor data provided by the domain experts for the 11 historical projects. Next, they compared the importance of the factors indicated by weights to the importance ratings provided by the domain experts in the first iteration (Step 5). In this way, the analysts wanted to compare the importance of effort factors provided by the experts indirectly through the project data to the factor's importance they had rated directly in the first iteration.

This analysis revealed several inconsistencies where the analytically computed importance of a factor (weight) differed from the importance rated by the domain experts. The analysts presented these findings to the domain experts during a joint meeting. After some discussions about the data analysis, the domain experts decided not to revise the historical project data they had provided.

I2. Step 10: Building Effort Model

In this step, the analysts combined the quantified effort overhead model, the multiplier data, and the past project data within a CoBRA simulation tool. Using the tool, they computed the nominal productivities across the historical projects as a basis for estimating new projects. Because the nominal productivities obtained for the historical projects still varied, the analysts decided to use the median value across the 11 historical projects considered in this iteration as a basis for estimating future projects.

I2. Step 11: Validating Effort Model

The analysts validated the revised CoBRA model on the historical project data. Overall estimation accuracy improved in the sense that the average estimation error was reduced to 55 %. Yet, estimation accuracy still varied a lot across the historical projects. In particular, a few projects were extremely under- or overestimated. Moreover, only 8 % of the estimates had an estimation error of 25 % or less. Since these results were not acceptable, SISL decided to perform an additional iteration to revise the CoBRA effort model.

I2. Step 12: Analyzing Results of Model Validation

A detailed analysis of the model's validation results indicated several issues:

Development productivity: After the second iteration, the CoBRA model met the assumption regarding linear dependency between project effort and size better. However, it still did not satisfactorily explain the variance in development productivity. Several projects, including project P07, were outliers with respect to their nominal productivity computed by the CoBRA model. One of the consequences was that CoBRA was not able to estimate these projects properly.

Effort overhead: The analysts investigated the effort overhead of those projects that stood out with respect to their nominal productivity. They found that the effort overhead the current CoBRA model provided for these projects was inadequate for their actual productivity. Contrary to expectation, development productivity was hardly related to the projects' effort overhead. For example, three highly productive historical projects should have had much lower effort overhead than the CoBRA model actually assigned to them. And vice versa, an outlier project with low productivity should have had much higher effort overhead than the CoBRA model actually assigned to it.

The analysts identified several potential causes of the poor performance of the CoBRA model. On the one hand, the CoBRA effort overhead model might have been lacking some relevant effort factors that would have accounted for the missing effort overhead of the project with extremely low productivity. On the other hand, the currently considered effort factors seemed to allocate too much effort overhead to the projects with extremely high productivity. According to the analysts, one possible source of the latter effect could be that the effort overhead assigned by the domain experts to those effort factors that had their worst-case values in the three extremely productive projects was much higher than it actually was. One reason for that could be the low granularity of the applied 4-point approximately ratio scale. In order to understand this effect, let us consider a simple example. Let us define the worst-case value on the scale (3) for the *"Ratio of hazardous requirements"* effort factor as 25 % of the total requirements being hazardous. If two projects have a ratio of hazardous requirements equal to 25 % and 50 %, respectively, then they shall both be assigned the value 3 and the same amount of effort overhead, although in reality, the second project should be assigned much higher effort overhead because its ratio of hazardous requirements is twice as high as that the first project.

Moreover, the analysts indicated a potential inconsistency in project size and effort data as a likely source of the model's poor performance. For example, an analysis of the available project measurement data indicated reused lines of code as making a significant contribution to the variance in development productivity. This was, however, not used as part of the currently defined "Enhancement LOC" size measure. The analysts and the domain experts agreed that the amount of reused software source code should be considered while estimating project effort. The analysts suggested two alternative ways of including this aspect in the CoBRA effort model:

1. Adding it as an effort factor to the effort overhead model
2. Integrating it into the existing size measure for enhanced software code

Table 11.6 SISL: improvement potentials after iteration I2

Issue	Improvement action	I3
Some of the relevant effort factors might be missing in the effort overhead model. For example, an analysis of the project measurement data identified several project characteristics that have a significant impact on develop-ment productivity and that were not considered in the effort model.	Revise effort overhead model. Check if the model covers all factors that have a significant impact on productivity variance across the historical projects considered.	×
Current measurement data indicated much lower development productivity for project P07 than expected by the domain expert who knew the project.	Revise the size and effort measurement data for historical project P07.	√
Reused source code is not considered in the current size measure, although it is a widely acknowledged fact that it also contributes to the project's engineering effort. Moreover, application of the analytical factor selection technique on the available project measurement data confirmed that the reused lines of code had a significant contribution to the variance in development productivity across the historical projects considered.	Consider reused lines of code in the enhancement LOC measure. Modify the current size measure and re-collect the historical project data accordingly.	√
Information on the amount of reused source code is missing for most of the historical projects. Calculating the number of reused lines of code using other measurement data returned incorrect values. For example, the formula "Reused = Delivered−Added−Modified" returned negative values.	Review the historical project data regarding the size of the source code and check consistency.	√
The "Enhancement LOC" size measure is considered for determining testing effort, although the delivered lines of code should be considered. Enhancement activities on software code do not matter for testing effort because testing is always done on the delivered code – independent of how many LOC have been added, deleted, removed, or reused.	Consider delivered LOC instead of enhancement LOC for the estimation of testing effort.	×
The low granularity of the 4-point measurement scale used might potentially cause large variation in effort overhead, especially around the worst-case values.	Consider using more levels of the measurement scale or using a ratio scale for the effort factors.	×

Integrating reused LOC into the existing Enhancement LOC measure was preferred because other project control activities that use this size measure could automatically benefit from its update.

The analysts presented the results of the analysis to the domain experts during a joint feedback session. After some discussions, they came up with a list of several issues and corresponding improvement potentials. Table 11.6 summarizes them briefly. In the end, the analysts and the domain experts decided that in the next iteration, the current effort overhead model and project the size measures should be revised.

11.3.3 Iteration 3: Model Refinement

I3. Step 1: Preparation and Planning

The third iteration started with a brief preparation and planning of the activities and resources needed for implementing the refinements of the CoBRA model selected after the second iteration.

Model Refinements

Based on the analysis of the CoBRA model's performance after the second iteration and on the discussions with the domain experts, the analysts decided to address two particular issues in the third refinement iteration. It was decided that since reused source code contributes to overall project effort, it should be included in the size measure used for the purpose of effort estimation. After modifying the size measure, the historical project data should be updated accordingly. However, the direct measurements of the reused lines of code were not available for all historical projects considered in the study. Therefore, before updating the enhancement LOC data, the reused LOC measurement needed to be completed and validated first.

The domain experts decided that these should be the major model refinements realized in the third iteration. However, they decided to additionally review the effort overhead model and its quantification.

In addition to the refinement objectives, the analysts based their plans on the constraints of the refinement iteration, the results of the first iteration, and the experiences they had gained in the previous iterations concerning the resources actually needed for performing particular activities. Planning consisted of specifying the exact model refinements, identifying existing information sources, and planning the iteration steps with the available time, budget, and personnel resources.

I3. Step 2: Defining Size Measure

According to the decision regarding the most critical model refinements, the internal (SISL) and external analysts modified the *Enhancement LOC* software size measure used at SISL for the purpose of project effort estimation. The analysts based the modified definition of the size measure on the observation that adding, removing, modifying, and reusing the same amount of software code typically require different amounts of effort. Consequently, the analysts agreed that the outcomes of code enhancement—Added LOC, Modified LOC, Deleted LOC, and Reused LOC—should contribute differently to the overall value of the "Enhancement LOC" measure. Consequently, the measure should be defined as the weighted sum of these four elements instead of as a simple non-weighted sum as defined before.

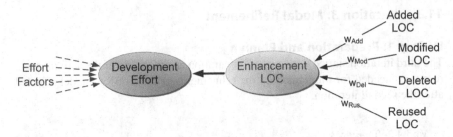

Fig. 11.5 SISL: software size model

In order to determine the appropriate weights for added, modified, deleted, and reused LOC, the analysts integrated the analysis of the measurement data and the expert judgments. This approach was actually similar to weighing the importance of potential effort factors the analysts had applied for selecting the most relevant effort factors in iteration I2 (Step 5). First, the analysts represented software size as a simple causal model. The idea was similar to the effort overhead model; only in this case, composite *Enhancement LOC* represented the causal effect (analogue to the effort overhead) and the four elements *Added LOC*, *Modified LOC*, *Deleted LOC*, and *Reused LOC* represented the influencing factors (analogue to the effort factors). Figure 11.5 illustrates this idea.

The objective of the weighting analysis was to determine the strength of the impact each size factor has on the total size. In the integrated approach, the experts first applied an analytical factor weighting technique on the available measurement data and then integrated the weighting results with the judgments of the SISL domain experts.

In order to apply an analytical factor weighting technique, the analysts needed measurement data concerning the four size factors (independent variables) and the composite "Enhancement LOC" measure (dependent variable). However, the "Enhancement LOC" was not known for the historical projects considered at SISL. In order to solve this issue, the analysts took advantage of the fact that the "Enhancement LOC" is actually an element in a causal chain between the four software size factors and the "Development effort[3]," as presented in Fig. 11.5. They used project effort as a proxy for the unknown "Enhancement LOC" measure and computed the numerical weights reflecting the strength of the impact the size factors had on effort. Next, they used these weights for approximating the strength of the impact the size factors had on "Enhancement LOC."

For the purpose of the analytical factor weighting, the analysts used the same RReliefF technique they had used in Step 5 of iteration I2 for identifying the most important effort factors. The analysts excluded from the analysis one historical

---

[3] In terms of causal modeling theory, "Enhancement LOC" was a latent causal mediator between size factors (Added LOC, Modified LOC, Deleted LOC, and Reused LOC) and "Development effort."

project, P08, for which the reused lines of code measurements (*Reused LOC* size factor) were missing and could not be acquired in retrospect. They then applied the RReliefF algorithm on the remaining set of ten historical projects.

The absolute numerical weights RReliefF assigned to individual size factors needed to be interpreted from the perspective of the relative development effort they required. The analysts considered developing new software as a baseline. As a consequence, adding new code from scratch corresponded to 100 % effort and should thus be assigned a baseline weight equal to 1. Relative to the newly added code, modifying, deleting, and reusing existing code required less effort and should thus be assigned weights lower than 1. Based on these assumptions, the analysts normalized the absolute weight RReliefF assigned to the "added LOC" factor to 1 and proportionally recomputed the absolute weights RReliefF assigned to the "Modified LOC," "Deleted LOC," and "Reused LOC" factors. The resulting relative weights were $w_{Add} = 1.0$, $w_{Mod} = 0.2$, $w_{Del} = 0.0$, and $w_{Rus} = 0.0$, where the value 0.0 should be interpreted as marginal influence rather than simply no influence at all.

The results of the analytical factor weighting indicated a certain trend but could not be used "as is" for defining the enhancement LOC measure. First, the results were based only upon ten historical projects and thus were not representative of the entire context considered in the CoBRA study. Moreover, they differed from the judgment of the involved domain experts and from the common experiences reported in the related literature, such as Dekkers (2004). The major difference concerned the contribution of deleted LOC and reused LOC. Both the domain experts and the related literature suggested that deleting and reusing existing software code contribute to overall development effort—though not extensively. Using these experiences, the analysts decided to use the following set of weights: $w_{Add} = 1.0$, $w_{Mod} = 0.25$, $w_{Del} = 0.1$, and $w_{Rus} = 0.1$. The analysts further used these weights for defining the new software size measure for the purpose of estimating the effort of the enhancement projects (11.3).

$$LOC_{Enh} = LOC_{Add} + 0.25\,LOC_{Mod} + 0.1\,LOC_{Del} + 0.1\,LOC_{Rus} \qquad (11.3)$$

I3. Step 3: Collecting Project Measurement Data

In this step, the analysts and the domain experts collected historical project data according to the changes they had made to the definition of the "enhancement LOC" size measure. In order to derive "Enhancement LOC" measurements, they first needed to collect data regarding added, modified, deleted, and reused LOC. Yet, the reused LOC had not been measured directly for all historical projects considered in the study. As a solution, the analysts decided to derive the reused LOC (11.4) using the available data on total LOC delivered (LOC_{Tot}), newly added LOC (LOC_{Add}), and LOC modified in the project (LOC_{Mod}).

$$LOC_{Rus} = LOC_{Tot} - LOC_{Add} - LOC_{Mod} \qquad (11.4)$$

I3. Step 4: Data Validation and Preprocessing

While collecting the historical project data, the analysts obtained a negative value for LOC_{Rus} for one of the projects. Since it was not possible to clarify the source of this inconsistency and thus to correct it, the analysts and the domain experts decided jointly to exclude this project from the study. The software size data for the remaining ten historical projects were accepted for developing and validating the CoBRA effort model.

I3. Step 5: Identifying and Defining Relevant Effort Factors

In this step, the analysts integrated the analysis of project measurement data and the judgments of the domain experts for identifying the most relevant effort factors. For this purpose, the analysts used the same analogue approach as in iteration I2. First, they applied the factor weighting technique (RReliefF) on the historical measurement data in order to identify those project characteristics that contribute most to the variance in development productivity observed across the historical projects considered. Next, they discussed the outcome of the analysis with the domain experts during a joint meeting.

The analytical approach showed that the number of different platform versions supported by the software system was factor that had a significant impact on development productivity. Moreover, the *"Platform experience"* and *"Programming language skills"* factors selected by the experts were reconfirmed as important effort factors by the analysis of the measurement project data. After discussing the results of the data analysis, the domain experts decided to use the effort factors included in the effort overhead from iteration I2 without any changes.

I3. Step 6: Identifying Relevant Factor Interactions

The domain experts decided not to introduce any changes to the existing causal effort model.

I3. Step 7: Quantifying Selected Relevant Effort Factors

The domain experts did not change the quantification of the effort factors in the effort overhead model. This refinement iteration adopted the factor quantifications from the previous iteration.

I3. Step 8: Collecting Historical Project and Multiplier Data

There was no need to collect project and multiplier data in this refinement iteration because (1) the effort overhead model was not changed and (2) the project and multiplier data collected in the previous iteration were considered as valid.

I3. Step 9: Validating Historical Project and Multiplier Data

There was no need for validating the historical project data and the multiplier data because they did not change in this iteration and had already been validated in the previous iteration.

I3. Step 10: Building Effort Model

In this step, the analysts combined the quantified effort overhead model, the multiplier data, and the past project data within a CoBRA simulation tool. Using the tool, they computed the nominal productivities across the historical projects as a basis for estimating new projects. Because the nominal productivities obtained for the historical projects still varied, the analysts decided to use the median value across the 11 historical projects considered in this iteration as a basis for estimating future projects.

I3. Step 11: Validating Effort Model

The validation results showed a high impact of the updated size measurement data on the model's predictive performance. The average estimation error decreased by more than half to 25 %. Moreover, the variation in estimation error across the historical projects also decreased, with 60 % of the estimates having an estimation error of 25 % or less.

I3. Step 12: Analyzing Results of Model Validation

A thorough investigation of the model's validation results showed several issues:

Development productivity: After the third iteration, the CoBRA model met the assumption regarding the linear dependency between project effort and size much better. However, it still did not satisfactorily explain the variance on development productivity. In particular, one project was an outlier with respect to its nominal productivity computed by the CoBRA model. One of the consequences was that CoBRA was not able to estimate this project properly. This project was also an outlier with respect to its actual productivity; it was a project with extremely low productivity. This suggested that the CoBRA model was not able to account for the productivity loss of this very project. This, in turn, indicated that the effort factors that were responsible for the productivity loss in the outlier project had either not been properly considered in the effort overhead model or had not been considered at all.

Effort overhead: The analysts investigated the effort overhead of the few projects that still differed regarding their nominal productivity. They found that the effort overhead the current CoBRA model provided for these projects was inadequate for their actual productivity. On the one hand, some projects were allocated much less effort overhead than implied by their low actual development productivity. On the other hand, a few projects seemed to be assigned larger effort overhead than indicated by their development productivity.

The analysts and the domain experts discussed the outcomes of the analysis in a joint feedback session. As a result, they came up with a list of two major issues and corresponding improvement potentials that needed to be addressed by future model refinements. Table 11.7 briefly summarizes the identified issues and the suggested refinements. The analysts agreed that revising the effort overhead model from the perspective of the productivity outlier projects would have first priority.

Table 11.7 SISL: improvement potentials after iteration I3

Issue	Improvement action	I4
The CoBRA model does not explain the productivity loss of a project with extremely low productivity.	Revise current effort overhead model with respect to its ability to account for the productivity loss of the outlier projects. The revisions should particularly focus on (1) identifying and removing any unnecessary/misleading effort factors from the model, (2) revising the appropriateness of the effort multipliers assigned to effort factors in the model, and (3) identifying and adding to the model any missing effort factors that have a significant impact on development productivity.	√
The modification of the Enhancement LOC size measure proposed in this iteration has an initial character.	The new enhancement LOC size measure needs to be validated by SISL in different scenarios and revised appropriately. Revisions should particularly concern the weights assigned to individual components of the Enhancement LOC measure, that is, Added LOC, Modified LOC, Deleted LOC, and Reused LOC.	×

However, due to the limited availability of the domain experts, SISL decided not to continue model refinements and improve the model internally at a later time using the knowledge gained during the pilot modeling. The analysts proposed running an additional refinement iteration based solely on the quantitative analysis of the project data collected in the previous modeling iteration—including the historical measurement data and the data acquired from domain experts. On the one hand, the analysts were interested in identifying potentially irrelevant effort factors and interactions that should (could) be removed from the model without decreasing its predictive performance. On the other hand, they wanted to identify effort factors and interactions that were potentially relevant and thus should be added to the model in order to improve its predictive performance, in particular for the outlier projects.

11.3.4 Iteration 4: Analytical Refinement

I4. Step 1: Preparation and Planning

The fourth iteration differed from the previous iterations in that it did not involve the domain experts. In this iteration, the analyst revised the effort overhead model based solely on an analysis of the available project data.

Model Refinements

Based on the discussions during the joint feedback session at the end of iteration 3, the analysts decided to revise the effort overhead model based solely on an analysis of the available project data. In particular, the analysis focused on identifying effort factors and interactions that (1) are incorporated in the effort overhead model but are potentially irrelevant and thus should be removed from the model, and (2) are not incorporated in the effort overhead model but are potentially relevant and should be added to the model.

Since this iteration focused on a quantitative data analysis and did not involve the domain experts, all the activities that typically involve the domain experts could be skipped in this iteration.

The analysts planned this iteration solely from the perspective of investigating quantitative project data. As no domain experts were involved in this iteration, the analysts did not have to plan any joint activities with the domain experts such as group meetings or interviews. As input for the planning, the analysts took the objectives and constraints of the refinement iteration and the experiences they had gained in the previous iterations concerning the analysis of the quantitative data.

I4. Step 2: Defining Size Measure
In this iteration, the analysts used the enhancement LOC measure defined in the iteration I3.

I4. Step 3: Collecting Project Measurement Data
In this iteration, the analysts used the project measurement data collected and modified throughout the previous iterations.

I4. Step 4: Data Validation and Preprocessing
The analysis of the complete project data did not reveal any further serious problems other than issues that had already been discovered and addressed in the previous iterations.

I4. Step 5: Identifying and Defining Relevant Effort Factors
In order to identify potentially relevant and irrelevant effort factors, the analysts applied the same analytical factor weighting to the measurement data and the effort factor data provided by the domain experts for the already completed—historical—projects considered in the pilot CoBRA application at SISL. The analysts used the same factor weighting technique (RReliefF) they had already used in Step 5 of iteration I2 and iteration I3. The objective of the analysis was to investigate the measured project characteristics and effort factors already incorporated into the CoBRA effort model with respect to their contribution to the variance in development productivity across the historical projects considered.

Analysis of measurement data: The analysis of the project measurement returned results analogue to those obtained in Step 5 of the previous iteration (iteration I3). It indicated that the number of different platform versions supported by the software system was a factor that had a significant impact on development productivity. Moreover, the *"Platform experience"* and *"Programming language skills"* factors

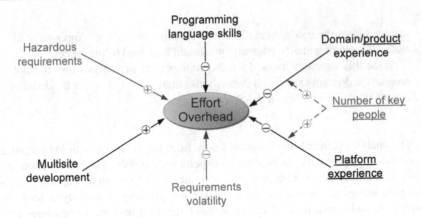

Fig. 11.6 SISL: reduced effort overhead model

selected by the experts were reconfirmed as important effort factors by the analysis of measurement project data.

Analysis of expert data: The analysis of the effort factor data provided by the domain experts indicated that some of the effort factors included in the effort overhead model do not contribute to the variance in development productivity across the historical projects considered. Particular effort factors included *"Hazardous requirements," "Requirements volatility,"* and *"Number of key people."* The analysts decided to exclude them from the model and validate how this would influence the model's predictive performance.

14. Step 6: Identifying Relevant Factor Interactions
After excluding the *"Number of key people"* factor, there were no indirect influences left in the model. The analysts decided to model all remaining effort factors as directly influencing effort and to refrain from modeling indirect impacts on effort. Figure 11.6 presents the reduced effort overhead model. The elements marked in gray were excluded based on the analysis of effort factor data provided by the domain experts.

14. Step 7: Quantifying Selected Relevant Effort Factors
For the effort factors remaining in the effort overhead model, the analysts used the quantifications that had already been defined in the previous modeling iterations.

14. Step 8: Collecting Historical Project and Multiplier Data
The analysts used the historical project and multiplier data that had already been collected in the previous iterations. They merely removed from the data repository those data associated with the effort factors and interactions that they had removed from the effort overhead model.

I4. Step 9: Validating Historical Project and Multiplier Data

There was no need for validating the historical project data and the multiplier data used in this iteration because they had already been validated in the previous iterations.

I4. Step 10: Building Effort Model

In this step, the analysts combined the reduced effort overhead model and its associated project and multiplier data within a CoBRA simulation tool. Using the tool, they computed the nominal productivities across the historical projects as a basis for estimating new projects. They used the median value of nominal productivity across the ten historical projects considered in this iteration as a basis for estimating future projects.

I4. Step 11: Validating Effort Model

The analysts validated the reduced CoBRA effort model using the data from the ten historical projects considered in the CoBRA pilot application at SISL. The model showed slight improvement of the predictive performance. The average estimation error decreased to 24 % with unchanged variance of estimates across individual projects.

I4. Step 12: Analyzing Results of Model Validation

Detailed analysis of the model's performance showed that the model suffered from similar deficits as the unreduced model in iteration I3. In particular, the model did not account for the extremely low productivity of an outlier project. The most likely reason was that although the analysts had removed irrelevant factors from the model, they had not added any factors that could potentially explain the extremely low productivity of this project. Based on these observations, the analysts came up with a list of several issues and corresponding improvement potentials that should be addressed in future revisions of the CoBRA model created during the four iterations of the pilot study. Table 11.8 summarizes them briefly.

Table 11.8 SISL: improvement potentials after iteration I4

Issue	Improvement action	Future
The CoBRA model does not explain productivity loss of a project with extremely low productivity.	Revise the current effort overhead model with respect to its ability to account for the productivity loss of outlier projects. The revisions should particularly focus on (1) identifying and removing any unnecessary/misleading effort factors from the model, (2) revising the appropriateness of the effort multipliers assigned to the effort factors in the model, and (3) identifying and adding to the model any missing effort factors that have a significant impact on development productivity.	√
The modification of the Enhancement LOC size measure proposed in this iteration has an initial character.	The new enhancement LOC size measure needs to be validated by SISL in different scenarios and revised appropriately. Revisions should particularly concern the weights assigned to individual components of the "Enhancement LOC", that is, Added LOC, Modified LOC, Deleted LOC, and Reused LOC.	√

11.3.5 Benefits and Costs

The pilot application of the CoBRA method has shown its significant contribution to the achievement of the objectives specified by SISL. During each iteration of the CoBRA model development, the analysts and the domain experts discussed the weaknesses of the estimation model as well as their potential causes and solutions. Identified improvement potentials concerned both the elements of the effort over-head model and the data upon which the effort model was developed. Throughout a series of group meetings, the analysts and the domain experts at SISL could learn about the most relevant factors influencing software development effort, which were at the same time the most relevant factors influencing development produc-tivity. Moreover, they could improve selected measurement processes related to effort estimation, which in turn had a positive impact on other management activities that used the same measurement data.

Figures 11.7 and 11.8 graphically summarize the improvement of the CoBRA model's predictive performance achieved through the various refinement iterations in the context of SISL. Figure 11.7 shows the mean magnitude of estimation error, whereas Fig. 11.8 shows the percentage of the historical projects for which estima-tion error was lower than or equal to 25 %.

Summarizing, the pilot application of the CoBRA method at SISL provided the following benefits:

- *Accurate project resource planning*: The obtained effort model enabled the project managers to make reliable (accurate) and repeatable project estimates.

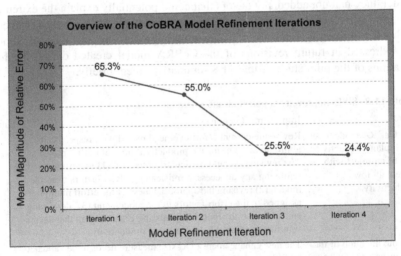

Fig. 11.7 SISL: mean magnitude of estimation error across modeling iterations

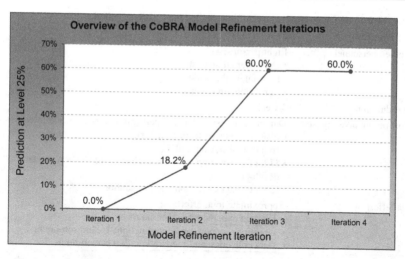

Fig. 11.8 SISL: prediction at level 25 % across modeling iterations

- *Effective project risk management*: The transparent and context-specific structure of the model indicating the most relevant factors influencing development
  productivity supported the project managers in analyzing potential project risks
  and created a basis for effectively negotiating project costs and scope with the
  involved stakeholders.
- *Effective productivity improvement*: The effort factors that consistently showed
  to have a negative impact on development productivity indicated areas of the
  organization that required improvement in order to avoid productivity losses in
  the future.
- *Effective process improvement*: The effort factors that consistently showed to have
  the greatest impact on increased project effort—due to productivity loss—
  indicated processes that need to be improved first in order to increase development
  productivity and reduce project effort. Moreover, the analysts identified several
  improvement potentials regarding the organization's measurement processes. On
  the one hand, inconsistencies in the project measurement data considered during
  effort modeling indicated several important improvement potentials. On the other
  hand, the most relevant effort factors provided a basis for building goal-oriented
  measurement system for the purpose of managing software project effort and
  development productivity. In the study, the project data for these factors needed to
  be acquired from human experts. Due to the inherent subjectivity and uncertainty
  of human judgment, this might have been the source of additional errors in the
  model. Including these factors into the measurement program would allow for
  gaining a quantitative basis for future estimates.

Moreover, the concise and reusable effort model supported SISL by reducing the
overhead for effort prediction—compared to predictions based on expert

Table 11.9 SISL: approximate costs of introducing the CoBRA method

Cost aspect	Cost
Involved personnel	Eight persons: • One external analyst • Four internal analysts • Three domain experts
Total duration	3 weeks
Effort per involved person	Domain experts: 28 h per expert (group meetings and interviews) CoBRA users (per team member): • 16 h of CoBRA tutorial • 37 h of direct support and coordination of CoBRA model development • 120 h of data collection and preparation
Total effort	Approximate total effort: • Domain experts: 84 person-hours • Learning, support, and coordination: 148 person-hours • Data collection and preparation: 240 person-hours

judgment—and by reducing the overhead needed for collecting measurement data for the purpose of estimation.

The delivered effort estimation model was a first step toward formalizing and integrating the effort estimation procedures at SISL. The model can (and should) be expanded to encompass more effort factors and more projects. The knowledge and experiences gained during this study should be used to maintain and refine the model as well as to build and optimize models for other project contexts, meaning other domains, development types, technologies, etc.

Table 11.9 summarizes the cost of the pilot application of the CoBRA model and of building an initial effort model.

Japan Manned Space Systems, Japan

12

This chapter summarizes the CoBRA application in the context of Japan Manned Space Systems Corporation, Japan (JAMSS). In this chapter, we will show how to adapt the baseline CoBRA model development process to the specific context of independent verification and validation (IV&V), which is different from the kind of software development to which CoBRA is typically applied. We will demostrate how to create CoBRA models for different IV&V objectives and how to address typical constraints of the IV&V context.

12.1 Context Characteristics

The CoBRA method was applied in the context of Japan Manned Space Systems (JAMSS), a company that performs independent verification and validation (IV&V) of space software systems.

Independent verification and validation can be defined as a process where software work products generated by a development team are verified and validated by a completely independent organizational entity. Independence is considered in terms of technical, managerial, and financial independence (IEEE-1012 2005).

At the time of the study JAMSS had been mainly supporting the functions of the Japan Aerospace Exploration Agency (JAXA) for over 10 years, in particular:

- Functions related to safety and product assurance of space systems such as the International Space Station (ISS), and
- Set up of initial operations and stationary operations of the ISS's Japanese Experiment Module (JEM).

The CoBRA method was applied at JAMSS in the context of the independent verification and validation of safety- and mission-critical software systems (Table 12.1).

A. Trendowicz, *Software Cost Estimation, Benchmarking, and Risk Assessment*,
The Fraunhofer IESE Series on Software and Systems Engineering,
DOI 10.1007/978-3-642-30764-5_12, © Springer-Verlag Berlin Heidelberg 2013

Table 12.1 JAMSS: characteristics of the CoBRA application context

Context factor	Value
Organization	Japan Manned Space Systems Corporation, Japan
Maturity	ISO-9002, ISO-9001, ISO-14001
Domain	Embedded safety-critical software systems (space systems)
Development type	Independent verification and validation (IV&V) of software systems
Life cycle model	*This characteristic does not apply to IV&V*
Programming language	*This characteristic does not apply to IV&V*

12.1.1 Constraints

The typical constraint of IV&V, as compared to classical in-house verification and validation (V&V), is limited information on the processed artifacts. On the one hand, there is limited knowledge about the software development environment; on the other hand, IV&V has to handle various types of mission-critical systems. This variety does not allow for collecting a lot of historical project data. Moreover, the involvement of three quite different groups of stakeholders (customer-, development-, and IV&V-entity) in the software development process contributes to frequent and unpredictable requirements changes. In such a context, managing an IV&V project's resources is critical and difficult at the same time.

Unlike typical CoBRA applications, the pilot effort model for JAMSS was not developed on site. The JAMSS representative who was to coordinate the application and learn the method (internal analyst) visited the external analysts. In addition, the internal analyst was responsible for communication with the domain experts at JAMMS who operated in their native language (Japanese). The JAMSS analyst performed all necessary data acquisition and feedback meetings with the domain experts via telephone and email.

12.1.2 Scope

The CoBRA application at JAMSS focused on IV&V of the software requirements specification documents using a document review technique. The document review process starts with a risk analysis to identify a software system's operational risks. Software requirements are then reviewed in more detail based on their operational risks with respect to one or more review objectives. In principle, the six review objectives defined by Kohtake et al. (2008) were considered as listed in Table 12.2.

Since the review process varied depending on its objective, JAMSS decided to build an individual CoBRA model for each objective. In summary, the context of the CoBRA modeling was limited to a review of the requirements specification with a single objective.

Table 12.2 JAMSS: IV&V objectives and corresponding project data

ID	Objective	#Projects
O1	Risk analysis	5
O2	State transition completeness and consistency	5
O3	Design completeness for exceptional behavior	5
O4	Timing correctness and consistency	4
O5	Interface correctness and consistency	3
O6	Traceability	5

12.1.3 Measurement Data

A survey about current estimation practices at JAMSS revealed that, in total, measurement data from around ten already completed projects had been collected within the past 10 years. Due to the strong uniqueness of the considered projects, the data suffered from large variability. Moreover, around 20 % of the data entries were missing. The IV&V *effort* was measured in person-hours and had been collected for five already completed projects. Yet, since some of the IV&V objectives were not addressed in each of the five projects, the quantitative data available for CoBRA modeling varied between three and five historical projects. Table 12.2 summarizes for each IV&V objective considered in the study the number of projects that could be used for building a CoBRA model. *Size* was measured in terms of pages of software requirements for objectives O1 to O5 and, in addition, the pages of the system[1] specification for objective O6.

12.1.4 Domain Experts

There were three domain experts involved in the study who provided their knowledge as input for building the CoBRA effort model. Project effort *estimation*—The project managers gained a systematic approach for making <u>reliable</u> and <u>repeatable</u> estimates at the beginning of a new IV&V project.

- *Project risk management*: The project managers obtained explicit information for analyzing and managing major risks jeopardizing project success, in particular information regarding the factors that have a significant negative impact on IV&V efficiency.
- *Justifying and negotiating project costs*: The project managers gained a reliable basis for justifying planned IV&V costs to the project stakeholders and for making informed decisions about accepting a particular IV&V project.
- *Process improvement*: The project managers obtained insights into those areas of the IV&V processes that have the greatest impact on increasing the costs of IV&V. In particular, the project managers learned which factors have the greatest negative impact on the efficiency of IV&V activities in a considered

---

[1] Systems refers to composition of software and hardware

estimation context. These factors indicated process areas that are responsible for major efficiency loss and thus should be the main target of improvement activities.

Moreover, the analysts and the domain experts at JAMSS benefited from the qualitative experiences gained during the pilot application of the CoBRA method. The most important lessons learned included:

- *Effort estimation scope*: Depending on the specific objective of IV&V, different IV&V activities are required and different personnel is involved. Consequently, different factors might influence IV&V effort for different objectives. Therefore, the scope of effort estimation, meaning the context for which an effort model is built and applied, should be limited to a single IV&V objective. Since different IV&V objectives involved quite independent sets of activities, the total effort of an IV&V project aimed at attaining multiple objectives can be estimated as the sum of the efforts estimated individually for each objective.
- *Size and complexity of review*: The complexity of a document under review should be considered as an effort factor in addition to simple size measures, such as the number of document pages.
- *Effort factors*: A very important aspect of effort modeling is to consider effort factors other than simply size, although this is typically the major determinant of project effort. The JAMSS analyst and the domain experts experienced that a single factor may multiply effort by as much as ten times. For example, if e software supplier does not perform risk assessment, the effort that an IV&V company must spend on independent risk analysis may increase by up to 20 times. Such an effect is impossible to investigate based only on historical size and effort data which are usually used in software industry as the only basis for managing development productivity and effort.

Table 12.6 summarizes the costs of the pilot application of the CoBRA model and of building an initial effort model.

Table 12.3 summarizes the expertise and experience of the domain experts involved in the CoBRA pilot application at JAMSS.

Table 12.3 JAMSS: characteristics of involved domain experts

Expert	Expertise	Domain experience [#years]	Estimation experience [#years]
E1	Safety reviews	7	8
E2	Product quality and safety assurance	8	9
E3	Safety assurance in operation	4	6

12.2 Estimation Objectives

Besides traditional estimation objectives, such as precise planning and tracking software resources, JAMSS required the CoBRA method to support project decision-making. In summary, the CoBRA method was expected to contribute to the following objectives:

- *Project effort estimation*: The effort estimation should support the project managers with a systematic approach for making <u>reliable</u> and <u>repeatable</u> estimates at the beginning of a new IV&V project.
- *Project risk management*: The effort estimation should support the project managers in the explicit identification of major risk jeopardizing project success, in particular factors that have a significant negative impact on IV&V efficiency.
- *Justifying and negotiating project costs*: The effort estimation should provide the project managers with a reliable basis for justifying planned IV&V costs to the project stakeholders and for making informed decisions about accepting a particular IV&V project.
- *Process improvement*: The effort estimation should support the project managers in performing a comprehensive investigation of those areas of the IV&V processes that have the greatest impact on increasing the costs of IV&V.

12.3   Model Development

Six CoBRA models were built in parallel at JAMSS—one model for each requirement review objective. Each model was developed following the same process summarized in this section. The resulting models were very simple and fairly similar to each other. Each model included just a few effort factors and many factors were shared by multiple models. At JAMSS, all CoBRA models were developed in a single iteration, meaning the modeling process finished after a model had been validated.

In the JAMSS case, direct meetings and interview sessions involved only one domain expert who played, at the same time, the role of an internal analyst. Besides learning the CoBRA method, she coordinated the study at the JAMSS site and communicated with the other domain experts involved in the pilot CoBRA at JAMSS. She communicated with the domain experts on site in their native language (Japanese) using telephone and email. She also translated all documents exchanged between the analyst and the domain experts (Fig. 12.1).

12.3.1 Step 1: Preparation and Planning

The transfer of the CoBRA method started with a 2-day tutorial where the detailed theoretical background for the CoBRA method was provided to the internal analyst of JAMSS.

The pilot application started with a kick-off meeting where the internal and external analysts defined the detailed objectives of effort estimation at JAMSS. Moreover, they determined the context of the CoBRA application at JAMSS and specified its characteristics. These included existing estimation processes and available information sources, particularly measurement data and domain experts. This context information was the input for the detailed planning of the CoBRA model development and validation. Planning included scheduling tasks and

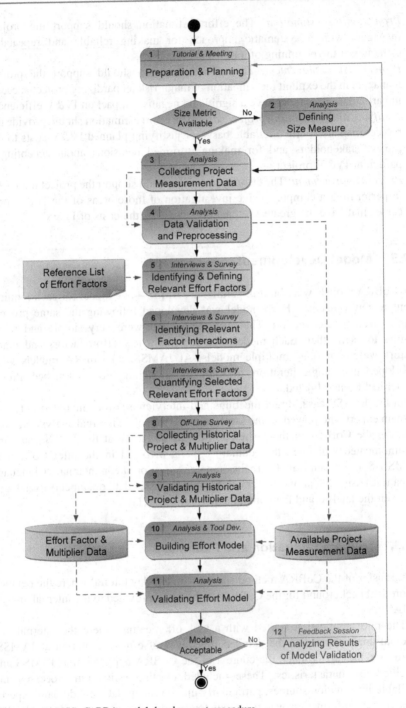

Fig. 12.1 JAMSS: CoBRA model development procedure

communication with the involved experts, collecting information regarding the sources of available measurement data, and preparing the necessary tools.

12.3.2 Step 2: Defining Size Measure

The purpose of the pilot CoBRA application at JAMSS was to estimate the effort required for reviewing—for different objectives—software and system requirements specifications. For the purpose of size measurement, the analysts agreed on the use of simple numbers of pages of the requirement documents under review.

12.3.3 Step 3: Collecting Project Measurement Data

After defining the size measure, the analysts collected size and effort measurement data from the five already completed IV&V project considered in the study. For this purpose, the internal analyst contacted the personnel responsible for data collection at JAMSS.

12.3.4 Step 4: Data Validation and Preprocessing

The analysts checked the historical project data for potential threats such as invalid or missing data entries. The analysis did not discover any serious issues.

12.3.5 Step 5: Identifying and Defining Relevant Effort Factors

In this step, the internal analyst interviewed the domain experts at JAMSS regarding the most relevant factors influencing the efficiency of reviewing software or system requirements. Next, the analyst consolidated the factors identified by the domain experts and prepared a questionnaire for rating effort factors with respect to their impact on review efficiency, their measurability, and their controllability. The domain experts were then asked to rate the effort factors off-line using the questionnaire.

The analysts checked the factor ratings for potential inconsistencies. Next, they used the impact and measurability ratings to select the most relevant factors, that is, those factors that have the greatest impact on review efficiency and are easy to measure at the same time. Table 12.4 summarizes the most relevant effort factors identified at JAMSS.

12.3.6 Step 6: Identifying Relevant Factor Interactions

The analysts presented the factor ranking results to the domain experts and asked them to review them with respect to the appropriateness of the selected factors as well as existence of potential factor dependencies. The domain experts decided to neither change the selected factors nor include any factor interactions. The

Table 12.4 JAMSS: the most relevant factors influencing development productivity

Effort factor	Factor definition	Objectives
Domain experience	The level of domain experience of the IV&V team	O1–O3
Requirements volatility	The extent of requirements volatility allowed within an initial contract	O2–O4, O6
Novelty of IV&V technique	The level of novelty of the applied IV&V technique for the IV&V team	O3
Interface complexity	The number of the system's interfaces to other (sub)systems	O4, O6
Time pressure	The extent of time pressure in the last IV&V phase	O5
Risk assessment by supplier	The level of risk assessment that was done by a supplier or customer	O1
IV&V for risk analysis	The extent to which the fault tree analysis (FTA) was done by the IV&V company	O1
Timing consistency evaluation	The timing consistency objective included in IV&V	O5
FPGA review performed	The extent to which a field programmable gate array (FPGA) review was performed	O5
New personnel	The extent to which the personnel involved in IV&V was new and inexperienced	O1

analysts used the most relevant factors for building six effort overhead models, one model for each IV&V objective considered in the study. Figure 12.2 illustrates these models.

12.3.7 Step 7: Quantifying Selected Relevant Effort Factors

The domain experts were then asked to quantify the effort overhead models, that is, define quantitative measurement scales for the incorporated effort factors. This step was accomplished throughout a series of "acquisition-and-feedback" cycles. In each cycle, the internal analyst first acquired the required information from the domain experts via telephone or email and then discussed the outcomes with the external analysts. If any issues or questions arose, the internal expert clarified them with the domain experts and got back to the external analysts.

Before quantifying the effort factors, the domain experts were asked to review them to make sure that none of the factors represented a complex concept and, thus, needed to be split into component aspects before quantification. The experts found no effort factor that would need such decomposition. Next, the domain experts quantified the effort factors using a 4-point approximately ratio measurement scale. Each measurement was precisely defined in order to ensure that subsequent values were equidistant and that all involved experts consistently understood them and could provide consistent project data for them.

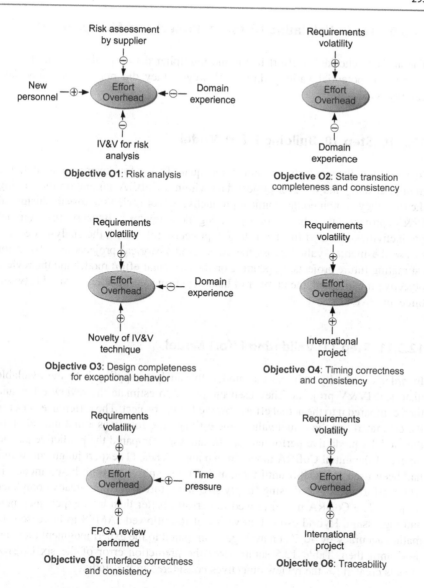

Fig. 12.2 JAMSS: Final effort overhead models

12.3.8 Step 8: Collecting Historical Project and Multiplier Data

In this step, the analysts prepared questionnaires for collecting the data required for implementing and validating the CoBRA effort model. One questionnaire regarded the effort factor data for the five already completed (historical) project considered in the study. The second questionnaire regarded the effort overhead introduced by each effort factor assuming its worst-case value. The analysts used these questionnaires in an off-line survey in which the domain experts provided the required data.

12.3.9 Step 9: Validating Historical Project and Multiplier Data

The analysts checked if effort factor and multiplier data provided by the domain experts for potential validity threats. However, they did not discover any data validity issues.

12.3.10 Step 10: Building Effort Model

In this step, the analysts combined the quantified effort overhead model, the multiplier data, and the past project data within a CoBRA simulation tool. Using the tool, they computed the nominal productivities for reviews across the historical IV&V projects as a basis for estimating new reviews. Because the nominal productivities obtained for the historical projects still varied, the analysts decided to use the median value across the considered historical projects as a basis for estimating future projects. Depending on the particular effort model and the review objective it addressed, the number of historical projects considered varied between three and five (Table 12.2).

12.3.11 Step 11: Validating Effort Model

In order to initially validate the model, the analysts applied it to the available historical IV&V projects. They used the model to estimate the review effort and then compared it to the actual effort observed in the project. The difference between the estimated and the actual value—the estimation error—was a first indication of the model's predictive performance. The analysts compared the predictive performance of the initial CoBRA model to two approaches: (1) expert judgment, which had been used at JAMSS until then, and (2) a simple regression-based model, in which effort is estimated using simply size and effort data from already completed projects. The CoBRA model proved to perform better than both expert judgment and regression. Hybrid estimation with CoBRA allowed JAMSS to increase estimation accuracy by 40 %, on average—compared to the expert judgment they had used until then. Table 12.5 summarizes the prediction error of the six CoBRA models created for the review objectives considered in the study.

Table 12.5 JAMSS: results of effort model validation

Effort model	Review objective	#Effort factors	Estimation error
1	O1. Risk analysis	4	18.2 %
2	O2. State transition completeness and consistency	2	25.4 %
3	O3. Design completeness for exceptional behavior	3	22.4 %
4	O4. Timing correctness and consistency	2	24.1 %
5	O5. Interface correctness and consistency	3	39.6 %
6	O6. Traceability	2	24.5 %

12.4   Benefits and Costs

Besides improving predictive performance, the CoBRA model provided several other benefits compared to the simple expert judgment JAMSS had been using before. The transparent and context-specific effort models supported the IV&V practitioners in achieving a number of project and process management objectives:

- *Project effort estimation*: The project managers gained a systematic approach for making <u>reliable</u> and <u>repeatable</u> estimates at the beginning of a new IV&V project.
- *Project risk management*: The project managers obtained explicit information for analyzing and managing major risks jeopardizing project success, in particular information regarding the factors that have a significant negative impact on IV&V efficiency.
- *Justifying and negotiating project costs*: The project managers gained a reliable basis for justifying planned IV&V costs to the project stakeholders and for making informed decisions about accepting a particular IV&V project.
- *Process improvement*: The project managers obtained insights into those areas of the IV&V processes that have the greatest impact on increasing the costs of IV&V. In particular, the project managers learned which factors have the greatest negative impact on the efficiency of IV&V activities in a considered estimation context. These factors indicated process areas that are responsible for major efficiency loss and thus should be the main target of improvement activities.

Moreover, the analysts and the domain experts at JAMSS benefited from the qualitative experiences gained during the pilot application of the CoBRA method. The most important lessons learned included:

- *Effort estimation scope*: Depending on the specific objective of IV&V, different IV&V activities are required and different personnel is involved. Consequently, different factors might influence IV&V effort for different objectives. Therefore, the scope of effort estimation, meaning the context for which an effort model is built and applied, should be limited to a single IV&V objective. Since different IV&V objectives involved quite independent sets of activities, the total effort of an IV&V project aimed at attaining multiple objectives can be estimated as the sum of the efforts estimated individually for each objective.
- *Size and complexity of review*: The complexity of a document under review should be considered as an effort factor in addition to simple size measures, such as the number of document pages.
- *Effort factors*: A very important aspect of effort modeling is to consider effort factors other than simply size, although this is typically the major determinant of project effort. The JAMSS analyst and the domain experts experienced that a single factor may multiply effort by as much as ten times. For example, if e software supplier does not perform risk assessment, the effort that an IV&V company must spend on independent risk analysis may increase by up to

Table 12.6 JAMSS: approximate costs of introducing the CoBRA method

Cost aspect	Cost
Involved personnel	5 persons: • 1 CoBRA external analyst • 1 CoBRA internal analyst at JAMSS • 3 domain experts
Total duration	1 month
Total effort	30 person-hours • Domain experts: 4 h per person for CoBRA model development meeting and interviews. In total, 12 person-hours • Internal analysts: 16 h for learning the CoBRA method (2-day tutorial); 2 h for supporting the external analyst and coordinating the pilot study. In total, 18 person-hours

20 times. Such an effect is impossible to investigate based only on historical size and effort data which are usually used in software industry as the only basis for managing development productivity and effort.

Table 12.6 summarizes the costs of the pilot application of the CoBRA model and of building an initial effort model.

Further Reading

- H. Nakao, A. Trendowicz, J. Münch, "Estimating Effort of an Independent Verification and Validation in the Context of Mission-Critical Software Systems—A Case Study." *Proceedings of the 20th International Conference on Software Engineering and Knowledge Engineering*, Redwood City, San Francisco Bay, USA, 1–3 July 2008, pp. 167–172.

  This paper reports on the pilot application of the CoBRA method at JAMSS described in this chapter. Yet, the authors do not focus on a detailed description of the CoBRA modeling process. Instead, they concentrate on an empirical comparison of the predictive performance of three alternative effort estimation strategies: expert-based, data-driven, and hybrid. For this purpose, the authors compare the estimation accuracy and precision of three methods that represent these strategies: expert judgment, ordinary least-squared regression, and CoBRA. A statistical analysis showed that in case of both estimation accuracy and precision, CoBRA outperforms the other two methods.

Appendix: Example List of Relevant Effort Factors

This chapter lists aspects of software project environments that proved to have the greatest impact on software development effort in industrial contexts. These factors can be used as a point of reference when identifying the most relevant context and effort factors during the development of a CoBRA effort model. On the one hand, the analyst may use selected factors to explain the idea of effort and context factors and the difference between them. On the other hand, the analyst may present the domain experts involved in the CoBRA model development process with an example set of effort factors to initiate a group discussion during which the experts are supposed to identify organization-specific effort factors.

Context Factors Versus Effort Factors

In the context of effort estimation, the term "effort factor" refers to product-, process-, or personnel-related characteristics that have an impact on the development effort. In practice, software size is the most important determinant of development effort and, as such, is always considered. Effort factors refer to the remaining aspects of software project environment, which cause the development effort per unit of software size to differ across projects. In other words, effort factors are factors that make development productivity differ across projects. In the CoBRA method, effort factors are defined as factors contributing to the increase of development effort relative to "nominal effort" and are modeled in the effort overhead model.

In practice, it is difficult to build a reliable effort model that would be applicable across a variety of environments. Therefore, usually only a limited number of effort factors are considered within a model; the rest is kept constant and described as the context in which the model is applicable. For example, building an effort model that would be applicable for both enterprise and embedded software systems would require covering a large variety of effort factors that play a significant role in both of these domains. In practice, it would be a very complex and expensive task to develop, use, and maintain a model that encompasses a wide variety of contexts. Alternatively, we may build simpler models independently, each for a specific domain. In that case, the factor "application domain" would be constant for each model and would determine the context of the model's applicability. We would refer to factors that describe a modeling context as *context factors*. On the other

A. Trendowicz, *Software Cost Estimation, Benchmarking, and Risk Assessment*, The Fraunhofer IESE Series on Software and Systems Engineering, DOI 10.1007/978-3-642-30764-5, © Springer-Verlag Berlin Heidelberg 2013

hand, factors that are included in the model in order to explain productivity variance within a certain context will be called *effort factors*. In practice, context factors determine effort factors; that is, depending on a specific context, different effort factors would have a different impact on development productivity and effort.

Context Factors

Table A.1 lists the context factors that are most commonly considered in the software industry for the purpose of modeling software development effort.

Table A.1 Common context factors

Context factor	Definition
Application domain	The domain in which the software is to be applied. Example domains include embedded software systems, management information systems, and web (Internet) applications.
Development type	Type of development. Example development types include new development, enhancement, and maintenance.
Programming language	Programming language(s) used to develop software, e.g., Java, C/C++, Fortran, etc.
Software life cycle model	The model of the software life cycle phases, e.g., waterfall, iterative, incremental, etc.

Effort Factors

For the purpose of systematically identifying of potential effort factors, we propose considering four facets of software project environments:

- *The product* facet covers the characteristics of software products being developed throughout all development phases. These factors refer to products such as software code, requirements, documentation, etc., and their characteristics, such as complexity, size, volatility, etc.
- *The personnel* facet reflects the characteristics of the personnel involved in the software development project. These factors usually consider the experience and capabilities of project stakeholders such as development team members (such as analysts, designers, programmers, and project managers), software users, customers, maintainers, subcontractors, etc.
- *The project* facet refers to various qualities of project management and organization, development constraints, working conditions, or staff turnover.
- *The process* facet refers to the characteristics of the software processes as well as the methods, tools, and technologies applied during a software development project. They include, for instance, the effectiveness of quality assurance, testing quality, quality of analysis and documentation methods, tool quality and usage, quality of process management, or the extent of customer participation.

Table A.2 provides example effort factors and sub-factors that are most commonly considered in industrial contexts.

Table A.2 Common effort factors

Effort factor	Definition
Team capabilities and experience	The extent to which the software development team possesses the skills and experiences necessary for the successful and efficient completion of the project (i.e., delivering software products of required functionality and quality within specified cost and time).
• Programming language experience	The project team's experience with the programming language(s) and technologies/tools (e.g., the development environment).
• Application experience and familiarity	The experience of the project team working with a similar type of software systems (i.e., providing similar functionality and operating in similar environments).
• Domain experience	The extent of the project team's familiarity and comprehension of the target domain in which the developed software system is to be applied.
• Platform experience	The extent of the project team's familiarity and comprehension of the platform for which the developed software system is intended.
• Communication capabilities	The ability of the project team to communicate easily and clearly within the team (with other team members).
• Project manager knowledge and experience	The ability of the project manager to efficiently manage resources, tasks, milestones, and project delivery dates as well as his or her ability to organize the project, including managing project goals, methods, schedules, or the clarity of the project team roles and responsibilities. The level of practical experience in managing similar software projects.
Software complexity	The complexity of the developed software system.
• Database size and complexity	The complexity of the database structure and the database operations. This may, for example, range from simple, such as arrays and basic database queries, to complex, such as distributed data coordination, triggers, and search optimization.
• Architecture complexity	The complexity of the software architecture used.
• Complexity of interface to other systems	The complexity of the software interfaces, including user interface and interfaces to other software systems. This may, for example, range from simple, such as device reads and writes, to complex, such as routines for masking, communication line handling, and operations at the physical I/O level.
Tool usage and quality/ effectiveness	The extent to which automated tools are going to be used for the project and the quality/effectiveness of these tools, ranging from basic editors and debuggers to integrated case tools.
• CASE tools	The extent to which CASE tools are going to be used for the project and the quality/effectiveness of these tools.
• Testing tools	The extent to which testing tools are going to be used for the project and the quality/effectiveness of these tools.
Project constraints • Schedule pressure	Additional constraints affecting the projects' feasibility. The extent to which the planned project schedule is reasonable to attain a system that meets all of the stated requirements.
• Distributed/Multisite development	The level of distribution of the project team (developers and users/ customers). Whether the project will be performed on one site or whether different geographically distributed sites will be involved, and if so, how distributed (e.g., nationally or internationally).

(continued)

Table A.2 (continued)

Effort factor	Definition
Software reuse	The extent and quality of reuse in the project.
• Reuse level	The extent to which existing software artifacts are reused in the project.
• Quality of reused assets	The quality of the artifacts reused in the project, in particular their documentation level and reliability. Moreover, the extent to which reused assets conform to the particular quality requirements defined in the project.
Requirements characteristics	The characteristics of the requirements specified in the project.
• Requirements volatility	The extent to which the requirements are expected to change over time, after the requirements freeze.
• Requirements novelty	The extent to which requirement are new to the development team (i.e., requirements refer to functional and nonfunctional software characteristics that have never been faced by the development team before).
Required software quality	The extent to which the software is expected to meet certain nonfunctional (quality) requirements.
• Required software reliability	The amount of attention that needs to be given to minimizing failures and ensuring that any failures will not result in safety, economic, security, and/or environmental damage, achieved through actions such as formal validation and testing, fault-tolerant design, and formal specifications.
• Required software maintainability	The extent to which the software is expected to be easy to understand and modify, achieved through actions such as information hiding, modularity in design, completeness and traceability of life cycle documentation, and the recording of design rationale.
Team size	The number of stakeholders (users, customers, developers, maintainers, etc.) directly involved in the project.
Stuff turnover	Personnel continuity on the project, i.e., the extent of turnover for the duration of the project.
Method usage	The extent to which certain systematic software engineering methods are implemented during the software development.
• Reviews and inspections	The extent to which peer review and inspection methods are implemented during the software development—whether inspections are planned, documented, supported, and consistently performed.
• Testing	The extent to which testing methods are implemented during the software development—whether testing activities are planned, documented, supported, and consistently performed; which tests (unit, integration, acceptance) and which particular techniques (e.g., regression testing, statistical usage testing, etc.) are implemented.
• Requirements management	The level of disciplined requirements management, e.g., the extent to which requirements are explicitly defined, tracked, and traced to design, code, and validation testing. This also includes the extent to which changes to requirements after their freeze are systematically managed (e.g., supported by the use of change management methods and tools).

(continued)

Table A.2 (continued)

Effort factor	Definition
Team motivation and commitment	The extent to which the members of the software development team are motivated and committed to performing their tasks and cooperating with the other project stakeholders (e.g., other developers, users, etc.).
Customer involvement	The extent to which the user/customer is involved in the project providing necessary/useful information, reviewing requirements documents, performing some of the analyses themselves, and taking part in acceptance testing.

Further Reading

- A. Trendowicz and J. Münch, "Factors Influencing Software Development Productivity—State-of-the-Art and Industrial Experiences," *Advances in Computers*, pp. 185–241. Elsevier, 2009.

  This article provides a comprehensive overview of the factors influencing development productivity and effort. The authors based their survey on a review of related literature and on numerous experiences gained in the software industry. On the one hand, the authors discuss effort drivers that seem to be universally applicable across various project environments; on the other hand, they provide factors that seem to apply only within particular project situations.

- ISBSG, *Estimating, Benchmarking Research Suite Release 11*. International Software Benchmarking Standards Group, 2009. Refer to http://www.isbsg. org/ for the most recent releases of the ISBSG benchmark repository.

  The International Software Benchmarking Standards Group (ISBSG) maintains a benchmark data repository of software development projects. Release 11 of the repository contains data on over 5,000 development and enhancement software projects. The repository covers a number of project aspects that proved, over the years, to have a significant influence on software development productivity and project effort. These project characteristics can be used within the CoBRA method for selecting relevant context and effort factors.

Glossary

Accuracy Estimation accuracy refers to the nearness of an estimate to the true value, i.e., a highly accurate prediction method will provide estimates very close to the actual, known values. In the context of software effort estimation, the *Relative Error (RE)* or *Magnitude of Relative Error (MRE)* measures proposed by Conte et al. (1986) are commonly used to measure estimation accuracy. They measure the difference between actual and estimated effort relative to the actual effort. See also *precision, bias, actual,* and *estimate.*

Actual Actual (outcome) refers to true outcome of a certain project activity or project condition (characteristic) observed after the activity or condition has already taken place. In the context of effort estimation, actual is typically used to refer to the actual value of effort required to successfully complete a certain work activity or to the actual value of the productivity of this activity. See also *Estimate, Effort,* and *Productivity.*

Best Case See *Nominal Case.*

Bias Estimation bias refers to a systematic (constant) error in estimates and is determined as the difference between the average of the estimates and the actual, true value. In the context of software effort estimation, the *Prediction at Level m (Pred.m)* measure proposed by Conte et al. (1986) is commonly used to measure estimation bias. *Pred.m* measures the percentage of estimates that are within m % of the actual value. In other words, *Pred.m* measures the percentage of estimates for which the magnitude of relative error (accuracy) is lower than or equal to m. See also *accuracy* and *precision.*

Causal Effort Model In CoBRA, the causal effort model (also referred to as *effort overhead model*) models the factors influencing software project effort and the interactions among these factors, and quantifies the impact of these factors on effort. See also *Effort Factor* and *Effort Overhead.*

Constraint of Estimation Estimation constraint refers to limitations regarding an organization's capability of applying an estimation method. In the context of the CoBRA method, estimation constraints refer to organizational limitations with respect to building, maintaining, and using CoBRA models. A very important constraint that concerns literally every estimation method is the capability of an organization to provide proper information as a basis for the estimates. In practice, this constraint has two facets: availability of appropriate project measurement data and availability of human expertise in terms of human experts'

A. Trendowicz, *Software Cost Estimation, Benchmarking, and Risk Assessment,* The Fraunhofer IESE Series on Software and Systems Engineering, DOI 10.1007/978-3-642-30764-5, © Springer-Verlag Berlin Heidelberg 2013

knowledge. Estimation constraints are closely related to the goals and purposes of estimation. An example relationship between estimation purposes, constraints, and objectives might be as follows. Let us consider an organization that possesses a large base of historical project data, has a limited budget for estimating projects, and wants to use CoBRA estimation for the purpose of managing project risks. Corresponding estimation goals could be that the estimation method (1) does not require much involvement of human experts, (2) is based on an analysis of quantitative data, and (3) provides estimates in the form of probability distributions. See also *Goal of Estimation* and *Purpose of Estimation*.

Context Factor Context factors refer to the characteristics of a software development project, which determine the feasibility of the CoBRA method and the shape of the CoBRA model. On the one hand, context factors refer to the constraints and capabilities of the software organization with respect to the requirements of the CoBRA method. Example requirements include the availability of certain measurement data and domain experts for the purpose of constructing the effort model. On the other hand, context factors describe the environment within which the project effort effects are expected to remain constant. Examples of common context factors are application domain (for example, embedded software or web applications), programming language, or development type (for example, new development, maintenance, or enhancement). See also *Effort Factor* and *Effort Driver*.

Context of Estimation Estimation context refers to the characteristics of a software development project, so-called *context factors*, which determine the feasibility of the CoBRA method and the shape of the CoBRA model. On the one hand, context factors refer to the constraints and capabilities of the software organization with respect to the requirements of the CoBRA method. Example requirements include the availability of certain measurement data and domain experts for the purpose of constructing the effort model. On the other hand, context factors describe the environment within which the project effort effects are expected to remain constant. The objective of the CoBRA method is to model these effects. For example, if we consider the application domain as a context factor, then certain effort dependencies will be common within one domain whereas they will vary across domains. See also *Goals of Estimation*.

Cost In the software engineering domain, *cost* is defined in a monetary sense. With respect to a software development project, it refers to the partial or total monetary cost of providing (creating) a certain product or service. In the software engineering literature and practice, "cost" is often used as a synonym for "effort". Yet, effort only refers to manpower spent on performing activities aimed at providing a certain product or service. As a consequence, project cost includes, but is not limited to, project effort. In practice, cost includes such elements as fixed infrastructure and administrative costs. Moreover, dependent on the project context (e.g., currency or cost of manpower unit), project cost may differ despite the same project effort. One way to notice the difference is to look at the units used. Cost in a monetary sense is typically measured in terms of a certain currency (e.g., $, €, ¥, etc.), whereas cost in an effort sense is typically measured as manpower (e.g., person-hours, person-days, person-months, etc.). See also *Effort*.

Effort In the context of software development, *effort* refers to manpower spent on performing activities aimed at providing a certain product or service. Effort results from a combination of the total supply of persons for completing a certain activity and the time they spend on this activity. It is typically measured as an equivalent of the time spent by one person on completing the work activity. Common units of effort measurement are person-hour (ph), person-day (pd), or person-month (pm). See also *Cost*.

Effort Driver See *Effort Factor*

Effort Factor Effort factors, also referred to as *Effort Drivers*, refer to aspects of a software development project that influence project effort. Effort factors include project, product, and personnel aspects of a software development project. Effort factors represent those aspects of the project environment that are assumed to change across software projects within a specific context. For example, the domain experience of the developers is an effort factor that varies across projects. See also *Context Factor*.

Effort Overhead Effort overhead is the additional effort spent on overcoming the imperfections of a real project environment, such as insufficient skills of the project team. Effort overhead refers to non-productive project effort spent in addition to the nominal effort. See also *Effort Multiplier* and *Causal Effort Model*.

Effort Overhead Model The effort overhead model (or *causal effort model*) produces an estimate of the project effort overhead. The effort overhead model consists of factors affecting the project effort within a certain context (so-called *effort factors* or *effort drivers*). The causal model is obtained through expert knowledge acquisition, for example by involving experienced project managers. See also *Causal Effort Model* and *Effort Factor*.

Effort Model Effort model refers to a model that captures effort dependencies within a particular context. Typical usage of an effort model includes specifying and explaining project effort, predicting project effort, and improving projects with respect to consumed effort. In CoBRA, an effort model consists of the *Effort Overhead Model* and the *Productivity Model*.

Effort Multiplier Effort multiplier refers to the qualitative impacts of an effort factor directly influencing project effort (direct effort factor) on project effort. In other words, an effort multiplier is associated with a direct effort factor and quantified the magnitude of the factor's contribution to the overall effort overhead. For a given direct effort factor, its effort multipliers refer to the percentage of effort overhead above that of a nominal effort this factor introduces. The value of an effort multiplier depends on the factor's value and is elicited through expert judgment. The multipliers for the effort factors are modeled as distributions to capture the uncertainty inherent in expert opinion. Triangular distributions can be used to reflect the experts' opinion about each effort factor's impact on cost by giving three values: minimum, most likely, and maximum value of a multiplier. See also *Effort Overhead*.

Estimation In principle, estimation is defined as "the act of judging tentatively or approximately the value, worth, or significance of something". Yet, in the context of planning and managing software development, the term estimation is used in the sense of forecasting and refers to the process of making statements about future events and conditions – events and conditions whose actual outcomes have not yet been observed. In the context of software project management, the terms estimation, prediction, and forecasting are used interchangeably. See also *Prediction*.

Estimate In the context of software effort estimation, *estimate* (or effort estimate) refers to the approximate, predicted value of certain project characteristics. In the context of effort, estimate typically refers to effort estimate and means the prediction of effort required for successfully completing a certain future project activity (activity that has not yet been performed). See also *Actual*.

Explanatory Power Explanatory power of the CoBRA model refers to its capability to capture the relationship between development productivity and effort overhead. More generally, explanatory power refers to the form and amount of information an estimation method provides in addition to simple effort numbers. Typically, additional pieces of information associated with effort estimates are the probability of extending these estimates and the means for reducing effort.

Extreme Case Extreme case (also referred to as *Worst Case*) refers to the worst project circumstance or state possible in a given context. In the CoBRA method extreme case is typically used in reference to effort factors and means the worst value of a factor in a given context. It is important to note that worst case in CoBRA does not mean "the worst" in general but "the worst" possible in a given context. For example, let us consider the tool support aspect. In general, the worst case would refer to a situation where none of the project activities is supported by appropriate tools. Yet, in practice, such a situation is hard to find and the worst case would rather refer to tool support for some basic project activities. See *Nominal Case* for comparison.

Goal of Estimation Estimation goal refers to the expected performance of the CoBRA method in terms of the goodness of the estimates and the additional information it provides. A typical example of an estimation goal is estimation accuracy. Estimation goals are usually derivatives of the estimation purposes. In other words, the purpose for which CoBRA is going to be used determines, at least partially, the objectives the method should accomplish. For example, using the method for the purpose of risk assessment requires that besides simple effort estimates, the method provides associated information to support assessing and reducing effort-related project risks. Estimation goals are derivatives (at least partially) of estimation constraints and estimation purposes. See also *Predictive Power* and *Explanatory Power*, *Purposes of Estimation*, and *Constraints of Estimation*.

Historical Data Historical data refer to project data collected from historical projects. The data encompass project environmental characteristics such as product-, process-, resource-, and project-related characteristics. In particular, historical project data encompass data on software size, project effort, and effort factors considered in an effort model. Historical project data can be collected via measurement or expert judgment. See also *Historical Project*.

Historical Project A historical project is a project that has been successfully performed in the past and has already been completed. In CoBRA, successfully completed projects are used as a basis for building and initially validating the effort estimation model. The criteria for project success principally depend on the respective organization and may differ across organizations; yet, they should be consisted for the historical projects considered within one organization when building the CoBRA effort model. Examples of traditionally considered criteria of project success include completing a project within budget and time, and delivering a software product with the expected functionality and quality. See also *Historical Project* and *Successful Project*.

Informative Power Informative power refers to the form, the amount, and the quality of the information an estimation method provides in addition to simple effort numbers. Typical additional information associated with effort estimates includes the probability of extending these estimates and the means for reducing effort. In the context of the CoBRA method, informative power can be interpreted as generalization of the explanatory power objective, which refers to the ability of a CoBRA effort model to explain the dependency between effort overhead and development productivity. See *Explanatory Power* and *Predictive Power* for comparison.

Nominal Case Nominal case (also referred to as *Best Case*) refers to the best project circumstance or state possible in a given context. In the CoBRA method, the nominal case is typically used in reference to an effort factor and means the best value of the factor in a given context. It is important to note that best case in CoBRA does not mean "the best" in general but "the best" possible in a given context. For example, let us consider the tool support aspect. In general, the best case would refer to a situation where all project activities are supported by appropriate tools. Yet, in practice, such a situation is hard to find and best case would rather refer to tool support for majority of the project activities or for all of the most relevant project activities. See *Extreme Case* for comparison.

Nominal Effort Nominal effort is the engineering and management effort spent on developing a software product of a certain size in the context of a nominal project. A nominal project is a hypothetical "ideal" project in a certain environment of an organization (or business unit). It is a project that runs under optimal conditions, that is, a project where all environmental characteristics having an impact on project effort are at "the best" levels ("perfect") at the start of the project. Note that "the best" refers to realistic levels that are possible in a certain context; not to the best imaginable levels. For instance, the project objectives are well defined and understood by all staff members and the customer and all key people in the project have the appropriate skills to successfully conduct the project. See also *Actual Effort* for comparison.

Nominal Productivity In CoBRA, nominal productivity refers to development productivity under optimal project conditions, that is, the productivity of a nominal project where all effort factors have their best levels. In general, productivity refers (IEEE-1045 1993) to the ratio between a project's output and input. In the concrete case of software projects, development productivity is computed as the ratio between the size of the delivered software products and the effort consumed to develop these products. In real software projects, *actual development productivity* is decreased by non-productive effort spent on overcoming the imperfect character of the project. For example, a certain effort must be expended to train the development team. The factor by which productivity is decreased depends on the specific characteristics of an individual project. The difference between nominal and actual productivity (*productivity loss*) is proportional to the portion of additional non-productive effort, and in CoBRA it is accounted for through the effort overhead. In general, the higher the effort overhead, the higher the actual project effort and the lower the actual development productivity. See also *Nominal Project* and *Nominal Effort*.

Nominal Project A nominal project is a hypothetical "ideal" project in a certain environment of an organization (or business unit). It is a project that runs under optimal conditions, that is, a project where all environmental characteristics having the impact on project effort are at "the best" levels ("perfect") at the start of the project. Note that "the best" refers to realistic levels that are possible in a certain context; not to the best imaginable levels. For instance, the project objectives are well defined and understood by all staff members and the customer and all key people in the project have the appropriate skills to successfully conduct the project. See also *Nominal Case*, *Nominal Productivity*, and *Nominal Effort*.

Planning In general, planning refers to "the act or process of <u>making or carrying out plans</u>; *specifically:* the establishment of goals, policies, and procedures for a social or economic unit". In the context of software development, planning refers to planning a software project and includes identifying and scheduling the project activities, assigning the necessary resources and infrastructure, etc. In practice, planning is wrongly interchanged with estimation, in particular with effort estimation. Yet, effort estimation is only a part of planning and refers to forecasting the manpower required for successfully completing certain project activities. In this sense, the outcomes of estimation are inputs to planning. See also *Estimation* for comparison.

Precision Estimation precision refers to the degree to which several estimates are very close to each other. It is an indicator of the scatter in the estimates. The less the scatter, the higher the precision. In order to measure estimation precision, we can apply the well-known statistical measure of *standard deviation* (*SD*) upon multiple estimates. See also *Accuracy* and *Bias* for comparison.

Prediction In principle, prediction refers to "the act of <u>declaring or indicating in advance</u>; especially: <u>foretelling</u> on the basis of observation, experience, or scientific reason". In the context of software effort estimation, prediction is used interchangeably with estimation and refers to forecasting the outcome of a project activity that has not yet taken place; in particular to forecasting effort required for successfully completing a certain project activity. See also *Estimation*, *Effort*, and *Estimate*.

Predictive Power Predictive power refers to the capability of the CoBRA model to provide effort estimates close to the actual (true) effort. In the context of software effort prediction, predictive power is typically considered in terms of estimation *accuracy*, *precision* and, *bias*. For quantifying each of these three aspects, a number of measures have been proposed.

Productivity Baseline Baseline productivity refers to the "average" nominal productivity of a historical project. Baseline productivity is determined using the productivity model and is used for building the estimation model (meaning, it is a part of the effort estimation model). See also *Productivity Model* and *Estimation Model*.

Productivity Model The productivity model is the second base element of the CoBRA effort model (besides the *causal effort model*). The productivity model uses data from past similar projects for identifying a relationship between effort overhead and actual project effort, and for determining the baseline productivity of the nominal project. Note that this is a simple bivariate relationship that does not require a large data set. This is important, as it explains why CoBRA does not have demanding data requirements, as opposed to data-driven estimation techniques. In order to build up such a regression model, data from merely about 10 historical projects are needed. See also *Nominal Project*, *Nominal Productivity*, *Effort Overhead Model*, and *Effort Model*.

Purpose of Estimation Estimation purpose refers to what we want to use CoBRA effort estimation model for, that is, to the project scenario in which we want to use estimation. Example purposes of effort estimation include obtaining a point estimate of project effort, identifying effort distribution across project phases, identifying effort-related project risks, or identifying productivity-related process improvement potentials. See also *Goals of Estimation* for comparison.

Successful Project The CoBRA method often refers to a successful project. For example, while collecting historical project data for building the effort estimation model, we should consider only successful projects. It would not make much sense to take failed projects as a reference for the future. The usual definition of a successful project in the software community refers to a project that was completed within budget and time and to a software product delivered with the expected functionality and quality. A minimal definition of a successful project may refer to a project that delivered the expected software product without creating substantial financial loss. See also *Historical Project*.

Worst Case See *Extreme Case*.

Bibliography

P.D. Allison (2002), *Missing Data*. Thousand Oaks: Sage Publications, 2002. Quantitative Applications in the Social Sciences. p. 136.

V.R. Basili, G. Caldiera, and H.D. Rombach (1994), "The Experience Factory," J.J. Marciniak (ed.) *Encyclopedia of Software Engineering*, vol. 1, John Wiley & Sons, 1994, pp. 469–476.

V.R. Basili, M. Lindvall, M. Regardie, C. Seaman, J. Heidrich, J. Munch, H.D. Rombach, A. Trendowicz (2010), "Linking Software Development and Business Strategy Through Measurement," *IEEE Computer*, vol. 43, no. 4, pp. 57–65. April 2010.

S. Berkun (2008), *Making Things Happen: Mastering Project Management*, Revised Edition, O'Reilly Media, 25 March 2008.

B.W. Boehm (1981), *Software Engineering Economics*. Prentice Hall, 1981.

B.W. Boehm, C. Abts, A.W. Brown, S. Chulani, B.K. Clark, E. Horowitz, R. Madachy, D. Reifer, B. Steece (2000), *Software Cost Estimation with COCOMO II*. Prentice-Hall, 2000.

J. C. Borda (1781), "Mémoire sur les élections au scrutin," *Histoire de l'Académie Royale des Sciences*, 1781.

L.C. Briand, K. El Emam, and F. Bomarius (1998), "COBRA: a hybrid method for software cost estimation, benchmarking, and risk assessment," *Proceedings of the 20th International Conference on Software Engineering*, pp. 390–399. IEEE Computer Society Press, 1998.

L.C. Briand and I. Wieczorek (2000), "Resource Modeling in Software Engineering," J.J. Marciniak (ed.) *Encyclopedia of Software Engineering, 2nd Edition*, John Wiley & Sons, 2002.

F.P. Brooks (1995), *The Mythical Man-Month: Essays on Software Engineering, Anniversary Edition, 2nd Edition*, Addison-Wesley Professional, p. 336. August 1995.

S.D. Conte, H.E. Dunsmore, and Y.E. Shen (1986), *Software engineering metrics and models*, Benjamin-Cummings Publishing Co., Inc., 1986.

T. Dekkers (2004), *IFPUG Workshop on Function Point Analysis*, (presentation), Sogeti Nederland B.V., July 2004.

T. DeMarco and T. Lister (1999), *Peopleware: Productive Projects and Teams*, 2nd Edition, Dorset House Publishing Company, Inc., p. 245, February 1999.

B. Efron and R.J. Tibshirani (1994), *An Introduction to the Bootstrap*. Chapman and Hall, 1994.

N.E. Fenton and S.L. Pfleeger (1998), *Software Metrics: A Rigorous and Practical Approach*. Revised, 2nd Edition, Boston, MA, USA. PWS Publishing Co., 1998.

T. Foss, E. Stensrud, B. Kitchenham, and I. Myrtveit (2003), "A Simulation Study of the Model Evaluation Criterion MMRE," *IEEE Transactions on Software Engineering*, vol. 29, no. 11, pp. 985–995. November 2003.

R.L. Glass (2002), *Facts and Fallacies of Software Engineering*. Addison-Wesley Professional, 2002.

M. Hall, E. Frank, G. Holmes, B.d Pfahringer, P. Reutemann, I.H. Witten (2009), "The WEKA Data Mining Software: An Update," *Special Interest Group on Knowledge Discovery & Data Mining (SIGKDD) Explorations*, vol. 11, no. 1, pp.10–18. July 2009.

J. Van Hulse and T.M. Khoshgoftaar (2008), "A comprehensive empirical evaluation of missing value imputation in noisy software measurement data," *Journal of Systems and Software*, vol. 81, no. 5, pp. 691–708, May 2008.

A. Trendowicz, *Software Cost Estimation, Benchmarking, and Risk Assessment*, The Fraunhofer IESE Series on Software and Systems Engineering, DOI 10.1007/978-3-642-30764-5, © Springer-Verlag Berlin Heidelberg 2013

ISBSG (2009), Estimating, *Benchmarking Research Suite Release 11*. International Software Benchmarking Standards Group, 2009. Refer to http://www.isbsg.org/ for the most recent releases of the ISBSG benchmark repository.

ISO/IEC 20968 (2002), *Mk II Function Point Analysis. Counting Practices Manual*, 1st Edition. International Standardization Organization, 2002.

ISO/IEC 19761 (2003), *COSMIC-FFP A Functional Size Measurement Method*, 1st Edition. International Standardization Organization, 2003.

ISO/IEC 24570 (2005), *NESMA Functional Size Measurement Method Version 2.1. Definitions and Counting Guidelines for the Application of Function Point Analysis*, 1st Edition. International Standardization Organization, 2005.

ISO/IEC 29881 (2008), *FiSMA 1.1 functional size measurement method*, 1st Edition. International Standardization Organization, 2008.

ISO/IEC 20926 (2009), *IFPUG Functional Size Measurement Method 2009*, 2nd Edition. International Standardization Organization, 2009.

IEEE-1012 (2005), *IEEE Standard for Software Verification and Validation*, IEEE Std 1012–2004, Revision of IEEE Std 1012–1998, 2005.

IEEE-1045 (1993), *IEEE Standard for Software Productivity Metrics*, IEEE Std 1045–1992, approved by IEEE Standards Board on 17 September 1992. Approved by American National Standards Institute on 23 March 1993.

C.T. Jones (2007), *Estimating Software Costs, 2nd Edition*, McGraw-Hill Osborne Media, 2007.

M. Jørgensen and B. Boehm (2009), "Software Development Effort Estimation: Formal Models or Expert Judgment?" *IEEE Software*, vol. 26, no. 2, pp. 14–19. April 2009.

T.M. Khoshgoftaar and J. Van Hulse (2008), "Imputation techniques for multivariate missingness in software measurement data," *Software Quality Control*, vol. 16, no. 4, pp. 563–600. December 2008.

M. Klaes, A. Trendowicz, Y. Ishigai, and H. Nakao (submitted 2011), "Handling Estimation Uncertainty with Bootstrapping: Empirical Evaluation in the Context of Hybrid Prediction Methods," *Proceedings of the 15th International Symposium on Empirical Software Engineering and Measurement*, September 22–23, Banff, Alberta, Canada, pp. 245–254, 2011.

M. Klaes, A. Trendowicz, A. Wickenkamp, J. Muench, N. Kikuchi, and Y. Ishigai (2008), "The Use of Simulation Techniques for Hybrid Software Cost Estimation and Risk Analysis," *Advances in Computers*, vol. 74, pp. 115–174. Elsevier, 2008.

N. Kohtake, A. Katoh, N. Ishihama, Y. Miyamoto, T. Kawasaki, M. Katahira (2008), "Software Independent Verification and Validation for Spacecraft" *Proceedings to the IEEE JAXA Aerospace Conference*, pp.1–8. 2008.

P. Mahalanobis (1936), "On the generalised distance in statistics," *Proceedings National Institute of Science*, India, vol. 2, pp. 49–55. April 1936.

S. McConnell (2006), *Software Estimation: Demystifying the Black Art*, Microsoft Press, Redmond, MA, USA, 2006.

S. McConnell (1997), *Software Project Survival Guide*, 1st Edition, Microsoft Press, October 15, 1997.

A. Meneely, B. Smith, and L. Williams (2010), S*oftware Metrics Validation Criteria: A Systematic Literature Review*, Technical Report TR-2010-2, North Carolina State University, Raleigh, NC, USA. February 2010.

H. Nakao, A. Trendowicz, J. Münch (2008), "Estimating Effort of an Independent Verification and Validation in the Context of Mission-Critical Software Systems – A Case Study." *Proceedings of the 20th International Conference on Software Engineering and Knowledge Engineering*, Redwood City, San Francisco Bay, USA, July 1–3, 2008, pp. 167–172.

L.M. Laird and C.M. Brennan (2006), S*oftware Measurement and Estimation: A Practical Approach*. Wiley-IEEE Computer Society Press, 2006.

R. Likert (1932), "A Technique for the Measurement of Attitudes," *Archives of Psychology*, vol. 22, no. 140, pp. 1–55. 1932.

PMI (2007), *A Guide to the Project Management Body of Knowledge (PMBOK® Guide)*, 4th Edition, Project Management Institute, Inc. 2008.

D.J. Reifer (2000), "Web development: estimating quick-to-market software," *IEEE Software*, vol. 17, no. 6, pp. 57–64. November/December 2000

M. Robnik-Sikonja, I. Kononenko (2003), "Theoretical and Empirical Analysis of ReliefF and RReliefF," *Machine Learning Journal*, vol. 53, no. 1–2, pp. 23–69. October-November 2003.

L. Rosencrance (2007), "Survey: Poor communication causes most IT project failures. nadequate resource planning, unrealistic deadlines also cited in CompTIA study.," *Computerworld*, March 2007.

M. Ruhe (2001), *The Accurate and Early Effort Estimation of Web Applications*, Master Thesis, University of Kaiserslautern, Kaiserslautern, Germany, August 2001; supervisors: I. Wieczorek, D. Rombach, R. Jeffery.

M. Ruhe, R. Jeffery, and I. Wieczorek (2003a), "Cost estimation for web applications," *Proceedings of the 25th International Conference on Software Engineering*, 3–10 May 2003, Portland, Oregon, USA, pp. 285–294.

M. Ruhe, R. Jeffery, and I. Wieczorek (2003b), "Using Web Objects for Estimating Software Development Effort for Web Applications," *Proceedings of the 9th International Symposium on Software Metrics*, pp. 30–37, 2003.

J.L. Schafer (1997), *Analysis of Incomplete Multivariate Data*, Chapman and Hall, London, 1997.

R. Scheines, P. Spirtes, C. Glymour, C. Meek, and T. Richardson (1998), "The TETRAD Project: Constraint Based Aids to Causal Model Specification," *Multivariate Behavioral Research*, vol. 33, no. 1, pp. 65–117. January 1998.

D.J. Sheskin (2011), *Handbook of Parametric and Nonparametric Statistical Procedures*, 5th Edition, Chapman and Hall, 2011.

P. Spirtes, C. Glymour, R. Scheines (2001), *Causation, Prediction, and Search*, 2nd Edition, New York, N.Y.: Springer-Verlag, MIT Press, 2001.

K. Strike, K.E. Emam, and N. Madhavji (2001), "Software Cost Estimation with Incomplete Data," *IEEE Transactions on Software Engineering*, vol. 27, no. 10, pp. 890–908. October 2001.

J.E. Tomayko and O. Hazzan (2004), *Human Aspects of Software Development*. Charles River Media Inc., 2004, p.338.

A. Trendowicz, J. Heidrich, J. Münch, Y. Ishigai, K. Yokoyama, and N. Kikuchi (2006a), "Development of a hybrid cost estimation model in an iterative manner," *Proceedings of the 28th International Conference on Software Engineering*, 20–28 May 2006, Shanghai, China. ACM Press, New York, NY, USA, pp. 331–340.

A. Trendowicz, J. Heidrich, J. Münch, Y. Ishigai, K. Yokoyama, N. Kikuchi (2006b), "Development of a Hybrid Cost Estimation Model in an Iterative Manner," (in Japanese), *Software Engineering Center Journal*, no. 7, September 2006, Tokyo, Japan, ISSN 1349–8622.

A. Trendowicz, M. Ochs, A. Wickenkamp, J. Münch, Y. Ishigai, and T. Kawaguchi (2008a), "An Integrated Approach for Identifying Relevant Factors Influencing Software Development Productivity," in B. Meyer, J. R. Nawrocki, and B. Walter (eds.) *Balancing Agility and Formalism in Software Engineering*, pp. 223–237. Springer-Verlag, 2008.

A. Trendowicz, A. Wickenkamp, M. Ochs, J. Münch, Y. Ishigai, and T. Kawaguchi (2008b), "Integrating Human Judgment and Data Analysis to Identify Factors Influencing Software Development Productivity," *e-Informatica Software Engineering Journal*, vol. 2, no. 1, pp. 47–69, 2008.

A. Trendowicz and J. Münch (2009), "Factors Influencing Software Development Productivity – State-of-the-Art and Industrial Experiences," *Advances in Computers*, pp. 185–241. Elsevier 2009.

D. Wettschereck, D.W. Aha, T. Mohri (1997), "A Review and Empirical Evaluation of Feature Weighting Methods for a Class of Lazy Learning Algorithms," *Artificial Intelligence Review*, vol. 11, no.1-5, pp. 273–314. February 1997.

E. Yourdon (2003), *Death March*, 2nd Edition, Prentice Hall, November 2003.

About the Author

Adam Trendowicz is a senior consultant at the Fraunhofer Institute for Experimental Software Engineering (IESE) in Kaiserslautern, Germany. He has several years of experience on software project estimation.

He received his master's degree in software engineering from Poznan University of Technology (Poland) and his PhD in computer science from the University of Kaiserslautern (Germany). Both his master and PhD work concerned estimating software development projects.

Dr. Trendowicz has led software cost estimation and software measurement improvement activities in software companies of different sizes and from various domains (e.g., in Germany, Japan, and India). He has been involved in functional software size estimation (Function Points Analysis) and productivity benchmarking in organizations from both the industry and the public sector.

Dr. Trendowicz has taught several tutorials on software cost estimation and co-organized the International Workshop on Efficient Software Cost Estimation Approaches (WESoC). Moreover, he supervised the "Software Economics and Risk Management" and "Metric-based Quality Management" modules within the distance master studies program "Software Engineering for Embedded Systems"— a program developed jointly by the University of Kaiserslautern and Fraunhofer IESE. Finally, Dr. Trendowicz has co-authored more than 20 international journal and conference publications.

Dr. Trendowicz's other software engineering interests include (1) measurement-based controlling of software products and processes, (2) software quality modeling and evaluation, and (3) technology validation by means of empirical methods.

A. Trendowicz, *Software Cost Estimation, Benchmarking, and Risk Assessment*,
The Fraunhofer IESE Series on Software and Systems Engineering,
DOI 10.1007/978-3-642-30764-5, © Springer-Verlag Berlin Heidelberg 2013

The Fraunhofer Institute for Experimental Software Engineering (IESE)

Fraunhofer IESE in Kaiserslautern is one of the worldwide leading research institutes in the area of software and systems engineering. A major portion of the products offered by its customers is defined by software. These products range from automotive and transportation systems via automation and plant engineering, information systems, healthcare and medical systems to software systems for the public sector. The institute's software and systems engineering approaches are scalable, which makes Fraunhofer IESE a competent technology partner for organizations of any size—from small companies to major corporations.

Under the leadership of Prof. Dieter Rombach and Prof. Peter Liggesmeyer, the contributions of Fraunhofer IESE have been a major boost to the emerging IT hub Kaiserslautern for more than 15 years. In the Fraunhofer Information and Communication Technology Group, the institute is cooperating with other Fraunhofer institutes to develop trendsetting key technologies for the future.

Fraunhofer IESE is one of the 60 institutes of the Fraunhofer-Gesellschaft. Together they have a major impact on shaping applied research in Europe and contribute to Germany's competitiveness in international markets.

A. Trendowicz, *Software Cost Estimation, Benchmarking, and Risk Assessment,*
The Fraunhofer IESE Series on Software and Systems Engineering,
DOI 10.1007/978-3-642-30764-5, © Springer-Verlag Berlin Heidelberg 2013

Index

A. Trendowicz, *Software Cost Estimation, Benchmarking, and Risk Assessment,*
The Fraunhofer IESE Series on Software and Systems Engineering,
DOI 10.1007/978-3-642-30764-5, © Springer-Verlag Berlin Heidelberg 2013